Praise for John Gimlette's

WILD COAST

JOHN GIMLETTE

WILD COAST

John Gimlette has won the Shiva Naipaul Memorial Prize and the Wanderlust Travel Writing Award, and he contributes regularly to *The Times* (London), *The Guardian*, *The Telegraph*, *The Independent*, and *Condé Nast Traveler*. When not traveling, he practices law in London.

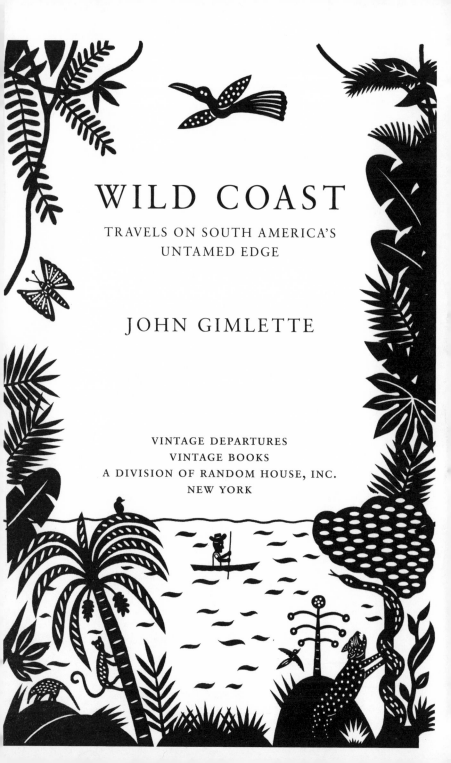

WILD COAST

TRAVELS ON SOUTH AMERICA'S
UNTAMED EDGE

JOHN GIMLETTE

VINTAGE DEPARTURES
VINTAGE BOOKS
A DIVISION OF RANDOM HOUSE, INC.
NEW YORK

To my sister, Philippa, and my brothers, Matthew and Edward

 FIRST VINTAGE DEPARTURES EDITION, JUNE 2012

Copyright © 2011 by John Gimlette

The Library of Congress has cataloged the Knopf edition as follows:
Gimlette, John.
Wild Coast: travels on South America's untamed edge / by John Gimlette.—1st U.S. ed.
p. cm.
Includes bibliographical references and index.
1. Guyana—Description and travel. 2. Suriname—Description and travel.
3. French Guiana—Description and travel. 4. Gimlette, John, [date]—Travel—Guyana.
5. Gimlette, John, [date]—Travel—Suriname.
6. Gimlette, John, [date]—Travel—French Guiana. I. Title.
F2373.G56 2011
918.81—dc22
2011009370

Vintage ISBN: 978-0-307-47362-2

www.vintagebooks.com

Printed in the United States of America
10 9 8 7 6 5 4 3 2 1

CONTENTS

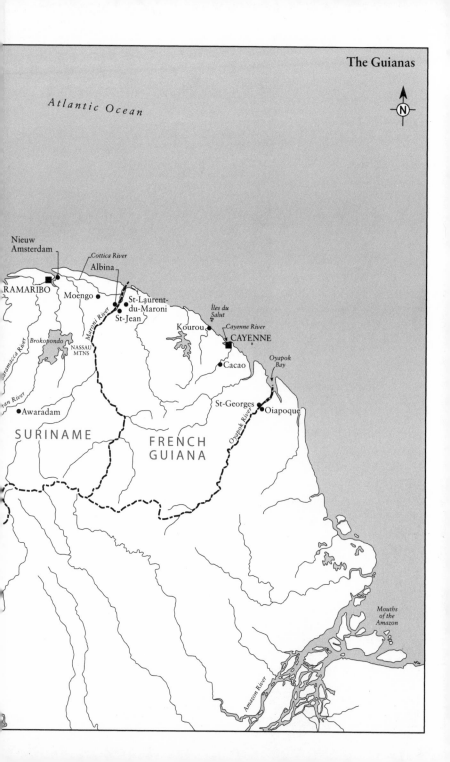

INTRODUCTION

Guiana is a country that hath yet her maidenhead, never sacked,
turned nor wrought.
> Sir Walter Raleigh, *The Discoverie of the Large, Rich and*
> *Bewtiful Empyre of Guiana*

The Guianas have fascinated me. It always seemed odd that
these three little gobs of empire should survive in the general
explosion of South American self-government.
> Evelyn Waugh, *92 Days*

No elaborate outfit is necessary. For day wear, drill or
palm beach shirts or light suits are general ... revolvers are
unnecessary.
> The South American Handbook 1947

AS FAR AS AMERINDIANS ARE CONCERNED, the land between the Orinoco and the Amazon has always been *Guiana*, the 'Land of Many Waters'. European explorers, however, took a while to appreciate this name. On early French and English maps the region was marked as 'Equinoctiale' or 'Caribana, Land of Twenty-one Tribes'. To the Dutch, on the other hand, this was – for a while – the original 'New Zealand'. Then they thought of a name which expressed what they felt. It had about it the promise of danger, risk, wealth and perhaps even desire. It was *de Wilde Kust,* 'The Wild Coast'.

Certainly nowhere else in South America is quite like it; 900 miles of muddy coastline give way to swamps, thick forest and then – deep inland – ancient flat-topped peaks. It's never been truly possessed. Along this entire shore, there's no natural harbour, and beyond the mud the forest begins. It covers over 80 per cent of Guiana, and even now there's no way through it. Such roads as there are stick mainly to the coast. Without an aeroplane, it takes up to four weeks to get into the interior, and there the problems begin.

With such an abundant canopy, most of Guiana never sees sunlight. Perhaps it's therefore no surprise that – both in science and history – the story of this land reads like a long, green night. Huge tracts of the interior are only vaguely described, and new species are always tumbling out of the dark. Even some of the more common ones make unnerving companions. Guiana has the biggest ants in the world, and the biggest freshwater fish. There are head-crushing jaguars, strangling snakes, rivers of stingrays and electric eels, and whole clouds of insects all eager to burrow in under the skin. To some this is hell. To others it's an ecological paradise, a sort of X-rated Garden of Eden.

But it is water, as the Amerindians recognised, that defines Guiana. Through this land run literally thousands of rivers (in Guyana alone there are over 1,500). These aren't like the little waterways that meander through the Old World, but vast sprawling torrents that thunder out of the forest and then plough their way to the sea. Some have mouths big enough to swallow Barbados. But, even the biggest of them – the Essequibo, Corentyne and Marowijne – are intolerant of shipping; beyond ninety miles inland, nothing larger than a canoe gets through without being battered to bits. Once it was thought that these furious rivers all linked up, and that Guiana was really an agglomeration of islands, bobbing around in the froth.

But whatever the layout, water still rules. It dominates development, trims opportunities and seals off the world. It makes islanders of tribes, and supports long-lost communities of prospectors, Utopians and runaway slaves. It feeds malaria and nurtures some of the world's most ambitious strains of dengue fever. Damp gets everywhere, rotting buildings and feet and making steam of the air. From the very earliest times human beings have realised that their best chance of surviving Guiana is by living right next to the sea. Even now, nine out of every ten of its inhabitants live on a long, muddy strip, barely ten miles wide.

It's curious, life in the silt. Most of the houses have legs, and every town is built on a grid of velvety, green canals. Meanwhile, the Atlantic Ocean here is the colour of plaster, caused, it's said, by sediments harvested in Peru, washed across the continent and disgorged by the Amazon. It makes for a beautiful world, luminously lush and drenchingly fecund. Not surprisingly, its inhabitants are proud of it and give it affectionate names. In Demerara they call their land 'The Mudflat' (and their neighbours the 'mudheads'). But not everyone's impressed. As one visiting English yachtsman wrote in 1882, 'It appears a hopeless land of slime and fever, quite unfitted for man, unless it be for Tree-Indians, a low race of fish-eating savages ...'

Naturally, this claggy, overgrown, fish-breathed coast was never immediately inviting. For years the newly emerging Europeans had steered well clear. In theory, Spain was the first to claim it (along with the rest of the western world) under the Treaty of Tordesillas in 1494. It was five years, however, before they sent a ship, and even then it didn't stop. Another thirty years passed before anyone tried to land, only to be eaten by the locals. After that, Spanish interest in Guiana shrivelled, and the only part they ever occupied was the north-west end, now part of Venezuela, called 'Guayana'. Meanwhile, the Portuguese colonised the southern flanks (now the Brazilian state of Amapá), and the bit in between was up for grabs.

It's this bit of Guiana – the chunk in the middle – that interested me, and eventually it became the setting for these travels. It's an area about twice the size of Great Britain, divided into three unequal, roughly rectangular shares: Guyana (formerly British Guiana), Suriname (formerly Dutch Guiana) and Guyane Française (also known as French Guiana). They are sometimes referred to – usefully, if a little inaccurately – as 'The Guianas', and form the only part of the South American mainland that was never either Spanish or Portuguese. What's more, they've totally resisted the influences of the continent all around, never knowing salsa or tango, Bolívar, *machismo*, liberation theology or even the liberation movement. In fact, independence for two of the Guianas arrived only some 150 years after the rest of the continent, and even today Guyane remains a *département* of France. It's almost as though the giant at their backs has never existed. Even as I write, there isn't a single road that leads from the Guianas into the world beyond.

The story of how this oddity came about is surprisingly bloody. After the Spanish lost interest, it looked, for a moment, as though England might quietly acquire this coast. In 1595 Sir Walter Raleigh propagated a rumour that there was a city of gold here, that the women were biddable and cute, and that there was a fat partridge draped on every branch. Although these claims were rather obviously over-puffed, there was plenty of interest. First off, in 1597, was a barrister called John Ley, although he never planned to settle. Plenty of others did. But insolvency killed off most of their ideas, and ridicule the rest. Even the Pilgrim Fathers briefly toyed with the idea of planting New England here in Guiana (before a more sober assessment prevailed). Eventually, however, in 1604, colonisation began, with a settlement of English gentlemen in what is now Guyane. Most were dead within the year.

Their colony, however, heralded the beginning of a murderous game of musical chairs. For the next two hundred years, the three great European powers – France, Britain and Holland – scrambled around on this coast, snatching colonies and killing the previous incumbents. These wars always began and ended in Europe, and there were nine in all (First Dutch, Second Dutch, Grand Alliance, Spanish Succession, Jenkins' Ear, Austrian Succession, Seven Years, American Independence and Napoleonic). At the end of each round no one was where they'd started, and the coast was in ruins. Modern-day Guyana changed hands nine times, Suriname six and Guyane seven. All three were seized at one point (1676) by the Dutch, and at another (1809) by Britain. Even today, the Guianas – as I'd soon discover – still reel from the impact of this antique chaos.

Warfare has also left a curious mess of the map. The original Guianese, the Amerindians (who make up about 3 per cent of the population) now find themselves scattered through all three Guianas, and into Venezuela and Brazil. As for the borders, they're almost accidental, the upshot of wars begun long ago, and over 4,000 miles to the east. As the fighting drew to an end, in 1815, the Europeans carved out shares that broadly reflected their prowess at arms. Britain got a slab of land about the size of itself (83,000 square miles), while Dutch Guiana was half this size. France, meanwhile, was left with what's still the smallest territory on the continent, a damp, unworkable inferno known for a while as Cayenne.

But still the borders are dangerously vague. Deep in the watery, green anarchy of the interior there's little agreement as to who owns what. Vast areas of the map lie blank except for the words 'FRONTIER IN DISPUTE'. Everyone claims a piece of each other. Venezuela claims almost 70 per cent of Guyana, which it marks on its maps as *'La Zona en Reclamación'*. Elsewhere, the contenders for this vast, unoccupied space attack each other with gunboats and build bunkers in the forest. Their claims are usually as wild as the jungle itself. Often they're based on ancient Elizabethan maps, drawn up by dreamers who thought there was a golden city here, and a tribe of headless men.

These days no one's quite sure what the fight is for – perhaps oil, perhaps gold. But for the old sea powers, there was something much more valuable at stake: sugar. By the 1700s Europe was addicted to the stuff, and anyone enterprising enough to plant it could double his capital in less than three years. In places such as Bristol and Amsterdam it created a new class of millionaire: the exotic, silk-slippered nawabs of Wild Coast sugar. Meanwhile, the Guianas themselves were transformed. Sugar dominated the economy for over 300 years, creating its own ruling class, known as 'The Plantocracy'. Even on the eve of its decline in about 1860, sugar still accounted for 95 per cent of British Guiana's exports. The region's history since then could almost be summarised as the struggle for life after sugar.

Nowhere is sugar's hold on Guianese life more obvious than from the air. Examine this coast on Google.earth and you'll skim over mile after mile of ghostly oblongs. These are the old cane fields, each one a work of almost pharaonic effort. For every square mile of cane it was necessary to dig over sixty-five miles of drainage canals, and shift over 10 million tons of earth. None of this, of course, was done by the Europeans. It's entirely the creation of slaves.

For me, grappling with the concept of slavery was one of the most troubling aspects of this Guianese journey. On the one hand, slavery seemed to have disappeared completely; the 'yards' have gone, the impedimenta have rotted away, and across the entire region there are barely a handful of monuments. On the other hand, slavery was everywhere, even in the food and the way people lived. Sometimes I felt as though slavery was like some weird metaphorical telephone exchange and that every strand of Guianese life somehow led back to this point.

This, of course, is to say nothing of the difficult questions we Europeans must ask. How did we manage to suspend a basic tenet of humanity for almost 300 years? Was slavery a last relic of medieval thought, or was it the beginning of a modern phenomenon, where – if the price is right – anything goes?

Whatever the answers, the Guianese example is an unedifying tale. Almost everyone played their part. It began with the creation of a more comfortable moral climate for the trade, in 1454, with the papal bull *Dum Diversas* (which encouraged the Portuguese to go out into the heathen world 'and reduce their persons to perpetual slavery'). Once Portugal had made a virtue of slavery, the Dutch made it a business. In 1652 they brought Guiana its first slaves. After that, everyone piled in, including the Danes and the Swedes. But it was the English who made it an industry. (By 1760 they had a fleet of 146 slavers, with a capacity for 36,000 captives.) No one knows how many African lives were merged with the Guianese clay, but it must be hundreds of thousands. Worse still, this savage, unbelievable

Sir Walter Raleigh (c.1552–1618) gave Guiana a mythical reputation, which it spent hundreds of years shaking off.

trade continued in the Dutch colony until 1870, stopping just short of the Age of the Car.

Guiana has always had an uncertain place in English literature.

As I picked my way through Raleigh's great 1595 prospectus, *The Discoverie of the Large, Rich and Bewtiful Empire of Guiana,* I realised how energetically he'd shaped our early impressions of this coast. He'd promised his investors not only plenty but perfection. Quite apart from golden cities and comely Amazons, here were diamond mountains, dog-headed mermen, week-long drinking festivals and men with their eyes in their chests. Better still, the locals were conveniently hopeless. 'Those Guianians', he wrote, 'are marvellous great drunkards, in which vice I think no nation can compare with them.' Reading all this, I sometimes wondered whether he'd been to Guiana at all. *The Discoverie*, it seemed, was a composite of Spanish tittle-tattle, salesmanship and a feverish classical education.

For all this, it made an unforgettable impression. Long before the first green shoots of sugar, Guiana became a byword for fertility and wealth. Even Shakespeare was taken in (his Falstaff flatters Mistress Page, as 'a region of Guiana, all good and bounty'). Milton too was entranced, and an 'unspoilt Guiana' pops up in the heart of

Paradise Lost. Two centuries later, Trollope went there himself and, in his praise, became uncharacteristically light-headed. 'Life flows along,' he wrote, 'in a perpetual stream of love, smiles, champagne and small talk.' Perhaps Raleigh had got to him too, or perhaps it was all that bubbly.

More recently, literary Guiana has seemed not so much enchanted as somehow cruelly jinxed. Evelyn Waugh found only a 'destructive and predatory civilisation' and predicted that it would disappear 'like the trenches and shell craters of a battlefield'. The Naipaul brothers would have no better news after their visits of the 1960s and '70s. V.S. found the whole place 'deceitful and sullen', and Shiva concluded that he was gazing at 'social collapse'. Both economically and poetically, Guiana, it seems, was sliding off into obscurity.

Several decades later, I'd hardly heard of it at all.

But then, in 2002, I caught a distant glimpse of Guiana while researching a journey through Newfoundland. Ancient trade routes, I discovered, had once run between the two; molasses heading north for fishermen, salted cod going south for the slaves (in fact, Newfoundlanders still drink Guyanese dark rum, known to them as 'Screech'). The two colonies even seemed to share a strange, Georgian vocabulary, and a taste for place-names such as 'Profit' and 'Success'. Better still, I discovered that I had a distant ancestor who'd played a role in both colonies, one after the other, with disastrous results.

Robert Hayman was a lawyer, poet, dilettante and layabout. Few men were less suited to either the challenges of the sub-arctic or the rigours of the tropics. Born into an up-and-coming Devonshire family in 1575, Robert spent his formative years floating around the universities of Oxford and Poitiers. If he'd ever had any aptitude for the law, by the age of forty-two there was still no sign of it. In desperation, his father – who had friends at court – blagged him a job in the colonies. The following year, 1618, he was appointed Governor of Harbour Grace, a wind-scoured inlet in northern Newfoundland, famous for nothing but fish.

As governor, Robert ruled with spectacular indifference. He hardly seemed to notice that all his men were dying of scurvy. He himself was not a man to get his ruffs dirty, and by his own admission he refused to lift a finger. Instead, he spent his time translating Rabelais ('that excellently wittie Doctor') before beginning work on his own, rather curious oeuvre: *Quodlibets, lately come over from*

New Britaniola, Old Newfound-Land. Epigrams and other fmall parcels, both Morall and Diuine. To call it 'parcels' is to flatter it with content. In reality, it's merely vacuous doggerel, distinguished only by the fact that it's probably the first English poetry to emerge from the New World.

By 1628 Robert's Newfoundland venture was drawing to an end. His plans for the colony had been almost as silly as his parcels. The best of these proposals he'd sent to the king, Charles I, through a lush mutual acquaintance, the Duke of Buckingham. In his letters Robert urged the building of a great new city out here among the fish. All it needed was a million men, but it would be known for ever as Carolinople. This hare-brained scheme finally fell apart only in August of that year, when an assassin managed to get his bodkin into Buckingham. With the end of Carolinople, Robert began to look around for an empire somewhere else.

To anyone with a flair for disaster, Guiana was a perfect choice. At that stage attention was still focused on the 'Wyapoko' river, in what is now Guyane. There, disease and Portuguese raids had already polished off several English colonies. Not that this would deter a man of great poetic vision. In November 1628 Robert prepared a new will before his departure 'by God's leave to Guiane'. Then, along with a hundred others, he set off from Gravesend in 'a shipp of London called the little hopewell.' Three months later they arrived on the Wyapoko, built a fort and prepared the land for sugar.

From an early stage I realised that Robert's travels would never become a template for a journey of my own. There was simply not enough of him. With disaster written all over their adventure, he and his friends were almost certain to vanish without trace. And that, of course, is exactly what happened. Within eight months Robert was in the grip of a 'burning fever' and died of 'the fluxe'. The following year the 'Little Hopewell' was wrecked off the mouth of the Amazon, with the loss of all but eleven lives. As for the colony, it was razed by the Portuguese, and no sign of it remains.

I often hoped that our paths would cross, but it was never the objective of this journey. Instead, I'd make my own route, travelling down from Guyana to Guyane. But although Robert may not have provided me with a dotted line to follow, it was he who'd ignited the interest. What, I wondered, had become of the Wild Coast he'd known? In 2008 – almost exactly 380 years later – I set out from London, like him uncertain what I'd find.

1

THE TOWN OF GEORGE

Despite its shortcomings and the marring effect of lawlessness
and banditry, Georgetown is a city of undeniable character,
unique attraction and indefinable charm.

James Rodway, *Guiana*

The number of children in Georgetown is frightening.

V.S. Naipaul, *Middle Passage*

There was plenty going on in Georgetown that week. An
unknown Dutchman shot himself on Christmas morning in his
room at a rival hotel, on account of feeling lonely.

Evelyn Waugh, *92 Days*

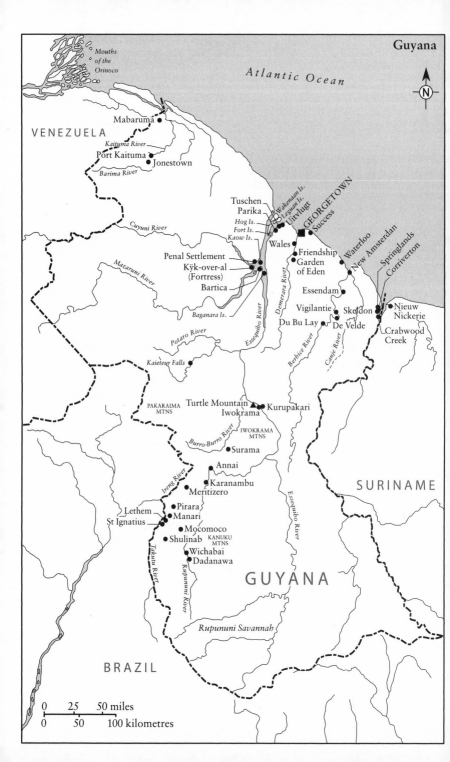

NOTHING SPOILS A GOOD LUNCH quite like the threat of a hand-grenade attack.

'But who's going to attack us?' I kept asking.

Around the table the politicians shrugged and continued with their chicken.

'Listen, man,' said the bodyguard slowly, 'we can't explain you.'

Bricko was no natural explainer. He was like a black Popeye, built out of tyres. I turned to the party's chairman, who was watching the street. It was mid-afternoon, and only the mule carts were working. 'Out there,' he said, 'there's a lot of disappointed people.'

'Like who?' I tried. 'Drug cartels?'

'Maybe. But there's some angry Indians too ...'

'... and people in big business ...' said his second.

'... and Amerindians ...'

'*And* the Africans,' growled Bricko.

More beers arrived, and foamed over the table.

'And then there's the Chinese ...' said the party secretary.

'And the other parties, the PNC ...'

'Or the PPP!'

I was puzzled. 'The *government*? They'd kill you?'

An old Nissan whirred past and stalled at the junction. We all stared.

'It's possible,' said the party leader, 'you never know.'

'But then that's just about *everyone*, isn't it? Everyone hates you?'

Across the debris of bottles and bones, no one said anything. From the very beginning theirs had been a political party caught in the crossfire. After a moment the chairman spoke. 'People,' he said, 'have lost faith in politics.'

His second nodded, 'That's why we got so many churches ...'

'... And rum shops! Numbs the pain ...'

'But has anyone *tried* anything?' I asked. 'Bombs or shooting ...?'

Bricko shook his head. 'Not here. Not *yet* ...'

The chairman frowned.

'But this is Georgetown,' he said, 'so anything could happen ...'

The Townies, or people of Georgetown, still made a spectacle of murder. In a country with no obvious theatres and only two ailing cinemas, the courtroom was often the next best thing. The trials were laboriously British, went on for weeks and weeks, and were then lavishly reported. In Guyana nothing else got attention like this. Small wonder that politicians seemed to aspire to be killed.

Soon after my arrival in the city I read about one of these trials and went along to watch. It was held in the Victoria Law Courts, a lingering fantasy of tropical Gothic. On the outside it looked like a vast tin palace, with corrugated gables and pillars made of iron. Inside, it seemed bigger still, and was richly inhabited by long-dead solicitors now whiter than ever in marble. There was even a statue of Victoria herself. I'd heard that, during the struggles for independence, a stick of dynamite had blown her head off. Now, I noticed, queen and bean had been solemnly reunited.

It was an unforgettable trial. In one sense, it was like a courtroom drama, circa 1790. The accused, Blacksam and Buggins, were old felons who drank in taverns and ate saltfish and souse. Then, one day, they'd picked a Georgian quarrel with their neighbour and dispatched him with a cutlass. Having entered their pleas, they were brought to the court in chains. Dozens of witnesses were called. Their villages sounded like old sugar ships: Garden of Eden, Providence and Friendship. Most wore their Sunday best, and there was earnest talk of 'coolies', 'larceny', 'house-breaking' and 'having carnal knowledge'. Somehow it seemed as though the last couple of centuries hadn't really happened.

In every other sense, however, the trial was like a snapshot of modern life in Guyana. The side walls of the court were open, and so the parrots sat in the palms outside, chattering through the evidence. Then the rains came early, and sounded like horses on the tin. Defence counsel, meanwhile, was – like almost half the population – Indian, and wore a black silk suit and robes. Whenever he could, he'd pound around the court, thundering away in a rich Creole, well larded with Dickens and Donne.

The other races too played their part that day. The judge and all the constables were – like a third of all Guyanese – 'African', while the jurymen made up the rest: 'the mixed races'. There, in their twelve furrowed faces was the story of Guyana, a hotchpotch of displaced souls: slaves, Amerindians, Dutch conquerors, 'Chineymen', Irish adventurers, Scottish cattlemen, pirates, pioneers and Pathans. Together, this volatile mix made up a population barely big enough to fill a little phone book. All that were missing were the whites, whose share of the whole was now a slice of 1 per cent.

'Ask not for whom the bell tolls …!' thundered the Indian.

Not that the jury heard. The whole building was shuddering under watery hoofs. Mercy, however, had survived, and the verdict was manslaughter. Off went the prisoners, grinning through their chains.

'Yeh, man,' said the constable, 'just now them been spared the noose …'

From the court a beautiful city, as light as feathers, fluttered off down the coast. Perhaps – like its people – Georgetown didn't truly believe it belonged here, and so it hovered over the water. Nothing was firmly attached. It was all built on canals and breezes, a city of stilts and clapboard, brilliant whites, fretwork, spindles and louvres. The streets were as wide as fields, and the cathedral seemed to drift endlessly upwards, reputedly the tallest wooden building in the world. One area was even called Lacytown, as though, at any moment it would simply take off and drift away, home perhaps.

Naturally, with so much kindling, Georgetown was always burning down. It was devastated five times by fire during the nineteenth century and then another four times in the century that followed. There's always a good reason for these fires – riots or an eruption at the Chinese fireworks plant. The latest victims, in 2004, were a cinema – one of the last in the city – and the Roman Catholic cathedral. Faced with these disasters, the Townies would simply cut some more sticks and start all over again.

Water too was a constant feature of the Townies' lives. At high tide the sea towered five feet above the city, all held back with a wall. It was all a permanent reminder that, tropical though the city may have seemed, it had the soul of Amsterdam. For 200 years – well over half its colonial existence – Guyana had been Dutch, and this was the town of Stabroek. Muddy, hot and flat, it may not have looked much, but during peace negotiations in 1802 it was considered a better bet than Canada. A few years later the British grabbed it again and named it after George III, the farmer king. Soon afterwards, the whole soggy colony passed to Britain, to be known as 'British Guiana'.

Two centuries on, the moisture was as vigorous as ever. People often told me how, a few years earlier, their city had all but vanished under several feet of water. Most of the time, however, it was just a low-grade skirmish with the damp. The forest was constantly trying to creep back into this city, along with the mildew. Even concrete rotted here, and cars seemed to moulder. By day the canals were silky and green, and by night they were operatic with frogs. 'Why? Why?' they'd sing, which made the dogs all howl. Nature, it seemed, was gradually reclaiming its inheritance.

Amid this riot of parrots and flamboyants, the Townies could still be fleetingly British. They'd talk about things like 'spring' and 'autumn' while the weather remained doggedly hot. They could even be a little archaic, with children peeing in 'posies' and having 'tennis rolls' for tea. In the shops, too, a little Britishness had survived; you could still buy Vicks VapoRub, a bottle of 'Nerve Tonic' or a stack of *True Confessions*. Meanwhile, Fogarty's department store was like a huge pink slab of Croydon, now quietly decomposing. Downstairs it had a 1940s' café, complete with skinny sausage rolls and dim lighting as though the war – like the café itself – was somehow still going on.

But nowhere felt quite so left behind as the city museum. Downstairs were all the odds and ends of colonial life, together with Britain's departing gift: a tiny Austin Rolls-Royce Prince. Upstairs, meanwhile, hadn't changed at all since 1933, when Evelyn Waugh called by. The same faint miasma of formaldehyde still lingered over what he'd described as 'the worst stuffed animals I have seen anywhere'. Not surprisingly, I had the place to myself, and so the curator pounced on me and made me take my hat off.

Out on the street, traces of the old empire were harder to find. Of course, almost all the civic buildings were notionally British – although they didn't always look it. Often even the queen's most loyal architects had let heat and fantasy go to their heads. Father Scholes's City Hall looked like a runaway doll's house, and Blomfield's cathedral had used up so many trees that, even now, it was at risk of vanishing into the mud. It was only in the details that Georgetown's streets were still lingeringly British; the Hackney carriages, the EIIR letter boxes, the statue of a great sewage engineer and a pair of Sebastopol cannons. Once, however, I did see a large building site called Buckingham Palace, although – sadly, perhaps – before any resemblance had taken shape, the financing had failed.

Despite these trappings, I soon came to realise that the Guyanese were neither British nor truly South American but lived in a world of their own. Sometimes it seemed that being foreign came so naturally to them that they didn't even understand themselves. There were several thriving dialects, and the city would grind to a halt not just for Christmas but also for Diwali, Eid and Phagwah. Depending on who I asked, the national dish was either roti, chow mein, a fiery Amerindian concoction called pepperpot or chicken-in-the-rough. Originally each race had had its own political party, but now there were fifty. Among a mere 750,000 people, this sometimes made Guyana feel like several dozen countries all stuffed into one.

I often felt this as I walked across Georgetown. One moment I'd be passing Chinatown, then a mosque, 'The House of Flavours', a Hindu temple, and the Pandit Council. Then I'd turn a corner and find myself in the middle of a 'Full Gospel Miracle Crusade' or a Mexican circus ('*With Real Tigers!*'). Occasionally the different cultures seemed to elide, creating tantalising hybrids. Who, I wondered, was behind all the duck curry competitions? Or the 'Festival of Extreme Chutney'? Most of the time, however, everyone kept to themselves. As I passed through each neighbourhood, the music changed – from reggae to Hindi, through soca and hip-hop, and back to calypso.

All this would be odd in a big city, and yet Georgetown was tiny. There was only one escalator in the whole town (and it still drew a crowd), and the rambling National Gallery received just twenty visits a month. Everyone knew everyone, even the men who sold horse-dung from their carts. You couldn't do anything, it was said, without word spreading outwards through the Spit Press ('You tell Tara,' as one taxi-driver put, 'and Tara tell Tara'). Only I was the odd one out: a *bucra*, or white man, in a town with everything but.

Most people I met told me a revolution was imminent. After a while I began to suspect this was merely a polite Towny way of saying that they were not to be underestimated.

Not that I ever did. They were like frontiersmen, an exotic blend of optimists, who'd arrived on the edge of not-very-much after a long, hard walk through history. Many didn't even have proper names, as though they'd simply jumped out of their lives. These nicknames were famously creative. I'd hear of 'Blue Beef', 'Prophet' Willis (who had a hotline to God), a sweet-maker named 'Who Sucking', and a man who made his living as a prize-fighter called 'Slack Foot Johnny'; then there were the villains like 'Jacket Wallah', 'Biscuit' Andrews, 'Banga Mary' and the lock-breaker 'Hocus Pocus'. But my favourite was the man who'd insisted he was white but was known as 'Walker the Nigger'.

But what really marked the Townies out was their sense of defiance. It didn't seem to bother them that they were either being flooded or roasted or picked apart by poverty. Everyone considered himself important, and his political views of interest. Each day the newspapers ran ream after ream of trenchant views, contemptuous of failure and wary of success. But this was nothing compared to the views being expressed on the market stalls, and in bars and shacks and abandoned vans. It sometimes seemed as though the whole place was about to break into a fight, which – remarkably – it never did.

'Something will turn up,' people would conclude. Often they were right. While half the city's workforce sat around wondering what to do, the other half were on the move. Either they drove mini-buses with names like 'Thug Life' or 'Try Jesus', or they sold things. It could be anything: watches, cane juice, kites, horse-dung or a sugary drink called swank. The most enterprising even headed out into the bush to do a little mining. Sir Walter Raleigh would have loved it: here was a city in the Guianas, inhabited by paupers, all with gold teeth.

'NO IDLERS', said the signs, 'NO TOUTS'. It was an impossible injunction. In Georgetown everyone was either one or the other.

The rich weren't much different, except that they had cars. Perhaps it was this mobility that made them hard to find.

'They's always out liming,' said a vendor on the sea wall.

'Liming' meant loafing around. 'Where?' I asked.

He shrugged. 'Out in them big hotels …?'

Being of the motorised classes was clearly not popular, so it took me a while to track them down. Eventually, however, I spotted some in a place on Middle Street called the Sidewalk Café. It was a remarkable evening, treacly hot and full of surprises. A man just like Marvin Gaye was singing a cappella, and the first person I met had no name at all. Known simply as 'The Man from Afar', he wore a black suit and used words so long and convoluted that – after two shots of El Dorado – I wasn't sure whether he was beginning one sentence or half-way through another.

Fortunately, I was rescued by the owner. At first I thought she was the next act, she was so omniscient and twinkly. But Cathy Hughes was always like this, and that night she towed me round, introducing me to her friends and clientele. Coming from a city as battened down as London, their collective generosity was almost disconcerting. They pumped my hand and asked me about life on 'The Outside' (as they called the world beyond). Some, even by Guyanese standards, weren't really rich at all. One was an old con man who went around telling people how he needed money for an old aunt or for petrol or a baby with galloping yaws. No one seemed to care; he was just part of the scenery – like missing manhole covers, the rum and Cathy's deep-fried cutters.

'He gets glorious,' she explained (when she really meant drunk).

The other guests were more determined survivors. That night I met gold prospectors, jazz musicians, a pilot, a beautiful Indian scientist called Racquel and Cathy's husband, Nigel, a giant Afro-Guyanese lawyer who'd once been chairman of the country's bar. The pilot told me he'd moved to Antigua and that there were now as many Guyanese working outside the country as there were at home. Another man, with a hard, stubbly head, said he'd gone all the way to America for work. By one of those strange twists of Towny fate, he'd ended up as a marine colonel, serving in Iraq.

Nigel drove me home, deftly avoiding the cows and the gaping holes.

'Life's not always easy here,' he said, 'but I wouldn't live anywhere else.'

'Home', for me, was an ill-defined area called Republic Park. It began on the edge of the city and petered out in the cane fields. As a neighbourhood, I was never quite sure if it was on the way up or on the way out. Half the houses seemed empty, or covered in razor wire, and the roads were merely long white furrows of powdery sand. Taxi-drivers used to love telling me who lived up here: drug barons, traffic cops and some fancy politicians. But the biggest house, which looked like a slice of Versailles, was owned by an evangelical pastor. 'Ah, yes,' they'd say, 'the church is some good business in Guyana.'

The house that I stayed in was the smallest of them all. It had so many bars and grilles that, from the outside, it looked like a cage finished off in concrete. But inside, it was cheery and cool, with burned-orange walls and African masks. I had my own bathroom, complete with a small yellow frog that lived in the cistern. In the mornings it made a noise like a tiny generator. I enjoyed this, the idea of a frog-powered house.

The arrangement I had was a bit unusual. Before coming to Guyana I'd spent weeks trying to find a family who'd have me to stay. This was obviously a novel concept in Georgetown. Why would a *bucra* want to stay in a Towny home instead of a big hotel? What will he eat? Will he need a pool? Undaunted, I sent out more emails, and they began to percolate into the Diaspora, spreading out from Canada to Israel. At last someone came up with a family, or at least half of one. Get in touch with Lorlene James, they said, who lives with her eight-year-old son.

I still laugh when I think of Lorlene. Although she was thin and light-footed, she had a fat person's gift for expression. Whatever she said was often, I realised, a hilarious distraction from whatever she felt. Of course, she could also be serious, coquettish, intellectual, furious and wry, but mostly she was funny. People loved her, and she could imitate anyone; the good, the straight, the cops and the people that ran the country. If there was rum around, she could even make herself laugh, and that's when I noticed that, between the gasps, there was always a chink of sadness.

We're all, I suppose, a product of the fortunes that have brought us where we are. The mystery, in Lorlene's case, was how her humour had survived the journey. She described a life buffeted along from one calamity to another. A beautiful Georgetown childhood had suddenly ended in the '70s, when the entire family was expelled. 'My father was editor of *The Guyana Chronicle*,' she told me, 'and had a radio show that fell foul of the dictatorship.' Canada offered asylum and seemed big and exciting at first. But it was no place to be black and hard up. Her father got a soulless job, vetting other immigrants, and his marriage fell apart. Bullied almost all the way to university, Lorlene realised that Canada was not for her. She decided to return to Guyana.

'I got back eleven years ago,' she said, 'and realised I'd missed it every day.' For a moment there were shoots of genuine happiness. Lorlene married, Floyd was born, and she threw herself into politics. She joined the AFC – Alliance for Change – a party whose novel claim was to represent all the different races. Soon, she became a member of parliament, and her bill for the abolition of corporal punishment was enthusiastically received. But this was a Guyanese tale, and so it was bound to end in surprises. First, her husband was killed by one of the country's only sports cars, and then her bill began to fall apart. 'The ruling party killed it off,' she told me; 'they weren't going to be told what to do by someone they saw as skinny, Canadian and AFC. I hated politics. It was so futile. There was *nothing* we could do.'

Floyd hadn't known his father, but somehow he seemed to absorb his mother's misfortune as though it was all his own. I've never met a child so acutely sensitive to the needs of adults. Once, after I'd taken him swimming, he asked his mother if I'd marry her. Lorlene explained that I already had a family, but Floyd never gave up. Every time I took off on one of my trips into the interior he'd hug me and start to cry. It still pains me to think of his tears splashing down my shirt, and his curious, ill-formed hopes. All he knew was that they had to emigrate, and he'd spent hours searching his books and comics looking for somewhere to live. Eventually he'd come up with the answer to everything, and that was Japan.

As Guyana's only landlady, Lorlene was hopelessly generous.

From the start she refused to accept any rent and instead threw a party. Her friends, both Africans and Indians, were like the people from the Sidewalk Café – except even more political. When the food appeared – a vast spread of spicy chicken, rice, fried bananas, huge pastries called 'doubles', stewed channa, fillets of Banga Mary and enormous flagons of punch – they gathered round it in a scrum. Soon the glasses were clinking and everyone was holding forth. It was like twiddling the dial of a radio and getting all the pundits at once. I was surprised how simple politics can sound. The AFC people said they'd been burgled, ostracised and completely excluded from public life, for daring to occupy the centre and courting all the races. For some of Lorlene's older, Trotskyite friends it was even simpler still: there were no such things as mishaps, life was a series of remarkable conspiracies. One lady solemnly told me that dark outside forces were responsible for everything here, from floods and robberies to the price of sugar. 'Even the AFC,' muttered another, 'are puppets of the CIA.'

Between these chicken fights Lorlene took me out on tours of the city. Being borderline solvent, she had a borderline car. It had no paintwork, no bumpers and no name. As it had no handles either, Floyd would have to climb in through the back window and burrow through the rubbish to release the doors. I enjoyed the idea that people thought this was a gift from the CIA. Once under way, it was like riding along in a skip – until we reached full speed. Then there'd be a gruesome howling sound, and everything would shudder. Several times we felt components detach themselves from the undercarriage and we'd watch as they clattered off down the road. 'Ah well,' Lorlene would say, as though they were bits of her life, 'we're still moving, aren't we?'

I loved these tours. We'd howl through rusty suburbs, drive along the edge of the blazing cane, visit a few fish shops – or bars – and poke our heads into all the public buildings. Although Lorlene kept insisting there was nothing to see, Georgetown was defiantly fascinating. It seemed that, wherever we went, people were trying to create a spectacle, with whatever came to hand. Even the dead were doing it, with their plumed horses and carriages of glass. Once, the draymen shut off the whole of Homestretch Avenue and had a mule race like something from *Ben Hur* (except with rubber wheels and distemper). Other spectacles were less ambitious, and involved rags and sticks and little creatures found in the forest. With these, people made kites and footballs, and the national sport was 'rackling'. To be a rackler, you had to put a tiny bird in a cage and then coax it to sing.

Our tours often ended by the pool of the Pegasus Hotel. There, for a small fortune, Floyd could eat fries and pretend he was somewhere

*A slave girl is given
200 lashes in 1773. The
brutality of that time
would leave an enduring
legacy.*

else. Around the pool there were plenty of others who, in their own small way, were escaping. Some were local girls, beautifully coiffed and primped, hopeful of a foreigner and available for marriage. Often too there were British soldiers here. Mostly they'd been doing jungle training and were now trying to reacquaint themselves with society through the medium of cocktails. AIRBORNE, read their tattoos, as though that said it all. The sight of the girls would make them dive off the tables and show everyone their buttocks.

'Is this *normal?*' asked Lorlene.

'Yes,' I replied, 'for squaddies, I'm afraid it is.'

Lorlene frowned. I'd often heard it said that the Guyanese were prissy and that it was only deep below the surface that there was a rich seam of philanderers and lovers. In the full glare of daylight, explained Lorlene, it was a different matter.

'As you've seen,' she said, 'everything here has to be *just so.*'

There was only one place Lorlene refused to take me to: the old slave market.

'You'll be mugged ...' she said.

Her friends agreed. 'People have been raped in there ...'

'... choke and rob ...'

'... bodies dumped in the Demerara ...'

It seemed that, apart from brutality, only a name had survived. Once, the word Stabroek had suggested a promising Dutch city, but now it was mostly just the market. Any sign of the old Hollanders, however, had long since gone. In 1880, seventy-five years after their eviction, the British had covered the whole site with a monstrous mock-Tudor fortress, made entirely from iron and tin. I often wondered what 'mock-Tudor' meant to the descendants of the slaves. Unfinished? Other-worldly? Or just mildly daft? Whichever it was, they'd be right. This great lump of a place was originally supposed to have been a station, and from here trains were to fan out across the continent. But the fanning never happened, and the engines never came. As the idea of Georgetown Central faltered, the grim reality of Stabroek Market revived.

Despite all the warnings, I felt I had to go inside. I can still see myself slinking along: a slightly comical figure, conspicuously pale and furtive. I was convinced that, any moment, robbers would put a chain around my neck and then work me over like some sort of human ATM. But they didn't. Perhaps in the hot, meaty darkness they were far too astonished by the sight of anyone so colourless. 'Hey, whitey!' people exclaimed, 'Whiiiiiite boy!' Only one person assaulted me. She was an enormous, over-inflated African who gave me a half-hearted slap across the arse. 'Why you all so, man?' she bellowed, 'Come give Mumma a big fuckin' kiss!'

Everyone roared, and I pinked and wriggled off into the crowd. I ought to have known something like this would happen. Visitors were always being cautioned. Writing in 1912, James Rodway (British Guiana's greatest – and only – historian) advised that we 'must not be too fastidious for the negro women who crowd here are by no means choice in their language'. But it wasn't just in language that choiceness was deficient. I was now slithering along in the darkness through offal and open drains. Then the air filled with hot, wet gusts of mud, the gloom cleared and there was the river.

As my anxiety dissipated, an African market took shape. Outside in the mud were the dwarfs and scavengers, but inside business was booming. I came across wild honey, salted shark, crab oil and strips of meat like ancient bark. Some of the hunters also sold weapons and charms, and a deadly form of rum known as 'Cut and Load'. Then there were the stalls of the witches. Each one was piled with old sauce bottles, refilled with potions and unguents, marked 'Belly', 'Head pain', 'Cold' or 'Man Builder Tonic'. Although this last tonic sounded intriguing, it was just a jar of chillies pickled in fish-scales and bush rum. Whether this does anything for African manliness I don't know, but I had a feeling that it wouldn't do much for mine.

I did, on the other hand, experience an archaeological moment. Perhaps it was just the sweat and the darkness, but I suddenly felt that I'd stumbled on an earlier age. Had the old Dutch market felt something like this? Well, maybe – except that, back then, the merchandise was altogether different.

By all accounts, the sale of people was once a source of celebration here.

Almost everyone dressed for the occasion. According to one Dr Pinckard, who was here at the turn of the nineteenth century, 'it was quite a holyday'; the planters wore their 'gayest apparel' and permitted their slaves to don 'holyday clothes'. The whole of town would turn up to see the new arrivals. For the planters, here was the opportunity to buy new workers and breeders, while for their slaves, here was the chance of a wife. Sometimes the planters let them choose their own women, and – occasionally – if they were later unhappy with their choice, they'd bring them back and let them choose another. Sales day in Stabroek was not to be missed.

For the new arrivals, now docking in the mud, the mood was rather less festive. Many would have been captured months earlier, in places such as Niger or Benin, and would already have changed hands several times in exchange for bells or gloves, red hats and beads. Then they'd endured the long voyage – the 'Middle Passage' – sustained only by horse beans and oil. Not surprisingly, the survivors would be in a pitiful shape.

Once off the river, the slavers then set about getting their goods well scrubbed up. The captives had already lost their names, their clothes and all their possessions, and now they'd lose their hair. Then, to make these human lots look sleek and attractive, they were dressed in a compound of lime juice, oil and gunpowder. They were finally ready for sale.

In 1800 a good African was worth £50–100, which at today's prices is about half the price of a family car. Pregnant women were worth more, and so were pretty girls, and slaves that could read or sew. Once purchased, most were carted off to the plantations, but some stayed here, tending the Dutch in their homes. Either way they'd be given a new name – such as Smith or Hughes or Amsterdam – and handed over to an old slave for six weeks of instruction. During this time they'd learn the language of slavery (which happened to be English) and recover from the voyage. 'From living skeletons,' wrote a Scottish officer in the 1770s, 'they become plump and fat, with a beautiful clean skin, til it is disfigured by the inhuman flogging of some rascally proprietor.'

But life for Stabroek slaves was by no means a series of floggings. In this abhorrent trade it's often surprising, the small liberties that survived. Most slaves kept their African gods, and their magic and their secret potions. Some ran little businesses and would return here, to the market, to sell whatever they'd made: honey, perhaps, or rum and salted shark. Others had smallholdings and were allowed out until eight at night (provided they carried a lantern). Some slaves even had their own slaves. There were also slave holidays, a slave ball (four times a year) and regular handouts of grog. What's more, Africans were encouraged to have children – particularly after 1807, when the import of new slaves was banned. That year one of the agricultural societies even offered a medal for the farming of human beings. It was given to the planter who'd raised the greatest number of baby slaves.

It all seems unreal now, particularly the concept of human property. The slaves weren't merely chattels, they were also a responsibility; their master was duty-bound to clothe them and feed them for life; he had to discharge all their liabilities (including the cost of imprisonment, at 5 pence a day) and to ensure that they were never a drain on the public purse. What's more, he was also the only person who was allowed to flog them, work them, free them, donate them or bequeath them in a will. Just as they defined his status (a European had to have twenty-five slaves in order to vote), so he defined their existence. As a matter of law, the slave's life was, in many ways, like the life of a valuable horse.

Georgetown's slavery has proved a difficult stain to wash away. This was partly because there was so much of it left behind. The older parts of the city were almost entirely the work of slaves. They'd cut all the wood and baked all the bricks. They'd started the roads and the sea wall, and cut out all the canals. Then they'd died, taking themselves off to their own huge boggy cemeteries, well away from those of the whites. Even now the outlying neighbourhoods were known as 'fields', as though all that mattered was work.

But it wasn't just things, it was also lives. Almost half the city's inhabitants had slave names, with no idea what they'd been before. They also sang slave songs, used slave cures and spoke the standard slavers' English. The food too – saltfish, yams and breadfruit – was slavish, all introduced to fuel human toil. It sometimes seemed as though even the most intimate aspects of daily life were still somehow tainted by slavery – including marriage. One of my taxi-drivers put it like this: 'The African don't like to settle down, get married. Sometime he have three child-mother. I guess it dates from slavery times. What did they call us? *Breeding bulls* ...'

'And what about you?' I asked.

'Me child-mother have two children,' he said, 'and me girl have another.'

Cruelty too still stalked the Guyanese. Out in the street, even perfect strangers could be flailed with words. ('Hey, coolie t'ing! Fat girl! Why you dis me?') As one woman told me, you needed a thick hide to survive downtown. But the abuse wasn't always simply verbal. Forty years ago V.S. Naipaul remarked that nowhere in the world did people beat their children more brutally than here. 'This could still be true,' said Lorlene. 'Child abuse was probably the reason I went into politics ...'

But slave culture also had another, more insidious effect, constantly eroding self-esteem. Being black, I discovered, was not a matter of pride but a question of degree. You had to be the right kind of black, ideally with a hint of white. It all dated back to the days when planters favoured their own half-caste progeny over the pure-bred children of their slaves. Once, this miscegenation had spawned a complex lexicon all of its own; there were *cobs* (a quarter white), *mulattos* (half white), *mustees* (three-quarters white) and *octoroons* (seven-eighths white). Even now, a slice through Afro-Guyanese society reveals not layers of class but a spectrogram of colours. 'I'm red,' said Lorlene, proudly. This meant that as much as her ancestors had been slaves, so they'd also been their masters.

But sometimes, she said, even being the right shade of black was not enough. 'If three people go into a restaurant,' she explained, 'the white man will always be served first, then the Indian, and then the black. It's the same whatever the colour of the waiter. And no one will ever say a thing ...'

This was a demoralising thought. Had anything really changed, I wondered, or did slavery still seep out of the earth like some debilitating gas?

I decided to cheer myself up, by going in search of abolition.

I didn't have to go far; churches were everywhere.

The Afro-Guyanese loved these places. Every variant of Christianity was represented, and their churches came in all shapes and sizes. There were pink ones, green ones, tabernacles, miracle halls, chapels on stilts and temples like rockets. God, it seemed, owned half the city. Although for some people devotion was merely a way of getting through the day, for others it was different. In quaint old structures like St James-the-Less they still sensed the first seeds of revolt. Throughout the 1820s it had been a rallying point in the bid for a human's life.

But that's not where I was heading. Instead, I walked back through Stabroek and followed a row of huge black railings to St Andrew's Kirk. Here the story looked different. Built in 1818, only fourteen years after the British takeover, the kirk was exorbitantly Scottish. Around the walls were Scottish saints and Scottish flags, and the whole thing was slathered in varnish the colour of ancient peat. What was odd was that, although slavery was already in retreat, this was a work of ecclesiastical forced labour. The kirk had even borne a notice on its door: NEGROES AND ANIMALS NOT ALLOWED. Clearly, even then, the established Church was no friend of the slaves.

I sat down in one of the pews and drank in the cool. The kirk's apartheid days hadn't lasted long. No sooner was the varnish dry than the debate began – not here, of course, but thousands of miles away, in the coffee shops of London. In the end it was won by a coalition of ideas. On the one hand were the Evangelists, on the other the adherents of Adam Smith. Together, they'd argued that propping up a bloated, slave-owning plantocracy made neither moral nor economic sense. In 1834 slavery was banned.

Meanwhile, in the colony, there was one last gift for the slaves, and that was God. Guiana was flooded with missionaries. It ought to have been the beginning of harmony, but instead it was an age of dissent. A vague sensation of suffering became a burning sense of injustice. After the riots of August 1823 hundreds of slaves were executed. Their heads were stuck on poles, and displayed in the little gardens next to the Sidewalk Café.

At the far end of the kirk two girls began to sing. Their beautiful African voices filled the church and drifted upwards, out through the open doors and across the city. I could see people stop and turn to listen. In the gorgeous cascade of notes there were both waves of human happiness and centuries of regret. This, I imagined, is how redemption would sound.

And so it might – except that, in the minds of many, the fight had yet to end.

Out on the housing schemes, revolt was about the only commodity in limitless supply.

One day I got an Indian driver to take me to Timehri. All the way Ramdat Dhoni chattered on about the Blacks. 'They never saves nothing, they lives for today, and they always lies ...'

I said nothing. As long as I was compliant, he kept his eyes on the road.

'... They got lots of women, and most of them is teefs ...'

'What about work?' I ventured.

'Lazy!' squealed Ramdat.

'What do you mean?'

'Ever since slavery, never been back in the fields!'

'And what if they don't get work?'

'That's when they ends up in places like this, Timehri ...'

We were now churning along a sandy road, tall grass on either side.

'It's a no-go zone,' said Ramdat grimly. 'Get a puncture, you don't stop ...'

From among the stalks, matted heads peered at us blankly.

'... all they got is guns and dope ...'

And shacks, I noticed, made of cinder blocks and plastic.

'Not exactly housing,' I said.

'In Guyana, a housing scheme is never no more than a good idea.'

Ahead of us a child was sharpening a cutlass, or a machete. Ramdat swerved.

'They all teefs,' he said bitterly. 'All the Africans is teefs.'

Obviously Timehri brought out the worst in everyone, including Ramdat Dhoni. With his open, chubby face and his swaggering waddle, I had no idea then that his anger went so deep. I thought he was merely doing what so many Guyanese do, sowing a little verbal carnage among the neighbouring races. Generalisation was the general rule. Among the Asians, I would hear Ramdat's words time and time again, throughout the Guianas. Even V.S. Naipaul – himself an Indo-Caribbean – had considered the Africans slow, sullen and impulsively deceitful, and would write of the 'malarial sluggishness' that stalked their kind.

But the Afro-Guyanese would probably agree with the Asians on one thing: slavery had transformed the concept of labour. It was not as though abolition had suddenly switched off the power. No, Africans would happily work in a town, or in a uniform, or – better still – for themselves. (The biggest of the 'housing schemes', Buxton, was originally an African co-operative.) They'd even half-kill themselves digging for gold upriver. But what they wouldn't do was work that involved a boss, dirt and an affront to their new-found dignity. If this was the only option, they'd rather revert to dissent. Despite a shortage of cane-workers, thousands of Guyanese lived like this, in impoverished defiance. Often it meant retreating to the margins of society, to a place like Timehri.

'The police still doesn't come here after dark,' said Ramdat.

His son had done his military service in the housing schemes.

'Tell you, Man, every night was like a little civil war ...'

That was when the city got its razor wire and began to feel under siege.

'We still got a murder rate three times that of the USA ...'

I asked Ramdat what the fighting was all about.

'Dunno,' he said. 'People here's nuts. Like they want some kind of revenge.'

Everyone remembered this sudden surge of congenital fury. Those that could got out, including all of Ramdat's family. Worse, however, was to come. First, in 2002, New York gathered up all its

Guyanese criminals and sent the whole lot home. Then, four years later, the GDF – or Guyanese Defence Force – managed to lose a huge consignment of AK-47s. After that, people began to hire little armies of their own. Foreign embassies turned into castles, and at night the streets were shackled in chains and then abandoned to the outlaws.

I asked Ramdat whether things were any better now. He hesitated.

'Probably, yes. Especially since we killed Fineman and Skinny.'

People would often tell me the story of Fineman and Skinny. It was like Robin Hood, except with no obvious sheriffs, no heroines, a crate of Kalashnikovs and twenty-five Robins, who stole mostly from the poor. I'd often seen Fineman's poster, still pinned up in shops and garages, and plastered over trees. WANTED, it said, FOR MURDER. Sometimes he was wanted alone, sometimes with his band of men. They didn't really need identikit pictures. It seemed that behind the killings was a macabre gang of runaway carica-tures: Coolie Boy, Baby James, Not Nice, Chucky Daniels, John Eye, Dread, Capone, Bullet, White Boy and Ratty.

No one knows why Fineman started killing.

'Came into Lusignan,' said Ramdat, 'shot twelve Indians, just like that.'

Soon the police had him everywhere, killing everything that died. Ramdat could list them all: ' ... a government minister, a TV pre-senter ...' Others, such as Lorlene, were less convinced.

'Fineman was the bogeyman,' she'd said, 'our one-man wave of crime.'

'Even kids talked about him!' said Ramdat, 'and dreamed of him at night ...'

Then it ended. Several months earlier the army had found him, here in Timehri.

'And this is where they shot him!' said Ramdat, skidding to a halt. 'Right here! Blew his head off!'

We peered out. There was nothing there but the seething grass.

'And what about the gang?'

'They're still finding them.'

Sure enough, over the next few weeks the rest of the gang were shot. Their posthumous portraits always appeared in the papers; bluish skin, muddy hair, eyes like marbles, and faces shot away. It was, I suppose, the modern equivalent of heads on sharpened sticks.

We drove back, looking out for little bits of India.

The horizon was just a long green curve of sugar. It was like being out at sea, moving almost imperceptibly through the swirling currents of cane. Every now and then Ramdat spotted what he was after. Temple! Mosque! Prayer flags! Occasionally we even bumped through little clusters of pink stilted houses, which he called the 'estates'. Only Africans, he told me, lived in 'villages'.

Then we'd be back in the cane. Once I saw some tiny figures working through it, with machetes and burning torches. The air was like hot, wet pulp, and the figures moved as though they were wading through the heat. I imagined that the slaves had looked something like this – until abolition. After that, most of them had refused to cut the boss's sugar at all, even for his poxy wages. Without muscle, this ocean of sugar would have reverted to mud.

'So that's when my family got here,' said Ramdat, 'about 1840 ...'

'Do you know where from?'

'Of course. We're from Bengal!'

Ramdat made an unusual Bengali. Neither he – nor any of the Ramdat Dhonis before him – had set foot in India for the best part of 200 years. He no longer spoke the language or wore the clothes, and he wasn't even sure where Bengal was. But, for all that, he was still obstinately Indian. He wobbled his head, worshipped Hindu gods and – whenever we went out – he brought bundles of dhal and rice, wrapped up in paper and string. It was almost as though he was just quietly waiting to head back to the home he'd never known. This, after all, is what his forebears had always intended. 'They signed a five-year contract,' he said, 'but then they never had the money for the passage home.'

Most Guyanese Indians could tell a similar tale. Between 1838 and 1917 almost a quarter of a million of them had arrived in the colony. It was like Exodus in reverse, a flight into bondage. Under the terms of their indentures the 'coolies' (as they became known) were no better off than the Africans before. Not only were they confined to their plantations but they'd also inadvertently agreed to being fined, starved, locked up for absence, abandoned, underpaid, flogged and doused in salt pickle. It was hardly the Promised Land.

In the century to 1950 there were at least sixteen major revolts. What else could they do? Like Ramdat's ancestors, few had enough for the journey home.

'So here we are!' he laughed, 'in a place we didn't want to be!'

I've often thought about this. Perhaps it would be Guyana's epitaph? Apart from the few Amerindians and a handful of adventurers, almost the entire country was descended from people who'd rather have been somewhere else. As between Africans and Indians, however, there was a difference. While the Africans were stripped of everything, the Indians carried on living in a world of their own; they never intermarried, never took anyone else's god and never changed their names. They even cornered off the cane fields, undercutting African wages and buying them off the land.

'So no wonder you don't get on?' I asked Ramdat.

The head wobbled. 'They think we're rich ...'

'And you think they're lazy?'

Ramdat paused. 'I can't forget how they killed my father ...'

Ah, I thought, the piece that's been missing all along.

Ramdat broke the silence. 'He was a water engineer.'

'And who were they?'

'Big crowd of Africans. Beat him down in 1963.'

He told me what happened, and then neither of us said much for a while. We just sat, watching the cane blurring past. I shall probably never understand how Ramdat senior's brains had ended up on the kitchen floor, or how so many others like him had died, but I could at least get some feeling for how the present had begun. To do this, I'd visit a dental surgery and meet a man whose parents had been republican royalty, and for whom he had nothing but contempt.

As the Age of Sugar waned, the Rule of the Dentists began.

It took me a while to find their surgery. Charlotte Street was like a riverbed, rippling along through old rocks and cataracts of tarmac. Occasionally the surface vanished altogether, offering eerie views of the world within. But even when I found my footing, I struggled to find the address. This was not uncommon in Guyana. Houses often had no number at all, or a wrong one, or one that bore no relation to those before. Sometimes I'd be making good progress along a street when, suddenly, twenty houses would disappear, only to reappear half a mile away in the opposite direction. It was almost as though the forest spirits had come into Georgetown one night and shuffled it all around.

Several times I asked the way. 'Excuse me, where do I find Cheddi Jagan's surgery?' This was like wandering around London and asking for Number 10. Everybody knew Cheddi, and people often talked about him as though he was still alive. In a sense he still was. 'Jaganism' was everywhere. To Africans it just meant being Indian and Marxist. But to Indians it meant being free of imperialism and free from Africans. Inspirational it may not have been but – to them – it was predictable, professional and reassuringly painful, a bit like dentistry itself.

Eventually I found the surgery. After fifty years of Jaganism I'd expected something dynastic, perhaps with a drawbridge and minarets. Instead, it was a low concrete box with a grille across the front. Cheddi's name was still painted up on a sun-bleached sign. He'd never had much money. His father, I'd read, had been a labourer, who'd married as a child, had ten children himself and then died in his fifties when his leg turned green. Cheddi was one of the only offspring not to emigrate. During his few years in America, at dental college, he'd survived by washing dishes and selling patent cures. This place was all he could afford when he returned in 1946, at the age of twenty-eight.

'You want something, mister?'

A woman had appeared at the bars. I explained my curiosity.

'You better come in, see Dr Jagan'.

I must have looked puzzled.

'Dr Jagan,' she said, 'is Dr Jagan's son.'

She ushered me in and then heaved herself back to her desk. We were in a long, narrow room that felt like a pipe. There was a large tank of fish and some brittle foliage, and everything was painted dark blue as though we were on the seabed. I was surprised to find Jagans still here. In his lofty autobiography, *The West on Trial*, Cheddi had never mentioned any children. Perhaps he hadn't noticed them. I wondered what it did for a son to be ranked in his father's memory somewhere below the price of rice, a meeting with British trade unionists (1951), and his thoughts on cricket and Cuba.

Then Joey appeared, angry from the start. It was an alarming sight: a big man with hands like haunches of boiled beef and a beefy head topped with silvery bristles, breathing smoke. He wore a pale blue military shirt and seemed to barge around as though there were people always in his way. For a moment his gaze settled on me, and I wondered what I'd done wrong. But it soon passed, and he gave a dragon-like huff and agreed to a two-minute talk. I followed as he barged off down his strange undersea hall into a submarine study.

'This is where my dad practised,' snarled Joey, 'all his life.'

'What, even when he was the president?'

Joey sat down behind an empty desk. 'Yup, needed the money.'

Around the walls were photographs of his father: Cheddi with generals and other presidents; Cheddi in knitted ties; Cheddi receiving honours, or handing them out to Marxist rebels. Among these pictures Joey had added a few touches of his own: a mail order collection of the classics, a life of Pol Pot and a boom box with tiny, flashing lights. Strangely there was nothing here of his mother.

Joey shrugged. 'I don't see her that much.'

I had, however, seen her picture before. She was famously white and Jewish, and notoriously waspish. Cheddi had met Janet Rosenberg during his Illinois days, and the day they married her father had threatened to shoot her. Janet herself was one of those rare creatures, an American communist, but she was also fiercely loyal to her dental hero. She served Cheddi here, as his hygienist, for the rest of his life. She even took ministerial posts in his governments, and then – when he died in 1997 – she took over his job and became the head of state. That made Joey one of the few people in the world both of whose parents had held presidential office.

I asked him if that had ever made him feel excluded.

Joey crushed out his cigarette. 'They were married to politics. Communism. That's why I was called Joey – after Joseph Stalin. Jesus! I was even a communist myself for a while. I had a beret, and was arrested for rioting in Montreal ...'

'But not now?'

'Hell, no!' snorted Joey. 'You know what? If I was running this place, I'd kick out all the communists. I'd hold a panel of inquiry and ask everyone a simple question: are you a communist? If so, I'd throw them! Send them to Cuba.'

'Isn't that a bit like McCarthyism ...?' I ventured.

'Nope. McCarthy picked out people who'd done nothing wrong. These people are communists.'

'So you'd send your mother to Cuba?'

'She's a communist, yes.'

'And do you want to run the country?'

Joey said he did. Although he'd spent all his life as a dentist, he still had a vision of power. He said that Africans would vote for him, and so all he needed was 10 per cent of the Indian vote. He'd already formed the Unity Party of Guyana. It stood for clean streets, no crime and an ambitious policy abroad. He told me he'd happily take out not only Venezuela's Hugo Chávez ('a fascist') but also Syria and Iran. 'In my view,' he said, 'we should implement a limited nuclear strike.'

I said I'd follow his progress with interest.

'I got to build a website,' said Joey, 'I'm not ready yet.'

Guyana, it seems, still has some time to wait before a return to dental rule.

A previous generation of tooth-pullers had fought a much bloodier fight.

To begin with, no one could find the enemy. During the colonial elections of 1953 the Africans and Indians had united under Cheddi and won. There wasn't even a struggle for independence. Britain couldn't wait to get shot of Guiana, and the only thing that worried it – and its ally, the United States – was Marxism. Cheddi could never see this and soon started spouting Soviet policy. London reacted by suspending the constitution, imposing an interim government and dispatching two destroyers, an aircraft carrier and an army of occupation. For the British, this would be one of the biggest wars they'd ever fought with an enemy that didn't exist. The troops had been told they were here to suppress a dangerous coup. Instead, they found nothing. Even now, they're remembered wandering the streets, asking 'Where's the fighting? Anyone seen the war?'

In the absence of revolution Britain cast around for an enemy within. On Fleet Street the Jagans were depicted as traitors. The *Daily Express* even suggested that Janet the Hygienist was trying to 'ape the Mau Mau terror'. Soon the colonial police were bashing down the door of Charlotte Street, and confiscating books that would have been perfectly legitimate in London. Then, in 1954, both Cheddi and Janet were imprisoned for travelling without permits, and a few literary infractions. Cheddi spent six months in a penal colony deep in the bush.

I asked Joey whether this had left him resentful.

'Nope,' he replied, airily, 'he always admired the British.'

What no one had spotted was that the enemy was everywhere, among the people themselves. The great fault line that runs through Guyanese society began to crack open. The first casualty was Cheddi's party, the PPP. Stimulated by the prospect of power, the Indians declared *Apan Jhaat* – or 'each to his own'. Meanwhile, in 1955, the Africans broke away. 'The coolies,' declared their leader, 'have taken over the party.'

It wasn't long before the insults turned to rocks. Over the next few years the abuse escalated into strikes and scuffles and then full-scale riot. It infuriated the African faction (now called the PNC) that they couldn't defeat the Indians in the elections of 1957 and 1961, and so they abandoned Marxism and unleashed their fury across the city. Whole neighbourhoods were burned, Indians were looted and the police were caught in the crossfire. More troops arrived, only to be hated by both sides. It didn't help that one of the first regiments to turn up was called the Black Watch.

Soon the colony was barely functioning at all. The Indians discovered that they could close down the countryside, while the Africans turned off the city. Nothing stirred except the flames. In desperation, Cheddi's government sought help from Cuba, while the Africans had Washington's support. British Guiana had become a little sugary pawn in a much bigger game.

Then the killing began. Ramdat's father was only one of hundreds to die. Both sides casually ambushed their victims and then hacked them apart. Grenades were tossed into buses, and there were acid bombs and dynamite. Over 1,400 homes were destroyed, and 15,000 people were displaced. A ferry and several cinemas were also blown up, and at Plantation Leonora a group of Indian strikers were mown down with a tractor (one of them, Mrs Kowsilla, being famously cut in half). But the worst place of all was Wismar. There a crowd of 18,000 Africans descended on the town, with petrol bombs and knives. 'Kill the coolies!' they screamed, and the entire Indian population of 1,300 was jeered all the way back to Georgetown. Along the road eight women were raped, one man was decapitated and another burned alive. The rest never returned, and – later – the town was renamed Linden, after the African leader.

'It were a warning,' said Ramdat, 'of the power of the mob.'

But not everyone remembers it like this. I once met an old boatman on the Berbice River, and I asked him about the Indians of Wismar.

He thought about it for a moment, staring deep into the black water, and then shook his head. 'They got what them deserved.'

I often walked back along the old battlefields.

All quiet now, it was hard to believe the violence of fifty years before. The trees had grown back, and the scorch-marks had long since faded away. Sometimes I'd walk through Stabroek and Lacytown, where the fires had flourished, reducing whole neighbourhoods to little stumps of charcoal, but there was no sign now of this self-inflicted blitz. Fretwork and fancy carpentry were blooming once again. Occasionally I'd pass down Water Street and Robb Street, where the rioters had once screamed at each other under a blizzard of tear gas and rocks. Nowadays this was the place to haggle for a boom box or cover yourself in trinkets. But it was also here that a colonial police superintendent called MacLeod was standing one turbulent morning in February 1962. Just as he was wondering how his life had come to this, a burst of gunfire smashed through his lungs and brought it to an end. All he learned that day is that you never know where you are with Georgetown until it's far too late.

Other times I'd duck back across the centre. Here the city was at its most beguiling, swooning with parks and gardens, and more than a touch of denial. These days no one admitted to having joined the riots. Anybody would have thought the upheaval was seismic in origin and had happened all by itself. But the trouble with this was that so many hideaways had somehow survived. I was always coming across places where plots were supposed to have been hatched: hotels, offices, bars and even a school of ballet. Perhaps the most conspicuous of all was Congress House. Everyone agreed that the PNC had spent most of the '60s here, cooking up homemade bombs.

It would soon be the turn of the Africans to rule.

Over on the seaward side of town was the last bastion of Indian rule.

Cheddi, it seemed, had chosen a residence that looked the way he felt. The Red House was grand and yet spartan, and covered in bristly crimson shingles. At first I thought it was abandoned: the shutters were bolted, and the grass grew long in the yard. But then I noticed that the front door was open, and so I went inside. It was breathlessly hot, and all I could hear was the furious bandsaw of flies. There was no furniture, just highly polished floors and my own reflection, wandering around, upside down and slightly perplexed.

After a while an Indian appeared. She wore the clothes of a child but had the face of an older woman. When she moved, she made no sound at all, and I half-wondered if she'd been there all the time. I asked her if I could see where Dr Jagan had lived, and she tilted her head and gestured towards the stairs. I clattered upwards through the gloom and the thickening stratum of heat and flies, while she floated along behind. We stopped only when we got to the attic. There were only two rooms to see. One had a glass case full of gifts: a silver dish from the Americans, a carriage clock from the Queen and some pieces of rock from Zambia. I nodded approvingly, and the little apparition floated off, beckoning me to follow.

The second room was Cheddi's study, looking exactly as it had the day he fell from power in 1964. There was his hammock, his old driving licence, a roll-top desk and an armchair with freshly laundered antimacassars. For three years he'd worked away up here, controlling the currency, dreaming up taxes and closing down the newspapers. I noticed that his armchair tipped up, so that – like his patients – Dr Jagan could lie back and contemplate the pain.

Behind me, the little sprite hovered in the shadows.

'What are these?' I asked her.

On the desk was a large collection of old jars: mints, toffees and humbugs.

'He loved sweets,' whispered the girl.

It was the only thing she ever said, but it left a powerful impression. While all around him the city burned, the Great Comrade–Dentist was up here, secretly ruining his teeth. By the end the colony was in such poor shape that even the Trinidadians were suggesting it be placed under UN control and run by New Zealand. But Britain and America had other plans. They'd spotted that, by tweaking the electoral system, they could put the Africans in charge. All it involved was a switch from 'first-past-the-post' to proportional representation. Although the Indians would still have the most popular party, the Africans could then unite with the Portuguese and the Amerindians and oust them from power.

Cheddi howled at the unfairness of it all, and soon it was the Indians letting off bombs. They burned part of the railway and blew up the US Consulate (injuring, among others, Miss Guiana, now better known as Shakira Caine). But none of this changed anything. Once in charge, the Africans began to negotiate independence. Two years later, in 1966, the old colony was renamed Guyana, and the British departed in a great display of feathers and tootling trumpets.

'Madness,' Joey told me. 'We shouldn't be independent, even now.'

So began the next twenty-eight years: an African dictatorship in the margins of South America.

Lorlene often talked about the man who became the *kabaka*, or African king. It was almost as though her life could be divided into three parts: the time before Burnham's reign (idyllic), the time during it (catastrophic) and the time since (yet to be decided). If only she could understand the world of Linden Forbes Sampson Burnham, then everything else would fall into place.

'Is there anything left of him?' I asked. 'Around the city?'

'Not much,' she said. A concrete memorial and the place where he'd lived.

One day we all got in the car and went over to Castellani House.

'I haven't been here for years,' shuddered Lorlene as she drove up the drive.

It was a huge wooden barn of a place in the fringes of the zoo. For Burnham it was perfect: a life spent among flamboyants and peacocks, trees that sprouted cannonballs and reptiles that lived for ever. In the photographs that have survived he looks exotic and well groomed, as though he himself had a tail full of plumes. Everyone agreed he was charming and articulate. V.S. Naipaul said he was the best public speaker he'd ever heard. With his heady blend of Christianity, Marxism and liberal democracy Burnham had soon emerged as the Africans' champion. Only his sister was suspicious. On the eve of his election she published a pamphlet called *Beware of My Brother Forbes*.

Nowadays his old house was used as the National Gallery. Here was Guyana depicted from every angle, slathered in colour, contorted, post-modernised, pre-Raphaelited, reassembled from egg boxes and draped in nudes. All that was missing was Burnham. Every trace of him had gone – from his cabinet rooms down to the last drop of Chivas Regal. It was a remarkable act of sanitation (which had all the hallmarks of Janet Jagan, who'd refurbished the gallery). The life of one of the world's most exuberant black politicians had simply been painted over.

It was the same on the floors above. This was painful for Lorlene, to discover that her nemesis had vanished. There was nothing left to be shocked by or to mock, or even to understand. It was typical of Burnham to be like this. Right from the start, his rule had been artfully insidious. To begin with, it had seemed no more than a change of décor; the Union Jack was exchanged for the Golden Arrowhead, the statue of Queen Victoria was moved to the zoo, and – in parliament – a portrait of Sir Walter Raleigh was taken down and replaced with one of Burnham, looking equally Jacobean. Even the Americans still loved him at that stage, as he'd renounced Marxism and slapped a huge tax on anything communist. Guyana was the perfect former colony.

'Then, in 1969,' said Lorlene, 'we became a republic.'

Nobody much minded this, but it was a sign of things to come.

'A year later, we became a *co-operative* republic.'

'What did the co-operative bit mean?' I asked.

She didn't know, and nor did anyone else. Burnham promised that it would 'make a small man into a real man', and his ministers began signing themselves off, 'Yours co-operatively'. But it was more than just a game of words. At heart were old African anxieties. Burnham fretted that he was too compliant, too much the product of a master and only outwardly black. It was time to reassert the communal values of his ancestors and become more African again.

Castellani House had never seen anything like this before. Burnham began striding around in dashikis and calling himself *kabaka*; he threw his piffling weight behind the liberation movements in Angola and Mozambique, and allowed Cuban planes to refuel in Guyana en route to war. Then, just to complete the picture, he recognised China and nationalised sugar and all the mines. As the Americans withdrew, they were replaced with Zambian advisers and North Koreans. Among their more ludicrous ideas, the Koreans came up with rice terraces. 'Imagine that!' said Lorlene. 'Rice terraces! Here, in a country short of everything but space …'

We'd reached the top floor, a maze of smaller rooms. Lorlene stopped.

'This is where they brought my father,' she said, 'the night we were expelled.'

Having rearranged his friends, Burnham then turned on his enemies.

First he fixed the Indians. By the time of the 1968 election they significantly outnumbered the Africans and ought to have won. But once again Burnham had changed the rules. This time overseas voters were allowed to vote, and he invented an entire electorate of ghosts and Mickey Mouses, and Guyanese with addresses in the fields. Jokes like this could be run and run, and kept the PNC in power until 1992.

Next Burnham turned on the dissenters. He suspended the constitution and the right of habeas corpus, and announced the 'paramountcy of the party'. Every public building had to fly the PNC's flag, and every military officer had to swear an oath of party loyalty. Meanwhile, the army was about the only organ of state still in development. It absorbed a sixth of the government's budget and 3 per cent of the workers (almost all of them African). With its socialist movements and red militias, it became an assiduous enforcer of the chaos.

But even if these ragtag outfits failed to scare anyone, there were always a few thugs that would. Most impressive was the House of Israel. Although it was run by an American fugitive, its goons would do anything for Burnham. They wore PNC colours, broke up strikes and called themselves his 'church'. Funnily enough, they always seemed to be around whenever his opponents were getting a bayonet in the guts or a bullet through the head.

That left only the media, and people like Lorlene's father. The papers were easy enough: they could be starved of newsprint or charged with 'public mischief'. But for people who also worked in radio, a different approach was needed. Just like Lorlene's father, they were summoned here at midnight.

'And what did Burnham do?' I asked her.

'He was charming, as usual. He just said you've got a nice family, and you should think of them.'

With charm like that, the Jameses were gone within the week.

'I hate to think what would have happened if we'd stayed.'

We were standing at one of Burnham's windows, looking out across a canopy of scarlet blossom. 'This city is like paradise on Earth,' said Lorlene, 'until you know what goes on beneath.'

As we drove back, I began to see not so much a city built by slaves as one worn down by Burnham. Beneath its beautiful canopies and fretwork the infrastructure had long since crumbled away. The canals were clogged, the roads had collapsed, the drains were imploding, and the last of the railways were now just a streak of cinders. Everyone agreed that it hadn't always been like this.

'The trains were the first to go,' said Lorlene. 'He sold them to Nigeria.'

After that, people told me, the buses failed, followed by the post office. Guyana, it was said, had the first postal system in the world that stopped for the entire weekend. Even now, no one had any realistic expectation of letters or parcels, or a public bus from A to B. But this was nothing compared with the malevolent spells that Burnham had cast over the country's natural wealth. Rice was cursed because it was the source of Indian wealth. Sugar simply failed through neglect and became unavailable for a while, even though it grew everywhere like weed.

Then, as scarcity took hold, Burnham banned the import of food. Potatoes and wheat, he said, were tools of the capitalist West. After that, almost all imports were banned. Engines failed, and there were no alarm clocks, fan belts or tractors. Production halted, as scarcity stalked every aspect of public life. For much of the dictatorship there was a black market in lipstick, and aspirin could only be acquired through the racketeers. 'We became a nation of smugglers,' said Lorlene, 'and, in many ways, still are ...'

She waved an arm at the cars. 'Almost all contraband, from Suriname ...'

After cars, she said, came fuel, drugs, guns and girls.

'Smuggling is now instinctive, a way of life ...'

The concept of collapse still has the Guyanese heading for the exits. To begin with, emigration was just a steady trickle. In the first eight years of Burnham 22,000 people left, followed by 28,000 in the four years after that. The poor slipped over the borders, and the rest took to planes. Burnham tried to stop them for a while. Watching the Guyanese at the airport was (as one foreign journalist put it) like watching caged animals getting their release. Soon the trickle became a torrent. Since independence, almost a quarter of the country has left. Even now, some 93 per cent of tertiary graduates pack up their bags and leave. Google 'Guyanese Club' and you'll find that almost every Canadian town has one. Another

70,000 headed to Britain. There, in a country they found education-
ally slack, they and their families had often thrived. Among them
were surgeons, lawyers, sportsmen (Mark Ramprakash), politicians
(Baroness Amos, Bernie Grant and Trevor Phillips) and performers
(Eddy Grant and Leona Lewis). The sheer breadth of their talents
speaks volumes for the depth of Guyana's loss.

'The only people still here,' said Lorlene, 'are those who either
have a passion for the place or can't afford the ticket out.'

A few weeks later, I had tea with an old bomb-maker, who'd led
the resistance. We'd arranged to meet at the Cara Lodge Hotel. I
loved this place, and occasionally stayed there whenever I needed
to be downtown. In a city of lacy buildings, this was the laciest of
all. From the outside, it reminded me of a wedding dress, all spot-
lessly white and frilly. But on the inside it was dark and breezy, with
wide open decks and wooden walls that creaked and yawed like a
ship. Once it had been the home of a family called the Taitts, and
here they'd hosted the colony's first philharmonic orchestra, its first
Marxist party, its first basketball team and its first school of ballet.
Even Cheddi and Burnham had conspired here, before they fell out.

'That made it inviolable,' said my host. 'Burnham wouldn't
touch it.'

'So it became the centre of resistance?' I asked.

'Well, yes, I suppose it did. We all lived in the rooms upstairs.'

'And is it still the Taitts' house?'

'Yes. They fled after the assassination, so we run it for them, as
a little hotel.'

Dr Roopnaraine was sprawled in a cane chair, before a tray of
untouched tea. Everything about him sprawled; the long, thin legs
dangling over the armrest; the jeans and shirt slightly too big; and
the boyish hank of silvery hair, flopping over his forehead. Even
his stories sprawled, bounding along in immaculate tally-ho Indian.
As he talked he smoked, and his hands swooped around making
vapour trails, like a dogfight in front of his face. He was thrillingly
articulate but not always easy to follow. Sometimes we were fighting
in Grenada, then we were at Cambridge (picking up a cricket blue)
followed by Cornell, then a childhood spent with Burnham (and
parents who were 'through and through Bolsheviks'), and then we'd

be back near the present, setting fire to the sugar cane or running a college, or making films, and researching the history of art.

I asked if he ever regretted the resort to violence.

Roopnaraine hesitated. 'No,' he said, 'democracy had failed.'

For the rest of teatime we lost ourselves in revolt. At times it all sounded weirdly parochial; Roopnaraine had been at the same school as not only Burnham but also Cheddi, the head of the army, the man who tortured him in prison, and at the same time as an awesome Pan-Africanist called Dr Walter Rodney. ('Politics in Guyana,' he said wryly, 'is still very much a family affair'.) But in another sense it all looked like something new, a revolution in reverse. Instead of the masses taking up arms, it was the tiny, intellectual élite. In 1979 they joined up under an incongruous name – the Working People's Alliance – and began to set fire to the cane. 'Fire terrified Burnham,' said Roopnaraine happily, 'and he started to lose his edge ...'

In front of us, the tea had gone cold, so we ordered tumblers of rum.

'And what did you do then?' I asked.

'Well, I wanted an armed insurrection! What a fuck-up. We'd been stockpiling timers, explosives and arms, right here in the room upstairs. I thought the army would come out and join us, but Cheddi disagreed and argued – on Leninist principles – that without the army the coup would fail ...'

Roopnaraine shook his head, smiled and lit another cigarette. 'So anyway,' he went on, 'that July, we burned down the PNC's head-quarters and the Ministry of National Development, and then, a few days later, we were all arrested ...'

The gang of scholars hadn't fared well in the days and months that followed. Although they all eventually wriggled out of the charges, several of them were murdered, some fled abroad and others disappeared. Their movement began to fall apart. Lorlene told me that none of them had ever married; the WPA was their life. Of the three vaguely Marxist parties that have dominated Guyanese politics, it was probably the most intelligent, as well as the most embracing and the most out of touch. But now it had almost gone. It had no money and no MPs, and only a figurehead in Rupert Roopnaraine. With his reputation for almost inhuman honesty, he was the *éminence grise* of the Guyanese left, as well as its *enfant terrible*.

'Tell me about the assassination,' I said.

In Guyana, all the most memorable murders happen outside the Camp Street jail. I'd often passed it, on the way to somewhere else. At one end of Camp Street itself was an empty space where the ministry had stood – before the scholars burned it down – and at the other was a steel fortress, the length of a block. Although it looked like some vast extraterrestrial biscuit tin, this was the city jail, mounted with a thick black fuzz of razor wire and arc lights. Occasionally, I'd see women standing outside, bellowing through the tin, and then – from inside – I'd hear faint voices in reply.

But it was not a place to hang around. There were even coils of wire across the street. Lorlene once told me they'd been there since the great break-out of 2002. A gang calling themselves Five for Freedom had somehow escaped and then used machine guns to blast a path across the city. 'It was like a film,' she said, 'I saw schoolchildren running for their lives, and a man just firing wildly down the street. After that, Guyana never felt quite the same …'

But the jail had seen atrocity before. One day in June 1980 a car pulled up and parked on the other side of the prison. Inside was the great Pan-Africanist Dr Walter Rodney, along with his brother Donald. There was also another man, a soldier called Sergeant Smith, in a house nearby with a triggering device. The Rodneys talked for a moment and then the car exploded. Donald was left with a large shard of glass lolling from his throat, and Walter lost most of his head. It seems odd to think of all this as merely a 'fuck-up'. Africans everywhere had been deprived of a champion. Some 35,000 people attended the funeral, and protests came in from all over the socialist world. Burnham the bomber! Ruthless Burnham! In all the accounts I'd ever read of Walter's death, he'd been killed by a radio set in which Sergeant Smith had secretly hidden a tiny bomb. Even the *Encyclopaedia Britannica* has him assassinated like this, with an exploding walkie-talkie.

'In actual fact,' said Roopnaraine, 'there was never any walkie-talkie …'

'So the bomb was *yours?*'

'Yes,' he replied, much to his own surprise, 'yes, it was.'

'And I don't suppose it was meant to go off?'

'No. There was no explosive in the device. It was simply a wooden box with an electronic receiver. The activity was intended as a loyalty test for Smith, who, it later emerged, had a background in electronics. It turned out he was an agent and that he'd somehow succeeded in loading the device with explosive. Next thing we know, BOOM! Walter's dead.'

'And Donald?'

'He's in a terrible state but we got him back here, found a friendly surgeon and performed an operation right where we're sitting now.'

'And he survived?'

'As good as new,' said Roopnaraine, and he smiled, as though insurgency was just like cricket, except without the blue.

It was time to leave Georgetown and begin my forays into the rest of Guyana, otherwise known as the bush.

I was sorry to be leaving. Somehow the city had created the illusion of familiarity. Within a few weeks I'd acquired somewhere to live and a few friends, and I had a rough idea of where everything was. But more than this, there was something about the city – its breezy architecture, its see-through homes, its open arms and its open drains – that made me feel I understood it, and that here was a place with nothing to hide.

Even at the time, I realised this was folly. There probably isn't a city in the world that's so physically transparent and yet so mentally opaque. Even those living in Georgetown didn't really understand it. They didn't know who owned anything, how the rich got rich, who was behind the politicians or who was running the country. Some thought America called all the shots, others that Britain was about to resume control (in return for carbon credits). When the Minister of Agriculture was mown down by a cadre of commandos, it didn't seem to surprise anyone that the inquiry had ground to a halt. People had got used to mysteries. Many still hoped that, one day, a revolution would sweep it all away. But how many decades had they waited? In the meantime they'd busy themselves in the struggle for work or fuel or a telephone that worked, or in the search for simple facts. As Shiva Naipaul once wrote, 'In British Guiana it is impossible to find out the truth about any major thing.'

In retrospect, I only caught occasional glimpses of hidden Georgetown, usually in hotels. Just as Cara Lodge had been the centre of revolt, so the Pegasus was now the centre of power. I never went there without seeing some or other government minister lunching with large Canadians. Everyone had bodyguards, and with so much shiny cloth and hired muscle it could sometimes seem like the court of a medieval king. Once I managed to talk to one of the oil men (or was he gold? I forget). He told me that he flew in every week and that he never left the lobby without his special forces. 'Guyana is complex,' he warned, 'there are wheels within wheels.'

Another hotel with a window on the world within was The Tower. It too ought to have been a hotspot of political intrigue. In an earlier incarnation it had been Georgetown's finest hotel (and even Evelyn Waugh had stayed there, making it, briefly, the head-quarters of his contempt), but then the fires had reduced it to ash, and a tube of concrete had erupted in its place. It sometimes seemed that this strong, new profile had made it a hotspot of something else. The lobby was satisfyingly perfunctory and anonymous, and housed a large condom machine with a notice: 'ACT SAFE. ROCK AND UNROLL.'

I only stayed there once. Although few guests ever seemed to use the public areas, I did meet three unlikely English pedlars, sitting in the bar. They said they enjoyed travel books, and were making their way round the world selling England football shirts and some-times a little cocaine. None of this seemed at all odd at the time, and soon I was joining in and throwing back the rum. 'Here's to Waugh!' hooted Dezza, a boy the colour of carrots. 'A toast to the grumpy old bugger!' It wasn't much of a salute, but then, as an old Waugh-haunt, The Tower wasn't much of a successor. As the bar staff slithered quietly out of sight, I made as though to go. But a powerful orange hand caught me by the arm. 'We'll see you again,' said Dezza, 'you'll find us at the Appleby Horse Fair.'

I then clambered off, up through six storeys of concrete. My room, somewhere near the top, was all white and metallic like a fridge and had a mirror along one wall. I remember thinking how novel it was, the quiet and the cold. For a long time I just lay there, pondering the mysterious fragments of another Georgetown day.

Almost exactly thirty years earlier another guest had lain here, somewhere on this floor, contemplating the ill-fitting pieces that made up her life.

She was convinced she was being hunted down by men with auto-matic rifles and bazookas, and perhaps she was. In her terror she slept in the bath and made the desk staff swear they'd never seen her. But she was not a person it was easy to forget. Even in her state of nervous disintegration she still had about her a smouldering beauty and an air of volatile youth. Perhaps that's why no one believed her when she talked about the guns, the punishments and the hundreds of people about to die. To anyone that met her, Debbie Layton was just a flaky Californian – callow, bush-crazy and probably drugged. She would fly home the next day, and The Tower would be rid of her for ever.

But Debbie Layton was more resilient than anyone imagined. True, her life was confused, but its components had left her resourceful and resistant to defeat. She'd survived a neurotic Berkeley childhood, years of self-harm, a spell in a bike gang and a period of exile at a boarding school in Yorkshire. Then came the cult. Seven years earlier, in 1971, she thought she'd stumbled on her destiny, in the shape of a preacher with oily black hair and full wet lips. At the age of eighteen she gave the Revd Jim Jones everything she had, including her virginity. He took it while they were riding along in his church's bus, and then he enjoyed her again in a public toilet. It wasn't the first time Jones had helped himself to his flock, and soon the press were on his trail. As the allegations began to entangle him, Jones moved out to one of the remotest areas of Guyana in 1977, along with his church, 'The People's Temple'. In December of that year Debbie Layton followed, and then – six months later – she was back in Georgetown, hollow-eyed and running for her life.

The cult, she claimed, was on the brink of catastrophe, and of course she was right. Through all the shards of her own broken youth she'd somehow spotted the impending disaster.

The calamity she'd predicted would not be long in coming. A few months later, in November 1978, Jones's private Promised Land would fail in a way that the world had never seen before. The Jonestown Massacre, as it's now known, would wipe out an entire community and kill over 900 people. Aside from acts of belligerence and natural calamity, it would be the biggest single loss of life in modern times. People didn't know what to call it. Suicide? Genocide? Or both? For years the slaughter would generate films, books, investigations, inquiries, elections and countless theories, but it has never been fully explained – and probably never will be. These days, it's all things to all pundits: a conspiracy, a collective failure of mental health or the end of the psychedelic era.

But to the Guyanese the massacre was something different again.

The Wall Street Journal once described it as 'the most famous moment in Guyanese history', and no one really disputed this. Thirty years ago the eyes of the entire world had settled on Guyana. But as well as being its most famous moment, Jonestown was also its most forgettable and its most forgotten. There was no memorial, and now even the facts were vague. As Rupert Roopnaraine warned me, 'Jonestown has no real part to play in Guyanese history. It was an American affair.'

So once again Georgetown's mental undergrowth had triumphed. Jonestown was now almost mystery, or at least a place best forgotten. For some reason this made me more determined than ever, and so I made a decision: before going anywhere else in Guyana, I would head for Jonestown first.

Most people were appalled at the idea of my trip to Jonestown. It wasn't just the name that made them shudder. Any trip that involved the Interior was unappealing. To most Townies, what happened beyond the city limits was beyond the pale – a vast, malarial dystopia of stinking swamps, thorns, bandits, bugs the size of rats and dark carnivorous forest. 'You gonna find nothing, Man,' they'd say, 'the bush swallow everything. You can't see you hand in front of you face ...'

The girl at the travel agent was a little more optimistic. Jonestown was no longer marked on the map, but we could find a nearby village. Between there and Georgetown were 250 miles of solid green – which I presumed was forest – threaded with nameless rivers. There were no railways at all, and the roads heading north petered out shortly after the city. There used to be a ship, said the girl. It headed up the coast to Mabaruma, but it was a dangerous voyage and perhaps the ship no longer ran. The only other option, she said, was to fly to the old port. Eventually she found me a plane, and I bought a ticket. After that, I'd have to finish my journey by river, another fifty or sixty miles.

Lorlene was intrigued by all these arrangements. 'I remember the People's Temple,' she said, 'they had the house next door to ours.'

On my last day she drove me over to her childhood home. It was out in Lamaha Gardens, a little suburb that had once been affluent. The Jameses' house was right on the edge of the sugar cane, but it was not what it had been before. Now the paint was peeling, and there were people asleep in the grass. Lorlene said nothing but drove on, grinding over the potholes until we came to the Temple's house. It was a shapeless yellowish villa with a tall metal fence and a few blank, meshed windows, leaking tropical mould.

'It always looked unlived-in ...' said Lorlene absently.

We both peered up at the windows, as though expecting to see Jones's people inside, manning the radios and cooking up plots. Despite its aura of emptiness, the villa had been the Georgetown base of the People's Temple for several years. From here they'd ordered the guns and cyanide, and had dispatched supple girls to politicians' beds. It was here too that the orders of the Revd Jones had found expression, crackling over the ether. When, that day in November, he'd issued his final command, it was received here by his last disciple and bleakly obeyed. Sleepless, brainwashed and devoted, Linda Amos climbed the stairs to the room with the blank, meshed windows and carefully drew the blinds. Then she took her children and cut their tiny, soft throats before turning the knife on herself.

It was these last details that troubled me most of all. If Jones had exercised power like this over the airwaves, what sort of power had he exercised in the jungle, hundreds of miles to the north? Even more troubling, how much of this malevolence still lingered on, and where would it end?

2

THE TOWN OF JONES

In this foreign and forbidding place it was impossible to have a sense of forward or backward. Everything looked the same – green, brown and dense. I came to realise that the jungle served as our prison bars, a barrier we couldn't punctuate.

Deborah Layton, *Seductive Poison*

Take our life from us! We got tired. We didn't commit suicide. We committed an act of revolutionary suicide protesting against the conditions of an inhuman world.

The last speech of Revd Jim Jones

ABOUT HALF-WAY THROUGH THE FLIGHT I began to wonder if all this was a good idea. Down below, the landscape began to change. For a while there were the comforting strips of sugar. They looked like the spines of books, stacked deep inland and then all the way up the coast. Then the patterns ended, with the mouth of a river almost as wide as the English Channel. It was the Essequibo, looking as though it had drained the continent of silt. After that, the land darkened to a sort of stygian green, with veins of silvery-black. There was no order about this, nor any sign of life. It was just an uneven vegetative darkness, as though the land had swallowed the night.

Perhaps the Townies were right: I'd find nothing. Perhaps I'd just wander off the airstrip only to be lost in the gruesome prickly dark. I'd meet strange people, mad with damp and sores, but they'd never have heard of Jones. Then I'd get diarrhoea and yaws, and my skin would begin to weep. After four days of this, blundering around looking for the light, I'd eventually emerge in a clearing. By then I'd no longer care about Jonestown, and I'd look like Debbie Layton: hollow-eyed, panicky and howling for a plane.

I tried to reassure myself, but nothing seemed to work. I was travelling to a place I wasn't sure existed, and which had once been the epitome of despair. I'd never met anyone who'd been there, and now here I was in a tiny plane with a tractor tyre, two cases of rum and

a box of brand new Bibles. Even my fellow passengers were a dis-
couraging sight. One was a pork-knocker – or gold prospector – and
was dressed in shorts and orange rubber boots, and carried a pump-
action shotgun. Another had with him a little bird, about the size
of a grape, which he chatted to all the way. Meanwhile, the woman
next to me, who was already flooded with sweat, peeled open the
Old Testament and started murmuring chunks of Leviticus.

'Where you going?' said the birdman.

'Jonestown,' I said, without thinking.

'You won't find their gold,' he grinned. 'They had *bunkers*
underground.'

My heart sank. Already I could feel myself encircled in coils of
local myth. Jonestown was famous for this. To survive it, I'd brought
with me my own version of the story, assembled back in London.
It included several hand-drawn maps, a hefty bundle of notes and
dozens of grainy pictures. I'd even transcribed parts of 'The Death
Tapes' – the recordings Jones made as he ordered his people to die.
None of this would tell me what went on there now – but at least it
was better than the birdie version.

As man and finch began to tweet, I pulled out my notes and
started to read.

In the short, peculiar life of Jim Jones what stands out most is his
relentless metamorphosis. The old coverings are constantly falling
away as the new ones form in their place. By the end he even acquires
a blank insectile gaze, and a voice that clatters and whirs. Perhaps
he knows where the transformations will inevitably lead. Not that
it frightens him. 'Death is nothing!' he'll be heard to say. It's merely
the shedding of a used-up layer.

Ever since he was born, in 1931, Jones has been wriggling out
of whatever he was before. His family are descended from Native
Americans. They are poor and live in Indiana, and Jones's father is
a Klansman and an angry veteran, enfeebled by poison gas. This,
Jones decides, is not the life for him. As a child he plays the preacher,
and by the age of twenty-two he's established a church of his own.
Jones likes the multicoloured skins of the poor, which seem to give
him a certain beauty. By 1963 he's head of the human rights commission, and his disciples assume a new name, the People's Temple Full

Gospel Church. Two years later he shrugs off Indiana and moves to California. According to an article he's read – in *Esquire* – it's the only place that'll survive if there's ever a nuclear war.

As he waits for the war that won't happen, another change occurs. The Prophet, as he now calls himself, acquires some of the powers of God. He tells his followers that he's the reincarnation of Lenin and Christ, and soon he's performing wonders with chicken giblets and hauling out dangerous tumours. By the end of the '60s, no one knows who loves him more: the politicians or the poor. Now the dispossessed are giving the Temple everything they've got: their children, their trust and all their possessions. In time the cult amasses over $10 million, in fifteen different accounts. Even the Revd Jones is surprised: 'Everything I touch,' he thrills, 'turns to gold.'

But soon there are no more layers to shed, and the sheen begins to fade. The Prophet now has to colour his hair and thicken his sideburns with an eyebrow pencil. He also finds that he has to rekindle his potency with the youngest girls and steady his hand with Scotch. Virgins like Debbie Layton are made to promise that they begged him into bed, and that they'd never seen a man so big. As the Prophet's powers dwindle, he even begins to press them on the boys. This only excites the interest of the police. One day he finds himself at the back of a Hollywood theatre, grappling with a fluffer (who works for the LAPD). He's accused of lewd conduct, a pitiful charge for a man so close to God.

So it is that the coverings begin to crack. But as they do so, the cult that surrounds Jones seems only to strengthen. He calls his followers 'darlings', and then tells them they'll never leave his church alive. Sex is often the only hold he has over people, so he keeps them all on film. Now there are always guns around, and curious ceremonies, to bless the Father's fetishes. Look at Idi Amin, he says, 'we should learn to emulate his wild actions'. Soon 'The Cause' will have its own fleet of buses and its own little army, which goes training in the hills.

It's now time for a final transformation. By 1977 California has become hostile, and it's time for the Prophet to fly. He's already bought a piece of Promised Land: 27,000 acres of distant Guyanese forest. There he will rule like some mystic king. In his eyes this country's perfect; it's been shunned by the world, and its officials are now starving, and candidly corrupt. They'll do anything for money, or a night with a teenage girl. Unsurprisingly, nothing seems to function,

except a ministry of thugs. Even better, Guyana is cranky and socialist, and run by a man called Burnham who thinks he's an African
chief.

Late that summer the planes are all block-booked. Over 900
believers will fly out to Georgetown and then transfer to ships.
Among them are both the hopeless and the hopeful: fundamentalists, former addicts, charismatics, ex-cons, Vietnam veterans, hundreds of African-Americans and a handful of white progressives.
These include a former CBS television presenter, Mike Prokes, and a
woman who escaped the Nazi death camps. She's there with her son
Larry – who will eventually start shooting people – and her daughter, Debbie Layton. Finally, there's Jones himself. He looks puffy
and distracted. All that sustains him now are faith and voodoo, and
powerful draughts of prescription painkillers.

Finally they get to Mabaruma. After two days at sea, there's
relief as they clamber ashore. But what no one knows is that this is
an act of metamorphosis. It's a process that can never be reversed,
and has only one conclusion.

Mabaruma was not quite what I – or the faithful – had expected.
While it wasn't exactly a Land of Milk and Honey, nor was it dark
and carnivorous.

From the airstrip I got a ride to the village, which was built high
above the forest on an enormous whale of green. Up here, running
along the spine, was an avenue of stately rubber trees and a pleasing sprawl of orchards, paddocks, tiny wooden farms and tobacco-
coloured cows. There was also a miniature hospital, an ambulance
without any tyres and a shop that sold nerve tonic, barbed wire and
jeans. It was run by a man called Mr Chan A Sue, who was part
Amerindian and part Chinese. He told me that this was once the
garden of Guyana and that every week the ships had left stuffed to
the gunnels with fruit.

These days the fruit ships no longer called, and the great sleep
that had overwhelmed Mabaruma was now in its third decade.
The paint had peeled, the machines had stopped and the mangoes
plopped – unclaimed – into the grass. I stayed at the government
guesthouse, which had an ancient bulldozer outside, nesting in the
leaves. The evening meal was served at lunchtime, and then everyone

went home. I ate with the local doctor, who happened to be Cuban. He hadn't understood anyone for months and almost wept at the sound of Spanish. The garden that he described sounded more like Eden than Guyana: idyllic, lonely and haunted by snakes. 'I see a lot of people with bites,' he said thoughtfully, 'and most of them die.'

It wasn't just snakes that made people mawkish. Across the road was the police house, quietly flapping apart in the breeze. There was always a drunkard on the porch, and once I asked him if he remembered the people of Jonestown. He fixed me with a meaty red eye, 'White boy,' he rasped, 'only one's thing is certain: we all is going to die.'

Then a corporal appeared, and I asked her the same. She had nervous, pretty eyes like a fox, and her stripe was fixed to her sleeve with a pin. 'They was lovely people,' she said, 'they had a band, and they often came here and sang. Right here, under the trees. Their girls was always beautiful. *Beautiful*. I can't believe they're gone.'

From the top of the guesthouse, I could just see Venezuela. It was hard to tell exactly where the trees lost their English names and where the Spanish ones began. The doctor said the border was ten kilometres away, but that no one ever went out there except 'piratas y contrabandistas'. We spent ages peering down into the jungle. There are few frontiers in South America that have tempted so much war, and perhaps we expected to see a patrol, or a little army on the move. Instead, all we heard were the monkeys and the call of a screaming piha.

But people still worried about the Venezuelans. Many felt that one day their rich, hot-blooded neighbours would come pouring through the forest, armed to the teeth. It was well known that Venezuelan schoolchildren were taught that over half of Guyana was theirs, and that clawing it back was a matter of national duty. Caracas was always threatening them. In the 1890s the issue had brought Britain and America – for the last time – almost to the brink of conflict. Eventually the tension between imperialism and the Monroe Doctrine had been resolved by the Tsar. But it wasn't the end. The row flared again in the 1960s and '70s, with occasional exchanges of gunfire, and it has smouldered ever since.

Some think Washington was behind these spats, trying to humiliate Burnham (better Venezuelan than Marxist, went the thinking at the time). But if it's true, Burnham outwitted them. He'd always

For the Amerindians of Guiana, the arrival of outsiders has often spelt disaster. To the first Europeans, their women were exotic and easy.

wanted some sort of leverage over the United States. Then into his lap fell Jones. This kinky, drug-befuddled crackpot not only had guns and a bank full of money, but was also willing to live in the benighted north-west and place thousands of vulnerable Americans right in the path of the enemy's army.

Guyana opened its arms and let the Temple in.

From here my trip upriver felt like a journey backwards through the Amerindian past. To begin with, everything felt reassuringly contemporary. I walked down off the hill to Mabaruma's port, known as Kumaka. It had a long street of bright red earth, with a few stalls selling contraband from Venezuela, mostly shotguns and beer. Several people still remembered the Temple. They'd sold embroidery here and kept a lodge called the Dewdrop Inn. One of the Indian traders wished me luck finding the gold and slipped me a can of illegal beer. 'Look out for my cousin,' he told me. 'Lost all his fingers in the Jonestown sawmill, but he knows where everything is.'

Along the river was a waterfront, made of timber and zinc. Here I met Ivan, an Arawak boatman, who had thick, square hands, long blue hair and a canoe with a powerful engine. He could take me as far as Port Kaituma, he said, first along this river – the Uruca – and then the Barima and Kaituma. It was about fifty miles, and we'd leave as soon as he had fuel.

As I waited on the wharf, I began to get a sense of the past closing in. First of all a large blue-haired family appeared, with an ancient sewing machine. The children, who were all naked, swooped off the woodwork like swallows and flapped around in the water for a while, until a boat like an old tree trunk appeared, and they all climbed in and paddled off. Then suddenly there was an old man next to me, inspecting my face very closely. Eventually he spoke: 'You got glasses. I'd like you to give them to me.' I explained that I couldn't see properly without them, and he explained that he'd never seen properly at all. This, however, had never stopped him making canoes, one a week, chopped from a tree.

Then Ivan reappeared, and soon we were soaring along between two ribbons of forest. To begin with, there were occasional Arawak farms: a canoe, a tiny, painted house and a plot of neat little vegetables coaxed from the edge of the jungle. But then the river narrowed and darkened. The water here was black and inert, like tarnished silver, and, above it, the morphos seemed to flop around as though they were caught in molten metal. Here the people too were different, glimpsed through the trees. They had narrow, roasted faces and knots of dusty hair. At first, I waved but they just stared back, as though they'd seen nothing at all.

'They're Warau,' said Ivan, and I suddenly understood.

The Warau were famously different, like a link with a long-lost age. It's said they gave mankind its first dugout, and would probably give it its last. In hundreds of years they'd hardly changed at all. Although it's likely they were the first Amerindians to encounter Europeans, they were also the most resistant. They'd never been persuaded to work and had no interest in learning the language of others, or in the world beyond their own. For centuries they'd been merely a vessel for everyone else's contempt. 'They just Bucks,' said Ivan, 'dirty, lazy Bucks!'

But it was their simplicity that had probably saved them. There were now about 3,000 Warau living in these swamps. Even their huts had a pared-down, essential feel. They were just stacks of branches and woven grass straddling the water. There were no crops, no ornaments and no discernible gods. Traditionally, the bodies of the dead were stripped down by the piranhas, then daubed with ochre and hung inside the hut. For all I knew, the Warau still did this, and the bones were their only possessions. That's how they'd survived: by having nothing of their own that anyone else could possibly want.

The experience of the other Amerindians hadn't always been so simple.

To begin with, all seemed well. At this end of the Guianas there was little resistance to the Europeans, who'd often assumed that the natives had been provided for their pleasure. Even the things explorers took home – *berbekots, kanoas, hamakas,* and *marákas* (barbecues, canoes, hammocks and maracas) – seemed to suggest an easy life of indolence and leisure. The men too made good souvenirs, and there are records of the 'Guianians' serving not only the English Tudors but also the court of the Medicis.

But most pleasing of all were the women, who were biddable and plump. 'Whoever lives among them,' wrote one early adventurer, 'had need to be the owner of no less than Joseph's continency, not at least to covet their embraces.' Even the good Sir Walter Raleigh found his continence severely tested. ('I have seldom seen a better favoured woman,' he pants, 'she was of good stature, with black eyes, fat of body ...') Before long the Europeans were lavishing the Amerindians with their appreciation. It is now widely believed that, in return, the Amerindians had another innovation for their guests: Europe's first cases of syphilis.

Then came sugar, and everything changed. By the early seventeenth century the Dutch were gathering up the natives and trying to make them work. But it failed. Like the Warau today, the Amerindians would rather die than do what they were told. They wouldn't even work for baubles and periwigs, and so the import of Africans began. Only then did the Amerindians have a role, as manhunters and captors of runaway slaves. In 1686 it became illegal to enslave Caribs and Arawaks, and for the next century and a half they became a minor aristocracy, just below the whites.

None of this bode well for the emancipation of slaves. In 1834 Africans were suddenly in the interior, scraping out farms and looking for gold. Even now the Amerindians fear them for their size and their strength, and their potential for revenge. As the new population began to sprawl inland, so did the smallpox. By 1900 the population of indigenous Guianese was down to 18,000, a fraction of what it had been before. The survivors were those that lived in the swamps and the mountains, or three weeks' journey inland. But they were still like vagrants in their hunting grounds, despised by those that worked.

Then came the age of the museum. For much of the twentieth century the Amerindians have lived like specimens, preserved in their own domain. It was made illegal to visit them, and they all became wards of the Crown. Sex with an Amerindian was now a crime, like the seduction of a child. It wasn't quite what the tribes had wanted, but at least they began to revive. There are now 45,000 Amerindians living in nine different groups. In fact, it's the only section of Guyanese society whose numbers are increasing.

But the modern world is still fraught with danger. In the last fifty years the Amerindians have had to cope with drug gangs, illegal logging, mercury poisoning (from the gold mines) and a new and virulent plague. Ivan explained: 'The big thing just now is HIV. The girls go to the camps, and they works with the miners, and then they comes back here. If one of our men dies, then, in our culture, his brother must take on his wife – and so him die too.'

The dangers have constantly changed. In 1977 there was an altogether different threat to the Amerindians of the north-west. It was the beautiful people, with their embroidery and cookies. Come and join us, they'd say, we've found paradise on Earth.

After several hours Ivan dropped me at Port Kaituma. From here it was only seven miles to Jonestown, over the ridge and out in the bush. 'But watch out,' he warned, 'there's bad people around.'

I thanked him and smiled bravely. But it was not how I felt. I realised that, the nearer I got to Jonestown, the more insistent the warnings became. It was as though I was now closing in on the target, and some internal radar was beginning to beep. As far as people downriver were concerned, Port Kaituma was a sort of tropical Gomorrah, a place of whores and smugglers, and fortunes made in gold. The only people who ever came up here were the mad, the desperate

and those on the run. It seemed that these were the Guyanese badlands, and now, here I was, wondering what to do next.

I took a deep breath, and clambered onto a pier. Around me was
a small black inlet, cluttered with stilted slums. The mud stank and
made the air feel oily and burned. I followed a path of planks that
led upwards through the stilts. Many years earlier Amerigo Vespucci
had seen huts like this – also Warau – and had called the place Venezuela, because they reminded him of Venice. Clearly he'd never seen
Port Kaituma.

This was no Venice. As for the town at the top of the bank, it
wasn't even remotely Venetian. For a start, I could see right through
it, along a furrow of crimson mud. It looked as though something
huge had plunged through the shacks, scraping up a layer of stalls
and cardboard and starving dogs before vanishing into the forest.
Then I discovered what the plunging object had been. Through the
mud ran long, broken trails of silvery metal. It was all that remained
of a railway line that had closed in 1968. Most of the wagons were
still there, scattered along the ridge. A few were inhabited, and –
where they'd clustered together – this was the centre of town.

I soon learned that much of this had sprung up in the recent
goldrush. But, although Port Kaituma looked like the work of an
afternoon, there was a pattern, of sorts. Along the top of the ridge
was a rim of rickety churches. They had grandiose names like the
Tabernacle of His Glory Revealed and the Assembly of God, and
from here the town spread out, in descending levels of sin. First
there was a strip of old British army trucks. This is where the miners
worked, constantly loading up drums of fuel and roaring off into
the bush. Next came the gas-sellers, who were always swearing and
drinking and playing cricket in the sludge. Then there were the little
people – the prostitutes, pedlars, rappers and junkies – who lived in
a sort of human piggery of pens and stalls tumbling down the hill.

Finally, at the bottom, was the long red scar left by the rails.
During my three days in Port Kaituma it was always here that I felt
most wary. Each of the rum shops played its own techno, enveloping
everything in waves of interlocking sound. It was like being caught
in some devastating electronic crossfire. Often people looked as
though they'd already been mechanically deafened and now just
stood and watched. Once a man who was almost naked came over
and screamed at me, waving some wounds in my face. I couldn't even
tell what language he was speaking, but his breath smelled of paint.

It was quieter up the other end, away from the port. Up here there was a large, clapboard guesthouse – where I stayed – and a matching clapboard shop. They were both owned by an African ironmonger, called Mr Charles. There was also a row of little eateries, each with stools around the stove. The best of these was called BIG D'S FOOD MALL. It was painted toothpaste green, and – instead of techno – it emitted gentle chirrups of gospel choir.

'Big D' herself – or Denise – was clearly not the woman she once had been. Life was constantly diminishing her. Now she just sat, looking small and surprised. First, she said, she'd lost her schoolfriends, then her husband (to a woman half her age), and then she'd lost a breast. Even now she wondered when the missionary doctors would return and take other bits away. All she had left was her mall and her skinny girls, who hung around like a pack of hungry whippets. I think she liked the idea of a new customer, as though I was somehow reversing the trend. Every mealtime she'd roar when I appeared, and the girls would scatter backwards into the kitchen and return with something new.

Inevitably we'd talk about Jonestown, and this is the story she told.

This community was smaller then. We was only thirty families.

I remember Jonestown well. I was thirteen at the time. It was a real nice place. I visited on Sundays. They had a doctor, who used to see patients there, or you went to relax. It was a nice place, sort of normal. We were always given things to eat, good food like sandwiches. They had a nice band, played mostly church music. And there were persons dancing with snakes. I remember they had a chimpanzee too, called Mr Muggs. We were a bit scared of him. But, man, it was a nice place! *Clean*. Everyone worked hard. Sometimes, they also gave out foodstuffs, which was very acceptable at that time. We never had enough to eat.

Yes, I think it was a happy place. I had some friends there who was going to my school. There was Tommy, who was a white kid. I'll never forget Tommy. And Paddy! She was fat! A lovely girl. I still cry when I think of her. And Derek Lawson, and David George, who was Amerindian, and Jimmy Gale. Jimmy was adopted by the Revd Jones, but I think he died soon after. They seemed happy. It was a happy place, that's what we thought. Later, I heard terrible things about what happened there, but we never see them.

I didn't hear the shooting because I was away at the school. It was a real shock for me, and I couldn't catch myself. I am still wondering what could spark a man off to do such things.

I never went back. Never went near it in thirty years. But now I want to, I don't know why. I'd just like to see it again. Perhaps one day I will.

While Denise was enjoying the sandwiches and snakes, Debbie Layton had a different tale to tell.

People still don't know what to make of the affidavit she swore on her return to the States, or the book she wrote much later. In them she describes an evil dystopia, a plantation of religious slaves. People are beaten, starved, bullied and harangued, and then punished with sex and stupefying drugs. Life is a brutal cycle of denial, and even toothpaste and knickers are banned. Work becomes a way of crushing the spirit, and the day ends at midnight and begins again at three. No one can escape; nobody knows where they are, and they have no passport and no money. Besides, everyone's an informer, and the forest's full of guards. Even if defectors do get away, they'll be hunted for the rest of their lives.

At the heart of this vision is Jones himself. He's now fabulously mad and broadcasts six hours a day. There are even loudspeakers out in the fields, so that no one misses a word. As for 'The Cause', it's now whatever he says. One theme, however, seems to recur: we're surrounded by mercenaries, says Jones, the capitalists are closing in. He makes everyone practise for a grand, communal death. These drills are called 'White Nights' and involve little cups of coloured fluid. Refusing to drink this, says Jones, is an anti-revolutionary act, and no one dares to disobey. On the orders of its Prophet, Jonestown dies over and over again.

In Debbie Layton's account there's no room for happiness or jolly Sunday teas. Like their parents, the children are repeatedly made to rehearse the moment they'll die. Meanwhile, affection is outlawed. Even the youngest children are brutalised and taken from their parents. If they were to survive childhood, they'd never forget it. Often they're dangled upside down in the well or nailed up in a box and left for days on end. There's even a chimpanzee in this version, although now he's a figure of terror.

For many, Debbie Layton's story was just too much. People assumed it was imagined. Writing years later, Shiva Naipaul said it was 'beyond the reach of reason', and that her Jonestown was an 'incarnation of comic book evil'. This was a shame, because Layton had a point: something was rotten in this state within a state. When her affidavit was distributed, in June 1978, only one paper ran with the story, The *San Francisco Chronicle*. Even the US government remained unpersuaded. That year embassy officials paid four visits to Jonestown, and – although they were later criticised for their naivety – they never found anything wrong.

But there was one man who wanted to investigate further. Leo Ryan was a large, slightly beaverish man with thick grey hair and an aptitude for trouble. Although he'd been a Congressman for years, he'd never quite found his cause. There'd been seal hunts in Newfoundland and abuse in American prisons, but Ryan was often on his own. Now here was something new, the People's Temple. Soon he became a rallying point for those with relatives in Jonestown. Eventually he made a momentous decision that would change everybody's life: he'd go out there himself.

Nothing could persuade him not to go. He received over a hundred letters of warning, and Debbie Layton told him he'd be killed. But Ryan had already made up his mind. When the cult's lawyers warned him against 'a witch-hunt', and threatened the US government with a 'most embarrassing situation', Ryan replied that he wasn't impressed. On 15 November 1978 he arrived in Georgetown with thirteen of the relatives and nine journalists, including an NBC film crew.

Two days later, they arrived in Port Kaituma.

As Port Kaituma has only ever had one place to stay, most of the delegation ended up, like me, as guests of the African ironmonger.

The old clapboard house now made an unusual hotel. It was a brilliant baby-blue, and along the front there were coloured lights and a large pink painting of a couple having sex. The blueness continued inside, although the pink people, it seemed, had long since packed up and gone. These days most of the guests were miners, Rastafarians with Amerindian girlfriends who padded around like cats. I always liked these miners. They were friendly and reckless and gave themselves nursery rhyme names, such as King Charley and the Golden Cat. They were like drop-outs in reverse, people who'd run away to lose themselves in work.

'My father was a gold miner once,' said Kenwin, the owner's son.

'But the money was better in iron?' I ventured.

Kenwin said nothing. He was unhappy. If his older brother hadn't killed a man in Georgetown, he wouldn't be here at all. He was a geologist and saw his life in stone, anywhere but here. He also knew he'd never be the man his father was. Before Mike Charles disappeared – to rescue his beleaguered heir – he'd been the biggest man in Port Kaituma. Not only was he an ironmonger but he also owned a transport business. 'And he ran the trucks for Jonestown,' said Kenwin.

'And what about this place?' I asked.

'Also his,' he replied. 'Used to be a nightspot, called the Weekend Disco.'

My room, as I soon discovered, had been built on the old dance floor. The walls were so thin and impromptu that, where they'd cracked, I had an unwelcome view of the room next door. At night I could hear my neighbour breathing and muttering in his sleep. It was almost as though the walls weren't there any more, and we were lying on the dance floor – just as the Americans had, thirty years earlier.

For the journalists it had been a pointless day. There was almost nothing to report. Soon after they'd arrived in Port Kaituma, Kenwin's father had driven them out to Jonestown. It had taken an hour and a half, and they'd arrived in the dark. Jones's wife had greeted them, and they'd all eaten sausages and sung the Guyanese national anthem. Congressman Ryan was impressed. Then Jones himself had appeared. He was eccentric but not obviously deranged. He'd said things like, 'I understand hate. Love and hate are very close.' The only troubling aspect of the evening was that – although he'd let Ryan stay the night – he made the reporters leave. Mike Charles had driven them all back in his truck, and had put them up at the Weekend Disco.

That night, on the dance floor, the journalists drank and smoked and slept. One of them, Charles Krause, of the *Washington Post*, recorded his frustration. He didn't believe the stories about beatings and automatic weapons. 'I couldn't understand,' he wrote, 'why there had been such fuss.' His colleagues agreed. It had been a wasted day. What they didn't know was that – for three of them – it would also be their last.

At ten the next morning, Saturday 18 November 1978, Mike Charles drove them back again to Jonestown. Now they could see it in the light: a camp of neat white huts, with nurseries and class-rooms, a large tin pavilion sitting in the middle. Another ordinary day threatened. There was no evidence of maltreatment or starva-tion, and Krause even found himself admiring the cult. It wasn't much of a story.

But then things took a different turn. Jones appeared, looking sickly and aggressive. When accusations were put to him, he would flare up with rage and self-pity. 'That's rubbish! I'm defeated!' he'd wail, 'I might as well die!' Then people started to cry, and some of the families said they wanted to leave. Jones was now at breaking point, and in the tension a man appeared with a knife. He made a lunge at Ryan but was overpowered and cut himself, spraying Ryan with his blood. It was time to go.

As Ryan prepared to leave, it was agreed he could take fifteen defectors with him. Jones gave them each their passports and a small bundle of cash. Then, when they were all aboard the truck, Debbie Layton's brother Larry stepped forward and said he too wanted to leave. No one stopped him.

Soon the truck was off. This time it was heading straight for the Port Kaituma airstrip. They must have made a curious sight: the weeping defectors; the reporters, unsure of what they'd seen, and a congressman spattered in blood. Did a flight from paradise always feel like this? And did it taste of sick and fear? No one seemed to know what to think any more.

Nor did they realise that Larry had a gun in his pocket, and that behind them was another truck and a tractor with a trailer. On board were half a dozen men armed with the Prophet's own peculiar brand of madness, and automatic rifles.

For those that know this story – and perhaps live it every day – it now unfolds like a collision in slow motion. The impact will be catastrophic not because events happen quickly but because of their terrifying momentum. It's like watching a railway line from above, and the ponderous piston action of two locomotives as they billow towards each other, gradually closing the gap. In the carnage that follows, you find yourself asking, what's the last point at which this could have been prevented? And then you look down the line and there's nothing there to see.

One man who'd lived most of his life with this scene was Big D's uncle. Fitz Duke had a face of sun-scorched hardwood, and his goatee was wiry and white like a clump of platinum filaments. One of his thumbs was missing, and he wore huge shorts and a pair of industrial boots that made tracks like a tank. But despite his demanding appearance, he was a man of reluctant words. At first I thought it was me, but then I began to realise that most things left Duke candidly unmoved. I now wonder whether it was the events of that November that had done this, and whether the shock of having felt so much so suddenly had now left him emotionally inert.

My second morning he agreed to drive me down to the airstrip. It was only a mile away, along a road of brilliant crimson. As he drove, I tried to assemble a conversation from syllables and grunts. But then we turned through a gap in the forest, bounced through some barbed wire gates and there before us lay the airstrip. It was here that Congressman Ryan and his party had come to meet their two small planes.

The sight of this weirdly open space had an immediate effect on Duke. He suddenly began to talk as though all the different strands of thought had now been gathered up as one. He told me where the planes had stood, where Ryan had waited, where the villagers had assembled to watch the planes, and where the gunmen had appeared, through the same barbed wire gate. At this point I suddenly realised that not only had Duke seen what happened next, but that it was all still like a film inside his head. 'They shouted that they had a sick person on board,' he said, 'and then their tractor drove between the planes ...'

What followed is like the clippings off the editor's floor, a series of events in uncertain order. A tarpaulin flies back, and six armed men appear. There's smoke and a cackle of gunfire. Tyres explode with a perfunctory plop, and there's the ding and thwap of holes bursting in aluminium and in human tissue. A camera whirrs blankly at the sky, its operator gone. Ryan too looks different now, with part of his head swept away. A man called Big Anthony is firing a machine gun from the tractor, expertly selecting Americans and punching them down. The dead look like rag dolls caught in a moment of flight. A diplomat is stumbling through the hail shouting 'Get me a gun! Get me a fucking weapon!', and the jungle clatters back. Larry the impostor pulls out his gun, but it jams, and he's beaten to the ground. There are hats and shoes in the dirt as the villagers flee for the trees. Krause the reporter is tucked behind a wheel and can feel his teeth cracking, as he wonders if he's already dead. Then suddenly it stops.

'They'd accomplished their mission,' said Duke, 'they'd killed Ryan.'

They'd also killed three newsmen and a dissident, and had left five others badly wounded. The bigger of the two planes no longer worked, and the pilots then took the smaller one and fled. The survivors were now alone. As the gunmen sped off down the road, people began to emerge from the trees and dragged the wounded clear. One of them had an arm that was hanging on only by a thread. 'And we also found the camera, still running,' said Duke. 'We didn't know what to do with it. We'd never seen one before.'

There would be no more planes that night; it was dark and – just as now – the runway had no lights. The nearest settlement was a mining post at the end of the airstrip, called Citrus Grove. But despite its winsome name, there was little there, and it was better known as Bottom Floor. All that the survivors found were a few shacks and a grog-shop called the Rum House. Here the dozen or so Americans would spend the most frightening night of their lives, listening to cries of pain and the sound of a tropical forest screaming itself to sleep.

But it wasn't just that they were alone. 'As the killers left,' explained Duke, 'one of them shouted, "We'll be back for Port Kaituma".'

Bottom Floor has never forgotten that evening either. Little there had changed, except that the Rum House had long since burned down. There were the same lemon trees, the same stilted shacks and the same shadowy lanes. One woman I spoke to said she'd never been back to watch the planes, and that she dreamed about the killings almost every night. I also tracked down a lemon-seller called Poppy Speed. People told me he'd been playing football on the airstrip that day, and that he'd caught a bullet in the thigh. I found him hobbling around his trees, and I asked him to tell me his tale. His eyes narrowed, and his hands began to tremble. 'How long will it take?' he murmured.

'Whatever you like,' I said. 'Five minutes?'

'Five minutes is a long time ...' he said blankly, 'but OK.'

Then I pulled out my Dictaphone, and he turned and fled up his ladder.

'I'm not saying nothing!' he cried, 'Not now! Not ever!'

I suddenly felt guilt rise and catch me in the throat. 'I'm really sorry ...'

But he'd gone, and all I could hear was him crying like a child.

Duke wasn't surprised by this, when I got back to his jeep.

'People here are still frightened,' he said. 'They don't know what happened, or who anyone is. They hardly ever seen any white men before. The only ones they saw were people from the Temple, who then starts killing them. Are you surprised they're still afraid?'

We drove back along the crimson road.

'This is where we set up an ambush,' said Duke, remotely. 'We didn't have much. A few men trained in the military and a couple of handguns. They had assault rifles. We thought they'd come back and kill us. It was a long night, a *bad* night. Then in the morning one of the survivors came down the road from Jonestown. He told us what had happened but of course we didn't believe him ...'

An unforgettable night was about to become an unbelievable new day.

Duke said he'd drive me out there, tomorrow at sunrise.

'And bring your boots,' he said. 'There's a lot of snakes.'

I didn't sleep well that night, at the old Weekend Disco. Perhaps it was the breathing that came through the cracks, or too much of Big D's boil-ups. I lay awake, taunted by the anguish of Poppy Speed, and the woman who dreamed of gunfire. Even when I did sleep, it felt like a dark trap, haunted by snakes and broken people and enormous lemons. Then at some point there were two explosions in the hall, and I woke in panic, unable to disentangle the imagined from the real. Perhaps the shooting had started again? Remembering that my windows were barred, I crawled across the floor and hid in the shower. Then, after an eternity of silence, I crawled back to bed and lay there, fitfully sifting the sounds of the night. In the morning I told King Charley about this, and he laughed. 'Kids!' he said. 'Kids with squibs!'

A surreal night was as good a preparation as any for a trip out to Jonestown. For almost an hour Duke's jeep soared through the jungle, cresting one great rib of laterite before swooping down on another. The only people we saw were some schoolchildren with umbrellas and a group of Amerindians who rode along with us for a while, never saying a word. Duke didn't say anything either, until we reached a clearing and a parade of blackened stumps. 'Fruit trees,' said Duke, 'all planted by the Temple.'

Then we turned off the track, between two posts; the old entrance. There had once been a sign here – 'WELCOME TO JONESTOWN PEOPLE'S TEMPLE AGRICULTURAL PROJECT' – but it had long since been devoured by the damp, along with a sentry box. 'Security was very tight,' said Duke, 'they even had a watchtower, so they could see all around.'

Not any more. Now the jungle had closed in again, and the path ahead was only a few feet wide. As the jeep passed through, I could hear the thorns squealing down our sides. Duke said you couldn't walk through this stuff – Tiger Teeth and Hold-me-back – and it occurred to me that our day would end like this, lost in the prickles and dark. But then, suddenly, the trees fell back, and we were out in a miniature savannah. 'Jonestown,' announced Duke grimly. 'This is where it happened.'

I peered into the long grass. Out in the middle was a very tall plum tree, and beyond it a distant brocade of forest. From this rank scattering of weeds and scrub it was hard to reassemble the past. Everything had gone: classrooms, offices, a cassava mill and housing for a thousand souls. No one could even agree what it had looked like. Debbie Layton had said it was 'squalid', and Shiva Naipaul – who turned up three weeks later – said it was a 'dismal constellation, half-ordered, half-scattered'. But the reporter Krause had described it as idyllic, like an old, antebellum American plantation. Who was right? Was this really an agricultural Utopia, or just a cranky sanctuary for the lost and dispossessed?

I walked forward and pushed into the long grass.

'Be careful,' said Duke, 'you don't know what's in there …'

I hesitated, but then I noticed that he was following. I'd already detected that beneath Duke's outer layer of indifference there was a vivacious seam of drama. We walked on. All around us the stalks swished and cackled, and little gnarly claws of thorn snatched at our legs. Along the way we found a 'Made in the USA' window fitting and an outpouring of giant amber ants.

'Yakmans,' said Duke. 'Never try and stop them. They eats anything in their path – rats, insects, even snakes ...'

Stepping over these unstoppable gourmands, we found ourselves on the edge of the clearing and squeezed between the trees. Here was what I was looking for: the leprous hulks of the three tractors, a boiler, half a dozen engine blocks, a vast workbench and the crumbling chassis of an old army truck. Whatever else was happening in Jonestown at the moment it imploded, it was in the throes of agricultural effort.

Duke looked sceptical. 'They wasn't farming. It was something else ...'

I said nothing, and we walked on. The undergrowth was being quietly snipped up by leaf-cutter ants, building a farm by instinct, uncluttered by ideas. At one point we came across an area where the soil seemed to have boiled up, or been ransacked by badgers. 'People,' noted Duke, 'looking for small scraps of metal.'

Further along, there was an old miner's cabin, made from twigs.

'This is where Jones had his house,' said Duke.

'Did you know him?'

He nodded. 'Funny guy. Always in shades. Never looked at you straight.'

'And did you see inside this place?'

'Nope, never crossed his gate.'

We both peered through the twiggy framework. There was nothing there but ant-works and Tiger Teeth. Duke explained that in the days following Jones's death looters had picked the place clean. I'd also heard that they'd discovered a grisly, parallel economy; the Prophet lived quite differently from his disciples. Apart from the trappings of office – books, electric lights, a fridge full of del Monte fruit, a double bed, cotton sheets and two dead mistresses – there was also a large quantity of Thorazine, sodium pentathol, chloral hydrate and Demerol. It was like a sort of pharmaceutical armoury, with every weapon you'd ever need in the practice of coercion.

'The Pavilion was over there,' said Duke, pointing back to the plum tree.

We set off towards it. Above us, in the tree, a chicken hawk watched, coldly appraising our vulnerability. Then something caught my eye. It was a tiny rotten fragment of a shoe: a woman's sandal, white with slingbacks.

'This is where the bodies were,' said Duke. 'All piled up, three deep.'

Here's what happened to the lady in the white slingbacks.

Shortly before dusk, she heard the tannoys blast into life. 'Alert! Alert! Alert!' She made her way to the Pavilion. The gunmen had returned from the airstrip, and Jones was calling a meeting. She could see him on his throne, beneath a notice that read: 'THOSE WHO DO NOT REMEMBER THE PAST ARE CONDEMNED TO REPEAT IT.' Over 900 people now pressed towards their leader. He was recording his last great speech, a valedictory. 'Death is not a fearful thing! It's living that's cursed …'

She could also see that there were guards posted around the pavilion, and that the doctor was supervising a concoction of Flavor Aid and chemicals. She didn't know that these included cyanide and tranquillisers, but she knew that this was no rehearsal. It was the final 'White Night', and this time even the cooks weren't exempted from the drill. 'It's over, Sister,' rasps Jones, 'we've made that day! We made a beautiful day …'

Everyone's frightened, and there's wailing on the tape. 'Stop this hysterics!' snaps Jones. 'This is not the way for people who are socialist communists to die!' But it was the children who went first, with a squirt in the mouth from a toxic teat. 'Take our life from us!' drones Jones. 'We got tired. We didn't commit suicide! We committed an act of revolutionary suicide …'

Then it was the turn of the woman in white shoes. The crowd were still compacted around her. She could hear The Father's voice above the moans of grief and pain: 'Die with respect! Die with dignity!' Few of her friends had disobeyed (and those that did had been dragged to the ground and injected with the poison). She'd watched as those around her took their little cups and drank. They'd wince at the powerful industrial taste, and then lie down as they began to feel the breath no longer working in their lungs. It was not an instant death, she'd notice, but a determined, chemical asphyxia. Confused and panicky, she'd gulp down her own dose and then take her place among her friends. No one would ever know the agonies she experienced in those last few minutes. She, like all the others, would be found in an attitude of sleep. It was almost as though they'd just lain down for a moment, not even bothering to remove their shoes.

A few weeks earlier I'd met a man who was one of the first outsiders to get to Jonestown, once news of the massacre broke.

Joe Singh, it seemed, had been present at almost every momentous event in modern Guyanese history. As a soldier, he'd quelled revolts, fought the drug gangs, negotiated truces with Amerindians and beaten off foreign incursions, and then – eventually – taken command of the army. During the African years this was no mean feat for an Indo-Guyanese. He had the almost unique status of a hero among each of the races. People were always writing to the papers asking that he be made president, or that a street be named in his honour. He was, I suppose, the nearest that Guyana had to a national institution. He also happened to be a friend of a friend, and so we agreed to meet.

The secret of his survival was soon obvious. Although Joe was generous and magisterial, with his dark tropical suit and hair like silvery pins, he was also deftly illusive. It was as though he only ever revealed a fraction of what he felt. He didn't even appear in his own stories very much – nor did anyone alive. Instead, he preferred to foray deep into the past, well out of range of possible ambush. I wondered whether Jonestown was far enough back in the temporal hinterland, and so I asked him. For a moment I could see him calibrating the possible fall-out. As the old Georgetown adage goes, whatever is said today is on the president's desk tomorrow.

He hesitated. 'Yes. Of course, I remember. How could anyone forget?'

This is the soldiers' story:

News of trouble came through that afternoon. By midnight the army had managed to fly some troops to the far end of the ridge. Under the command of Joe Singh – who was then a colonel – they'd marched all night and reached Port Kaituma at dawn. Later that day they reached Jonestown.

The sight that greeted them was incomprehensible. At first they thought that the clearing had been strewn with rags, and then they realised they were people. The bodies lay on their fronts, some with dried blood in their nostrils. Jones himself lay on the altar in the

Pavilion. He'd not taken poison but had got someone to shoot him, and now his shirt was bloody and pulled up over his head.

It was impossible to count all the bodies, such was the tangle and stench. At first, there seemed to be only 400, so a helicopter was sent out with a loudspeaker, urging the others to come in from the forest. 'We were there some days,' said Joe, 'just searching the site.' Then the bodies were counted again. There were 909, including 276 children. Even the dogs and cows had been poisoned, and Mr Muggs the chimpanzee.

Few survivors emerged. Among them was a 76-year-old woman, and a handful of others who'd fled. Strangest of all was the TV presenter Mike Prokes, who turned up with a gun and a suitcase full of money and said he was heading for the Soviet embassy. (Six months later, I discovered, he gave a press conference in a motel in Modesto and read out a forty-page testament before retreating to the bathroom and shooting himself in the head.)

Looters had already begun to prise the place apart. Martial law was imposed. There'd been some curious pickings: spice racks, boxes of Flavor Aid (which no one dared drink) and books donated by the Russians. Meanwhile, Joe's soldiers would retrieve twenty bows and arrows, thousands of dollars in cash (together with half a million in uncashed welfare cheques), about forty automatic rifles and a trunk containing 800 American passports. As for the mountains of foul, stained clothes, all the soldiers could do was scrape them into heaps and set them on fire.

The dead had been harder to deal with. It was obvious the soldiers couldn't cope. There were said to be only thirty body bags in the entire country. What's more, the heat was relentless, and – as his parting gift – Jones had poisoned all the water. For days nothing happened. When the journalists called by (including Krause and then, later, Shiva Naipaul), the troops just waved them through at gunpoint. 'Keep moving! Don't touch anything!' they screamed. They'd had as much as they could bear, and now it was time for the United States to come in and scoop up the mess. 'Well,' said Joe, defiantly, 'it was their problem. Jonestown had nothing to Guyana.' Most Guyanese believed this. As Naipaul put it, in life the disciples of the People's Temple had been hailed as socialist heroes, and in death they were 'hopelessly American'.

A few days later another small army arrived. They were specialised battlefield technicians, the people who clear up the pieces once the pruning of humans is done. Under the command of four colonels they moved among the dead, tagging, heaving, bagging, zipping and boxing. They untangled every corpse and gathered every document. Then they sprayed the clearing with so much disinfectant that, according to pilots, it's never been quite the same colour again. People like Joe were so astonished at the speed and complexity of the American operation that they began to wonder if they'd prepared it all in advance. ('It was as though they knew something,' he said, 'or at least had something to hide'.) Then they were gone: a vast dead decampment, shuttled away in relays of Jolly Green Giants.

For the sad, swollen followers of Jones the ordeal was not, however, over. As I'd soon discover, they had a journey ahead of them that's never quite come to an end. But it was different for Jonestown itself. Haunted, lifeless and antiseptic, it would now lie empty, probably for ever.

'Since that sad day has strucked,' said Duke, 'no one has ever lived here.'

We were walking back across the clearing, watched by the hawk. Duke was now deep in thought, and I asked him how the locals had reacted when the town next door had died. He stopped and turned, looking back over the scribble of thorns and rust. At first, it seems, people had hardly given it a thought and seen only a field of booty.

'Nothing went to waste,' he said. 'They took the tin and the windows, and all the timber. There's still plenty of people in Port Kaituma with bedsheets from Jonestown, or perhaps a couple of chairs. I remember they had a big freezer. It was full of food. Full! I tried it, but it was locked ...'

We walked on. Others had told me that, once everything portable had gone, the urge to forage was replaced with doubt. No one could quite believe that a town just like theirs – except bigger and richer – had simply self-destructed. A greater agency was at work. Suddenly mythology was sprouting everywhere, like luxurious clumps of forest. Duke himself thought that Jones was mining uranium, and that there were tunnels deep beneath the forest. 'That why they never found the cement he ordered. Five hundred bags! You see any concrete now?'

I couldn't. 'But that's only two truckloads?' I tried.

Duke wouldn't have it, and nor would anyone else. Back in Port Kaituma I met people who believed that Jones was still alive, that he and his assassins had escaped by plane, and that there was a massive cache of gold. Meanwhile, in Georgetown, it was often assumed that the CIA were involved, and that Jonestown was a dangerous psychological stunt. One politician even told me that the Russians had placed a missile silo there, and they'd all been killed by special forces.

'So there was no treasure?' I asked Duke.

'Nah,' he sneered, 'no one find nothing.'

This wasn't what everyone said. In fact, Duke's father was famous for having found $250,000 in cash. His mistake was to tell everybody. He was murdered a few weeks after Jonestown, on the path to Venezuela.

Jonestown carried on killing for years after the massacre. It was a curse, like one of those ghostly plastic gill-nets that breaks free of its trawler and travels the oceans in a state of perpetual slaughter. To begin with, there were the unfinished suicides, such as the woman who trimmed her children's throats in Lamaha Gardens, and television producer Mike Prokes, who ended it all in Modesto. Then there were the reprisals. Even years after the cult's demise, defectors were still being hunted down and killed. Perhaps the saddest story of all was that of Bonny Mann, the Guyanese ambassador to the United States. Two years after Jonestown he discovered that his lover, who was also the mother of his child, was not the girl she said she was. Instead, she'd been planted in his life by the People's Temple and had recorded all their trysts. As Mann's world fell apart, he killed both mother and child, before turning the gun on himself.

But it wasn't just the cult's survivors who were restless; so were the dead.

'Ask Caroline George,' said Big D. 'Her brother was among them.'

Ah, yes, David George, the Amerindian boy adopted by the Revd Jones.

Caroline George had a small shop, which sold salt and dried fish, out in Bottom Floor. On my last day I walked out there and found her stall, up to the eaves in weed. Inside, standing at the counter, was a customer with huge, knobbly hands like claws, and a face as wild as the forest. When he heard me mention Jonestown, his eyes widened, and I found myself staring upwards into two great rings of curdled yellow.

'If you kill one man,' he growled, 'you're a murderer. If you kill nine hundred, you're a conqueror!' With that, he tottered imperiously for a moment, and then lurched for the door.

Miss George looked at me without any perceptible expression. She was a short woman, rounded by poverty and thickened by work. Yes, she murmured, she'd tell me what happened. I thanked her, and then I must have hesitated, uncertain what I'd find when I clicked the latch of this person's grief. She sensed my anxiety and forced an unhappy smile.

'I think about Jonestown,' she said, 'almost every day of my life.'

A heartless saga emerged. She told me that her mother was a Carib, that she'd been born at the mouth of the river and that her father had died when she was small. For much of her childhood she and her siblings had drifted around like human flotsam. They'd fished and begged, and lived on the water. All that they'd had was each other. At some stage they'd ended up in Port Kaituma, and then into their lives came the Revd Jones. He was adopting Amerindian children and took on three of the siblings: Philip, Gabriella and 'Baby' David, who was ten.

'Jones said he would do better things for them,' said their sister. 'They all changed their name to Jones and called him Dad. I think they were happy at first, but we weren't always allowed to see them.'

Suddenly her eyes filled with tears.

'After it all happened, I went up to Jonestown to look for them. I'll never forget that day. By then, the dead were all black and swelled to a size. I tried to find Baby George and the others, but I couldn't stomach the smell, and I had to leave. I've always imagined that they died in there, but I've never known for sure. My mother never recovered from the loss of my brothers and sister, and died soon afterwards. I'd give anything to have them back again. They were beautiful children. I often wonder what happened to their bodies. Someone said they were buried there, but how can anyone tell? Sometimes I feel that they're still here, and that's why I stay. I don't ever want to leave them.'

But Baby George and the others were no longer here, or even in Guyana.

Later I discovered what had probably become of them. In death, the Amerindians had travelled further than they'd ever dreamed of in life. There were perhaps eight of them altogether, including the pseudo-Joneses, and they'd all have been scooped up in the great American airlift. In Georgetown this great, long-dead expedition was disembarked and packed onto transports. They were then flown to Dover in Delaware, where they sat for months in giant refrigerators built for the Vietnam dead. During this time they were fingerprinted by the FBI and then worked over by some thirty-five pathologists and twenty-nine morticians. By the end, it was still a mystery who everybody was. Once the relatives had retrieved those they wanted, a bewildering 410 bodies remained behind. Of these, sixty didn't seem to have any ties at all.

For the Amerindian Joneses, there was still another journey ahead. Boxed up with all the other unclaimed bodies, they were flown to California. There they were buried in Oakland, in a large, unceremonious mass grave.

As I flew back to Georgetown, I tried in vain to make sense of all I'd seen. Way below, the forest heaved and blackened like unsettled sky. Great whorls of green gathered together, swelled up, reshaped themselves, formed into vast billowing, black masses of chlorophyll and then burst, swirling off into the distance. Perhaps Jonestown was like this, I thought: not something made, but a series of random patterns. Take away any single feature from the whole – the diseased prophet, the badlands, the broken discipleship, the bush and the threadbare state – and the landscape would have looked completely different. In fact, Jonestown would probably never have taken shape at all, and the endpiece vanishes altogether.

But not everyone sees it like this. For many, particularly in America, Jonestown has an inevitable quality, and there's almost a straight line between the promiscuous '60s and the tubs of grape-flavoured cyanide. This is to say nothing of the belief that sinister agencies had somehow hustled the tragedy along. Every day on the internet more undergrowth is added to this jungle of myth. Some of it is planted by the descendants of the Temple, but the rest is seeded more despairingly, by those who insist that, in the absence of God, it's some human authority that determines our fate.

For the Guyanese there had been no patterns about Jonestown, and nor had it sat at the end of a line. As far as they were concerned, the whole thing had appeared from nowhere, like a visit from Outer Space. But they also knew that, whether they liked it or not, that day had changed them. 'For months afterwards,' said Joe, 'the eyes of the world were upon us.'

But what those eyes had seen had not always been easy to understand: private armies, stacks of Thorazine, a semi-feral theocracy, trunks full of cash and a Ministry of Hoods. After that, the great South American African Forbes Burnham had never quite regained his composure. Was he really a great liberator, or just a despot from the swamps? Six years later he found himself in the middle of a self-made famine, and – without any antibiotics – he died from a cough. It was the end of the African years, and the beginning of Indian rule. In 1992 Guyana held its first untarnished election for thirty years, and an ailing Cheddi Jagan was hoisted into power.

Jonestown could now be forgotten.

Back in Georgetown the events of 1978 still had people swooning with denial. Even the rebellious Dr Roopnaraine added his voice to the chorus of indignation.

'It was an American matter,' he told me, 'nothing to do with us.'

But, despite this energetic case of amnesia, Jonestown had proved difficult to bury. Every year, the *Stabroek News* would unearth the facts and parade them over its pages. It was almost as though readers needed reminding that the Temple was part of their story. Some joked that it was the only part. I once spotted a T-shirt in Stabroek market that depicted a map of Guyana under the heading 'Sights of Interest'. All it featured was Jonestown, marked with a skull and crossbones.

I sometimes wondered if the government had taken this taunt to heart. Only a few years earlier the Minister of Tourism had suggested that Jonestown be re-opened, to promote 'dark tourism'. In fairness, every other scheme had failed (including a refugee camp for the Indochinese). But tourism? I remember asking my driver, Ramdat Dhoni, about this soon after my return. Was it his cup of tea, a resort for the chronically morbid? Would he be booking his grandchildren in, and his son, and Mrs Dhoni?

'Don't shit me, man,' he giggled. 'You been too long in the bush ...'

Had I? I suddenly realised that I'd only been away for a week. It felt like months. Perhaps that was the effect of the bush, to render time endlessly elastic? Perhaps that's what had finally toppled Jones's sanity, an affliction like Dorian Gray's? This was not a particularly comforting thought as I contemplated my next move. The following day I'd be heading off – back inside – this time far deeper than before.

3

THE GOLDEN RUPUNUNI

The Empyre of Guiana is directly east from Peru ... and it hath more abundance of golde then any part of Peru, and as many or more great Cities ...

> Sir Walter Raleigh, *The Discoverie of the Large, Rich,*
> *and Bewtiful Empyre of Guiana*

Or there was the Rupununi savannah; several white people lived there and even a white woman, but it cost a great deal to get there and you might be drowned on the way or get a fever.

> Evelyn Waugh, *92 Days*

Ants in Guiana are very numerous, various and troublesome. They form themselves into a kind of a republic, governed by laws, like those of Europe.

> Edward Bancroft, *An Essay on the Natural History*
> *of Guiana in South America*

We stood on the borders of an enchanted land.

> Robert Schomburgk, *Reisen in Britisch Guiana*

THE RUPUNUNI SAVANNAHS are the wrong side of a forest several hundred miles wide.

Even by South American standards, this forest is overwhelming. There are parts that have never been properly charted, holes that have never been plumbed and lumps that have never been climbed. As for what's under the canopy, most of it has lain drenched in uninterrupted darkness for tens of thousands of years. New creatures are always turning up here, and, if trucks and planes get lost, they often vanish for ever. There's only one road through, and from the air it looks like nothing more than a tiny, bright red scratch. Meanwhile, the rivers are either huge and spectacularly violent – like the Essequibo – or thin and slinky, carnivorous and black.

Then suddenly the forest ends. It's like flying out of the night and bursting into sunlight. Ahead stretches a great, golden grassland the size of Scotland. This, of course, is only the wrong side of the forest if you feel a need for the outside world. The Rupununi doesn't. It is its own world, a fabulously impenetrable land, viciously defended by forests, and – at the southern end – walled in by some of the oldest mountains on Earth. These are said to be the last flat-topped columns of a lost super-continent, Pangea. It's not surprising that they should end up here, on this vast ocean of straw, where the lilies grow five feet wide and all the trees are armed. Even the animals feel curiously Jurassic. Here are the world's largest ants, otters and anteaters, and its biggest fish – the arapaima, a bearded monster as big as a horse.

All this makes the Rupununi's humans look rather vulnerable and small. Throughout the entire land there are still only 30,000 people. Some squares of the map are completely empty except for lumps of yellow and the names of dried-up explorers. No European managed to settle here until 1860. Even then, the only way in was on foot or by canoe. It remained like this until the age of the Dakota. There are still a few around who remember the gruelling journey – four weeks paddling upriver and then a couple of weeks on foot.

I soon realised that I didn't have the time (or the sanity) for a month in the Guyanese gloom, and so I did what the locals do and hopped on a plane.

The place where the plane dropped me was like the setting for a novel by Evelyn Waugh.

Annai, with its little grass village, was often said to be the gateway to the Rupununi. Out there on the savannah the horizon was so wide and bowed that it took me a moment to take it all in: an unearthly half-finished land, rimmed with mountains like purple teeth and dappled in brilliant birds. Sandpaper grew on trees, and the anthills looked like hooded monks emerging from the earth. I'd heard that during the rains it all turned to glue, but that then the waters would recede, and once again it would be what it was now, a sea of thorns and light and bony lagoons. To Waugh, who passed through here in January 1933, it was ideal, like a punishment from heaven.

I could almost imagine him pounding along, kicking up the dust. He looked unhappier than ever in his outsize shorts, ill-fitting boots and a brand new homburg hat. The Rupununi came at a bad time for Waugh. The failure of his marriage had left him shrivelled with rage and shame. All he seemed to want was to suffer, to find some distant and barbarous place, and to go there and hate it. Eventually he chose Guiana – not that he cared much about it. This was not supposed to be a voyage of enlightenment but a punishment. Even the book he wrote, 92 *Days*, sounds like a sentence. He arrived that new year, and after hating Georgetown (too big, too dull, too much sugar), he set out to hate the interior. 'It is by crawling on the face of it,' he wrote, 'that one learns about a country.'

At one level, Waugh's Rupununi journey makes an unedifying read. He's a fractious travelling companion, always moaning about poor gin-swizzles, servants, children and 'revolting meals'. No one escapes his withering scorn. But perhaps hardest hit are the Amerindians. Waugh despises their 'blank Mongolian faces', their 'stupidity and lack of imagination' and their 'nauseating hospitality'. One Patamona woman he describes as 'slatternly and ill-favoured even for one of her race'. The Guianese had not been described like this for years. It was, as one biographer put it (generously, I thought), a 'pre-Columbian and pre-enlightenment view of the world'.

But at another level his book is unmissable. Despite his pique and prejudice, Waugh is a master craftsman, deftly capturing character and sculpting the moment. Remarkable too is his journey, a slog of hundreds of miles, most of it by horse. Along the way he samples every variant of Guyanese discomfort: fevers, saddle sores, boils, rashes, 'deep and tenacious' ticks, and bites 'like circles of burning flesh'. Somehow he makes an art form of it all, and – as a work of mortification – his ordeal is a triumph. But there was even better to come. Among all his fears of being forgotten and lost, Waugh dreamed up a masterpiece, *A Handful of Dust*.

My host in Annai might easily have tumbled from the pages of Waugh. Colin Edwards had something about him of the caricature. He was a sort of broad, ruddy, bouncing squire – half Welsh, a bit Basque, wild in his dreams and loud in reproof. He told me he'd arrived as a road-builder twenty-odd years before. It was he who'd bashed the long, narrow road through the forest. 'And I'll tell you something,' he'd say. 'It was me who linked this country to South America.'

'And was that a good thing?' I said, half joking.

'My dear chap, of course! Stopped our absurd reliance on the coast …'

No doubt Colin would have carried on bashing trails through the continent but for these savannahs. The very sight of the Rupununi had transformed him from a man of the roads to the lord of the manor. He'd married the daughter of a local chief, imported his ageing parents and settled down in a large crumbling mansion shaped like a crown of thorns.

It had been a curious transformation, like a journey back to a long-lost age. Rockview now had rooms for travellers, a pet tapir and a shop called the Dakota Bar, which sold rum, bras, cutlasses and 'Anglo' spam. Meanwhile, the wilderness had been marshalled into tidy rows – limes, mangoes and breadfruits – and a small army of liveried Amerindians kept everything brushed and polished. There was even a little cemetery nestling herbaceously in this scene of content. It contained Colin's parents, a dog killed by a snake, the wreckage of a visiting helicopter and the man who'd built the house of thorns. As to this, his strange spiky home, it had hardly changed at all – except for the library, where a vast collection of leathery classics was now being enjoyed by the weevils.

All this would have appalled Waugh. Rockview was like something from a latter-day version of *A Handful of Dust*, with Colin recast as the new Mr Todd. It wasn't just the incongruous mansion, the Welshness of the tribe or the half-eaten books, but the whole idea of perpetuity. To Waugh this would have been unspeakable. Here was a man, not unlike himself, who'd stumbled in on this raw, uncivilised land, and who would now probably be here for ever.

From Annai, I went to stay with a hunter, who lived deep in the grass. To get there, I hitched a lift with a chief called Bradford Allicock. He was a thoughtful man, with skin the colour of ox-blood, and with an old school bus, covered in go-faster stripes. Riding along with him was like flying, except without the wings. Soon we were blasting across the savannah, following the edge of the forest. On the horizon I could just make out a grass fire, fizzling along like a gunpowder fuse. Then we dropped down and swooped in among the trees. This was the vicious vanguard of the forest beyond: trees sprouting daggers and poison, or – like the water cedar – densely bristled in cocktail sticks, each one brittle and black. Then eventually we emerged squealing into the sunlight. Here were more savannahs, miniature versions of the one outside, except enclosed by prickly hills. All of this, Bradford told me, was Makushi territory, for hundreds of miles around.

It hadn't always looked so well defended. Until the 1790s, the grasslands of the northern Rupununi were regularly raided by Caribs and *bandeirantes*, or slavers from Brazil. It was like a park for hunting humans. There's even a description of a raid in 1838, which reads like a leisurely duck shoot.

'Thousands of our people were lost,' said Bradford, 'but then we learned to fight, and we chopped them, and killed them, and now this land is ours.'

'And how many Makushi are there?' I asked.

Bradford sucked his teeth and whistled. Counting Makushi was like counting the ripples on a pond. Sometimes there were a lot, sometimes there were none. In his grandfather's day it was measles that almost wiped them out. Then, in 1943, a wild strain of malaria got in among them, leaving only 1,600 survivors. As for the number now, Bradford could only guess. 'Maybe 13,000. Half here, and the rest in Venezuela and Brazil.'

His own family were, however, like a subset of the tribe. They hadn't all been Makushis. Peering upwards into his family tree, Bradford could see mostly Caribs and Arawaks, but also a Scotsman perched in the branches. It was the irrepressible Mr Allicock, a strapping Victorian farmer. At some low point in the Makushis' evolution his potent genes had got mingled in, and now there were Allicock chiefs all over the savannah.

'Like this place,' said Bradford, 'which was run by my Uncle Fred.'

We'd arrived in Surama, where I was to stay. It was a memorable arrival, if only because I hardly noticed it at all. All I could see was grass. Although Surama was the size of central Paris and took an hour and a half to cross, only 240 people lived there. Even they were hardly ostentatious. Most of them lived around the edge of the savannah, in houses the colour of straw. Their great grandparents, according to Bradford, had settled here to service the cattle trail. But now the trail had long since gone, leaving the village with nothing but a few iron way-markers and an appetising name: *Surama*, 'The Place of Roasted Meat'.

There were few other signs of life: a little church, a school without any walls, a shop that sold bows and arrows, and a weather station. This last unnecessary gizmo had lasted only three months before the spirits had tired of it and blown it to bits with lightning. The church, it seems, had fared better, with only a plague of termites. Perhaps this was because (as one old Rupununian put it) 'The Makushis worship mostly the Anglican god – as well as lots of others.'

As we passed each leafy household, Bradford called out the names. Everyone seemed to be an Allicock. They lived in concentric rings: Uncle Fred surrounded by his sons, who were in turn surrounded by theirs, all half a mile apart. It was like a galaxy of Allicocks, all radiating power from Uncle Fred. In time I'd get to meet most of them: Ovid the guide; Sidney, who saw the future, richly cluttered with tourists; Velda, who distrusted the sea, and dreamed of a digital camera; Veronica, whose gold teeth were decorated with hearts and stars to ward off evil; and poor Sidney Junior, who'd gone to Georgetown once, discovered traffic, clashed with an old car and never walked again. Then, finally, there was Dango, the man with whom I was about to stay.

'I think you'll like him,' said Bradford, 'they call him the Jungle Commando.'

Dango Allicock once told me that the two most important things in his life were barbed wire and solitude.

He was never an easy man to understand, but Bradford was right to say I'd like him. Dango was huge and shy, barrel-chested, splaytoed, uncomfortable in the open and happy in the shadows. His hair was still rich and black, and although he only ever wore shorts, he could be surprisingly formal, even stately. But in his polished mahogany features there were always furrows of concern. In another world he'd have been a judge or bishop, but this was the Rupununi and so he was a hunter. He told me he prayed for the souls of those he was about to kill and then disappeared for days.

'And before I go,' he said, 'all I do is burn my mouth with peppers, so that my eyes are bright and sharp.'

'And what about all your gear?' I asked.

'Just a bow and arrows,' he said, 'some matches, and a little bit of salt.'

It wasn't hard to appreciate the role of solitude in this. The Makushi were famously lonely, always coveting isolation and the world's disregard. Resources were scarce, outsiders were dangerous and every nip of protein had to be wrestled from the land. Everyone was a competitor. That's why people scattered themselves across the savannah, and why Dango and his wife, Paula, lived so far out in the straw. It was as though even the prospect of a neighbour was too much to bear. Here we were in the heart of old 'Macoushia', and the only sound was the rattle of the leaves.

Barbed wire had a more complex role. For a start, it was one of the few imports from the outside world. Everything else was woven, carved, harvested, slaughtered or cut right here. It seemed like an idyllic life, at least in texture. The Allicocks had three long, stooped houses, made of sticks and mud, and fronds of ité palm. There was no water or electricity, and we washed in a waterhole out in the grass. Every mealtime a huge family gathered and ate whatever their father had killed. Then, as night fell, Dango would climb into a tree to sleep (he thought beds made him ill), while the rest of us – nine in all – would cram together in a single stilted hut. All night there was whispering and the rustle of feet, and everyone would tell stories until they fell asleep. These felt like ordinary lives except stripped of clutter: no chairs, no doors, no cash and no concept of time. Paula had made only one other concession to the present: walls plastered with pictures of mythical white women torn from the pages of *Vogue*.

But barbed wire was more than just an innovation. It was like a sort of elongated currency, the outward sign of a man's wealth and his prospects of survival. The more wire he had, the more forest he could clear and enclose, and therefore the more he grew. Without enough wire, either his farm was too small or the neighbouring cattle ate his crops. Without enough food, the family would die or move to the towns (which was much the same). So it was true, life still hung by a single strand of old barbed wire.

'And what about the tapirs?' I asked. 'Will the wire stop them?'

'No,' said Dango, 'their skin's too thick. But at least we can eat them.'

Each day I set out with Dango on one of his Herculean strolls. Sometimes we'd walk half a day into the jungle. We always followed the paths made by big cats, triggering a discordant symphony of screams. One unseen creature announced us wherever we went with a hoot of high-pitched raspberry. ('The anti-man,' announced Dango, 'the curse of the hunter'.) But this wasn't the only invisible musician. Everything in there thrummed and whistled or emitted blasts of cacophonous pain. Even the forest swamps had their own dank, crepuscular song. They'd be happily oozing and whirring, and then there'd be a crack and a muffled splosh as something slid back into the gloop, dragging a bundle of legs.

'Dangerous water,' said Dango. 'Lots of piranhas and electric eels.'

'But who comes off worse?' I asked. 'You or the piranhas?'

'Me,' he said modestly, and showed me his calves and the bits that were missing.

'It looks like you've been attacked by a dog,' I gasped.

'Yes,' he said, 'a dog with teeth like a saw.'

On one of these walks we stopped at his farm, deep in the forest. It was an astonishing sight. At first I thought there'd been some great disaster. The entire clearing was still smouldering, and great trunks of smoking ash lay scattered everywhere, like the columns of a plundered city. Perhaps the spirits had called down a meteorite? Or this was the tapir's revenge? But then I noticed Dango's pride. In a few days he'd done the work of a mechanical excavator, reducing this patch of forest to the garden that he needed. It would feed his family for the next two years, until the soil was spent. Within the wire there'd be yams, cassava, sugar cane and melons. It would even provide him with shafts for his arrows.

As we were leaving, Dango picked a few stems of arrow-wood, and that night he set to work. By dawn he'd produced a seven-foot bow and four arrows. Each was perfectly adapted for the killing in hand: barbs for a monkey, a detachable head for fish, a punch for birds, and a dagger for the tapir. After breakfast Dango presented them to me, to take back to London.

'And whenever you use them,' he said, 'you'll think of us.'

There was another side to Makushi life, lived around the hearth.

Dango despised the kitchen house and never went there, except to eat or to drink cassiri. This was a brew of fermented cassava, purple potatoes and human spit. According to Sir Walter Raleigh, it was what made the Amerindians 'the greatest carousers in the world'. I, however, took mine gingerly because it was like whisky blended with cabbages and socks. Dango, on the other hand, would seat himself up in the thatch and drink it by the tubful. At these moments he was like an old churchwarden: craggy and dark and only sleepily in charge.

In Dango's absences – physical and spiritual – his wife came into her own. I adored Paula. She was round and exuberant, had a tattoo on her face and was dressed in a Guyanese flag. Her variant of motherhood seemed to absorb everyone, and her kitchen was always a hub of scavengers and hopefuls. There was a daughter, Pinky, several sons-in-law, all their babies, an orphaned grandson, six chickens and a large apologetic hunting dog called Bully. If they waited long enough, there was always something going spare: bakes, okra stew, a local couscous called *farine*, fried plantains or a slice of barbecued tapir. Evelyn Waugh hated Makushi cuisine (he thought *farine* tasted like brown paper), but then he'd never eaten at Paula's. It was like all the best food in the world, the brilliant joint venture of sunlight and poverty.

But Paula wasn't just a conjuror of food. She also possessed something that was much rarer among the Makushi, the gift of talk. Over forty years she'd gathered up all the stories, the history, the myths, the gossip, the recipes and the cures, and now she was prepared to retell it to anyone who'd listen. Never before had I met an Amerindian like her, who talked with such candour about a lifestyle now slowly ebbing away. Perhaps she felt that her boldness would somehow staunch the tide. There was nothing she wouldn't talk about: it might be magic and sorcery, or the three gods of the Makushi world, or her mother, whose legs had been bound with twine to cut off the blood supply and accentuate the calves, or the old punishment for children (a peppery paste smeared on the anus), or her own forced marriage, or the birth of Pinky, when she was only a child herself. It was, said Paula, a beautiful world.

'And now,' she said, 'all the children want is DVDs and money.'

'But they still hunt, don't they?' I asked.

'Not many. They can't even make their own arrows ....'

The beautiful world, she said, was vanishing all around. Now that the cattle trail had gone, even the forest was closing in. With the darkness came a new plague, or perhaps it was an old one: jaguars. Dango told me they'd eaten all the village horses and were now killing all the calves. 'It won't be long,' he said, 'before they start on Man.'

But jaguars weren't the only monsters in the beautiful world of Macoushia. Like Paula, everyone had their ghosts. A life that had seemed idyllic was actually infested. One man told me that ghosts had drowned his cousin, breaking his neck with a paddle. Another described building a house on land that was cursed, and watching his plates as they started to bleed. The horror was always like this, richly surreal. During my time on the northern savannahs I'd come across supernatural rocks, giant worms, mischievous sprites and trees that turned you grey. There were even libidinous boulders that could make a girl pregnant, and stones that could fly. Evil spirits were everywhere, said Dango, and they entered the body through the eyes and ears, and even up the anus. That's why the women had symbols carved into their teeth – to ward off these impish intruders.

'People are afraid,' he warned. 'These aren't just stories.'

Some places, I realised, were worse than others. Graves, in particular, seemed to emit waves of malevolence, like a radioactive field. You couldn't eat where the dead had died or walk where they'd been carried, and cemeteries were regarded as so spiritually toxic that only the strongest could visit. But it wasn't just graveyards. Almost every aspect of Makushi life was haunted, and most people seemed to live their lives in a state of perpetual anxiety. Their worst fear was to have an enemy blowing evil in their face. Once a Makushi believes he's cursed, then – as everyone knew – he'll simply lie down and die.

Only one person could intercede on a man's behalf, and that was the magician.

'Maybe you want to meet him?' said Dango.

I said I did, and so we set off, an hour's walk across the savannah.

'I think we're too late,' said Dango as we got to the *piaiman*'s hut.

In the distance we could just see the sorcerer battling through the grass, off on a magical mission. His wife hailed us from her hammock. She must have been over eighty and was wearing only a pair of shorts. I was surprised how deflated the female form could become. She looked like a suit of human pelts.

'I'm sorry …' I began.

But she didn't understand. Perhaps I ought to have been relieved by this, that there was no call for English in her ghoulish world.

Somewhere in the great labyrinth of the Makushi mind there's always an avenger, known as the *kanaima*.

'We had one here once,' said Dango, 'about twenty years ago.'

Paula said he was a hired killer, or sometimes a *piaiman*. But the *kanaima* wasn't always a person. To some it was a murderous will-o'-the-wisp, a roving concept of indefinable dread. The *kanaima* was the reason children died, and was behind every death that couldn't be otherwise explained. Here was a constant reminder of man's vulnerability, a spectre that was soundless, ruthless, invincible and everywhere. I once met a Makushi near Annai who said that his brother had been hunted down by the *kanaima*. 'It could change itself into an animal,' said Hendrik, 'and move at a hundred miles an hour.'

'What had your brother done?' I asked.

'He had a girl in the Pakaraima Mountains, and then he left her.'

The *kanaima* was always assiduous in revenge. Most people thought that he, or it, could be hired, at the cost of an unmarried daughter, to effect some elaborate killing. I'd often heard these hits described, and they were nearly always the same. First, the *kanaima* smears himself with anaconda fat, which makes him instantly invisible. Then he takes up a club of purple heart and sets off after the victim, covering his tracks with secret spells. When he finds him, the killer hides among the rocks, biding his time with lethal precision. 'Then,' said Hendrik, 'he lash you, and black you out.'

After that, the mutilation varies from story to story. Sometimes the *kanaima* forces a poisonous snake's tooth through the victim's tongue, so that it swells up and, over several days, chokes the man to death. Other victims are found with their limbs twisted in the sockets, or their heads so thoroughly pulverised that they've become all shapeless and soft. But some *kanaimas* have a more visceral interest. They force a stick up their quarry's rectum, twist the intestines around it, extract them and knot them, and then ram them back inside.

'With my brother,' said Hendrik, 'the *kanaima* cut out his anus, and then took off his face with a knife.'

'And did you tell the police?' I asked.

Hendrik looked at me strangely. 'No, we went to the *piaiman*.'

After that, he didn't mention his brother again. Perhaps he'd realised that we came from different parts of the spiritual map, separated by thousands of years in the forest.

From Surama I set off across the savannah with a young archer called Hubert. He was a very different man from Dango. With his bulldog shoulders and his rolling gait, Hubert was always farting, and was boisterous and eager for the fray. It was like being with a bowman from *Henry V*. Once, he showed me how to kill a beer can at eighty yards. While he could pin it out like a moth, I could barely twang the string. 'It takes practice,' said Hubert, kindly. When he was a child, his grandfather had tattooed a scorpion across one of his ample biceps. It was supposed to bring him luck in hunting and success with women, and now – in both, it seemed – his aim was true. Although Hubert was barely twenty-five, he already had two families. We passed his latest household as we left Surama. It was a small wooden shack, profusely leaking children.

'And here come my friends,' said Hubert.

Along the track came a succession of hunters.

'Anything?' we asked

'Not even a monkey,' said the first.

'Nothing,' said the next, who was riding a bicycle loaded with arrows.

Then came another man, with a tiny capuchin perched on his shoulder.

'What's that?' I whispered. 'His bait? Or his lunch?'

'It's an orphan,' said Hubert, 'so now it helps with the hunt.'

After that we saw no one, and by early evening we'd reached the end of the savannah. Ahead lay the Pakaraima Mountains, looming up like great blue shards of broken forest. Hubert said that some of them had never been climbed, and that from now on there was nothing but the trees. As we stepped into the darkness, I thought of the hunters – and their monkeys – creeping around for game. No wonder they were away for days. The only creatures I ever saw were things that were trying to eat me.

Some of these tormentors were more insistent than others. One of them was the kabouri fly. It was a sort of microscopic mugger, slyly inconspicuous until the very moment it drove its white-hot pin deep beneath the flesh. There was nothing that could be done about it, although it didn't like the dark. Others were more flexible; nippers, stingers, itchers and puffs of poisonous mites. We even found a whorl of milky froth, a telltale sign of mosquito worm. This ambitious little tunneler likes nothing better than to colonise the scalp. But, as Hubert said, this wasn't the worst of them. 'If a screw worm gets inside a dog's head,' he told me, 'it will eat it from the inside out.'

In this exchange of proteins, only one creature offered itself for ingestion: the flying ant. Whenever one came into range, Hubert would pluck it from the air and pop it in his mouth. 'Delicious,' he'd say, through the succulent crunch of thorax, 'tastes just like a nut.'

Eventually, at dusk, we reached the Burro-Burro River. It was like a streak of blackened glass sliding away, off through the trees. There, high on a bluff, we slung our hammocks and ate some chunks of catfish. It tasted of trout with an extra dollop of pond. Then we

opened some rum, settled in our hammocks and waited for the show
to begin.

I had no idea the forest could be so wonderful at night. As the light
failed, the airborne eaters receded, and the tweeters began. At first
it was just a flurry of nightjars and a gentle lullaby of croaks. Then
came the crickets and cicadas, and a ludicrous bug like an aerial
lawnmower, trimming through the heat. At the same time a cloud
of fireflies appeared and flickered around as though they were the
cosmos, on a visit to the flowers. Then, all of a sudden, the evening
was torn apart by the sound of a sawmill bursting into life. It was
all the work of a single beetle, who'd waited fourteen years for this
moment and had twenty-four hours to live.

'Ah, the six o'clock beetle!' cried Hubert, as though it were just
on time.

But the beetle didn't just work through cocktail hour. It carried
on sawing all night: through bedtime, the witching hour, the small
hours and the early morning dew. It was still at peak production,
when – at four – I finally drifted off into a light industrial sleep. I
could hardly blame it. When you've only got two six o'clocks in your
life, you want to make them last.

Dawn was simply the evening thrown into reverse. The glass
reappeared, the eaters returned, and the tweeters fell quiet. The
last to go was the lawnmower, bumbling off to bed. That left only
a distant, constipated roar. It was the howler monkeys, with their
usual public announcement: Approach at your peril, and we'll pelt
you with dung. But even they stopped when the sun broke through.
Soon it had burned off the cool, clammy vapours of the night, and
torpor was restored.

Days on the Burro-Burro have probably always opened like this, even
in 1812. But one day towards the end of that year a new character
appeared, splashing up the river. He was six feet tall, horse-faced
and barefoot. Apart from a shirt and light cotton trousers, he was
wearing only a cocked hat and braces. With him in his canoes were
twelve warriors, who he chatted to in both Makushi and deepest
Yorkshire. Although unknown at that time, this man would soon
be the darling of Georgian society. Even now, he remains probably
the most enjoyable figure ever to have slogged through the southern
savannahs.

Walton Hall, a corner of Guiana in the heart of Yorkshire.

He is Charles Waterton, naturalist, eccentric, and master of Walton Hall. Here is his story.

By the time the twenty-seventh Lord of Walton is disgorged – bitten and blistered – by the Burro-Burro River, he's almost thirty-one.

It's been a rumbustious life so far. He's spent his childhood on the family estate, climbing trees and communing with owls. Shoes have never agreed with him, and nor have guns, foxes and protestants. There's been an attempt to educate him, but all Stonyhurst has taught him is how to catch rats. There's also been a period in Málaga, working for his uncle. Spain, however, will be remembered only as a series of biblical disasters. First there was an outbreak of 'black vomit', which claimed 14,000 locals, and then came an earthquake, which killed several thousand more. Wracked with the Spanish spasms, Charles was only just able to button himself back into his 'unmentionables' before bolting back to Wakefield. But Yorkshire proved much too small to contain him. Soon he'd be prancing around in a blue body coat with real gold buttons (much to the horror of the local police). By 1804 his father had made a momentous decision; it's time the boy was exported to Guiana.

Eight years have now elapsed since the young Waterton first arrived. The old Dutch colony suits him well. He's improved his outfit with the addition of gold epaulettes and a cocked hat, and has joined the Demerara militia. He's also done a spell on the family sugar estates, known – of course – as Walton Hall. But he's not been happy with plantation life. ('Slavery,' he says, 'can never be defended'.) It's only with the death of his father that Waterton becomes the man he wants to be. Armed with a dangerous curiosity (and a huge inheritance), he sets off into the interior. Between 1812 and 1824 he'll undertake four of these stupendous forays, each lasting up to fourteen months. Along the way he'll meet the tribes, learn their languages and gather hundreds of specimens, many of them previously considered scientifically absurd. What's more, he'll always travel alone, unsupported, barefoot and theatrically attired.

It's on the first of his trips that we find him paddling up the Burro-Burro. He makes an impressive sight, astride a mound of fur and feathers. Every now and then he jumps out of his canoe or scrambles off into the trees. At one point he leaps astride an alligator and rides it like a jockey (a feat of horsemanship he attributes to his years spent riding to Lord Darlington's hounds). Another time he comes face to face with a ten-foot boa and punches it full in the mouth. The poor snake is so surprised that all it can do is wrap a bit of tail around its astonishing assailant and give him a useless squeeze. At least it manages to fight. Another fourteen-footer finds itself wrestled into a ball and lashed down with a pair of gentleman's braces.

Waterton is deterred by nothing, not even the bouts of malaria. Whenever he feels peaky, he simply lets a little blood – which he calls 'tapping the claret' – or swallows a draft of mercury with 'calomel and jallop'. Remarkably, these ministrations don't make him worse, just more inquisitive. He leaves his feet out at night so he can watch the 'vampires' eat him. (In vain, as it turns out. Bats clearly don't like mercury-flavoured humans.) Then, the next morning, he's up again, out in the grass or climbing trees. He thinks nothing of shinning up fifty feet into the canopy. (A few years later, on a visit to Rome, he'll climb up St Peter's and plant his glove on the crucifix. It's said that when Pope Pius VII can't find a steeplejack willing to retrieve it, Waterton will happily oblige and climb back up again.)

The public will love these stories. Every time he gets home, the indomitable squire bundles up his adventures, and they're a publishing sensation. Eventually they all end up in one chaotic volume: *Waterton's Wanderings in South America*. It's a magnificent rambling yarn, bursting with improbable creatures, affection, family history, half-told stories and misplaced narrators. The critics mock it, but the readers love it. During his life it will be republished four times and earn Waterton a place in the National Portrait Gallery (depicted in a gold-buttoned coat, with a decapitated cat). The book will inspire not only Darwin, who's still a boy, but also a whole generation of infant scientists. As an introduction to the weirdness of an untamed continent, *Wanderings* is the best there's ever been.

As a guidebook, however, it's a disaster. Waterton doesn't care where he is and seldom gives us names. All I can be sure about is that, at some stage, he comes paddling up the Burro-Burro, perhaps stopping here to tussle with the snakes.

In order to stand a little longer in Waterton's footsteps, I'd have to pay a visit to Walton Hall. As the Guyanese version was now merely a name, that left only the original, back home in England.

I went there some months later, on a brittle February day, when the lake was frozen hard. All around lay Waterton's parkland like an etching in the snow. Everywhere there was the hoot and clank of wildfowl. It was almost a Guyanese scene, depicted in negative. Perhaps, as the years lengthened, that's how Waterton had remembered his 'magical woods'. I could just make out the wall he'd built, eight feet high and three miles long. It was supposed to wall off a bit of paradise and keep out the foxes and poachers. The result was the world's first wildlife park. There were artificial rookeries, stumps for owls and a grotto for the bats. On the weekends the local millworkers had visited, and Waterton would boil up water for their tea. He was a much-loved man and always had some stunt, such as wearing birds' wings or barking like a dog. Even at the age of seventy-seven he could still scratch his head with his foot.

The hall was exactly as he'd described it, on an island in the lake. There was the same iron bridge, and a barge for the coal. I even found the bullet-holes around the gatehouse door (the work of heretics, said Waterton, who'd besieged the house in the name of Oliver Cromwell). Only the inside had changed. It was now a hotel, and smelt of curious innovations such as peach-flavoured air-freshener and skinny cappuccino. But the biggest change was the departure of the Guyanese fauna. Once these hallways had teemed with lifeless wildlife, including a ten-foot caiman, several armadillos, an anteater and over 300 twitterless, glass-eyed birds. Now they'd all gone, having migrated down the road to Wakefield Museum.

All that remained of South America was a giant stone otter above the door. After his fourth expedition Waterton had never been back, although, in a sense, Guiana came to him. In 1829 he married the granddaughter of an Amerindian chieftain. Anne-Mary was only seventeen, and it's hard to know what she made of her husband's Yorkshire-Rupununi. He, on the other hand, declared himself 'the happiest man in the world'. It was, however, a happiness that wouldn't last. The following year Anne-Mary died giving birth to their son, Edmund.

Waterton never got over the blow and mourned her for the rest of his life. From then on he never slept in a bed again but spent his nights under a portrait of St Catherine of Alexandria, with only a plank for a pillow. Fortunately for Edmund, Anne-Mary's two sisters moved in and became his substitute mothers. Although the four of them made occasional trips to Sicily, to watch the migration of birds, there were no journeys back to Guiana. The two Amerindian sisters are buried in Scarborough, where they eventually retired.

Waterton himself is buried at the far end of the lake that he so loved. On his grave it says simply, 'Pray for the soul of Charles Waterton, whose weary bones are buried here.' It had been an agile life, right to the end. At the age of eighty-two he could still climb the highest tree in the park to watch the birds and read some Horace. Later that year, however, he tripped and landed on a log. Within a few hours he was dead.

On 3 June 1865 the Squire of Walton Hall was placed aboard the coal barge and rowed down the lake. Behind his coffin came a procession of boats draped with laurels and crêpe. Among the mourners were a bishop, four canons and thirteen chanting priests. It was all a far cry from the curious ensemble that had paddled down the Burro-Burro over fifty years earlier. This time the wildlife fell silent. It's said that only as the coffin was lowered into the grave was any sound heard: a single bird offering its song.

Ironically, Waterton's most enduring legacy was a gift to humankind.

I asked Hubert about this, as we were walking back.

'Blowpipes?' he said, 'I know how to use one – but none of us do.'

Waterton would have been disappointed to hear this. He was fascinated by blowpipes and, with an eye to his readers, had called them 'The Tubes of Death'. But it wasn't so much the pipe that intrigued him as what came out of the end. Each little dart was tipped in a remarkable compound known as *woorali*. This brown, syrupy gum was concocted from vines, ants, snakes' teeth and Indian peppers. To taste it or eat it would do no harm at all. But if it entered the bloodstream – even through the tiniest nick – it would induce an extraordinary death. 'It destroys life so gently,' wrote Waterton, 'that the victim appears to be in no pain whatever.' Poisoned creatures, he noticed, just seemed to lose the will to move and drowned in their own inertia. What was this poison, he wondered, and what could it do for us?

He wasn't the first explorer to be intrigued by *woorali*. Raleigh said it was the most curious thing he'd ever seen (and thought the antidote was garlic). It was also described, in 1759, by the French explorer Charles Marie de La Condamine, who added an intriguing detail: *woorali*, he said, was always cooked up by those condemned to die. (The potion was ready when its cooks fell lifeless to the ground.) Ten years later an English physician, Dr Bancroft, tried a few experiments of his own but got some in his eye and had to plunge his head in the Demerara River. Alexander von Humboldt brought a little more *gravitas* to the learning in 1800, with his discovery that the only active ingredient was the vine (now called *strychnos toxifera*). But Waterton would take matters much further: he struck a deal with the Makushi, acquired a vial of the priceless poison and brought it back to Yorkshire.

'Our *woorali* was easily the best,' said Hubert.

'How do you know that?' I asked.

'Because it killed all the Caribs.'

Back at Walton Hall, the squire set to work. It was already suspected that life could be prolonged by assisted respiration, and Waterton now tested this, using a donkey. After a massive shot of poison, he ventilated the animal with a pair of bellows, and after a while the animal began to rally. (It survived for another twenty-five years, until 1839.) In this rather crude experiment Waterton had conclusively proved the essential properties of a new drug, curare:

it was a muscle-relaxant and brought on temporary paralysis of the victim's respiratory muscles. But what could it be used for?

Waterton himself thought he'd stumbled on the cure for rabies. Later, doctors started using curare in the treatment of psychiatric illness. But the true importance of the Makushis' poison wasn't understood until 1942. It (or rather, its synthetic sister) would become a key component of general anaesthesia. By chemically relaxing the muscles, it was possible to reduce the dose of dangerous sedative. Now, every day, around the world, this simple idea saves thousands of lives. I like to think it all began with a small Makushi vial, now sitting in Wakefield Museum.

When I told Hubert about the donkey, he frowned.

'Did it taste good?' he asked.

'I don't think Waterton ate it.'

Hubert huffed. 'My grandfather never wasted his *woorali*.'

Two days later I said goodbye to the Allicocks and Hubert, and set off in search of the water monkey. Across the Guianas I'd come across several versions of this monster, but the worst of them lived in the rivers. No matter who was describing him – or when – he was always the same: long-haired, humanoid, clawed, with teeth like a tiger and an appetite for belly. The Amerindians told Evelyn Waugh that it would drag a man to the bottom and smash every bone in his body. As though this wasn't bad enough, the beast had another nasty trait. In 1769 Dr Bancroft (the physician who'd plunged his head in the Demerara) brought the world news of a Guianese 'orang-outan' that clambered from the rivers to 'ravish the female of the human species'.

I often wondered about the origins of this entrail-eating sex pest. Some say he's a horribly mutated variant of the West African gorilla, who survived in the imagination of the slaves. But all Guianese seem to claim him – and fear him. (Once I even met a Hindu woman who told me which rivers were haunted.) It's no great surprise, therefore, that his name tends to vary. To the Amerindians he's the Water Tiger, or the Dai-Dai. To most Africans he's the Massa Couraman, but to the descendants of the runaway slaves he takes on a deviant female form: the Ouata-mama. Perhaps, however, the most grotesque name of all is that on which Evelyn Waugh alighted; this was no tiger, it was the Water monkey.

Of course, I didn't actually expect to find him or break the rules of mythology and come running back with proof. Instead, all I wanted was to slip quietly through his watery domain and hope that something would happen, if only understanding. What better way of doing this than by taking a tiny metal boat up the Rupununi, with two Amerindian storytellers called Tiberius and Joe? They would drop me three hours upriver, at Karanambu. 'Just be careful,' they said, 'and keep your hands inside the boat.'

From the start it was a beautiful, well-toothed voyage. The great river seemed to trot along, nervously skirting the golden sandbanks and the bursts of luxuriant green. Everything here was either about to eat or to be eaten. Some creatures looked as though they were just waiting to be chosen – such as the capybaras, who were rabbity and plump, and helpfully myopic. Then there was a selection of delicious-looking birds – ibises, kiskadees and herons – all dutifully taking their place half-way up the food chain. Another, the piping guan, even had a call that sounded like a dinner bell.

As for the predators, they were mostly in the river.

'Caiman!' shouted Joe, as we passed a long black thug, slumped in the sand.

But the alligator was merely the tip of a predatory iceberg. Below us in the water was a vast society of flesh-eating beasts. My guide-book had this to say: 'Beware of swimming in Rupununi waters. The nine-inch perai is drawn to the smell of fresh blood. Stingrays and electric eels – the 500-volt variety – also inhabit the otherwise tranquil waters.'

Back in 1769 there was even worse news, from Dr Bancroft. Ducks' feet, he said, were frequently being amputated, 'as have been the breasts of women and the privities of men'. This last indignity could be avoided 'by tying a napkin or handkerchief around the waist'. Was he joking? Who'd be mad enough to dip *anything* into this liquid meat-shredder (with or without the serviette)?

I asked the boys what they felt about the swimming.

'Sure, we got plenty of perai …' said Tiberius.

'… and eels,' chimed Joe. 'They makes a big, blue flash …'

'… sometimes knock you out …'

'… and then there's stingrays …!'

'… they got a spike,' said Tiberius, 'can lash you open …'

Soon the stories were gushing free. Joe's ancestors had used the spikes in warfare. They were good for fighting because they always snapped inside the body and left a bit behind. The venom could be cured only with the spoil from an earthworm's burrow. Other injuries were harder to repair. Everyone knew people who'd lost fingers and ankles (and perhaps the occasional privity). But the worst creature, agreed the boys, was the water camoudie, or anaconda. Tiberius said he'd known it creep up behind someone, unclip its jaws and swallow him whole. I then remembered something that Dr Bancroft had once said about this snake (he could always pip a good story with one of his own). His version of the anaconda was also known as 'the sodomite snake' because it killed its victims by creeping up on them and shoving its tail right up their arse.

'Aieeee!' screamed the boys and then lay down in the boat and laughed.

I was pleased that my story had had this effect. It meant that there was a frontier, weaving its way between fact and myth. Even in these bloody waters some things were real and some things weren't. I wondered which side of the boundary the water monkey stood. Waterton knew. ('Ludicrous extravagance!' he declared. 'Pleasing to those fond of the marvellous and excellent matter for the distempered brain.')

But Tiberius wasn't so sure and refused to discuss it.

'Not here,' he said, 'not so near the river.'

Anyway, we'd almost arrived. On the left-hand side of the boat were some low black cliffs, like chunks of cinder toffee. Joe said that this was a holy place for Makushis, and that these were the bodies of a defeated enemy. As I gazed up into the smooth, dead crags, a bowman appeared. He was almost naked and carried a bundle of razor-toothed fish.

'Welcome to Karanambu,' he said shyly. 'I'll take you to Miss McTurk.'

There have been McTurks in Guyana ever since the departure of the Dutch. For the first hundred years they were pillars of the coastal community. They'd been doctors and planters and had sat in the Court of Policy. Then they'd bought ships, and for a moment it looked as though they might leave for ever and set up home in Liverpool. But then Grandfather Michael stowed away on one of his father's boats and returned to Guiana. It was the beginning of a

new generation of McTurks, this time slightly feral. Michael's greatest achievement was a survey of the Venezuelan frontier in 1895,
which almost sparked a war. Then, two decades later, his son Tiny
wandered off into the interior, and that was the end of the coastal
McTurks.

As a place to settle, the Rupununi was still an odd choice in 1922.
It took as long to get to Georgetown as it took for Townies to get to
London. There was no doctor, no government and still a handful of
tribes who'd shower you in arrows. But Tiny McTurk didn't seem
to mind. He was an enormous, plough-jawed man with an appetite for hardship. He taught himself to hunt with a bow, and could
survive on a diet of turtles' eggs. Once, when bandits tried to steal
his cattle, he followed them back to Brazil, snatched all their guns
and burned down their houses. After that, the Rupununi eagerly
adapted to Tiny McTurk. He even acquired a riverside ranch, above
the cinder toffee cliffs. There he built himself a sort of palace, a vast,
rambling structure, shaped like a beehive and made out of leaves.

The remarkable thing about Tiny's life is that he managed to
find a beautiful English girl willing to share it. Constance arrived
in 1927, and together they became the savannah's new aristocracy.
Apart from Waugh, almost every notable visitor to the Rupununi
paid them a call. Over the next fifty years they received visits from
princes, presidents, David Attenborough, Gerald Durrell and all the
world's best zoos. It was always a slightly uncertain grandeur. No
one ever wore shoes, and a goat ate all the books. Even more disconcerting were the young McTurks, the children that came tumbling
out of the trees. Among them was Diane, the present incumbent of
the Karanambu estate.

'I was born here,' she told me, 'in 1932. A wild child.'

In some ways not much had changed since Tiny's day. Karanambu
was still a large gravel clearing, planted with mango trees and
cashews. Scattered around the edge were the old ox carts and a few
antique trucks, put out to grass. The beehive too had survived, with
a mop of brand new thatch.

Inside, it was like a Makushi stately home. The walls were hung
with war clubs, bows, combs, quivers, hair-clippers and gun car-
tridge-fillers. There was even the remains of the goat-chewed library,
although the goat had long-since gone. ('He was accidentally killed,'
said Diane, 'by a Makushi with a hammer.') Now there were other

animals playing the role of furniture: a three-legged cat, several parakeets, two giant otters, a racoon called Bandit and a colony of fruit bats. All day the thatch creaked and snuffled as though it were a jungle canopy.

'This place was only meant to be temporary,' said Diane. 'My parents had always intended to build a really fancy residence, and they even bought the timber. But somehow they never got round to it, and the shingles got used for firewood. So here I am, still living in a *benab* ...'

Diane was constantly surprised by the curious turns her life hadn't taken. It was almost as though the timelessness of the Rupununi had got to her, carefully preserving the past. Perhaps that's why she'd ended up exactly where she'd started. Of course, she was older, but otherwise she was still the sylph who'd dangled upside down in front of the zoologists: willowy, fair, fleetingly fierce and effortlessly charming. Even the years away had hardly made an impression. There'd been a spell at drama school, a little, light skirmish with marriage ('a disaster') and then a few glamorous years in Chelsea. All of this had changed nothing except her consonants, which were now beautifully clipped into place.

'And when did you finally come home?' I asked.

'Crikey,' she said, 'I'm not awfully sure. It must've been '77.'

'And the giant otters?'

'Oh, I've always had them. I think I've reared more than forty.'

In the distance I could just see one: *Pteronura brasiliensis*, a ripple of chocolatey fur.

'An orphan,' said Diane, 'brought in by Makushis.'

Once again there were zoologists beating a path to Karanambu. Although during my stay I was the only guest, hundreds of others had been this way. To meet demand, Diane's Makushis had built four small guest huts, each from thatch and mud. It made a curious hotel. Just as in Tiny's day, there was no certainty what would happen next. In the few days that I was there, a planeful of food got lost, a fridge exploded, the heavens burst open, and there was a festival of toads. I loved it and would have happily stayed for weeks.

Karanambu and the otters also cured me of my deep-seated fear of the river. When I saw all the bowmen splashing around in the shallows, together with the giant otters and all our laundry, I decided to plunge in too. It was like swimming in lukewarm tea.

In the water the otters were half-puppy, half-torpedo. These ones were only young, but one day they'd be as long as a man. When they swam, everything would fold flat – claws, ears and spatula-tail – and they'd slink off, like some fish-seeking missile. On the sandbank, however, they'd look like a series of arches, slightly comical and ungainly. Although, strictly speaking, they were super-sized weasels, the giant otters were originally referred to as 'water dogs', and it wasn't hard to see why. They had huge knobbly paws and thick whiskers, and a bark like a foxhound. Diane said they were always hungry and were always hunting. Their high metabolism made them one of the most voracious predators of all.

'They must eat you out of house and home,' I said.

'Oh, yes, each one gets through a bucket of catfish a day.'

That explained all the bowmen, with their fish-killing arrows.

'So, not much of a pet then?' I suggested.

Diane smiled. 'No, not a pet at all.'

When the bowmen brought them their piranhas and catfish, the otters snatched the fish in the paws and frantically gobbled them down. Nothing was left, not even fins and teeth. Then the pups would yelp and squeal with rage, lurch down the bank and spiral off into the murk. Occasionally they caught their own fish, corkscrewing through the water, as though wringing it of life. But it didn't take much to bring the otters back to us. I only had to squeak and they'd be streaming towards me, exploding to the surface. Curiosity like this has always been their downfall. The otters are easy to hunt, and their velvety pelts once made popular collars. Diane said that, even now, they were hunted in Brazil. These days Guyana is one of the few places in South America where these remarkable beasts still thrive.

During my last swim a baby giant swam up and pressed his face into mine. Along the Rupununi, I don't suppose farewells get better than this: a flash of murderous teeth, followed by a spine-chilling kiss.

From Karanambu my plan was to travel west, parallel with the attenuating spine of the Kanukus, and then duck around its coccyx.

First, however, I'd have to get a boat to Yurupakari. There the river would veer south through the mountains, while I would carry on along the edge of the range, through a mysterious golden land first described by Sir Walter Raleigh.

The boat to Yurupakari was owned by a South African.

'It's abart twinnee-four kilometus,' he said.

In all but accent, Ashley Holland made a convincing Guyanese. It was as though he'd just deftly swapped the continents around. Although he was only young, already he had a Makushi family and a bilingual dog and could honk like a jabiru stork or clang like a piping guan. But listening to him talk, as we skimmed along, had a disastrous effect on my internal atlas. I kept thinking we were out on the veldt, and that any minute elephants would come bowling out of the trees. But Ashley had other beasts in mind. Here in the Rupununi he'd discovered a passion for the black caiman. Over the last few years he'd been part of a scientific project that had captured and micro-chipped almost 400 of these armour-plated killers. In scientific terms, this was a herpetological heaven.

'You make them sound quite nice,' I protested.

But Ashley wouldn't hear a word against his gnarly friends.

'You got more chawns of bin kilt by a bus.'

Yurupakari too, I discovered, was grateful to the alligators. It was built on the top of a grassy hill, a little way back from the river. As Waterton once said of a place like this: 'The finest park that England boasts falls far short of this delightful scene.' Yurupakari's history, however, hadn't always been so delightful. Between the wars it had become a trading post, dealing in balata. Someone had discovered that this tough, rubbery gum – derived from the letterwood tree – was the perfect coating for submarine cables. Suddenly the world wanted balata, and so Guiana was set to work. This little hill began to boom. Almost all the characters that Waugh had met, scattered through the bush, had ended up here. But no sooner was Yurupakari a thriving centre of the gum trade than it became a soulless slum.

Even now there was a hint of the old disappointment that had stalked this hill. On the far slopes there were still rich little pockets of rubbish, some of it strangely arresting; pieces of wild animals, helmet-sized tortoiseshells and dozens of Chinese shoes. Once I saw a man with a face like a strawberry and eyes of melting glass. I like to think he'd been on the beer, but it was probably engine fuel. Brazilian *álcool* could be bought throughout the Rupununi for just a few dollars a quart. It was a miserable leveller of Amerindian life. If ever there was a case of a broken wife, there was always a drinker with broken hands. The lead-free husband is a strange lover. Once he had been the standard model in Yurupakari. But not any more.

Everything changed, people said, when the scientists arrived.

Working out exactly who the scientists were was hard, because no one would talk about them. All I could establish was that they'd arrived from New York, studied alligators, criticised the government and then been expelled. Even in modern-day Guyana that was enough to render them officially forgotten. All that had survived was the science of herpetology and an enormous stockade. It was like Fort Apache, straddling the hill. Inside, there was a grand, red library, finished in hardwood, and all day it cheeped with children and computers. It also contained over 20,000 new books and was now radiating literacy across the plains. Perhaps it was power like this that had somehow spooked a distant government.

With the New Yorkers gone, Caiman House – as it was called – was now renting out its rooms. I slept in a turret above the gate. It was all decorated with polished panelling, four-poster beds, Amerindian tapestries and handsome reptile skulls. I don't know what you call this style. Makushi chic? Whatever it was, this had to be a first: an alligator-lover's boutique hotel.

That night Ashley took me down to the river to try and catch a caiman.

'I'll be in the first boat, trying to get a noose arand his nick …'

Meanwhile I sat in the second boat, with the B-team of alligator catchers. At first we couldn't see anything in the torchlight except a blizzard of moths and giant orange wasps. But then, suddenly, the first boat seemed to bob around in boiling water before plunging across the river in a magnificent squall of spume. It didn't last; soon the caiman had expended its explosive burst of energy and was hauled up onto a sandbank. There it just lay doggo: ten ugly feet of cedar-bark armour and bulldozer claws. Perhaps this was respect for those it thought were about to eat it? Whatever it was, this was not an easy creature to admire. All about it there was an air of menace, and the delicate scent of carcass. I was relieved when – the micro-chipping done – it was untied and pointed at the water. For a moment it looked stunned at the prospect of its own survival.

Then it tensed itself, like the sinews of a catapult, before blasting off into the darkness.

The Makushis watched as the bubbles dispersed.

'The perfick killa,' said Ashley, 'We doan even know if it fills any pain.'

From the village of the alligator lovers, it's only three miles to the lost city of El Dorado.

As to how such a grand and conspicuous city ended up here, adrift in the straw, it is a long story. Most people like to think it begins with an explosion deep in Venezuela and ends in London with a severed head.

The explosion is the responsibility of Captain Juan Martínez de Albujar, who is the munitions master on an expedition up the Orinoco in 1570. Martínez is a hapless lout, and during one of his moments of haplessness his cargo ignites and a precious barge is blown to bits. As a punishment, Martínez is bound hand and foot and set adrift in a canoe. He floats around for days and is on the brink of death when he's discovered by some Amerindians. Curious at the sight of what appears to be a man – although repulsively white – they salvage Martínez. He then disappears for the next sixteen years, only to re-emerge in Trinidad in 1586. Although he's probably spent most of this time shacked up with an Amerindian, he has a gourd of golden beads and a curious tale to tell.

He says that the Indians who rescued him were Manoans, from the city of The Gilded Man. Everyone knows about El Dorado. He's the great king who lives on a lake and has his subjects cover him with powdered gold. For years people have been looking for his city. Now here at last is a man who's been there! Martínez says his new friends took him, blindfolded, on a fourteen-day walk to their golden city. The place was so vast that it took a day to walk across it, and everything he touched was made of gold. For seven months, he says, he stayed there, before helping himself to a baggage train laden with golden pebbles. This would have made him the richest man in the world, if only he hadn't been robbed. Now all he has is this little calabash and a few remaining nuggets.

Despite the silliness of this tale, it has a powerful effect. Years later Voltaire will mock it, and the general foolishness of mankind. (In *Candide* his reconstituted Martínez leaves Manoa at the head of a train of bright red sheep.) But, for now, the tale of the wandering captain is believed. This is mainly due to the reports coming back from another adventurer, Antonio de Berrio. He's a slightly less bombastic figure than Martínez, and has been scrabbling around in the rainforests (of what's now Venezuela) for much of the 1580s. At some stage he's been told of a distant tribe that had 'come from the west' and had 'lived in splendour at a city on a lake surrounded by high mountains'. Doesn't this confirm what Martínez says? Although it's not much to go on, the development earns de Berrio the deliciously curly title of Gobernador de la Provincia del Dorado.

But de Berrio's career then receives a blow from an unexpected quarter. At the age of sixty-five he plans one final, determined expedition in search of Manoa. Unfortunately, however, in 1595 he's captured off Trinidad, by a dangerous romantic. It's Sir Walter Raleigh, who's also on the hunt for El Dorado. He's read all there is to read on the subject, including Martínez's account, and now assumes de Berrio's role. He and his men then travel 400 miles inland, in open boats, struggling with heat, rain and a bowel-stopping diet of endless dressed meat. Raleigh even loses one of his best negroes ('a very proper young fellow') to a *legarto,* or caiman. Manoa, however, cruelly eludes him.

In fact, his venture is a total failure in all but the literary sense. He doesn't conquer a single inch of anything and returns without a speck of gold. But Sir Walter is nothing if not a master of words. In a book that compacts gossip, aspiration, theories, a few first-hand accounts and more than a little deceit he recasts the entire fiasco as a triumphant reconnaissance. Investors are encouraged to believe in diamond mountains, a population of servants and roads that are dressed in gold. Even the title tends to suggest that a great scheme is already in place, and that all it needs is finance: *The Discoverie of the Large, Rich, and Bewtiful Empyre of Guiana, with a Relation to the Great and Golden Citie of Manoa (which the Spanyards call El Dorado).* Unsurprisingly, there are few takers, although the book itself is a runaway success. It's enjoyed as a rollicking yarn and is reprinted several times, in English, Dutch and German.

Raleigh is disappointed by the ridicule of his peers. They are, he says, 'blockishe and slothful dullards'. To prove them wrong, he sends out another expedition in 1596, led by an Oxford mathematician called Lawrence Keymis. At this point Raleigh still thinks of 'Guiana' as an inland territory, with 'but one entrance to the sea'. His new expedition, instead of battling up the Orinoco, will approach it from the seaward side. In this, Keymis is partly successful. He sails up the coast of the Guianas, identifying fifty-two rivers, of which forty have never been seen before. He deduces that several of these lead to the lost city, but that the best bet is the Essequibo. The Amerindians tell him the journey takes twenty days by canoe, followed by another day on foot. Then, reports Captain Keymis, 'afterwards they return to their canoes, and bear them like-wise to the side of a lake, which the [Amerindians] call Roponowini, the Charibes Parime, which is of such bigness that they know no difference between it and the main sea.'

It's here, on Lake Parima, says Keymis, that Manoa can be found.

'Is that really true?' I asked Mr Li.

We were standing in the local school, where Mr Li was the headmaster.

'See for yourself,' he said, 'I'm heading that way tomorrow.'

'Any chance of a lift?'

'Sure, I'm off north, to the end of the savannahs.'

'Great,' I said, 'me too.'

'OK. And we'll stop at the place Keymis describes.'

Mr Li was the perfect companion for such an unpromising venture. He was whiskery, slightly stiff, spectacled and sceptical. Among his ancestors he could count Amerindians, Chinese, Africans and Portuguese traders. Between them, they'd left him with the powerful impression that man was an instinctive wanderer, that he never quite knew what he was looking for and was invariably lost. I wondered if that's why he liked the idea of Manoa, a capital city for the chronically displaced. For him, Captain Keymis, the sailor–mathematician, was the hero of the El Dorado story. While everyone else was chasing fantasies, he was a scholar off in pursuit of geo-graphical truth.

'And he was seldom wrong,' said Mr Li, 'although it cost him his life.'

We were now driving along a hot, crumbling ridge that led south from Yurupakari. The grass here was shiny and yellowish, like a haze of burnished metal. In places – where the Makushis were clear-ing snakes – it was on fire, and the long brittle stalks would explode in the heat. Everywhere the anthills watched. They no longer looked like monks but a great muddy army, crouched in the straw, eight feet tall and as hard as bullets. Beyond them, in among the undulations, were 'bush islands', tufts of straggly forest, erupting wherever there was moisture. Out in the grass, however, few trees survived: just the sun-crazed Caiambés, whose foliage was smiley green and sandstone rough, and the Parikaran trees, which looked like cracks that had come to life.

Suddenly, the ridge ended and the ground fell away.

'This is it,' said Mr Li, 'this is Lake Parima.'

Below us, stretching away as far as the eye could see, was a plain of billowing gold. It wasn't quite as Keymis had envisaged it, with 'infinite numbers of canoes'. There weren't even any anthills to mar the horizontality – or bush islands, or farms, or slits of cleansing fire. It was just a beautiful shimmering flatness. I wondered what Raleigh's men would have made of it. He often talked of a form of madness called calenture. It afflicted sailors, who after months at sea would begin to see it as land and jump from their ships. Here they'd have suffered the opposite and found themselves swimming through the stalks or drinking the dust.

'I don't understand,' I said, 'why is this a *lake*?'

'Because it is,' smiled Mr Li, 'at certain times of year.'

He explained that we were standing at a watershed. From here the water ran off to join the tributaries of Essequibo in one direction and the Amazon in the other. During the wet season these two mighty river basins were linked by floodwaters, and the eastern Guianas became – if not exactly an island – completely encircled by water. The first person to recognise this phenomenon was the great explorer and hydrographer Alexander von Humboldt, in 1800. He also recognised that, in the absence of any other lakes of maritime size, the flood plain had to be 'Lake Parima'.

'And that,' said Mr Li, 'is right where we're standing now.'

So Captain Keymis was right after all, although he'd never known it. In 1616 he and Raleigh set off on one last search for the city of Manoa. Unwisely, they took the landward route, via the Orinoco, and were soon tangling with the Spanish. As the expedition disintegrated into a bloody brawl, it was obvious that a twenty-year quest had come to an end. Keymis took himself off to his state-room and blew a hole in his chest. When this failed to deliver the certainty he sought, he placed the tip of a dagger under his breastbone and drove it upwards into his heart. Raleigh, too, would soon be dead. On 29 October 1618 he was brought before an audience in the Old Palace Yard, Westminster. Among the onlookers were a group of 'Guianians', brought back as samples. To them, the ways of their much-bejewelled captors were never more mysterious than now. After a flurry of feathers and taffeta, Raleigh made a great speech and then knelt before an axeman and was trimmed of his head. With that swipe came to an end English hopes of a gilded city.

I now stared out across the lake of golden grass.

'This,' I suggested, 'would have been a disappointment for Raleigh.'

'Perhaps,' said Mr Li.

'Only perhaps?'

'Well, yes,' he said genially, 'because there *might* be something out there.'

Few other visitors have been so generous. Waugh is typically sniffy about the non-existent lake. Even Waterton becomes uncharacteristically snappish when he gets here and finds nothing but the dust. 'So much for Lake Parima,' he writes, 'and so much for El Dorado.'

Half an hour south, a peculiarly British El Dorado had briefly resurfaced.

We were now back on the ridge, swooping around in the gravel. Nothing grew up here, except a light, yellowish stubble and a bush that sprouted claws. Mr Li said that, in the rains, these hills became the headwaters of the Pirara. At that moment it was hard to imagine water at all, on this surface something like Saturn. Then, suddenly, the gravel seemed to swell up and part, and ahead of us appeared a hill like an enormous purple egg. Mr Li swerved off the track and drove up its side.

'Look!' he said, 'we're almost in Brazil!'

All around us, the savannahs began flattening out, like the features on a map. In any given direction it would have taken days to reach the horizon. But much closer in – only a mile to the west – was a fringe of knotty scrub. That, said Mr Li, was the international border.

Back in 1838 the proximity of mighty Brazil had caused a ripple of indignation. At its source was a little man with a 'damnable temper' and a taste for spiffy uniforms and hats. Brazilians, in his view, were savages and drunkards, their language was profane, and they were slavers by nature, and popish at best. The solution, he said, was the creation of an imperial counter-balance, a British Utopia in the image of Sir Walter. There'd be a new boundary, marked out with stakes. On this side, promised the little imperialist, the Indians would become Her Majesty's subjects, and enjoy her protection. As a first step, on 24 May – the Queen's birthday – he clambered up onto the purple egg and planted the Union Jack.

The odd thing about the man with the flag is that he wasn't British at all, but a cartographer from Prussia. Robert Schomburgk had somehow ended up in the wrong empire and then made it all his own. No one would get to know British Guiana better. Over a period of eight years he'd hack his way into almost every corner of the colony; he'd conduct at least six astonishing surveys, all in the name of the Crown; he'd discover dozens of new creatures, the source of the Essequibo, the highest mountain in north-east Latin America – called Roraima – and the world's largest lily (which, naturally, he named *Victoria regis*); best of all, he'd delineate the boundaries with both Suriname and Venezuela, much to Britain's advantage. With so much credit to his name, it's hardly surprising that London went along with his Brazilian venture and lent him a tiny army.

The expedition to the purple egg got off to an inauspicious start. Instead of police officers, as he'd requested, Schomburgk was given thirty-five soldiers of the West India Regiment. They were a resentful, work-shy lot, who wore slippers instead of boots and took a month to build their boats. When they finally set off, there was a squabble over titles, and Schomburgk insisted on marching – in an outlandish uniform – right at the head of the column. As they moved upcountry, he left bossy little messages in champagne bottles for those coming up behind. Naturally, the other officers soon had him down as a cad.

Eventually, in February 1842, this trifling, dandified troop reached the top of the purple egg. The soldiers were horrified. This, wrote one, is 'the last place God Almighty made'. The Colonial Office, however, was more upbeat. It immediately announced 'The Liberation of Pirara' (adding, at a stroke, a curious footnote to its imperial

For over four hundred years, the Guianas have thrilled and appalled Europeans in equal measure. One of the first explorers was Sir Walter Raleigh (visiting what is now part of Venezuela). His account of his travels, called *The Discoverie of the Large, Rich and Bewtiful Empire of Guiana* (1596), would lead men to believe in a golden city, and a land of limitless wealth and comely Amazons. The truth, however, has proved rather more complex.

These days, across the Guianas, Amerindians make up only about three per cent of the population. Initially, they were treated like souvenirs and brought back to Europe as gifts (there are records of Guianese serving at the court of the Medicis). Later, however, they became a minor aristocracy, respected for their skill in tracking down runaway slaves.

The Macushi farmer and hunter, Daniel Allicock. He will stay in the jungle for up to a week with only some matches, salt, and his bow and arrows. He fears nothing but ghosts and wild pigs.

In the water, giant otters are half-puppy, half-torpedo. This one is only young, but one day it'll be as long as a man. When it swims everything folds flat – claws, ears and spatula-tail – like some fish-seeking missile. Although strictly speaking, they're super-sized weasels, giant otters were originally referred to as 'water dogs' and, because of their high metabolism, they're always hungry. This makes them one of the most voracious predators of all.

Charles Waterton (1782–1865), left, was the first to bring back news of the extraordinary wildlife of the Guianas. He also helped unlock the secret of the dart poison, curare, and opened the world's first wildlife park. Today, the task of protecting the wildlife falls to – among others – Diane McTurk (right). Her family have been in Guyana (formerly British Guiana) for over 200 years.

Throughout the Guianas, there are no natural harbours, no railways, and only a handful of roads inland. Forest covers four-fifths of its surface, and without a plane it can take up to four weeks to reach the interior. Here, an ex-British army truck overturns in the Rupununi, and the crew will simply have to right it themselves.

For the Wapisianas of southern Guyana, life is a constant struggle with spirits and dengue fever. *Vaqueiros* or cowboys (left) rest at Dadanawa, after an exhausting round-up. The ranch loses up to 400 cattle a year to jaguars (right), who are considered so common that they are shot as pests.

In 1977, the Rev Jim Jones (1931–78) led his followers to a promised land in remotest Guyana. As his sanity unravelled, so The People's Temple imploded. The murder/suicide at 'Jonestown' left over 900 dead (right), and is still – war and natural disaster aside – the biggest single loss of life in modern times. Today, it's all things to all pundits: a conspiracy, a collective failure of mental health, or the end of a psychedelic era.

Jonestown now. Since 1978 no one has lived here, and they probably never will. All that remains are rusty machines and old shoes. After the killings, Mr Duke (above) was one of the first on the scene. 'This is where the bodies were,' he said. 'All piled up. Three deep.'

No people have died for the Guianas quite so willingly as the Dutch. They were on this coast from 1595 to 1977, arriving long before the English, and leaving long after. The river banks of the Essequibo were, for a while, the richest farmlands in the world, and were soon a hot bed of debauchery and decadence (left). But there was nothing feeble about their forts. Vlaggen Eyland, or Flag Island, is still a formidable sight, although Fort Nassau (below) succumbed to the bloody revolt of 1763.

Slavery has left an indelible impression on the Guianas. Not only did it transform the population but also the landscape. Fly along the Guyanese coast, and you'll see nothing but sugar fields (and, for each square mile of cane, over ten million tons of earth was moved). Meanwhile, in Suriname, the runaway slaves fled inland, where their descendants (above) still live ancient, African lives.

With the end of slavery came the beginning of indenture. Between 1838 and 1917, almost a quarter of a million Indians arrived in Guyana (above), and in Suriname there were also the Javanese. It was like The Exodus in reverse, a flight into bondage. Under the terms of their contracts, the 'Coolies' (as they became known) were no better off than the Africans before. Not only were they confined to their plantations, they had also inadvertently agreed to being fined, starved, locked up for absence, abandoned, underpaid, flogged and doused in salt pickle. Many had thought they were coming to an earthly paradise and, in the century to 1950, there were at least sixteen major revolts.

Even today, the Guianas are not easy to understand. Guyana alone is riven by over 1,500 rivers, and much of it is barely accessible. Meanwhile, although Suriname is the size of Florida, its population would barely fill a London borough. Almost one in six of the inhabitants is descended from maroons, or runaway slaves (above), and, at night, the country all but disappears, producing too little light for the satellite cameras.

history). Whether the Brazilians were impressed by all this flouncing and flummery is hard to say. They positioned a few troopers along the fringe of knotty scrub, and then the two sides settled down to a long, hot game of savannah chess.

The castle the British built is still there: a giant doughnut of piled-up gravel.

'Welcome to Fort New Guinea,' said Mr Li.

'*Guinea*? Isn't that in Africa?'

'Yes,' said Mr Li, 'I don't think they knew they were still in Guiana.'

We got out, clambered into the ditch, and then up onto the rampart. It wasn't much; 166 years of wind and rains had gnawed it down to a lumpy outline. But across the compound the gravel was glittering with glass. It looked like the debris left by some wild, interplanetary party. There was brown glass for ale, and green for champagne. Liberation, I mused, can be full of surprises. For Her Majesty's newly liberated subjects – the Amerindians – perhaps the greatest surprise was smallpox. By the end of the campaign there were at least three tribes well on their way to extinction.

Fort New Guinea is a fitting tribute to an old myth. Like all El Dorados, this hollow ring of gravel had yielded neither gold nor perfection. Six months after they arrived, Schomburgk's troops were ordered home. As they left, they scattered their bottles and set fire to the stockade. They'd achieved precisely nothing. Within days the only sign of their endeavours was the giant purple egg, now topped with a crown of ash.

At the end of the northern savannahs, Mr Li dropped me in Lethem.

'This,' he said, 'is the only town in the Rupununi.'

It was also the only town in southern Guyana. That meant it served an area the size of Britain, which – to Mr Li – gave it the feel of a bustling city. He described drugs and electricity, reckless development and plenty of drink. Just as I was getting used to the idea of an urban sprawl and the stifling hug of concrete, I realised that we were already in Lethem and had nearly driven through it. Another triumph, I noted, for the Makushi principle of human dispersal. In Lethem a mere 12,000 people had managed to spread themselves out over a plot the size of London.

'Good luck,' said Mr Li, 'and be careful.'

Over the few days I spent in Lethem, I never really discovered what it was that had worried Mr Li. Perhaps it was just the thought of compacted people? Anyway, I never saw any junkies or pimps; most of the time I never saw anyone at all. Maybe it was different during the rodeo. Every Easter, I was told, the population doubled, and the *vaqueros* – or cowboys – came to town. For four days they performed heroic feats of drinking before tumbling around on their horses. That, I decided, was probably the time for more urban activities like mugging and whoring and pelting your neighbour with Precambrian rock.

So I had Lethem mostly to myself. After a while, I began to enjoy this. It was that same feeling that, out here, the savannah was in charge. All the roads were made of dirt, and so were the bits in between. The poor and the Amerindians even had their own mud-brick suburb, called Culvert City. Meanwhile, everyone else was scattered through the sedge. A few still had old, wooden bungalows, now bearing the ravages of Nature's buckshot. But most people here were new. Their houses had a more temporary, flat-packed feel, as though at any moment they could just fold them up and run screaming for the coast. No one had a garden. If there'd ever been a hint of horticulture, it had long since been churned up, in an orgy of pigs and trucks.

Eventually I located the centre, or at least a place where buildings clustered. It was here that I found somewhere to stay: a set of solid, concrete lodgings known as the government guesthouse. Just beyond it was the River Takutu, a gloop of orange that kept Brazil at bay. Some people, mostly Amerindians, sat here all day, catching fish for their boily-boily. The water, they said, was only shallow, and never too deep for a stolen horse.

The border had a powerful effect on downtown Lethem. It meant that, like all good frontier towns, this little cluster could be both wildly exuberant and determinedly prim. Most people seemed to be either missionaries or cowboys. Everywhere there were notices saying 'No Indecent Language', and yet people were free with the rum and drove like fighter pilots (often both at once). By day, they enjoyed an internet café, a cow roast and a Brazilian pornographer, but at night it was all shut down, and off went the power. Meanwhile, the supermarket was called Savannah Stores, and was stocked with everything you'd need for a life in the grass: saltfish, cast nets, catapults and grog.

On my last night I had dinner at the government guesthouse with a splendidly desiccated character. Gordon Forte was an old friend of Diane McTurk and had wandered the Rupununi on and off for sixty years. The experience, it seems, had left him shrunken and sinewy, and desperate to talk. He hardly touched his food, but dipped in and out of his curious life. It was a lovely, fragmented story, full of things half-done and things half-said. There was philosophy, Catholicism, some Chinese grandparents, books (followed by insolvency), travels in half a Land Rover, thoughts on Schomburgk, a semi-detached wife and the remnants of a marriage. Being half-brilliant, Gordon had half-lived dozens of lives, sometimes simultaneously. Over the years, he said, he'd done everything from selling mosquito-proof shirts and recycling torches to transcribing the proceedings of the Guyanese parliament. His latest venture was the pursuit of suffering.

'I've moved into the St Ignatius Mission.'

I remembered the mission: a scattering of painted huts some way out in the Lethem scrub. In the middle was a large, plain building, on which the savannah winds had spent almost a century sharpening their claws. It was obviously a good place to plan a little penance, as Gordon had discovered.

'My wife said I was financially irresponsible, so now I've taken a vow of poverty.'

'Just poverty?'

'Yes, I couldn't stand the idea of obedience …'

'And chastity?'

'I'll leave that to nature.'

With that, he went outside and came back with an enormous cardboard box.

'I'm giving everything away, starting with these books.'

'And you want me to take them?'

'Well, you're going to the southern savannahs, aren't you?'

'Yes,' I said. 'Off to Dadanawa tomorrow.'

'Good. Then you can give them these. Some of my favourites.'

'What are they?' I said, expecting Sir Thomas More or perhaps a little Locke.

Gordon brightened a little and pushed the box towards me. 'Dick Francis,' he said, 'the complete works. I won't need them any more.'

So that's how I ended up, the next day, waiting in the early morning mist with a rucksack, a bow and arrow, and a vast consignment of horsey thrillers.

My lift turned up, a few hours later than expected, like a wagon train out of the dust.

Nothing about that day was quite as I'd envisaged.

A sedate jaunt around the tail of the Kanukus seemed suddenly to transform itself into a full-scale war party led by the Wild Bunch. For a moment I just stood and stared. The cavalcade now grinding to a halt in front of me consisted of two partially mangled pick-ups, half-a-dozen boys with ponytails, a beautiful Amerindian girl in designer combat gear and the warrior queen herself, who was short and wiry, and had reddish hair and bright blue nails. Almost everyone had some sort of knife or sword, and only the commando girl wore shoes: a pair of startling, gold high heels.

'Hi, I'm Sandy de Freitas,' said the lady with blue nails.

'Great,' I said. 'Quite a reception.'

She beamed, and gave a little shrug.

'Sorry my husband's not here. He's up in town with bushy arse.'

This, it turned out, was not a disease of piracy but a case of leishmaniasis.

'A little sandfly,' said one of the boys, 'starts to eat your face.'

Other aspects of that morning took longer to work out. I discovered that this was the monthly shopping trip for the Dadanawa ranch. The ponytail boys were just willing outriders, with nothing much else to do. They were all half Makushi and half something else (either Welsh or Irish), and always spoke softly with a rich, grass-land twang. The swords were for castrating bulls, or trimming off slices of tasso, and the beautiful commando was the ranch cook. As for Sandy, she was born in the sugar fields and had a touch of Portuguese and a healthy blast of Scottish.

It took a while to get off the ground. First, the trucks had to be stripped down and all their parts laid out on a tarpaulin in the grass. Then it was all put back, along with a sack of salt, some bicycles, a month's supplies, a few bits of furniture, a box of bullets, six pallets of beer and a case of rum.

'Good to go?' piped Sandy.

'Good to go!' replied the voices from deep inside the baggage.

Then we were off, on a beautiful lurch around the Kanukus. After an hour we rounded the southern tip of the range, which felt like driving through the gateway of a primordial world. Even the road seemed to fail. We were now wobbling along through marsh and sedge, through slicks of brilliant ooze, grass like green fire, liverish pools and succulent bogs rimmed with pink. I remember lilies so purple they looked like the work of an imperial hatter. Then we'd drop down into a long, thready crack of gallery forest, plunge through a stream and then scramble back out, up a bank of black quartz. I secretly hoped that this ride would never end, and it almost didn't. It would take another four hours to cover fifty miles.

At some point we passed Shulinab, the last Makushi village.

'We're now in the southern savannahs,' said Sandy.

'Wapisiana territory!' said the ponytails.

Ahead of us the horizon was pimpled with ancient cones. Everything here looked slightly ancient. Once we spotted a savannah fox skulking through the grass. It was like some prehistoric husky, still millions of years from the human hearth. Even the jabiru storks seemed to belong to a long-lost age. They'd all stand around in their tatty coachman's livery, stabbing at the frogs and then tossing them back like shots of gin. Mankind, it seemed, had made little impression in this walled-off world. Just occasionally we'd come across a boulder that had been prised apart by roots and inhabited by ghosts. Wapisiana ghosts.

'They're terrified of dwarfs ...' said the ponytails.

'... and spirits underground ...'

'... they'll die if they see one ...'

'... so they put pepper in their eyes ...'

According to anthropologists, the Wapisiana have always lived like this, in a state of home-made terror. Shy and unassuming, the southern savannahs have long been their last resort. No one knows where they came from, or why. But, for at least 5,000 years they've lived here, deep in this inner sanctum, a fugitive tribe. According to a Dutch report of 1769, they spent their days in the grass, 'and at night they retired to the inaccessible rocks and caves'. Already they were under pressure, with Jesuits in one direction and slavers in the other. By the time the incursions were over, the Wapisianas were a much-diminished tribe. But at least, in transubstantiation and purgatory, they had new magic to add to their own.

I asked whether anyone knew how many Wapisianas there were today.

'Five thousand,' said one of the ponytails.

'Twenty,' said the other.

Not that it mattered. We didn't see anyone all day.

Then, suddenly, as the sun began to cool, the Rupununi reappeared. It was just as wide as before, but younger, and frothy. I could see that it was desperate to gulp up our trucks, and it nearly did. The only way to get across was on a raft made of petrol drums and sticks. It looked like the work of crows, and for a moment it bobbed around euphorically before spinning into the current. I felt sure we were about to be snatched up and sucked through the Kanukus, and then backwards through Guyana. But then I noticed some Wapisianas, paddling out from the opposite shore. They were glossy and powerful, like little bronze statues that had sprung into life.

The next thing I knew, we were back on sand, at the bottom of a rise.

'Here we are,' announced Sandy, 'the Hill of the Macaw.'

It was Dadanawa, a tiny empire built by a Scot who thought he'd died.

Apart from Jesuits and slavers, it took Europeans a while to settle the savannahs.

One of the first was a chancer called Harry Melville. Born in 1864, he was the son of a Presbyterian archdeacon with a flock in Jamaica. But Harry never had his father's appetite for God, and preferred the sight of gold. At the age of twenty-seven he decided to extract himself from Scottish Jamaica and set off in search of ore. His gold-washing brought him to Guiana. There, in 1891, he plunged into the forest and was soon cooking up a case of malaria. At the moment of death – the story goes – he was found by some Amerindians. Harry had no wish to die in the dark and asked for help to reach the light. With either payment or pathos, they agreed and brought the dying Scot out onto the savannah. There he liked what he saw and lay down to die.

Death on the savannah suited Harry well. The next thing he knew, the grass was his home. He acquired two Wapisiana wives and settled down to become a trader in the finest fish hooks and trinkets. It was good business, and after twenty years he was the most powerful man on the savannah. Not only was he now the father of ten children; he was also a cattle baron, a district commissioner and the Laird of Dadanawa. It was the largest ranch in the world, and covered an area about the size of the Lowlands of Scotland.

'HBC', as he now called himself, had arrived. All Dadanawa needed was some sort of link to the rest of the Empire. On cue came the First World War, and a surge in demand. British soldiers would march to Berlin on Rupununi beef. It was an appealing image, and the funds flowed in. By 1917 Melville had begun work on one of the most ambitious private trails in the world. Soon Dadanawa would be pumping cattle up into the heart of Guyana, and then off to the coast.

Or so he said.

Life at Dadanawa still looked as though it had ground to a halt in 1923. At the top of the rise was a large and shady Brazil nut tree. All around it were the ranch buildings and the peeling gran-deur of Melville's design. There were several workshops and saddle stores, barracks for the *vaqueros*, slung with rows of hammocks, an abattoir, a tannery, two kitchens with huge ranges and drying-lines dripping with buttery tripe, half-a-dozen water towers and an ancient wind-pump that sometimes stuttered and stopped, a small brick cottage for the foreman and the enormous wooden halls of the management – all finished off in the Melville livery, balance-sheet white and Highland green.

'You're in the big guesthouse, sir,' said the cook.

'Hope you don't mind the bats,' said the ponytails.

I didn't mind anything by then. Dadanawa was enchanting. It wasn't just the livery and the lovable staff, and the distant blue hills, melting together. It was the sense of a peculiar past, all around. My room was high up on stilts and looked as though it had been quietly – and elegantly – flaking away since the First World War. Then there was the manager's house, which was like the officers' mess of an Edwardian army. Around the walls there were weapons and saddles, and at sundown we'd all sit on the balcony drinking punch. As the ranch no longer had electricity, we were soon in the dark and begin-ning to itch. 'Time for dinner!' Sandy would trill, and then – with all the ponytails – we'd fumble our way downstairs. There we'd sit in Melvillian splendour, dining on tablecloths adorned with his crest. As we sat working our way through three great courses of soup and mutton and chocolate mousse, the bats would come wheeling in through the windows and squeal around our heads.

But even better than this was the ranch store. This was the place to buy a stirrup, or a beer, or a single cigarette. At night people gathered here to listen to the distant crackle of the BBC, or for the cook – armed with a needle – to dig the jiggers from their feet. But, as well as a bar and a clinic, the store was also the repository of almost a century of grassland junk. There were jaguar skins, giant fish skulls, several antique guns repaired with tape, a truncheon, a pickled snake and endless Land Rover parts, going all the way back to 1950. Even things too big for the store were never thrown away. Just behind it was a collection of old army trucks, now green and hairy and reverting to soil.

I often met the old tanner at the store.

'I think I'm eighty, but I never go to school.'

I liked Uncle Cyril. He had a big, shapeless face, full of scrunched-up smiles, and he was wide and squat like an old leather chair. People said that he was all that remained of the Atorads, a tribe that had perished in the Great Spanish Flu. Perhaps it was this brush with oblivion that had made him a tanner. In his tank of preservative he had three jaguar skins.

'But aren't they endangered?' I protested.

'Jaguars? Not here! They attack us every night!'

'It's true,' said the ponytails, 'they kills four hundred cattle a year.'

I asked Uncle Cyril who did all the shooting.

'Not me. I was hit by a bull. So now I leave it to the boys.'

The *vaqueros* were certainly a lethal-looking crew.

'Nearly all Wapisianas,' said Sandy, 'I delivered most of them myself.'

Every morning they assembled at the store. There were fourteen *vaqueros* in all. With their long knives, El Greco faces and leather gaiters – clinking with buckles and spurs – they were like some ancient barefoot cavalry. Scowling and spitting, and shooting blasts of snot, they always looked impressively dangerous. I once watched them kill a calf. Their knives descended on it like a shoal of fish and swam around through the trembling flesh until suddenly everything was gone. It was said that Wapisiana men liked their women like this, with razor-sharp teeth filed into points, just like piranhas.

Sandy told me they were beautiful people, but hard to manage.

'If you ever shout at them, they just pick up their things and vanish.'

It was at least a day before they acknowledged I was there. The first to speak was the *capataz*, or foreman. 'I am Oswald,' he said, 'and these are my sons: Osbert, Oswin and Osmond ...'

Soon others were curious.

'What insults do you have in your country?'

I was taken aback. 'Oh, anything, really. Wanker?'

'We don't understand,' they said.

I explained, and they all collapsed, howling in the dust.

'We call people old foreskins!' they spluttered.

'... or horse-heads!'

Then a boy with long, crow-black hair pushed forward.

'Orvin wants to find you a giant anteater,' said Sandy.

I thanked him, and he galloped off into the grass. An hour later he found one, a beautiful sleepy specimen with a tail like a cloud. But I noticed that Orvin's arm was swollen, as though it were sprouting an egg.

'I got bitten by a snake.'

'Then you should rest,' said Sandy, 'and not do the round-up.'

But Orvin wouldn't be deterred. For the *vaqueros* the round-up was like a beautiful, violent game. They wore their best Brazilian football shirts, and, if they had saddles, these would be trimmed with jaguar and beads. Most, however, went bareback, and barefoot. The youngest, I discovered, was only twelve and sang as he rode. One of the older boys, who looked splendidly cruel, even had an MP3 player, so he could thunder along with his head full of screams.

Once I went to watch them, out in the corral. There was a bonfire for brands, and – high up in the rails – the boys clambered around, waiting for their moment to drop down and join the fight. Below them, in the arena, hundreds of animals swirled round, blind with dust and mad with panic. Whiplashes, forty feet long, sizzled over their heads, hissing and crackling like gunfire. Then the *vaqueros* dropped, knives drawn. What followed wasn't so much sport as medieval warfare. Horn and withers became tangled in rope, and – amid the bellows of terror – the knives began to dart around, nicking ears and emasculating bulls. At one point a steer seemed to explode from the melee and, like some huge and bloody meteorite, smashed through the rails and took off over the savannah. No one seemed to notice that they'd almost been killed. Even when the work was finished, the *vaqueros* weren't. Each found himself a furious steer, jumped on its back and then rode it for a few exhilarating seconds until the animal bucked him off.

'What can I do?' said Sandy. 'It's the only life they know.'

I didn't see the *vaqueros* again after that. By my last day they were far away, rounding up distant cattle. Across the ranch they had over a million acres to cover. While Dadanawa was not what it was in Melville's day, it was still twice the size of Suffolk.

Not that size was ever the issue. The problem for Dadanawa was an old one. Here it was, hundreds of miles from civilisation, in one of the most inaccessible spots on the continent. Cows still had a long way to go before they were beef.

Harry Melville had long recognised this, and so, in 1923, he took what he could and slipped away. It was years before his purchasers realised their mistake. Melville had even diddled them on the number of animals and the quality of grass. As for the cattle trail, it was a gruesome failure. At the first attempt to use it, over 70 per cent of the animals simply vanished in the forest. But still the company persisted. They bought more wire, and at the ranch they installed one drunk after another. Perhaps the worst was Mr Connel. 'Women were his hobby,' states the company reports, 'drink his downfall, and an aversion to work his ingrained habit.' (Eventually he conned an Indian princess into marriage, and they moved to the slums of Pimlico, where they drank themselves to death on a cocktail of red wine and methanol, known as 'Red Biddy'.) After that, Dadanawa only had a moment of prosperity. Then came the age of the plane, and in 1953 the trail was closed for good.

Meanwhile, Harry was long gone. Having abandoned his wives and children, he'd made it to London. There he took a third wife, a nurse called Ethel Barker, and they settled down in Twickenham. Suburbia was a strange choice for a man who'd spent so much of his life owning the horizon. But then, in July 1927, for the second time in his life Harry Melville died. He was rich, sixty-three and intractably malarial. This time he was carried to Richmond Cemetery and has never been heard of since.

I thought a lot about Harry, as we drove away down his ill-fated trail. I also thought about the ten children he'd left behind. The

Rupununi's twentieth-century history is rich in Melvilles. They crop up in all the books: Waugh, Attenborough and Durrell. Another, more distant Melville, Pauline, even became a novelist herself. After a life in British films she won the Whitbread Award for *The Ventriloquist's Tale*, a beautifully torrid tale of Rupununi life.

Meanwhile, back on the savannah, the Melvilles have been politicians, ranchers and legends. The oldest son, John, was known as 'Dynamite'. It's said he was immensely strong and could lift a pony over his head. He once challenged a senior New York zoologist to a duel, causing the entire expedition to scatter in panic. Then, in 1947, he brought the southern savannahs their first vehicle, delivered in a plane. But John had nothing of his father's ambition, and this was never the beginning of congestion.

Then, suddenly, towards the end of the century, the Melvilles go quiet.

'What's happened to them?' I asked. 'Where are they now?'

'There are still a few around ...' said the ponytails.

'... Don and Shirley ...'

I was puzzled. 'A few? There must be *hundreds* by now ...'

No one said anything. Then Sandy spoke.

'There was a terrible revolt,' she said, 'and all the others fled.'

The burned-out nucleus of the revolt was still there: the Lethem Hotel.

It was right on the edge of the dissipated town, next to the airstrip. Parts of the building had collapsed, and the windows were covered with mesh and bulging with rubbish. In its day this was the Rupununi's first work of concrete and its first hotel. But it was never much of a place. Harry's son, Teddy, had run it up quickly to service the planes. When Attenborough was here, in 1955, none of the windows had glass, and to V.S. Naipaul the whole place was 'rough'.

But, for all that, it was still, even now, the hub of airstrip life. Out at the front there were stalls, selling skewers of meat and Brazilian beer. There was also a large, dark shop under a mango tree. It was owned by Don and Shirley, the last of the Melvilles. Don was sad to see the old hotel crumbling away. In happier times, he told me, Uncle Teddy used to show movies here every Saturday night. They were always cowboy films.

'The Wapisianas loved them. Watched them over and over again.'

But then, in 1968, a new movie appeared. This time there were no cowboys and Indians, just voices of dissent. Uncle Teddy and his ranchers suddenly started talking about independence. They already regarded themselves as the lords and masters of their grassy domain. But, added to their flyweight feudalism, there was also anger. They saw their leases threatened; their candidates cheated at the general election, and an African government contemptuous of whites. What's more, they weren't the only ones who were angry. Promises made to the Amerindians had never been honoured. Just so they knew who was to blame, Teddy and his friends showed them a film. It had been made in the South Pacific, and depicted a black-ish people killing the natives and eating their flesh. 'That's what'll happen to you,' said the ranchers, and so – somewhat bewildered – their *vaqueros* lined up and joined the revolt.

It wasn't hard to find an armourer. Venezuela still claimed the Rupununi, and a lot more besides. They'd have moved in and grabbed the lot, if it wasn't for Brazil. Instead, they had to content themselves with this Ruritanian revolt. But was the map really about to be changed for ever? By who? Some hard-drinking cattlemen, a few thready cow hands and a family of hotheads known as the Melvilles? Somebody thought so. On Christmas Eve 1968 the rebels were secretly flown to Santa Teresa and recast as the gallant new army of *Guayana Esequiba*. A week later they were draped in guns and flown back to the savannahs.

I asked Don whether he remembered the day the fight broke out.

He shook his head. 'I'm not the person to ask.'

It was no good. Melvilles don't talk about what happened next.

'Speak to Esther. Her family was here, and were all expelled.'

Esther Park ran a mining company on the other side of town. She was a strange person to find, directing trucks. I'd expected some swarthy, industrial figure, but instead she was assured, intelligent, beautiful, part-Indian and oddly urbane. I later found out that, in exile, she'd been a model. 'But now I'm back,' she said. 'I love the Rupununi. During my time in Venezuela, I missed it every day.'

She told me her father had once been an administrator here.

'Then my brother got mixed up with the rebels ...'

I asked her if she minded bringing up the past.

'No. People must know. Come, I'll show you what happened.'

With that, we were out in her car, on a tour of the revolt.

'This is where my parents lived ...'

We were in the old colonial area. Esther pointed out the wreckage of a dance hall where a Chinaman had once sold tickets for a weekly dance. Then there was the Amerindian hostel, now quietly falling apart. I don't think Esther really saw the decay. For her everything was just as it was the day her childhood was snatched away: 2 January 1969. 'I was fourteen,' she said, 'when the revolt began ...'

We were now outside the old office of the District Commissioner. 'This,' said Esther sadly, 'is where the shooting started.'

It wasn't distinguished combat. The only casualty was Inspector Braithwaite, whose life and otherwise dignified career were brought to a sudden and undignified end. Most people agreed that it was a Melville boy that fired this shot. But whoever it was, there was no turning back. From here the rebels spread out across the savannahs in a collection of old farm vehicles and Mini Mokes camouflaged with branches. 'At first, I thought it was something to do with the feast of St John,' said Esther, 'and then I thought it was the Venezuelans, coming here to kill us.'

She drove on, stopping by the police post. Out on the porch two young 'ranks' were asleep in the sun. 'This was the worst place. Somebody threw a hand grenade through the window, and four young policemen were killed. Nobody knows who did it, even now. It was so senseless, so utterly senseless ...'

For the rebels it was also the end of the fight for Lethem. They gathered up the dead and put them in the abattoir, along with their prisoners, the government officials. They then blocked off the airstrip with trucks and declared independence.

The Rupununi was finally a republic, at least for the day.

The end for the republic came at Manari.

'I'll take you over there,' said Esther, 'it's just out of town.'

Manari was five miles away, deep in the thorn. It was an ominous place, with its long, empty airstrip, its ghoulish anthills and its mournful views of the Moco-Moco Hills. Esther said that a few descendants of Harry Melville still lived out here. One was his granddaughter, a retired doctor, known locally as Pixie. She lived in a new house by the runway, and just when I was wondering what kind of pixie she was, she suddenly appeared. With her pink bath-robe and cut-glass vowels, Pixie could not have been less puckish. But then, like Esther, she didn't really belong in this scene. She was the daughter of a notorious Polish rancher called Cesar Gorinsky, and, as she explained, she'd spent much of her life in England.

The occupants of the other house were more complicated.

Manari's old ranch-house was a sprawling fantasy of bricks. It had loggias, pagodas, terracotta heraldry and a mock-Tudor front. Once this had been the grandiose home of a Basque, called Orella, but now the wind had its nose in the roof and was peeling back the tin. Esther told me that Orella had married another of Harry Melville's daughters, and that their son Louis had only just died, deep in his eighties and fighting off doctors. Now his huge, gaunt mansion lay abandoned, with its furniture scattered all over the steps.

We walked round the outside, found a door and wandered in. It all seemed empty at first, but then we got to the kitchen and were surprised to find Louis's family still there, gathered in silence around his chair. With their long, Amerindian faces they looked like a por-trait of Victorian mourning. We tiptoed in and stood at the back.

'Louis had eleven sons,' whispered Esther. 'All a bit wild.'

Behind us, something stirred in the shadows.

'Don't I know you?' said Esther.

The man said nothing. He had lank, blue hair and lifeless eyes.

'We'd better go,' murmured Esther, 'this isn't good.'

'Who was that?' I asked, as we hurried away.

'Well, he calls himself Satan. He's a rustler, probably the most wanted man on the savannahs. I always feel nervous with people like that around. You never know if they've got guns. I think he's one of Louis's lot. He stole one of my horses once, called Skelly. I only got it back when I threatened to kill him.'

'Should we go to the police?'

'No point. By now he'll be back in the Moco-Moco forest.'

We drove away over the airstrip. Although I knew I shouldn't, I felt slightly exhilarated by the encounter with Satan. It was as though I'd stumbled on the Melville gene in its most mutated form: predatory, arboreal and well beyond the law. Forty years earlier the same gene, or an earlier variant, had shaped the great revolt. There'd been a Melville at its beginning, and there was another – right here – at its end. He was only eighteen, but the Melville who stood here in 1969, had been armed with a powerful machine gun. He stepped onto the airstrip, took a wild swing at the sky and began loosing off the rounds.

Above him was a plane full of soldiers, coming in to land.

As coincidence would have it, the officer in charge of the soldiers was Joe Singh, the same man who was at Jonestown ten years later. He told me that the plane was an old Dakota, with all the seats removed.

'And we were each loaded up with bandoliers and grenades. We came to Manari because it was the only airstrip the rebels hadn't blocked. I was up in the cockpit, and I suddenly heard "Tap! Tap! Tap!" They were firing at us! If they'd hit the fuel tank, we'd have had it ... I told the pilot to go higher. Go above it! We then circled with the gun firing at us, and landed at the far end. As the rebels were in a depression, they were in dead ground and couldn't fire at us, and so they took to their Mini Mokes, and fled ...'

'And what happened to them?' I asked.

'A few got away. The Venezuelans came to pick them up.'

'And then you marched on Lethem?'

'Yes,' said the general, 'without any trouble.'

Ahead of his soldiers, the population had fled. The Amerindians, believing they were about to be eaten by black soldiers, headed for the hills. The rest waded over the Takutu and took refuge in Brazil. Among them were the Melvilles, and all of Esther's family. None of them ever went back, she said, and they lost everything. Eventually, Caracas – which still regarded them as Venezuelan – offered them a home. Esther's father ran a café for the rest of his life, and the Melvilles were last heard of working on the roads. Even now, Melvilles in the Rupununi are the subject of suspicion.

Meanwhile, the army began the search for remaining rebels.

'It was a straightforward mopping-up operation,' said Joe.

But not everyone agreed. There were still some who said that the army brutalised the Rupununi, that they killed a hundred Makushis, that they dumped them in mass graves, that they beat over four hundred people and raped eighty girls (even tethering one down and using a truck to crush her).

In these versions there were 'bodies in the river', but none to be found.

'It's all rubbish,' said Joe, 'I kept a very tight ship.'

'And the stories of genocide?'

They were all, he said, 'the product of a feeble mind.'

'So what do you say to people who tell these stories?'

'I've said I'll take them on a tour of the Rupununi. Let them find a single witness! There aren't any. It just didn't happen. Besides, I have great affection for the Amerindians. They've always been my eyes and ears.'

It was hard to be sure exactly where the truth lay. I liked Joe, and during my travels the charges of genocide never bore fruit. Of all the Amerindians I met, only a few mentioned beatings or the mistreatment of girls. In Surama there was a man who said he'd been chained up for a week on a concrete floor. But the suspects were soon released. By 1970 only ten accused remained, and they were all acquitted and left for Venezuela. Somehow none of this added up to an iron-fisted campaign – but nor was it kid-gloved either.

I asked the general why the missionaries were expelled.

'Well, we felt they were involved.'

'And what about the eight ranches left by the rebels?'

A jubilant president had referred to them as 'terrorist centres'.

'Yes, it's true,' said Joe, 'we burned them down.'

During my last week in the Rupununi I travelled out to the great ranch at Pirara, to see what was left. Evelyn Waugh had said that, in 1933, it was 'one of the most imposing and important houses in the district'. He described a schoolroom, fruit trees and a compendious library with books on every conceivable subject 'much ravaged by ants'. I paid it a visit with my friend Mr Li.

'I used to come here as a child,' he said as we reached the drive.

Ahead of us was a mountainous billowing of mango trees, topped with a wind pump. Beyond it we could just make out a river – the Pirara – like a long, thin lake, curling away through the hummocks of grass. Mr Li said he'd camped here in 1963 and had almost lost a finger, fishing for perai.

'The ranch was owned by the Harts,' he recalled, 'a rough-and-tumble lot.'

I asked what he meant.

'Like something from a Louis L'Amour. Fantasists.'

Everyone had stories about the Harts. They were descended from

a giant American who'd arrived in 1911, after a spell digging railways in Brazil. Ben Hart had weighed over 200 lb, and the sight
of so much space was clearly to his liking. He settled and married
another of Harry Melville's daughters, Amy. Waugh remembered
him as 'a kindly middle-aged American of wide experience' and
piety. But it was a curious type of piety. By night Ben led moonlit
processions through the grounds, accompanied by his six wild sons,
their governess and their Wapisiana grandmother. By day the boys
were 'tumultuous' and spent their school hours reciting the rosary
and getting whipped. But Waugh was clearly taken by their governess, a Creole who wore shorts. She was, he wrote (with uncharacter-
istic fervour), 'as lithe and vital as an adolescent Josephine Baker'.
Even she, however, managed to exercise only a 'precarious care'.

'No wonder the boys were so wild,' said Mr Li.

We were now almost at the mango trees, churning through the
sand.

Waugh's tumultuous urchins had, it seemed, turned into natural
rebels. 'They used to hold rodeos here,' said Mr Li, 'and parachute
jumps. I think two of the boys had been in the US army, and had
served in Korea. But all of them were always fighting! I think most
were involved in the uprising …'

Beneath the mango trees, all trace of the old ranch had gone.

Mr Li stopped and stared. 'I still find this hard to believe …'

In front of us an imposing mansion had vanished, along with its
schoolroom and its compendious library of half-eaten books. The
army had burned and destroyed everything, even the corrals and the
fences. The Harts had fled, every single one. President Burnham had
regarded their Pirara as 'the centre of the operation', and this was
his terrible revenge. Now all that remained were a few shoddy brick
structures erected in the 1980s, and abandoned ten years later.

From one of them an Indian emerged, grinning and waving. 'Me
truck broken down on the road,' he said, 'I been here two days now!'

He said that, although he was surprised by the fruit, he'd not felt
easy here.

'Something not right,' he beamed, 'too many ghosts.'

A few days later I left the Rupununi and flew back to the centre of
Guyana, and the beginning of the forest.

Down below, the colours of the grass and bog seemed to melt and implode, simultaneously livid and inert. The optimist in me announced that this would probably always be one of the most magnificent, untrampled corners of our planet. Isolation was a beautiful price to pay for all its crimes: for the obstinacy of its environment, for failing to produce a golden city, for daring to rebel, and, of course, for being a republic that lasted a day. Isolation had even become government policy after the revolt. For years it was illegal for anyone living in the region to keep an aircraft overnight, and they had to have the word 'RUPUNUNI' stamped in their passport, like the mark of Cain.

Even now, the coastlanders could hardly bear to contemplate the savannahs at their back. Perhaps for people who saw themselves as Caribbean it was all just too South American. Nobody ever went there, and even the idea of a road made them bristle with disgust. As for the plan to fly out frozen cows, that too had been dropped. Now the only planes that ever ventured in and out of the Rupununi were like mine, carriers of the quick and not the dead. Even then, only three out of twenty seats were taken.

Behind me was a travelling oncologist, out from New York. 'I love the Rupununi,' she said, 'but I'm always pleased to see that forest.'

I must have looked surprised. 'Why?'

''Cos that's when I know we're soon back in the present.'

4

A PARLIAMENT OF ANTS

There is no country which yieldeth more pleasure to the Inhabitants, either for these common delights of hunting, hawking, fishing fowling and the rest, than Guiana does.

Sir Walter Raleigh, *The Discoverie of the Large, Rich and Bewtiful Empyre of Guiana*

The people come out to Demerara and they drink and they drink, and they die, and then they write home and they tell their friends that the climate killed them.

James Rodway, *Guiana*

Demerara is the Elysium of the tropics ... the Happy valley of Rasselas, the one true and actual Utopia of the Caribbean Seas, the Transatlantic Eden.

Anthony Trollope, *The West Indies and the Spanish Main*

AT THAT MOMENT THE FORESTS of central Guyana didn't feel like the beginning of the present. Even at the best of times, I've only been grateful for woodland, never really fond of it. Now here I was the wrong side of one of the oldest, thickest, darkest, dampest and least-inhabited forests in the world. Seventy per cent of it has never been possessed and only barely explored. From the air it had looked like a sort of compacted vegetable fog. Nothing about it had conveyed the present. Now all I could see ahead was some vast pre-historic frontier and a long, last plunge through our primeval past.

On my map there was no real certainty as to where – or whether – this forest would end. Not only was everything green but an over-imaginative mapmaker had also added a few touches of his own. He'd shifted towns around, obliterated Colin Edwards's road, rein-serted the cattle trail and then added a trans-jungle highway and an enormous American airbase. As a map, it was more aspirational than useful, but at least the coast was there, and two great sinuses, the Demerara and the Essequibo. Between them – several hundred miles to the north – I could also make out a spattering of old place-names: Uitvlugt, Enterprise, Harlem. This, I realised, was the heart of old Guiana, and it was here that I was heading.

I lost count of the hours I spent bouncing down tracks that led to the coast. Being completely encased in foliage, it was like travelling down a pipe that arched and bowed, and occasionally flexed to the left and right. Sometimes I could see almost a mile ahead, as though Colin's men had created this road by blasting it out with some earth-hugging rocket. At other times I could hardly see anything at all, just a silvery gash in the canopy above. The rhythm of it all, and the endless stream of greenery, was inspiring in its way. On either side of me the flanks of the forest were as formidable and dense as city walls, and in the larger trees – the mora and the silk cotton – I began to see great, grey buttresses like the limbs of a cathedral. I tried to imagine how it would be to walk this track and to feel the same landscape endlessly repeat itself, tree after tree, for weeks on end. After a while you'd begin to wonder whether it was you that was moving or just the orange soil, flowing south beneath your feet.

My eyes were soon craving incident, or some sort of visual punctuation. For hours there'd be nothing, and then a feast of occurrences. I always noted them. It might be a toucan, a log the size of a truck or a mysterious cluster of hammocks. Once there was a real treat: a policeman in silver buttons, sitting in a hut plastered with posters of wanted villains. Another time we passed an overturned truck, with its driver and crew camped underneath. They all looked so happy and domesticated that I wondered whether – one day – their unfortunate accident would turn into a village.

There was only one stop, a small collection of painted huts, called 'Kilometre 58'. I liked the idea of a place that had defined itself purely in terms of somewhere else. In fact, everything about it was faintly apologetic. 'We used to have horses,' said a man on a bicycle, 'but the jaguars ate them.'

Km 58 did, however, have the only eatery in central Guyana.

'What's for lunch?' I asked.

'Wild cow,' said an Amerindian, crouched among the pots.

I bought two boxes of stew and gave one to my driver.

'Tapir!' he said gratefully, tipping his head back and pouring it all in. I did the same. It was like a rich boeuf bourguignon on a salver of cardboard.

I had several different drivers on my journey north. The last one was so Indian and so strongly accented that I began to wonder whether I'd ended up on the wrong continent. But for the first part of the journey I got a lift with a man called Stephano, whose father was Brazilian and part of the gang that built the road.

'This were meant to be Brazil's gateway to the Caribbean …'

'Oh,' I said, 'it doesn't look like it now.'

'No, they all finds a quicker way, up through Venezuela!'

I enjoyed Stephano's distorted outlook and his jungly chatter. He said that, when he wasn't driving, he was cutting trees, and had girls all over the forest. There were over a thousand different types of tree, as well as creepers, epiphytes, blood-sucking loranths and strangler figs. They all had their uses, he said. Did I know that purple heart was poisonous to termites? Or that aromata was used for ringworm, and greenheart for ships? Or that the best cure for scorpion bites was a little blob of earwax? If you ever saw a mango tree, that's where the cattle trail used to pass. And under every silk cotton was a grave of murdered slaves.

I'd like to have travelled all the way with Stephano, but then – suddenly – the forest ended, and a huge expanse of mad, thrashing water appeared. We'd arrived at Kurupakari, the place where the old cattle trail had crossed the Essequibo River. It was here that I'd decided to break my journey for a few nights. So, while Stephano headed back to his girls and his trees, I made my way down to the field station on the banks of the river. It rejoiced in the name 'Monster Worm' but is better known as Iwokrama.

I shall remember Iwokrama as one last moment of gentility before plunging back into the forest.

It was an arresting scene: grassy banks, acres of buttery sunlight and the pleasing rumble of water. I was sure this was the place that Waterton had in mind when he wrote: 'This delightful scenery of the Essequibo made the soul overflow with joy and caused you to rove in fancy through fairyland.'

While I was never quite moved to fairy-like roving, I knew what he meant. Sitting here, watching the river turn purple and fireflies sifting through the trees, it was impossible not to feel a certain surplus of joy. In fact, Mankind has probably been here, quietly overflowing, for almost 6,000 years. Down among the waterfalls were the comments of some of Iwokrama's earliest visitors, gouged in the rock. I'm no reader of runes and glyphs, but I'm sure I could make out 'nice water', 'good fish', 'occasional famines', 'straight sticks' and plenty of fat things with little short legs.

Nowadays the visitors tend to be less expressive but far more numerous. Almost everyone who comes to Guyana gets here at some stage or other. And why not? Its wooden cabins, arranged in an arc along the bank, felt like the ringside seats at an extraordinary spectacle. First to call by were a pair of macaws in a state of perpetual carnival. Then came a bright pink snake, thousands of moths, a friendly old caiman and a sloth, which – in torchlight – looked like a teddy-bear mounted with meat-hooks. But what was even more remarkable was that this great, savage menagerie extends backwards over an area the size of Rhode Island or Essex. As reserves go, this may not be vast, but it's completely unmolested. This is one of the few places on Earth where Man – apart from the odd petroglyph – has barely made a mark.

Because the field station had tiptoed so lightly into this forest, we often saw no one at all. Food would appear and beds would be made, but none of it seemed to involve clatter or dialogue or even people. But then, at around dusk or dawn, I'd be aware of someone standing at my shoulder. It would be one of the Makushis from the village, here as a guide.

Most of the time I went off with a young hunter called Edgar. At first, it was disconcerting to turn and find his face so close, peering into mine. Most of his teeth were broken into little points, and on one side they were missing altogether, which gave him a leer like a wolf. But he was a thoughtful man and knew the forest like his larder. During our walks he was always finding me teas and greens and edible grubs. He was also an energetic pharmacist, advising on cures for everything from BO (tonka beans) to whooping cough (an infusion of ground-up baboon ants). There was nothing Edgar wouldn't treat, and I was always testing him, thinking up fresh disasters.

'What happens if you crack your skull? Or break a leg?'

'Easy. Kill an anaconda, smear on the fats and tie it up with leaves.'

Edgar seemed to enjoy all these questions. It's always hard to know whether a professional guide feels any more for you than a vague sense of investment. But at least my curiosity seemed to humour him. I think he thought I was daft, not knowing how to deal with colic or fix a fractured femur. He was even more surprised that I'd never heard of the Monster and the Worm. It took him a whole boat ride and half a mountain to tell it as it should be told, but here's the gist of it.

The Makushis were being slaughtered by the Caribs, and so they asked the monster Ok' Kraimî to help. This he did, but then he turned on the Makushis and started eating them. He also had a side-kick called Iwo, who was a giant worm, with a nasty habit of pulling people's heads off and lapping up their innards. It was a while before the Makushis were able to bring this outsize pest under control, but they did. Eventually they killed both Iwo and Ok' Kraimî, leaving nothing but a name: Iwokrama.

By the time we'd finished this story, we were five miles down the Essequibo, and half-way up Turtle Mountain. But myth was almost nothing compared to the peculiarity of life up here. We were now surrounded by giant amber crabs and vines as fat and smooth as transatlantic cables. Meanwhile, up in the canopy, there were balls of mud, assembled by the ants, the size of cars. We could also make out troupes of monkeys, way above, trickling through the sunbeams. Everything here seemed to cackle and scream. I asked Edgar what he used to hunt, and he told me racoons, squirrel monkeys and porcupines. But those, of course, were not the words he used. Instead, he reverted to the old, bosky language of the hunter: 'Crab, sakiwinkis, dogs and pimpla hogs.'

As our little boat clattered back upriver, Edgar told me about the voyages of his childhood. From the age of eight, he and his father had set off every year canoeing to the mouth of the Essequibo. It was a journey of over 200 miles and had taken almost a month. Along the way they'd slept in the trees and traded fish for salt and clothes. Then, when they'd got enough, they'd paddle home. 'It was slower then,' said Edgar, 'against the current.'

This wasn't a new journey, I realised. Europeans had been paddling up the Essequibo ever since the seventeenth century. The Dutch had even had a trading post, just below Turtle Mountain. Now it was almost impossible to follow them downstream. Nobody went by boat any more, so I'd have to take the road.

'Yes, a long road,' said Edgar, 'up through the forest.'

Behind me, the Essequibo hauled itself away, off on its watery adventure.

It was another week before I found myself back on the banks of the Essequibo. In the meantime it had been transformed from a riotous, ten-lane adolescent to a swathe of inland ocean. There was now no doubt about its status: the greatest river within the Guianas. Since its source – over 1,000 kilometres inland – it had gathered up millions of tons of gaily coloured sediment, whole rafts of forest and hundreds of smaller rivers.

One of these tributaries was the Potaro. I flew up there once, on a day tour from Georgetown. The river itself would have been worth the trip, like a gorgeous seam of folded jet. But then suddenly it just ended. It poured over a lip and vaporised as it fluttered away into a deep abyss. These were the Kaieteur Falls, and without having seen them they'd have been hard to imagine. Every minute, the equivalent of twenty-four Olympic-size swimming pools was falling twenty-seven storeys. In other words, one moment a river the width of the Thames was looping through the jungle, and the next it was dropping from a ledge the height of Telecom Tower.

Somehow our little plane managed to land on this ledge, and we all got out and crept towards the rim. It was like watching all the whisky in the world tumbling into an explosion of weather. Way below, we could just make out the river, reassembling itself from the clouds and then swirling off through a canyon. Conan Doyle would have loved it up here. It would have confirmed his belief that there were Lost Worlds, and that they were right here in Guyana. Among the oddities living on the edge were swifts that could fly through hundreds of tons of falling water and a tiny yellow frog that spent all its life on a single bromeliad, swimming in its cistern.

Only one man lived up here, called The Caretaker. He was very thin, and the roaring loneliness had given him hot pink eyes and fiery breath. Just when I was wondering how one cared for anything so huge and unruly, we set off on a tour. The Caretaker obviously hadn't seen anyone for weeks, and in his excitement he skipped off over the rocks, leaving us all behind. Later we caught up with him and found him chattering away in Creole and addressing his plants in Latin. 'Heliconia!' he'd squeal, 'Digitalis! An ere is de local Viagra!'

I'd like to think that in this wonderland of canyons and microscopic frogs it's always been the rivers in charge. But that's not so. Every now and then Man has blundered in and asserted his stupidity. The worst time was in August 1995, at the junction of the Potaro and the Essequibo. Here a Canadian company had established the biggest gold mine of South America, called Omai. It was producing not only 300,000 oz a year (imagine eight little cars of solid gold) but also 20 million tons of rock and a lake of industrial cyanide. It was not a happy combination, and one day a dyke burst, and the lake and river merged. A billion gallons of cyanide set off down the Essequibo. For days the world's media watched as this great toxic surge bubbled towards the sea, killing everything before it. To the Guyanese, cyanide on this scale felt like the ghost of Jonestown, trickling back through the heart of the country. To the rest of the world, it was one of the worst environmental disasters ever known. It was ages before the Essequibo was safe again to drink.

Surprisingly, for this superhuman error no one was punished. Within weeks Omai was back in production, spewing out dirt. The Guyanese have always hated it. ('The mine dug out de heart of dis country,' said The Caretaker, 'and we gets nothing at all'.) I remember seeing it once from an aeroplane. It was huge and red, and streaming with slurry. Too late, Guyana had discovered that its El Dorado was not a golden city but a suppurating boil.

At the point where I rejoined the Essequibo it was ten miles wide. From here I was expecting a long, empty day, travelling forty miles up one of the continent's most magnificent estuaries. As it turned out, it was certainly magnificent but never empty. People were now back in the landscape, with bundles and stories, and all their pomp and mischief.

There were plenty of boats going upstream, but I got a lift with Captain Cesar. He was a large hairy African, covered in scars and baubled in gold. His boat was different from the others. Most people were paddling around in corials and balahoos and other forms of tree trunk, but Captain Cesar's boat was owned by a mining company and had two aero-engines and a cabin like a cockpit. Packed inside were several months of provisions, including over 400 toilet rolls. When it shuddered to life, it felt like we were airborne, off to bomb Dresden with a payload of shopping.

'Be there in an hour!' roared Cesar.

As we flew along, he greeted the islands and called out their names.

'Leguan! Wakenaam! Lau-Lau and Hog!'

Cesar said that on the Essequibo there was one island for every day of the year, and that he could identify them all. Sometimes it sounded more like gossip than geography. Some of the islands had secret little beaches, and others had villas and love-nests, or a camp full of misfits. It seemed that anyone who was anyone had a bolt-hole here, for when the heat got too much. There was an island for drug barons, and Khaow for the lepers. The singer Eddy Grant even had an archipelago of his own, mounted with a palace. Then there was our island, Baganara. It was owned by the mining consortium, and through the trees I could make out an enormous lozenge of fuel and a company airstrip. Cesar dropped me at the far end, by a colonial-style mansion, now the company hotel.

'Enjoy your stay,' he said, crushing my hand in his.

I said I would, and of course I did. It wasn't hard. Baganara was a beguiling place. The beach was like sifted sugar, and the water was dark and warm. Even the names of the birds – tanagers, tyrants, plovers and snipe – sounded collectively decadent and louche. At sundown there were cocktails on the terrace. Most of the other guests were Europeans, working in development. I don't suppose they were much different from the colonists before, at least in terms of poise. One was an Italian banker, who'd arrived on a yacht. Another was Swiss, and the more she drank, the more her make-up migrated. After a while it became hard to focus on her, she was so blurred around the edges.

One of the other guests was harder to place. He was always heading out on lavish cruises and throwing back the beers. 'I'm going to Bartica,' he'd say, 'and get me some girls.' He told everyone he was the son of the American ambassador (who also happened to be black). This was so obviously absurd that I thought it was some kind of Guyanese joke. But not everyone got it. It was only three weeks later that I learned the full extent of his deceit. According to the *Kaieteur News*, John Spence was just a boy from the sugar fields with the gift of the gab. Both the Italian and the Swiss had given him hundreds of euros, and the hotel was down by $2,000. For the boy, it was a little adventure that would cost him a year in the Camp Street jail.

But Baganara would survive its guests, whoever they were. When you live on the edge of an enormous forest, you can never be sure who'll turn up next. There was a picture of Mick Jagger in the bar.

But even more surprising was the British army. They'd been riding around in helicopters, buzzing the river for days. Captain Cesar said they'd stopped over at Baganara the week before. ('Big men,' he confided, 'I see one drink seventeen bottles of beer'.) As coincidence would have it, the island had been one of their earliest bases, back in the nineteenth century. But before that it had been a camp for another army, this one far more brutal and ambitious. It was, of course, the Dutch.

No people have died for this river quite so willingly as the Dutch. Others would die in greater numbers, but in the white-hot heat of commerce it was only the Dutch who died so freely.

Take the case of Laurens Storm van 's Gravesande. He served the West-Indische Compagnie from 1738 to 1772, rising from secretary to director-general. His greatest achievement was making money, and under his management the two colonies, Essequibo and Demerara, ran at a fabulous profit. But it also came at a heavy personal cost. During his period of office he lost not only several infant children but also his wife, a grown-up daughter and three adult sons. By the end he himself was utterly spent, and three years later he was committed to the dirt for which he'd given so much.

It's been an enduring sacrifice. The Dutch were on this coast from 1595 to 1977, arriving long before the English and leaving long after. Here, on the Essequibo, these riverbanks were, for a while, the richest farmlands in the world. In the peace treaties of the seventeenth century they were accorded the same value as vast chunks of West Africa, or the city of Madras. It was like a tropical Holland, with all its dimensions exploding outwards. But not anyone could turn it to profit. Only the Dutch had got what it took: a nose for finance, the brass for a fight and an aptitude for drainage.

To get some idea of this long-lost Holland, I decided to visit its earliest fort.

The hotel lent me a boat and a guide, called Leon. Together we set off into an enormous tangle of rivers, like a knot made out of Danubes. First we had to double back up the Essequibo and then loop past the mouth of the Cuyuni, before turning back on ourselves and up the Mazaruni. The fort turned out to be a small nob of jungle, out in midstream. How had the Dutch found it, in this gigantic labyrinth of water?

That was the point, I suppose. Although by 1616 Holland was one of the greatest landowners in the world – with vast possessions in Africa, Indonesia, Formosa and Ceylon – it was not yet master here. This was still the 'Wild Coast', contested by Spaniards, unpredictable savages and English privateers. To survive, any fort had to be unobtrusive, well inland, heavily armed and easy to defend. This one even had a vigilant name: *Kijk-over-al*, or 'Watch over all'.

Leon found a jetty, and we pulled in to land.

'Careful where you step,' he said, 'it's very overgrown.'

Nature had spent the last 300 years throttling the fort. Huge roots were now levering up the masonry, and a large mango tree had sunk its claws deep inside the rock. Leon said it was a very old tree. Perhaps once it had supplied the garrison with fruit, and now it was prising it apart. An account of 1669 describes a dinner here of 'roasted water-hare' washed down with barrels of brandy and rum. It must have been like life on a petrified ship. The crew had spent their time learning Carib, and at some stage the commandant had married an Amerindian princess.

Now all that remained of the grandeur was a large brick arch. In architectural terms it wasn't so much a door as an exclamation mark. It declared that this was the beginning of a great Dutch world. From here plantations would spread out downstream, fifty miles to the sea. But not just yet. At the time of the water-hare dinners this river was still deeply infested.

Every now and then piracy returns to the Essequibo, even today.

Soon after my fort excursion I left Baganara and got a boat down to Bartica. It was a gold-mining town, at the crutch of two rivers: the Essequibo and the Mazaruni. Everybody there was into gold. People no longer wanted a grand gateway to the coast, just an orifice into the forest. Every day great bladders of fuel arrived by boat and were then being hauled away on trucks. The beach was like a long thin junkyard of old steamboats, draggers and dredgers and other contraptions for sucking up ore. All around were things abandoned in the rush: machines, hovels, sawmills and dogs. Surprisingly, despite its temporary, impatient feel, Bartica was now the largest town in the Guyanese interior.

Work went on all day and then long after midnight. No one seemed to notice it was dark, and that there weren't any lights. This made Bartica a hard place to contemplate once the sun had gone. I was for ever stumbling over hungry dogs or falling down drains and bumping into cows. The only place to enjoy the light was Auntie Chan's Massive Upper Level Restaurant. It was superbly misnamed (being African, earthbound and pokey), but it did screen soap operas like *Sexy Mistress*. The miners loved this and hooted with pleasure at the merest kiss. This only made the waitresses look sulkier than ever. They wore prim, lime-green uniforms and had seen it all before.

For many, the work had never brought much wealth. Although the rich had big pink houses like birthday cakes, everyone else had shacks. The very poorest lived in an enormous old iron barge, mounted with a slum. Most of the miners were Brazilians, which gave poverty here a paler complexion. It also gave it a bright red parrot, and a constant drumbeat like a thin, metallic pulse. These were precarious lives, of people easily bullied. I remember a notice outside the hospital which said, 'PATIENTS ATTENDING THE GYNAE CLINIC WEARING PANTS WILL NOT BE ADMIT-TED.' I don't think I've ever seen a sign so pointlessly demeaning.

I stayed down the road, at the government guesthouse. It was a towering tongue-and-groove structure, full of wobbly colonial furniture. The two crones who ran it took an instant dislike to me, and whenever I went near, they'd start muttering in proverbs. ('And thou shalt smite every male thereof! And eat the spoil of thine enemies!') I think the only time they spoke to me in post-Apocryphal English was when I asked for a key. 'The door doan lock,' they said. 'The watchman goan come.'

It was unusual to encounter such hostility. Most people in Bartica were curious to find a foreigner among them, and the miners were effortlessly friendly. One, an old man called The Sultan, even took the trouble to explain how things worked.

'Gold is easy to smuggle', he said. '*Very* easy, yes, Sir. None of it go through the lawful channels. Nearly all these rich guys here smuggle gold. And now they're into cocaine. They got islands out on the river, and airstrips in the bush. These people are *powerful*, man. I shouldn't even be telling you this. If they heard, they'd proba-bly come after me, and put a bullet in my head. Just like that. Bang.'

He looked up the street. 'You heard of Roger Kahn?'

I said I had. He was on trial in the USA.

'OK, he owned Khaow Island, and a lot of the interior. He even had his own little army. They were all ex-cops. Imagine that, man! These people runs everything, and they buys everyone. *Everyone!* They can have whatever girl they wants, and just send a taxi round to school. They got factories, planes, ships, politicians ... And those stupid pink houses! I hate to think what coke's doing to American kids but *this* is what it's doing to us! Bent cops, bent courts, bent government, and millions of dollars ...'

A new economy, it seemed, had settled on the river.

With such bloated pickings, it was inevitable the pirates would return. Just before leaving Bartica, I walked down to the wharf. It was a large barn of a place, full of reflections and smelling of brine. The only person around was an old Indian guard, in a uniform of crumpled claret. He was standing on the wooden *stelling*, staring into the water. It was here, six months earlier, that the water-thieves had clambered ashore. There were twenty of them; masked, camouflaged and clattering with guns. First they rounded up the stevedores, and then they forced them onto the decking and shot them where they lay.

'Just here,' said the Indian, 'five men dead.'

The divots in the timber were still ragged and fresh.

'But what did the killers want?'

The guard shrugged. 'They just goes robbing round the town ...'

I followed the bullet holes out through the wharf into the streets beyond. After shredding the police post, the pirates had stolen a truck and ridden around blasting at will. For over an hour Bartica was forced underground while the raiders toured above. But were they really just robbers? No one seemed to know. The Sultan said they were after those that ran this town, the big-shots like Mango Man and Vulture. But they never found them, and nor was very much stolen. In the end eleven people died, and their killers vanished into nothing. Perhaps it was all a warning, or just a blast from the past.

Three miles upstream I reached the original, fortified plantations,

or what was left of them. It was a promontory of terraces, blooming with lemon trees, flamboyants, corolla, mangos and bamboo.
At the bottom of the slope was the Mazaruni – looking like a sheet
of mercury – and a cluster of bushy islands, including Kijk-over-al.
From here the Dutch had watched as their investment took root,
sprouted, flourished and turned into wealth.

The terraces were still in production, although now it was not
sugar but vegetables and music. Since 1988 there'd been a Benedictine monastery up here, on Mora Camp. I don't suppose the
house was much different from the sort of place the planters had
built: white-painted timber, loggias, louvred openings and windows
without glass. Inside, it was furnished mostly with books, and a few
simple pieces wrought from hardwood. Not a cent had been wasted
in the pursuit of pleasure. Along the hall there was a row of cowls,
and around each window a fringe of crusted lace. For a few dollars
the brothers gave me a room of my own. I was their first guest for
months and had a cell in the eaves.

'We rise at six,' they said. 'Matins at six-fifteen.'

It wasn't long before I was part of the clockwork of monastery
life. There were only two brothers, Pascal and Matthias, and an
elderly abbot called Hildebrand. But they lived their life to a split-
second *horarium*: matins, Mass, prayers (three times during the day)
and then vespers, supper and compline. At exactly the moment they
promised, their euphonious chanting would lift up out of the trees
and carry out across the river. Loosing off canticles into this vast
expanse of light and silvery water must have felt like addressing
heaven itself. 'The only way I can live with celibacy,' Brother Pascal
once told me, 'is by having all this beauty.'

I still have a recording I made of the chanting monks. It was a
gorgeous, sepulchral sound. By day it seemed to blend in with the
reedy hum of crickets, and by night with the chorus of frogs. After
a while I almost forgot it was the music of the thirteenth century,
filtered through the tropics.

I didn't always join them. Sometimes I swam out to one of the
islands or wandered over the hill. After sugar, Mora Camp had
become a rubber plantation, and there were still a few trees left.
Occasionally I found the glass cups used for tapping latex, or shards
of older glass that was bubbly and brown. When I took some pieces
back to Hildebrand, he smiled and produced a complete, unbroken
flask. 'Jenever,' he said. 'The Dutchmen liked their gin.'

Way across the river was another reminder of the days of the Dutch. It was a large collection of stone buildings, which was unusual for Guyana. Although little seemed to happen there, occasionally the whole place came alive with the sound of voices in song. This was said to be the most beautiful prison in the world: the Mazaruni Penal Settlement. It was here that Dr Jagan wrote his first political treatise, on toilet paper, in 1954. It was also here that the German explorer Carl Appun breathed his last in 1872. He was an illustrious chronicler of the Guianas (*Unter den Tropen: Wanderungen durch Venezuela, am Orinoco, durch Britisch Guyana und am Amazonenstrom*), but they also drove him mad. Believing that he was about to be eaten by his Amerindian guides, he swallowed a draught of carbolic acid. Puzzled by this gesture, his guides brought him to the prison, where he died in agony two days later. The prison was never as sweet as it looked. Even as late as 1918 every prisoner was 'catted' – or whipped – on arrival, and then again when he left.

'It's still tough,' said the Abbot, 'and no one escapes.'

The early Dutch would have been proud to hear that, in the prison at least, their regime had survived. The Essequibo of the eighteenth century was still a dangerous place. But by 1744 a new confidence was beginning to emerge. The planters were about to embark on one of the world's greatest feats of agricultural endeavour. It was time to sail downriver, and drain the coast.

I said goodbye to the abbot and set off in their wake.

The reason everything changed in 1744 was Vlaggen Eyland, or 'Flag Island'.

I stopped there on my journey back up the estuary. It was now called Fort Island, and from the river it looked like a tussock of floating jungle. But its appearance was deceptive. Commissioned that year, the fortress – although never Krak des Chevaliers – was better in a way. Here was a huge, unsinkable gunboat, moored right in the shipping lane, half-way up the estuary. I realised, as I scrambled up through the mud and bricks, that whoever possessed this outcrop controlled not only the river but also the thousands of acres of swamp all around.

At the top of the bank was a track that led to the fort. Along the way I met a drunk called Bobby, who had big, clubbed fingers and swollen feet. He was soon tagging along. 'You know what?' he began. 'Dere's a huuuuge secret tunnel runs right here! Under de river!'

Bobby was a terrible guide but an extraordinary magpie of planter life. From the folds of his tatty outfit he produced musket balls, clay pipes and trade beads. 'Take them,' he said, putting them in my hand, 'we gets lots of dis shit.'

We were now at the fort. Despite the encroaching undergrowth, it was still a formidable sight: a huge nest of ramparts, parapets, moats, scarps and counter-scarps. In the middle was a three-storey blockhouse, shaped like a diamond and built from brick. Every surface facing the river had been slewed through forty-five degrees, to deflect any incoming fire. It seems that the tireless Gravesande had ordered the very latest in military technology. His fortress – Fort Zeelandia – had been armed with over forty heavy cannon, and even now there were half a dozen left.

Bobby was still babbling on about tunnels and treasure. While he hobbled off to look for snakes, I took out my notes. This was a moment that called for Bolingbroke. No one had known the old Dutch colony like Henry Bolingbroke of Norwich. For seven years, from 1798, he travelled the colony, working as an articled clerk. His memoirs, *A Voyage to the Demerary*, describe Guyana right at the end of Dutch rule, and at the very pinnacle of wealth. So confident was the colony, it didn't need castles any more, and so Bolingbroke arrived to find this one in decay. 'The cannon are dismounted, and the fort is totally deserted, save by the wash women who find it a convenient place for hanging linen to dry ...'

When I read this to Bobby, he snorted with pleasure.

'Dat's my grandmuddah! She took washing!'

I didn't like to question this. Bobby lived in such a fragile world of possibilities and drink. 'I gonna show you de biggest fuckin building in Guyana,' he said suddenly, 'you wanna see it?'

I said I did, and so off we went, back down the path. At the far end of the island was a long brick hall. It had tall, shuttered windows, the bell-tower of a church and the body of a warehouse. Bobby was wrong to think it was the biggest building, but – forts aside – it was probably the oldest. Inside there was a large expanse of flagstones, a cluster of well-laurelled tombs and a colony of bats. This was another of Gravesande's creations (and it was often thought that he was still here, curled up under a slab). In its day the hall had been a church, an office, a college, a slave market and, most importantly, the Court of Policy. From here the great planters had declared dominion over an estate five times the size of Holland. They were men of exorbitant ambition, and each had a fancy title, such as the Predicant, the Captain-Commandant, the Vendue-Master and the Fiscal. Now all that remained of them were a few coloured pictures, each looking splendid in a breastplate and wig.

Bobby peered at them closely and puckered with contempt.

'Dis people ruled Guyana? Don't make me laugh!'

He was right in a way. It wasn't really rule. Of the land the Dutch had claimed, 96 per cent remained unvisited and unexplored. All they controlled was one brilliant, fertile edge. As for the rest, their dominion was illusory. Out there, this great hall might just as well have been a Council-in-the-Sky, or a Parliament of Ants.

Meanwhile, out on the edge, the Rule of the Farmers had taken shape.

Between the two rivers, the landscape had been transformed. Had I set off on foot from the Essequibo, I'd have spent days walking to the Demerara, across the featureless grid of Dutch design. Instead, I was grateful for a lift, and the road round the coast. Even then it was daunting: the sheer flatness of it all, the crushing parallels, the endless rhomboids of cane and the great canals – some, sixty feet wide – trailing off into infinity. I remembered how it had looked from the air, like book-spines stacked in their thousands. Now here I was among the spines, each the size of a public park. The planters had moved perhaps a billion tons of earth, as they rolled back the sea, flushed out the salt and poldered the mud. The process had not only continued up the rivers, but also – ten miles deep – all down the coast.

The road followed the sea wall along the shore. Out there the Atlantic looked sludgy and pink, like a desert of sediment except slightly more choppy. Just as I was wondering whether there was life in the silt, I spotted a heron, with charcoal plumage and eyes like spots of fire. The Guyanese were grateful for their wall. They called everything inside it the 'backdam', as though their whole world was a product of Dutch drains. But this wasn't the only legacy of Holland. The plantocracy it had created would survive long after the arrival of the British. Even now there's the sense that commercial life is controlled by the few. These days, however, the big houses are rarely Dutch: Booker, Correia, Banks and perhaps the occasional Gravesande.

But there was another, more immediate, reminder of Holland. It was the names, scattered through the landscape. Sometimes, in West Demerara, it felt as though the Dutch had never left. Among others, there was Roed-en-Rust and Vreed-en-Hoop, Blankenburg, Den Amstel, Tuschen-de-Vrenden (or 'Between Friends') and even a miniature Hague. I enjoyed these places. They were like fleets of little boats, moored in the drain. Everything was painted in glorious colours, for fear of not being noticed. I remember a huge old cinema, looking like a bridesmaid, and a small café called Christ's Professional Fish Shop. Did modern Zeeland still look like this? Somehow I doubted it. These were old plantations, and this was the landscape of slaves.

I stopped overnight at Meten-Meer-Zorg. It was built on a grid of canals and had a temple, a mosque and a market laid out on sheets. My hotel, the Toucan Inn, was – like the town – still sprouting upwards and outwards. For the owner, a Portuguese-Guyanese called Gary Serrao, his great concrete creation would never be complete. In the last few years he'd added staircases, annexes, outer defences, a crow's nest, a whole new storey and a series of gantries to link it together. Everything was white and gleaming, as though it had been iced. Inside, it was more like a contraption than a building, a tottering fantasy from Dr Seuss. There was even a swimming pool, right through the middle.

'I used to be a gas-fitter,' said Gary, as though that explained everything.

But, as well as his fantasy guesthouse, this was also his museum. Gary had spent his life gathering up the pieces from Guyanese history. There was everything from kitsch to stone axes. I've often wondered what it would be like to judge countries by their ephemera. Here, the British period would be remembered as a time of ginger beer and postage. The Dutch era looked far more impressive. There were cannonballs and manacles and giant jars of fish. It was also more persistent. Gary said that both guilders and the Court of Policy had survived well into the twentieth century, and so had the law. Two centuries on, land deals could still get tangled up in tracts of Roman Dutch.

'And then there's this,' said Gary.

Guianese slaves in the 1770s. Attractive women were expensive but could be rented two at a time.

He was standing in a room full of empties. There were flagons, demijohns, hand-blown wine bottles, decanters, crocks, pots and flasks. But mostly it was gin. Gary told me there were flasks everywhere, down every river and up every creek. As the old abbot had said, the Dutchman liked his gin. Perhaps it was more than this. If it's possible to read history from the rubbish, then a curious picture emerges: by the 1780s the planters were living a life of luxury, up to their eyeballs in gin and fabulously dissolute.

It was time to consult Bolingbroke, to see what he'd said. For this, I needed to get to the Reynestein estate so that at least our view would've been the same. Back in London, it had taken me days to find it, scouring old maps and books. I knew it was somewhere close to Zorg, up the Demerara River. Then I spotted it, an oblong of sugar, among a cluster of others. They sounded like brothels or old Dutch bars: Free and Easy, Jacob's Lust, Vive La Force, De Yonge Rachale, and Goed Verwagting. I also discovered that they were now all lumped together into a super-estate called Wales, one of the biggest in Guyana.

Next, there was the problem of getting there. Back in 1799, Bolingbroke had taken a tent-boat from Georgetown, rowed by some slaves. The journey had lasted two and a half hours, and throughout it the oarsmen had sung a song called 'Good Neger make good Massa'. With this option no longer conspicuous, I decided to call my old friend the driver Ramdat Dhoni. Any chance he could pick me up and take me to Wales?

Ramdat sounded puzzled. 'OK, but it's just a lot of sugar ...'

'That's fine,' I said, and so we were agreed.

Actually, it wasn't fine. In the back of my mind I still hoped there'd be something left of the Reynestein manor. Bolingbroke said it was a large white house of 'the greatest elegance of style'. He described billiards, good coffee, the finest linen, floors scrubbed with citrus juice, farmland 'like gardens', solid dinners ('salted ling, roast beef and Muscovy ducks, then Bologna sausage') and hammocks round the table. Scattered throughout this pleasing scene was a riot of semi-feral infants. The 'Massa' of Reynestein, noted Bolingbroke, was 'particularly fond of children and used to enjoy their antic nakedness.'

Sadly, all trace of this had gone, ploughed back into the mud. Instead, all we found was a sugar mill, which looked like an ancient tramp-steamer, puffing away in the mud. Next to it was a stilted, end-of-the-Raj clubhouse, for the bosses of today. Inside, everything was made of darkening hardwood and lavished in sepia and cobwebs. Around the walls were enormous metal trophies given not for Formula 1 but for dominoes and whist. There were no naked urchins or Muscovy ducks. We did, however, find a manager, who generously agreed to show us around. His name was Mr George, and he was skinny, half Indian, and wore a uniform of corporate khaki.

'This club is just for us,' he said, 'not for the cane-workers.'

I asked if the two ever mixed.

Mr George looked surprised. 'Never. We live very different lives.'

Back in 1799 the lives of the Dutch and their workers had often merged. It's not a chapter of European history that's easy to read. Even British visitors (such as Bancroft, Pinckard, Stedman and Bolingbroke) were less than charmed by what they found. Their journals describe a life of relentless duress, perfunctory intercourse and exalted greed. The planter, it was said, was 'like a petty monarch, as capricious as he is despotic and despicable', and his very existence was one long 'round of dissipation'. Here's a typical day.

The planter rises at six, when his coffee or chocolate is waiting. He then summons his girls on an ivory whistle that's always to hand. The finest young slaves attend, but they do not wash him. In contrast to the cleanliness of his house, the Dutchman prefers only to have himself dabbed with a napkin dipped in a glass of water. His is not an impressive physique. He weighs around eight stone, and his body is 'generally exhausted' by the climate and the vice. In the language of the slaves there is a term for this: *wishi-wassi*. It means 'being Europeanised', or enfeebled like a white.

As his slaves dress him, he enjoys a pipe and a flask of gin. A typical outfit might include the very best Holland trousers, white silk stockings, red or yellow Morocco slippers and a nightgown of chintz. He will then wear a nightcap 'as thin as a spider's web', and over that a beaver hat. If he's not going out, he'll have breakfast with his cringing slave-master, the *baas* or 'overseer'. They will have bacon, broiled pigeons, plantains, cheese, Madeira, Rhenish and Moselle, all the while being fanned by the most beautiful of slaves.

If he is going out, a boy will dress him in white silk breeches, matching waistcoat, buckled shoes and wig. He'll then set out to supervise the work of the estate, and to attend the daily flogging. If he's going by barge, it will be suitably furnished with fruit and gin. He is now smoking all the time 'to correct the effects of the strong drink'. If he's on horseback, a boy runs behind him with his 'segars and a stick of fire'. As the planter passes his slaves, they doff their hats and murmur *'Ja, weledele gestrenge Heer!'* ('Yes, great and honoured Sir!'). He affects not to notice them, even when they're being beaten. After each lash of the hempen whip, they call out *'Dankee, Masera'*, or 'Thank you, Master'.

At midday he rests, playing billiards, perhaps, or taking a nap. Then, at three, he rises and is dabbed down again and perfumed in time for dinner. This will be another spectacle of food, commencing at four with 'soop as in France'.

Typically, a table of gentlemen will be waited on by naked slave girls, who've been oiled and plucked, all the better to enjoy them. Carnality, however, can be a complicated matter, and there's often a moment of hesitation before debauching a slave. This is partly because the African is an adept poisoner, and is known to be passionate in revenge. The other reason is economic: a pregnant slave is an unprofitable one, and so it pays to avoid the casual conception. Owners, as Dr Bancroft notes, go to great lengths to prevent such mishaps, deploying noxious lubricants of ocro and gulley root. Often these leave the girls hopelessly infertile.

If the planter has a wife, she will preside over dinner, an extraordinary sight. Dr Pinckard writes at length about the 'astonishing supper appetites betrayed by some of the Dutch females'. On one occasion his hostess polished off a bottle of Madeira before tucking into the claret, and 'a solid substratum of two heavy slices of fat ham, after which I helped her to no less than fourteen other dishes'. With that lot gone, she then started work on the fruits and sweets.

If the planter is not married, he'll need to improvise. 'A European', writes Bolingbroke, 'generally finds it necessary to provide himself with a housekeeper or mistress.' Females can be either rented at the fortnightly Stabroek Ball ($12 for two) or bought. However, decent specimens are in such short supply that often they have to be imported from Barbados (a traffic run by coloured women, paid on commission). A good, well-trained girl, notes Bolingbroke, can be purchased for around £100 to £150, and 'they are tasty and extravagant in their dress'. The best can read and write, and 'most are faithful and constant once an attachment has been formed'. They embrace all the duties of a wife, and, if children are produced, they are generally sent to England for education 'at the age of 3 or 4 years'.

Dinner done, the planter rises to consider his next move. Whether he has a wife or mistress, this does not imply restraint. Here is how Stedman describes the end of the day: 'His worship generally begins to yawn about ten or eleven o'clock, when he withdraws and is undressed by one of his sooty pages. He then retires to rest, where he passes the night in the arms of one or other of his sable sultanas (for he always keeps a seraglio) …'

So it was that lives merged, in contrast to today.

Another aspect of Reynestein had remained eerily unchanged: work. All around us was the landscape of the seventeenth century. It was like stepping into a painting by Koninck or Van Ruisdael. The view was mostly of sky, but along the bottom there was a strip of flatness, busy with people and oxen and barges full of greens. Occasionally, huge brick *kokers* and sluices loomed up out of the ditches, and then – beyond them – stretched the cross-canals and 'Dutch beds', and endless miles of 'Middle Walk'. Mr George said modern machines would never survive in this and would just vanish in the mud. 'So it's all still cut by hand. Four thousand hectares by two hundred men!'

I asked him whether anything had changed in 300 years.

'Not much,' he said. 'I'll show you if you want.'

Mr George had a powerful new pick-up, and so we set off in that. At first, we drove around the edge of the estate, through the villages where the cane-workers lived. In Bolingbroke's time these were called 'niggeryards', and were staunchly African. In Reynestein he'd found some families in their third generation of slavery.

Now the Africans had long gone, and the villages were Indian and known as the 'schemes'. I thought they looked quaint, with their old Morris Minors and their bungalow-mosques. But often they were anything but. Every day the papers had some story of a murder on the schemes. These usually involved a girl in a ditch, or a piece of jewellery, or a man in a beer garden, run through with a cutlass. 'We never stop here,' said Mr George, solemnly. 'It's a drinking culture.'

Then we were in the cane. Ramdat hadn't ventured so deep into the sugar for years and was curiously excited. He gasped as we sped towards the vanishing point, and as the cane closed in, like a forest of long grass. At one point we came across a weeding gang. They were all women, dressed in overalls and gold. Nowadays everyone worked in the fields, said Mr George (although you could never ask Hindus to kill the rats). It was slightly different in Bolingbroke's day. Then, only a quarter of the slaves worked in the cane. The rest were an extravagance, there to service the lives of the Dutch.

Eventually, after about five miles, we came across a cutting gang. They'd just burned off the rats and the snakes, and the crop was still smouldering. Everything was sticky and black: cane, hands, clothes and hair. The chicken hawks had gathered in the hope of something charred, and one of the men was holding a deadly labaria, as long as himself but lifeless and limp. 'About every twenty years,' said Mr George, 'someone here dies of a snakebite.'

The work was still brutally hard. During his four-hour shift each man had to cut over 2½ tons of cane, tie it in bundles and then carry it down to the barge. There was no shade and no stopping, and the temperature was now somewhere in the eighties. The cane-worker had little to be grateful for. If he didn't achieve his target, his wages were docked. No wonder he was so famously angry. 'For these people,' said Mr George, 'it's a rough and bully life.' Only for the slaves had life been harder: their day, of course, was unpaid, spurred by force and three times as long.

As we drove back, Mr George suddenly stopped.

'I want to show you this,' he said.

We got out and sloshed through the clay, towards a patch of scrub. 'It's all grown wild,' said Mr George. 'I can't get anyone to clear it ...'

We pushed into the grass, and there in front of us was an old stone tomb. It was scrolled and grand, but the inscription had gone.

'Who is it?' I asked.

Mr George shook his head. 'Probably the planter.'

Perhaps it was the Master of Reynestein? Or the cringing overseer, after all that sausage and ling? I had a sudden image of a pale, thin man, with his silvery breeches and his flask of gin. It was unsettling to think he might be here, leering up out of the clay.

Mr George shifted uncomfortably.

'This thing terrifies my men. They won't even touch it.'

Two centuries on, an unspeakable violence still haunted the sugar.

What shocks me most about plantation cruelty is that it was so candidly commercial. Here was the beginning of a new era in human depravity. What was different was not so much the scale as the deference to profit. There was no passion or fervour, no diktats from tyrants or instructions from God. It was simply about gain, and managing the units of production. In these strange, new economics atrocity varied according to supply. That's why, as the slave trade began to falter, around 1807, planters began to consider less destructive means of control (such as cancelling holidays, or the stoppage of rum). Until then, however, mutilated slaves could be easily replaced, and the brutality knew no limits.

The quantity of violence usually related to the impact on production. Some aspects of the slaves' performance needed greater correction than others. The most serious aberrations were disobedience and absence. But because the slaves owned nothing, they were hard to penalise. All they could be deprived of were parts of their body – usually breasts, testicles, arms and feet. It would all be hacked away without either a trial or an anaesthetic. For the most demanding cases, the transgressor could be tied to a wheel and then pounded with iron bars until every bone was broken. Other transgressions were dealt with on a limb-by-limb basis. If a slave raised his hand in anger, it would be amputated. If he ran away, his Achilles tendon would be sliced through, leaving him 'hamstrung', or permanently lame. If he ran away a second time, the leg would be cut off altogether. For all other matters there was always the lash, or the 'Spanish whip', which not everyone survived.

In this vicious economy everyone had their price. For each judicial amputation the colony doctor was paid £6. The Amerindians, too, had set rates. For each runaway recovered, they received 400 guilders, or 200 for an arm (and in one year, 1795, they put in a claim for seventy arms). Meanwhile, overseers were paid on results, which only multiplied their malice. But in all this brutality the most surprising agents were the slaves themselves. With Europeans outnumbered by eleven to one, it was often Africans wielding the whips. According to Bolingbroke, 'Africans of all masters are the worst to one another.' He said that the greatest threat a slave could face was to be sold to one of his own. It was as though the machinery of slavery was now so great and violent that it could almost run itself.

But not all the slaves were so compliant. In fact, by 1763, the outer margins of the colony were ripe for revolt.

What happened next is still, for many Guyanese, the most important moment in their story. It's the only one they celebrate with holidays and statues. Other events – such as emancipation and independence – have an ambivalence about them, perhaps because they feel like donations or the start of some new trauma. But 1763 is different, at least for the Africans. For well over half their Guianese history, they've lived in slavery, and this was the moment when they grappled with control. It's also given them a hero, one of few in a long, hard search.

It all begins with a note from the planters in Berbice. 'For God's sake, send and help us in our hour of need.' The slaves had risen up and declared a republic.

5

THE BLOODY BERBICE

The River Berbice is shallow but broad; nearly a hundred plantations have been formed on its banks.

Henry Bolingbroke, *A Voyage to the Demerary*

Formerly a land of mud and money, it was now a wilderness of mud and mosquitoes.

James Rodway, *Guiana*

BERBICE STILL FELT LIKE ANOTHER COUNTRY. In Georgetown people talked about it as though it were another planet. They
said that upriver the journey was impossible, there were no roads or
telephones, and that often everything was flooded. One man told me
to expect giant frogs, marijuana plantations and strange, old people
jabbering in Dutch. Another said I'd find no one at all, just a lifeless
river and vast black forest. ('Take a gun,' he said, 'and a satellite
phone, although don't expect any help'.) All anyone would agree
on was that Berbice was remote, backward and different. It was
also relatively new, and had been a completely separate colony until
1831. Georgetown had yet to get used to its strange green neighbour.

All this made Berbice hard to understand. Few people went there,
and there was no useful map. Even the one I had was intriguingly
obscure. Along the coast I could see a road, dotted with breezy
English names (such as Waterloo, Whim, Gibraltar and Nigg). But
inland the marks faltered. There were just a few tracks, the thick
snakey river and a scattering of words, all stubbornly Dutch. Right
at the bottom, I could just make out the old Rupununi cattle trail,
wandering northwards before fizzling out.

Berbice didn't even appear much in books. In all I'd read there was
barely a mention. Schomburgk had called by, of course, and so had
Bolingbroke, dutifully noting all the belting and gin. But other visits
had been more cursory. Trollope had trotted along the coast (and

loved it), and Waugh had ploughed through the middle (and hated every moment). Attenborough remembered it as the place where he didn't catch a manatee, and Waterton avoided it altogether, as did Durrell and Keymis and Shiva Naipaul.

After a while it began to feel like an anti-destination, a place to be shunned. Least inviting of all were the history books. Berbice seems to have erupted in revolt at almost every great moment of Guyanese history; abolition, the arrival of the East Indians, the departure of the British, the election of an Indian and the African dictatorship. Was there anything left of it? What had become of its first revolt? And would I ever get there?

Just when I was giving up hope, someone introduced me to Alex Mendes. He was a rancher from Berbice and was up in Georgetown buying feed and ammunition.

'I can get you to the ranch, and you can stay the night. Then – from there – you can get a boat to the coast. We're about ninety miles upstream.'

He said the old name of his ranch was Peereboom, or 'Peartree'.

It was perfect. Ahead lay a journey through 1763.

All I remember of the drive to Berbice are trees and aluminium. First there were the trees, and then the road to the mines. This was an outlandish construction, four lanes deep but only half-an-hour long. Alex explained that it was all the work of an aluminium giant, ALCOA. They'd built everything: the bridges, the culverts and even the signs along the verge. Now we had it all to ourselves. It was like a short, wide stump of American freeway, lost in a country without any cars.

'It was a gift,' said Alex, 'in 1965.'

It was a funny gift, I thought, as I watched the road swooping around in the sand and scrub. Who exactly was it for? A new African regime or the American consumer? I suppose the clue was in the beautiful tarmac, heading straight for the sea. For over seventy years the United States had been scraping the bauxite out of Guyana. The busiest time was the Second World War. I'd often heard about the wartime aluminium. People liked to tell me how, once, the world's greatest airforce was two-thirds Guyanese.

Soon we were in the mining town, and then among the pits

themselves. These were huge orange holes, bruised with purple and black. Some were half a mile wide and sixty feet deep. This is how Mars would look if you blew it to bits. The dust got every-where, said Alex: in your teeth, in your hair and under your nails. You could wash your truck three times, and it would still come up a nasty pink. Things even tasted of aluminium. It was in the river and the water butts, and it powdered the forest. Alex told me that a few years earlier it had almost killed him. He'd spent his thirties break-ing bones and was in a wheelchair at the age of forty-two. It was the aluminium, mischievously mimicking the effects of old age. 'I'm better now,' he said, 'but I don't swim, and I never drink the water that comes off the roof.'

After the pits, the bauxite never really left us. The road was now brutally red and dived back into the trees. Five hours later we were still lurching along in the dark and dust when, suddenly, a white house appeared and, beyond it, the great black river.

It was Peereboom, the seat of the revolt.

All around the farmhouse was the wreckage of that day: 3 March 1763.

The house itself was a replacement for the one that was burned. It sat at the end of a long, steep bluff high above the river. There was nothing grand about it. A few large tree trunks had been set in the ground, cleaned up with axes and then stitched together with carpentry and planks. I could still see the axe marks as I lay in my bed. The man who'd built this place hadn't wanted a mansion. He'd just wanted a stopover, somewhere from which to pump cows into Europe. It was, of course, Harry Melville, of Rupununi fame, cob-bling together the end of his trail. He'd even given the place a new name, Du Bu Lay ('Double A'), which looked better on a brand.

Further along the bluff were the traces of a far more imposing house. Although the mansion at Peereboom was now no more than shingle, it had produced a lot of pieces. The fragments began on the bluff and then spread down the slopes and along the riverbank. Among them I spotted brickwork, tiles, lumps of earthenware and delicate slivers of Delft. There was also evidence of wine: not whole bottles but thick tufts of glass, like chunks of hand-cut thistle. A little distance back were a few of the drinkers themselves, tucked up in their fancy graves ('*Hier leyt begraven …*'). They all had elaborate, king-size headstones, scrolled and swagged, and finished off with a fetching skull and crossbones. Rococo details like this don't occur naturally in Guyana and must have been shipped out along with the claret and chintz.

'Looks like business was good,' I remarked.

Alex grunted. 'Maybe. But it's poor soil. All leached and acidic.'

He said he was trying new breeds of sheep, for the Islamic market. 'All they have at the moment is the old Black Belly.'

'Not a very appetising name…'

'Not an appetising sheep. It's just a reproductive skeleton.'

At three o'clock, a bell rang, and all the farm workers took off across the field. There must have been sixty of them – all African – shepherds, weeders, herders and ploughmen. Many still had their old Dutch names, such as Amsterdam and Linden. How odd, I thought, that in every waking moment, there was a reminder of the afflictions of the past. How would their descendants remember the present age? That depends on who survives, said Alex. Along the river, AIDS was now depressingly common. It was a mean twist of fate that, after centuries of fearing the outsider, people now feared each other.

When the workers got to the river, they stepped into their dugouts and paddled away. It was like watching a regatta for the chronically dispossessed. I tried to imagine a much earlier Berbice. Surely it hadn't always been like this, acid-cursed and Black-Belly poor? Once I saw a map of the river, made soon after the introduction of Angolan slaves, in 1714. It showed plantations on both banks, almost all the way back to the coast. Now, if I looked downstream, all I could see was a mirror-black surface and jungle spilling out over the water. According to Alex, there was hardly any work on the river these days, and people would paddle for miles just to get a job. 'Some of these workers,' he said, 'have a two-hour journey home.'

As the last of the canoes disappeared, I tried a little mental archaeology. I peeled away the jungle and cut back the trees for a mile inland. I scooped out miles of drains and ditches, and levelled the land for a crop of sugar. I also replaced all the shacks along the waterway, the kokers, the wharfs and the large thatched mansion at the top of the slope. Peereboom was almost ready. All I now needed was to recall the canoes (filled with ancestors and furious Angolans), and to have a riot of slaves – 600 strong – come tumbling out of the woods.

With everything back in place, the revolt could begin.

The owners of Peereboom had been expecting trouble. The previous week, on 23 February 1763, there'd been an outbreak of violence on the Canje River, fifteen miles to the east. There was no pattern to it, and no sign of leadership or strategy. The slaves had simply risen up in revenge, killed their overseers and then helped themselves to whatever they'd found: muskets, powder, cutlasses, waistcoats, fancy hats, white women and rum. As the gang moved upriver, they became a band, then a rabble and then eventually a mob. What they left behind was not pretty: burning mansions, and body parts in trees. It also took the colony completely by surprise. Throughout Berbice there were only about two dozen soldiers, and most of them were laid out with dysentery. The fury looked unstoppable.

Peereboom was prepared for a siege. As one of the few brick houses on the river, it became a fortress for those all around. The windows were barricaded and the fire buckets filled. Guns were primed, and preparations were made for an assault by barefoot slaves. All the wine bottles were smashed, and around the house was laid a thistle-bed of glass. No one would ever have imagined that this little detail would still be there more than two centuries later.

A vicious fight ensued. By the time the mob reached the Berbice, it was a full-scale rebellion. It had numbers, arms, leaders and the beginnings of a purpose: liberation. For some of the rebels it felt like an African war all over again. They'd even prepared missiles, bundles of hobnails wrapped in cotton, which they lit and hurled into the thatch. The planters managed to extinguish the blaze, but still the rebels came. Hands and arms were ripped away, and feet were cut with glass. The fighting was given a particular intensity by the thought of losing. It was always better to die furiously than to be calmly sawn up and dangled in the trees.

Eventually, however, stalemate was reached, and a dialogue took shape. The rebels were defiant negotiators. They said that Christians were no longer to be tolerated in Berbice and that the plantations were now theirs. If the whites wanted to leave, they could, and they'd be allowed to their boats. After some discussion the planters agreed.

What happened next would set the mood for the war to come.

The planters emerged from the house and gathered themselves on the bluff before heading down the slope. Then, as they reached the water's edge, the rebels opened fire. Most of the Europeans were killed, although a few got away by boat, or fled into the woods. For the rebels it was a bittersweet moment. On the one hand, the Dutch would not forget them. On the other hand, the day was theirs, and so was the booty. For themselves, there were guns, bottles, jars and Delft, and – for their leader – there was a plump white wench called Madam George.

Then, of course, there was Peereboom itself. Soon it would be burned and smashed to pieces. Up on the bluff, nothing would remain but lumps of brick and china, the wreckage of the day.

The next morning I got a ride downriver with an old marijuana grower called Fridge. It was a cruel name for a man so sensitive and black. But then, I suppose, he was also large and square, and seemed to occupy space like a household appliance. When I first saw him in his tiny boat, I wondered what it was that kept them afloat. Fridge, however, insisted on his buoyancy and said we'd easily make Fort Nassau, thirty-four miles downstream. It was here, I'd read, that the Dutch tried to make a stand. After the destruction of Peereboom, its survivors had paddled off to join them, and so – 245 years later – we set off in pursuit.

'How long will it take?' I asked Fridge.

He smiled. 'Softly, softly catch de monkey.'

It was a surprising morning. Even this far upstream, the river was several hundred feet wide and as dark as a pond. At first I couldn't make sense of anything. All I could see were patterns endlessly replicated, then vitrified and inverted and repeated all over again. The only time the trees parted was to admit a tiny church with a steeple, and then they closed in again like banks of bright green cloud.

For the enormous man sharing my little saucer of boat, all this was just a neighbourhood quietly flowing along. Fridge knew every tree and every creek. If ever we saw a boat, he knew whose it was, what they were doing and what they sold. His forest wasn't unfathomable but replete with drama. He knew who had AIDS, who did what and who'd had who. There were the Vandenbergs, the Van Lewins, Mr Vanderstoop (with the brand new outboard) and the slippery Van Sluytmans. Fridge said that everyone was up to something. He told me that the Amerindians were busy making land claims, and the Seventh-Day Adventists (who'd only hunt creatures with four stomachs) had eaten all the deer. There was nothing Fridge wouldn't talk about – except marijuana. That aspect of his life (I was later told) had all ended when he'd found someone stealing his crop and had rearranged him with a cutlass.

But what was even more remarkable about Fridge was his nose for the eighteenth century. He seemed to have some sort of innate extra sense for whatever had been there before. Although there was nothing left to see, he could still name all the old plantations: Juliana, Zeelandia, Lilienberg, Helvetia and Hoede Hoop. Wherever there's a giant silk cotton tree, he'd say, that marked a boundary. Once he even took a small, historical diversion, steering in under the trees. For a moment we bobbed around in a catacomb of roots, like a forest planted upside down. Then a mudbank appeared, and a stilted hut, made of strips of wet, black wood. 'Dis man,' said Fridge, 'still find all de tings what de Dutchman have left.'

From the hut a tiny wizened figure appeared and skipped across the mud.

'What you found now?' asked Fridge.

The mudlark said nothing but held out a coin, dated 1762.

'He sell dis tings in Georgetung. Must be making a mint!'

The mute grinned, pocketed his booty and danced off over the slime.

'Time we was gone,' said Fridge and turned his boat around.

Out on the river I had a sudden sense of desolation. Everything had died here and was now dying all over again. The mute had reminded me of one of those figures on the Napoleonic battlefield, collecting up knick-knacks and digging out teeth. It was almost as though the great revolt had only just passed through, leaving behind a trail of looting and disease. Even the butterflies now were funereal and black, and the egrets hung in the trees like handkerchiefs out to dry. Along this stretch of river little had survived the jubilation of the slaves. Every plantation was torched, and at Juliana the wife of a brutal manager had been decapitated, and her head mounted on a stick. The Dutch have never forgotten this horror, and even now they have an expression: 'Naar de Barrebiesjes gaan' ('Get thee to Berbice'), the equivalent of 'Go to Hell'.

'And here,' announced Fridge, 'is Hollandia.'

Through the trees I could just make out a small savannah. In the middle was a cluster of palm trees and a small, unpainted house. Once the mansion that had stood here had been the headquarters of the rebels, at least for a while. Now there was no one around except half a dozen children. They were mostly naked and fighting in the mud. It was a battle of impressive ferocity, and they only stopped when they spotted me. I wondered whether the younger ones had ever seen a white man before. They stared, and I stared. It was as though, suddenly, the years had dispersed and we'd all spotted ghosts.

Hollandia is probably best remembered for the letters written there.

The author of these letters was a man of rare dignity and unusual expression. His enemies are always 'excellencies' and are showered in greetings and praise. No one knows what Cuffy looked like. All that can be said is that both he and his lieutenant, Akara, were Akans from Asante (now Ghana). Cuffy may even have been a prince in his former life, but in slavery he'd been sent to Lilienberg to work as a cooper. After his role at Peereboom he'd been awarded not only the best of the spoils (including Madam George) but also the leadership of the revolt. In this he was a shrewd master of his meagre resources. Above all, he realised that, while it might not be possible to defeat the Dutch, they were capable of compromise. Already, in Suriname, they'd signed away millions of acres of rebel land. Five days after Peereboom, Cuffy sent off the first of his proposals, styling himself 'The Governor of the Negroes of Berbice'.

Over the next five months there were eight letters in all. They begin by demanding the surrender of Berbice, but within a month there's the suggestion of partition. 'The Governor will give Your Excellency one half of Berbice, and all the Negroes will go high up the river, but don't think they will remain slaves. Those Negroes that Your Excellency has on ships, they can remain slaves …' This wasn't exactly a declaration of rights, but it still horrified the Dutch. 'We will fight,' continued Cuffy, 'as long as one Christian remains in Berbice.'

The first letter didn't have far to go. It was addressed to the other governor of Berbice, now holed up in Fort Nassau, a few miles downstream. His name was Van Hoogenheim, and although he was only thirty-four, he'd already established a reputation as a canny governor, with some sympathy for slaves. But he was also Cuffy's equal in terms of resolve. Not for a moment did he intend to yield to a *negeropstand*, or 'Negro revolt'. He sent replies in one direction, stalling for time, and orders in the other, demanding troops. For as long as he was in command, he was determined that Berbice would not be lost.

Meanwhile, there was the small problem of how to defend Fort Nassau against 900 rebels, when all he had was ten fit soldiers and a few dozen planters ruined by Malmsey and vice.

Twenty minutes later, we arrived at the fort. I suppose I ought to have been more pleased at this arrival. I was leaving behind the haunted woods of the early revolt, and ahead lay the promise of a fortress. In one of the pictures I'd seen – a print dated 1682 – it looked like a large wooden cake, mounted with a Cambridge college. I'd noticed flags, weathervanes, cloisters and an elegant hall of crow-stepped gables. But now, peering up into the foliage, I wasn't altogether happy to be back, broaching a more familiar world. I'd enjoyed being with Fridge, and absorbing his revolt. Leaving him here felt like crossing over into enemy lines.

He dropped me on the riverbank, at a tiny clearing. It was like a niche in the forest wall. I was surprised not to see a castle, but at the back of the clearing was a small haphazard structure. It looked like something built by children and dropped from a tree. Fridge explained that this was the caretaker's house, and that Mr Grimmond had spent all his life defending the fort, and fighting the flora. Eventually the task had overwhelmed him and he'd taken his place among his forebears' bones. Now all that was left was his indifferent carpentry, a pile of 10 lb cannonballs, and his indomitable widow.

'She gonna look after you,' said Fridge, and then he was gone.

Actually we looked after each other. Mrs Grimmond was seventy-five, and everything you'd expect of someone whose ancestors were partly Angolan and partly blond. She was pale yet ebullient, glad of a guest and proud of her Dutch forebears. All that she had left of them were a few broken goblets, with delicate air-twist stems. I think she liked the idea of them dining at the hall, toasting *Colonie* and *Companie*. Not even the deformities of age would prevent her showing me around. On our walk through the jungle she'd be the brains and I'd be the banister.

'Careful of the pits! It's them people looking for treasure ...'

I enjoyed our tour at Zimmer-frame speed. Inside the forest it was cathedral-cool, and the path was rich in detail. We found the old ramparts, a small brick bridge, some glazed tiles and a stash of hand-blown bottles. Mrs Grimmond also found us food and cures, where I saw only mulch. If, by chance, one of her late husband's paths had led us astray, we'd have survived for months, lost in the wild. There were herbs and palm nuts, roots for constipation and 'bitter stick' for bile. We even had coffee – thanks to the Dutch – and a tree on which to summon help. The kumaka was like a waterfall of wood, pouring out of the canopy, and Mrs Grimmond said that, if we beat its buttresses, the noise could be heard for twenty miles around. Back in 1763 the booming of the kumaka would have signalled the start of the revolt.

'Nice, eh?' said Mrs Grimmond, 'we calls it the singing tree.'

Laxatives and yodelling trees were all very well, but what had become of my fortified college?

'You're already in it,' said the old lady.

She was right, of course. After we'd hauled each other over a giant root-ball, I hadn't noticed the shadowy outlines all around. We'd landed in an enormous hall. Only one account remains of this building, by a traveller called Hartsinck. In *Beschrijving van Guiana of de Wilde Kust* he'd described a structure 100 feet long and 50 feet wide, which had served as a church, a storehouse, the government and the home of the *'corp de guarde'*. Now all that remained was this diagram, and beyond it more rectangles: stables, according to Hartsinck, two smithies and some barracks. It was still like Cambridge, I suppose, except ground down, overgrown and ankle-high.

Mrs Grimmond sat down on a set of steps that led to nothing.

'Just think how great this place would be but for that revolt ...'

Greatness was not the planters' first thought when they heard the kumakas booming. Most acted with memorable funk. It's said that, at the approach of the rebels, the only sound from Fort Nassau was that of 'woeful lamentation and consternation'. Those who could, jumped in their boats and fled for the coast. Even Van Lentzing, the captain of the militia, tried to bluff his way downriver, along with two members of the Court of Policy. No one wanted to be around when the slaves were testing out their fury. It was an unedifying spectacle, the sight of officials making excuses. Perhaps the faintest of the fainthearts was the government secretary, Harkenroth. It wasn't panic, he blustered, just a matter of contract. 'I do not consider myself bound to stand here and be shot at for twenty guilders a month.'

Only Van Hoogenheim stood firm. He wanted to take on the slaves, although the odds were against him. Not only was he lacking a workable militia, but the fortress was rotten. The palisade that ran around the earthworks was now so old and wormy that, if the big guns were fired, the whole thing might simply fall apart. Van Hoogenheim, however, still thought the slaves could be held off until a warship arrived. But his colleagues were far less sure. His last chance of rallying them ended when a Dutch woman arrived, mad with terror. She said she'd come downriver and had seen the mutilated whites. It was the end of the debate.

On 8 March 1763 the guns were spiked and the fort was set on fire. The Dutch took to their boats and left behind the upper river. From that day on everything would change, and Fort Nassau would cease to exist. Once the flames and the rebels had finished with it, there'd be nothing left but glass and rubble.

The revolt too would be different from here. Ahead lay two new dangers; the first was the English, and the second euphoria.

The euphoria was easy to understand. The slaves had captured a beautiful river.

From the fort I got a lift with a water pilot called Mr Kertzious. He was a friend of Fridge and had a boat like a torpedo, which skimmed along on two magnificent plumes of spray. Suddenly a dank journey downriver had become a wild skedaddle through the afternoon sun. Suddenly, too, the banks opened up, revealing fields and fruit trees, with villages and farms. Everything now was lavished in ship's paint, and there were gardens sprouting marigolds and tyres. There was more traffic too. Often these were outlandish, home-made craft: floating cowsheds, motorised logs and carnival hulks. Optimism, it seemed, had triumphed over everything, including the laws of physics. Even the weekly ferry looked like a block of flats, bowling up the river.

We stopped only once, at De Velde.

'Just gonna visit my parents,' said the water pilot.

The Kertzious family had a smallholding on the edge of a savannah. They'd lived here so long that they no longer knew whether they were mostly African or nearly Dutch. Their house looked like a tiny stage-set and was painted baby-blue and pink. Inside, all the walls wobbled, the shelves were trimmed with lace, and there were rag-mats on the floor. For old Mr Kertzious the only mystery was why, of his nine sons, only one of them still lived on the river. 'I don't understand it,' he said, 'this is the most beautiful place in the world.'

'Nowhere like it,' agreed his wife, 'in Heaven or on Earth.'

As we prepared to leave, she pressed a bottle in my hands.

'Take it,' she said, 'we had it sitting here for years.'

It was a squat Dutch flask, bubbled and misshapen like an old glass bladder.

'Just a reminder,' said Mrs Kertzious, 'of our little Paradise.'

This was a pleasing thought, as we sped away. All round us were pretty smallholdings, cut and drained by those who'd once been slaves. It was true: each was, in a way, its own paradise, after all the years of brutality and toil. This was also the only land in Guyana ever to have been liberated by the slaves themselves. Their exhilaration is hard to imagine. It's said that for days they dressed up in beaver hats and chintz and rode around in tent-boats, mimicking the *massa*. Everyone wanted to be a soldier. Soon the slaves had their own army, with swords and generals and swanky parades. No one, it seemed, would ever have to work again.

Fifteen minutes downstream the river began to widen, and the jollity dispersed. I asked the pilot where we were, and he peered at the distant shore. A thin black soufflé of forest was now bulging over the banks. 'Dageraad,' he said.

We'd reached the limit of the rebel advance, otherwise known as 'Daybreak'.

Here the revolt develops a nasty English twist, convoluting loyalties.

Van Hoogenheim had passed Dageraad on 10 March 1763. The journey that had taken us a quarter of an hour had taken him two days. Along the way he'd run a gauntlet of musket fire and had stopped wherever he could to rescue the last of the planters. Here at Dageraad he'd again proposed a gallant stand, but nobody would join him. Reluctantly, he'd agreed to the evacuation of the colony. Berbice was on the brink of becoming South America's first and only republic of slaves.

Then the English turned up, and everything changed again. Quite why an English ship happened to be sailing by (with a hundred fresh new troops) is hard to explain. The effect, however, was startling. Suddenly, those slaves who were still in planters' hands found the courage of their convictions and rallied to the Dutch. Most were Creole, or born in the colony, and had no interest in an African war. The planters may have been pigs, but Cuffy was a savage. Colonial Berbice was saved. A few weeks later Van Hoogenheim returned to Dageraad at the head of a remarkable army, composed of his natural enemies.

The arrival of the English had also thrown Cuffy off his balance. At the very moment when he ought to have been delivering the *coup de grâce*, he hesitated. It was fatal. The English force was just sufficiently frightening to tempt him into diplomacy. He had no idea it was wracked with dysentery and couldn't even muster the sentries to man Dageraad at night.

It was two months before Cuffy attacked, but by then it was too late. The grim black soufflé of Dageraad was now latticed in ramparts and trenches. A hundred and fifty diseased defenders fought off an onslaught of 2,000 slaves. Meanwhile, from the river, three warships sprayed the rebels with canister and shot. For the first time, Cuffy was forced to retreat.

This defeat soon had loyalties back on the move. The treachery that had begun with the English now seeped in among the rebels. Field slaves turned against house slaves and Creoles against Africans. The Africans even began to turn against each other. On one side were those – like Cuffy – from West Africa, Asante and Dahomey. On the other was a far more warlike faction, from the Congo and Angola. Eventually, in about August 1763, Cuffy's leadership was challenged by a field slave called Atta. After only five months in power the greatest hero that Guyana has ever had conceded defeat. In the Akan tradition he gathered his closest supporters together and killed them, before turning a gun on himself.

By December the revolt had fragmented into countless civil wars. But it wasn't this that finished it off. Instead, it died of the victor's disease. In their triumph the slaves had defeated work and brought an end to human toil. It was a glorious sight, the fields set free. Now everyone was a boss, and for a while there was fattening plunder. Even after the raiding parties ceased, the celebrations went on. First there were feasts of cows and dogs and then, finally, just words.

Slaves paid a high price for revolt. On 'The Rack', every bone was meticulously broken.

The exhilarated slaves now lacked for nothing, except a bite to eat. Defeat had arrived in its most curious guise, and that was euphoria.

After Dageraad the river widened again. Ahead lay a great, blank estuary, the colour of sharpened knives. I remember thinking how bright it seemed, and how the only shapes were two straggly lines of attenuating mangrove. Out in the glare nothing moved except dolphins, forming soundless hoops of pink and grey before vanishing in rings. It looked like a film at the end of its spool. The blankness was compelling, as though anything could happen. This, it seemed, would have been the perfect place to watch the revolt in its final throes.

First I'd have seen the Dutch rushing their apothecaries to Dageraad. Berbice had proved reliably unhealthy. Its dysentery had resisted all manner of herbs and leeches, and was now liquefying the troops. On one ship alone, fifty-four men had died. Many didn't wait for the diarrhoea to come and kill them. The head of the militia, Lieutenant

Pronk, spent the entire campaign feigning illness. Another man, Captain Hattinga, decided to set off on his own mission, got blind drunk and shot everyone he saw. Not surprisingly, Dageraad became dangerously depleted. By October 1763 there were only forty-two men standing, and the only way to defend the place was by opening the sluices and flooding it in water.

Next, I'd have seen a small Dutch flotilla sailing up the estuary. News of the revolt had taken three months to reach Holland. The States-General then mustered an expeditionary force, but it was another six months before it arrived in Berbice. It was a humbling sight: two warships, two longboats and 260 soldiers. They'd go upriver and join up with a party of Amerindians, still being paid for each amputated hand. Dr Bancroft reports that these were prosperous times for Caribs; they became rich on severed hands and plump on human flesh. The manhunt had begun.

The following month, January 1764, an even more daunting spectacle had appeared on the river. It was a force of 660 volunteer marines, under the command of a cold-hearted killer called Colonel de Salve. He was here to gather up the colony's possessions, to capture rebels, execute their leaders and mutilate the rest. His arrival was so impressive that he soon had rebels changing sides.

Among the traitors paddling downstream were two that I'd hear of time and time again. They were Okera and Gowsary. Both had been close to the revolt's leaders, and each had made a crude assessment of his chances of survival. Living, it seems, was preferable to loyalty, and so they'd set off in search of de Salve. Not surprisingly, the colonel was only too happy to come to a deal. In return for their lives, the turncoats would tell him all he wanted to know. In fact, they did so well that de Salve later appointed them as drummers in his regiment. Meanwhile, he had everything he needed. Within two weeks of his arrival de Salve had found the rebel camp, burned it down and sent thousands of rebels reeling backwards through the bush.

It wasn't long before the ships were returning down the estuary, loaded with captives. Over the next three months some 2,600 slaves were recaptured. Atta himself held out until 14 April 1764, having wandered around like a hunted animal. In the end he was tracked down by his old lieutenants, Okera and Gowsary. It's said that they laughed as he was tied up over a fire. De Salve then ordered that Atta's flesh be torn away with red-hot pincers. For four hours Atta endured this before eventually dying. Observers say that throughout the ordeal he hardly uttered a sound. Having been tortured most of his adult life, he was, it seems, impervious to pain.

Far upriver, the revolt fizzled on until the end of the year. The last to give up were the Angolans. Some two hundred of them had established a tiny, nightmarish state, viciously defended by man-traps of sharpened bamboo. Inside, it was like Angola in miniature. Cannibalism was the source of all power, and there was a militia that ran on discipline and magic. The leader of this gruesome dys-topia was Accabre, a witch doctor from the Imbangala tribe. They believed that their women should not give birth but that the tribe should expand through abduction and theft. To join, all a man had to do was to kill an enemy and eat his flesh. Accabre's men would have eaten their way across Berbice if they hadn't been betrayed. Soon they too were back in their chains. It was the end of the revolt.

Along these banks the colony lay ruined. A third of the white population had fled or perished, along with half the slaves. Most of the Dutch had no appetite for rebuilding what was gone. Van Hoog-enheim pleaded exhaustion and resigned, aged thirty-five. Some of the colony directors even suggested abandoning Berbice, shutting it up and sailing away. But others saw a new future, out on the coast, and it was they who prevailed. The interior would never recover. The sad, empty river that I'd seen was entirely the product of 1763, a year of riot and revenge.

Meanwhile, ahead lay the coast, and the curious world post-revolt.

New Amsterdam still felt like an outpost at the end of a war. Although it was supposed to be the biggest city in eastern Guyana, it had all the exuberance of a temporary camp. Bars were booming, and so were shops selling shovels and lanterns and rolls of barbed wire. I have a lasting impression of lives lived outside; people dancing, canoodling and boiling up fish. All this was done with a certain intensity, as though all that mattered was now. I remember thinking how odd it was to drink this urgently, and to live every day like one last party. It was different at night. Then, there was no lighting or drama, and all the frogs squealed like incoming shells.

Somewhere in among this human furniture an old Victorian town was quietly picking itself apart. It had a bell-tower, a street

called The Strand and – like Georgetown – a large pink store called
Fogarty's. But the pavements had crumbled away, and nothing had
been painted for years. Grog-shops had wild apocalyptic names such
as Destiny's Guinness Bar or Diner's End. Then there was Good
over Evil, the barber, and an electrical supplier called EVIL EYE. I
couldn't decide whether, as a town, it was sad or mad or somewhere
in between. This was the place to come and buy a bag of dried-up
alligators or a hand-powered sewing machine. It felt like a long-lost
African colony on the brink of antiquity. Every street ended in some
sort of trench or catastrophe. Donkeys ran wild, and the police had
an entire garden full of rotting cars, like a patrol made of turf.

Even my hotel felt like a relic from an earlier age. The Hotel Aster
was built like a clipper, and had hardwood decks and a thick cream
hull. Inside, it was so dark and cramped that I had to wriggle my way
to my room. Like all good ships of its age, there was no unnecessary
luxury. My cabin was lime-green and contained only a washstand
and an old iron cot. Mr Kertzious, the pilot, had said this was the
cheapest hotel in town and had brought me to the door. It also happened to be run by his sister, Maylene. She, however, wasn't always
there, and at night the only other person around was a hefty rumi-
nant known as 'The Fat Girl'. But when Maylene did reappear, she
was always pleasingly Victorian. She was prim and dainty, and wore
a colourless frock and lace-up shoes. 'You're kindly welcome, sir,'
she'd say, as though the last hundred years hadn't really happened.

But of all New Amsterdam's oldness, nothing was more conspicuous than its hospital. It was all painted yellow and green, and was
three storeys high and two blocks long. When it was built, in 1881,
it must have been one of the grandest hospitals in South America.
Amid the grandeur I could see clapboard, frets, frills, crystal lights,
balconies, demilune windows, rooftop pagodas and an enormous
wrought-iron staircase cascading down the front. It was that particularly British style that's never seen anywhere else. I've always wondered what it's called. Neo-pavilionism? The Regatta Movement?
Or perhaps Seaside Realism? As no one was around, I decided to slip
through the fence and take a look inside.

It was only then that I realised the whole place was abandoned.
Everything was in place, but all the patients had gone. I climbed up
through the wards and the old dispensaries. There were bottles on
the shelves, and beds scattered down the stairs. It was as though
everyone had received terrible news and had just jumped up and

left. I came across a note for Mr Vanderbilt's steroids, and a coffin in the yard. I even found a photocopier, paralysed mid-copy and now richly slathered in droppings. I was surprised that no one was stealing all these things.

'But dey are,' said the waitress at Diner's End.

She explained that there'd been guards for a while.

'What happened to them?'

'Dunno. Even they's gone.'

'And now it's all quiet?'

'No, I don't sleep at night for de noise.'

'Noise?'

'Junkies, tearing up de zinc.'

'And you don't know what's going to happen to it all?'

The girl smiled wearily. 'Everything here fall down.'

With the future looking so sketchy, most people, I realised, had put their faith in prophets. This, like everything else in New Amsterdam, was not exactly new. Almost all the oldest sites in the town had some religious function. There were the Lutheran courts for the planters, a kirk for the Scots and a shady old tree for the slaves. Each new crisis seems to have brought a fresh new wave of prophets. After emancipation it was the Congregationists and the Wesleyans. Then, as the sugar failed, it was the Jordanites. They believed in polygamy and the divinity of a man called Mr Jordan. Now, however, the singular wife was back in control, but so were the Missionaries of Charity, the Shalom Full Gospels, the Church of the Nazarene, the Universalists and half a dozen others. They'd do anything to attract attention. Some had bright pink churches, and others had speakers mounted on the roof. Once I came across a bakery with a notice, tucked in among the rolls: 'This stall is covered with the blood of Christ.' It was certainly an arresting thought, if not an appetising ploy. Equally weird were the white evangelists. They wore ties and starched shirts, and stalked the town like the FBI.

For a while all this was pleasantly distracting. But then, after a day or two, I began to feel what the city had felt for years: a sense of purpose set adrift. It was time to move on and begin the journey east. But, before leaving, there was one more place I wanted to see. I rang Mr Kertzious and arranged to meet for a drink.

'Do you know where Fort Canje is?' I asked.

'Sure,' he said, 'why you want to know?'

'It's where the slaves were taken after the revolt.'

The old pilot tutted and whistled through his teeth. 'Well, it's still there ...'

'And will I get in?'

Mr Kertzious frowned and took a thoughtful swig of stout.

'Maybe,' he said, 'except it's now the city madhouse.'

Fort Canje, it seems, has yet to recover from the horrors of 1763.

It was always a sickly piece of land. Even now, few people live out here, on the swamps formed at the confluence of the Berbice and the Canje. The clay is always weeping oily water, and the air is itchy with mosquitoes. I remember thinking how fat and glossy they looked, as they settled on my jeans. This must have been a joyless posting for the Dutch. I could just make out their earthworks, bounding a plot in the crook of the rivers. There was no view beyond, just an enormous burning sky and a fringe of thick mangrove. At some stage the fort had failed altogether, leaving only the occasional outcrop of brick. Later, the British had replaced it with the only building possible in a place such as this: an asylum for those beyond the stage of caring.

Mr Kertzious announced me at the gatehouse and then shrank through the door. Behind a desk, a warden was watching cartoons on an old television. She was so fat that only her eyes seemed to move. 'What you want?' she murmured.

I explained that I was here about the revolt.

The eyes surveyed me coldly. I could see that she was working out how best to bully me, but my whiteness was confusing and so was my request. 'All right,' she said, eventually, 'but no photos of inmates.'

At first, we didn't see any inmates at all. The old British asylum was there, of course, tottering into the swamp. It was like the hospital in New Amsterdam, except pink, and more emphatically decayed. Much of the fretwork was fluttering away, and whole sheets of tin had wrenched themselves free and were flapping in the heat. In some places entire buildings had skewed and stumbled off their stilts, and lily ponds had formed in the wreckage of the wards. The plumbing of eviscerated laundries now lay sprawled across the weeds, and – round the back – we found an enormous boiler, cast in Glasgow, and now nosing out of the ooze like some strange, unearthly fungus.

Then, amid the debris, we spotted the inmates. Although they now had concrete barracks around the perimeter, some still preferred to wander the ruins. I was surprised how serene they looked. Perhaps the derelict mind finds comfort in chaos? One woman, who was whispering to the weeds, was luminously beautiful. It struck me that, however cruel insanity may be, it's scrupulously fair. Beauty probably didn't count for much up in the barracks. They had heavy steel locks, and wire across the windows. From inside I could hear the clank of metal, and a bitter miasma of urine and squeals billowed through the mesh. I don't think that – until then – I'd ever truly appreciated the sheer proximity of madness to pain.

Among the barracks was a small brick plinth, worn smooth by centuries of feet. I had an idea that here I'd stumbled upon the spot where one period of madness had ended and another had begun.

The conclusion to that savage year was perfunctory and grim. On 16 March 1764 fifty-three of the most prominent rebels were tried at the fort in a single day. They were charged with 'Christian murder', and not one of them was permitted to give evidence. All were found guilty. De Salve had wanted to have them locked in iron cages and put on perpetual public display, 'giving them too much food to die and too little to live'. But, perhaps mercifully, a more traditional view prevailed. The slaves were killed, as Dr Bancroft put it, 'with all the various species of cruelty for which the Dutch have long been notorious'. Fifteen were burned over slow fires, and sixteen were tied to the rab rack and broken up with hammers. Another twenty-two were dragged over the plinth and hanged at the gallows. The following month the whole exercise was repeated, and another thirty-four were killed.

Now, over two centuries on, there was little agreement about the revolt, or what it had achieved. Was all the slaughter worth it? Was this Guyana's proudest moment, or its worst? During the '60s, the rebels were re-cast as revolutionary heroes, which was a sure sign of bigotry to come. Even now there are Guyanese historians who describe the revolt as 'the first steps of freedom', although without any great conviction. Freedom was still too far away, and was not the work of violence. Besides, the rebels never spoke with one voice and were soon at each other's throats. Then there was the treachery, and men like Okera and Gowsary. Having betrayed the revolt, they then sailed off to Holland and joined the marines. There they'll be forgotten, at least for the moment.

Only Cuffy has a memorial. It's an angry-looking piece, cast in England and erected in Georgetown. What Cuffy would have made of this is anyone's guess: a statue of a man whose appearance is unknown, made by the old enemy and erected in a city that did not exist at the time, was in the wrong colony and took no part in the revolt. Meanwhile, Berbice has nothing – except the plinth, of course, and the anguished squeals of the chronically insane.

The road to forgiveness, it seems, is lined with Hindu temples.

Beyond the outskirts of New Amsterdam the walls of vegetation parted, and India appeared. Suddenly I was among paddy fields and coconut trees. I passed the Uttar Pradesh Pottery, and through a long string of villages painted lime-green and pink. It was exhilarating, the return of ornament and colour. There were prayer flags in the sugar and all along the sea wall. I remember concrete elephants and a Vedic healing centre, and a petrol station, called Vishaul and His Three Adorable Sisters. It was all so strangely upbeat that it was impossible not to feel a sense of restoration. Even my minibus was jauntily Indian. Its music was like an over-excited heartbeat, and across the windscreen were the words 'LOVE CONQUERS ALL'.

I also felt perversely relieved to be back among overcrowding. Perhaps I'd just had too much of empty hospitals and forest. It was exciting to be once again in the open, and among humankind, however tightly packed. Along the coastal strip the villages were so prolific they had numbers instead of names, and everything seemed to be richly clustered in people: piers, stalls, fishing boats and ghats. I even saw four people on a moped once, and cane-workers riding sixty to a truck. Of Guyana's 350,000 Indians, nowhere are they more concentrated than here in East Berbice.

After bouncing through the numbers I eventually arrived in a town called Springlands. It was a sleepless place, with two new minarets and yet more flags in the sea. Everyone here seemed either to fish for snapper or to sell stationery or teeth. In the market there was one man to pull the old teeth out and another to replace them. Most people got around in 'Tapirs', which were tiny home-made buses, with more paintwork than engine. All the beggars, I noticed, had parrots, and you could buy any god you wanted, made out of plaster. It all felt like some sort of unspecific festival, a celebration of nothing in particular. Was this the same Berbice that had almost imploded under the weight of discontent? Since the arrival of the Indians, it – or at least, the coast – had become a hotbed of something else; cricket, perhaps, or 'Grand Sari Pageants'. ('That's all we ever do in Guyana,' an Indian once told me, 'hold pageants'.) It was sobering to think that even the best-paid participants – the cane-cutters and pan-boilers – might earn as much in a month as an English plumber earns in an hour.

I stayed in a tall, thin hotel, almost on the sea wall. From my room I had a view of Suriname, way across the estuary. I also had a television, with two channels. One was in Dutch and had wafted over the river. The other was a Hindi channel, offering dances to the dead ('To Grandma, with all our love from Romel, Romeo and Robin'). There was no food in the hotel, and the only decoration was a portrait of Ganesh. The owner didn't even have his own room, and so he sat outside on the street. But at night he was replaced by a watchman, who had one wall eye and another for the ladies. He was disappointed that I hadn't brought him eye candy, so I gave him some beer instead. As we sat on the sea wall, dangling our legs, I asked him if India was anything like this.

'You joking, man? India some bad place, all that suffering and flies!'

I wondered about this, as I went off in search of food. Springlands had only two illuminated eateries. The first was a Halal 'snackette', which also happened to sell scent and anti-perspirant. The other was a curry shop, popular with farmers. I'd never seen Hindus in Stetsons before, and huge canvas boots. There were only three things on the menu: 'bush hog, chicken or iguana'.

This, I decided, was India all right but with a South American swagger.

On my last night in Guyana I watched the programmes from Suriname. It was a pleasing vision of life across the river. Smart, preppy-looking black people, chatting away in Dutch, sipped champagne and driving around in Humvees. It was like watching the American Dream, scrambled and encrypted.

Even the Guyanese were occasionally bewitched and would risk their lives for a piece of the dream. As darkness fell, I watched their lights, like sparks on the water. Each boat carried a payload of whisky and laptops, or human beings. Some moored next to the hotel, wedged in the silt. There the watchman studied them sadly. Hardly a month went by, he said, without some sort of unsung disaster. 'Usually, they hits the fish-sticks, the boat flips and everyone drowns.'

Guyana, I realised, always seemed to end like this, leaking smugglers around the edges. The watchman called them 'backtrackers', as though they were pioneers or scouts showing everyone the way. Was this the future for Guyana, a 'backtrack economy'? The watchman didn't think so. He told me something I'd often heard before: that here beneath this great, pink swathe of ocean lay the world's largest untapped oilfield.

'This place,' said the watchman, 'going to one day be like Kuwait.'

All that was holding the future back was the threat of a threadbare war. For years the Guyanese had been asking Canadians to set up a rig. But the last time anyone did so was in June 2002, when Suriname's response was to send an ancient gunboat. Guyana had no real answer to this, and so there matters lay.

I asked the watchman if he ever saw the Surinamese boat, out on the river.

'No,' he said, 'they can't afford the fuel.'

6

GOOD MORNING, SURINAME

In the distance I see a town which I think must be Surinam.
It belongs to the Dutch, you know. Our troubles are over and
happiness lies before us.

Voltaire, *Candide*

Surinam resembled, indeed, a large and beautiful garden,
stocked with everything that nature and art could produce to
make the life of man both comfortable to himself, and useful to
society.

John Stedman, *Expedition to Surinam*

'But this Surinam is a lost corner of the world,' he motioned
through the open cabin porthole toward the low-lying swampy
coast in the distance. 'Ten miles in there is nothing but sickness
and death, murder and Black Magic.'

Nicol Smith, *The Jungles of Dutch Guiana*

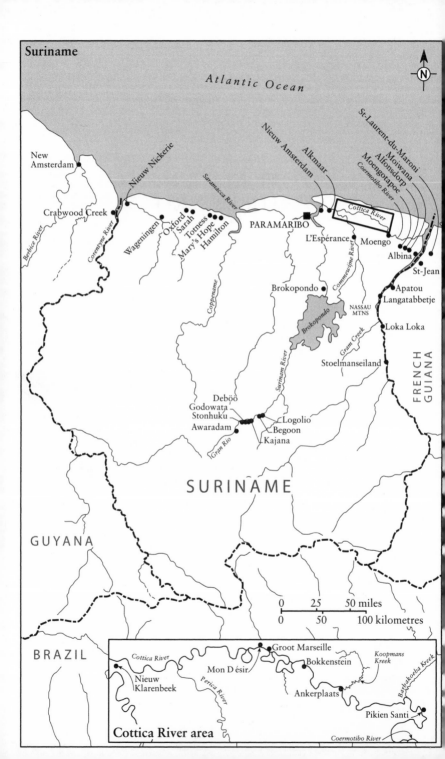

ACROSS THE RIVER LAY A PECULIAR LAND. The key to its peculiarity lies with its earliest visitors. They're misfits and dreamers, running away after years of destruction. They're also English, and wear sashes and lace, and beautiful wigs. Behind them are the charred remains of Edgehill and Newark, to which, they hope, they'll never return. But they haven't always had a common purpose. Some have fought for the King and others for The People. Their leader, however, Francis Willoughby, 5th Baron Willoughby of Parham, has fought for both sides, and in his portrait – which still hangs in the National Portrait Gallery – he is the very picture of well-groomed indecision. But about *Surreyham* (as this coast is quaintly known) he has no doubt. In 1650 he sinks the colossal sum of £26,000 into the creation of this, his own private heaven. It will be known, of course, as 'Willoughbyland'.

For the next seventeen years the coast flourishes and is a variant of paradise. 'It is commended by all that went for the sweetest place,' writes Willoughby, 'delicate land, brave trees and fine timber.' The new arrivals build a fort, and the Jews – recently expelled from Brazil – teach them the subtle arts of sugar. Soon over fifty vast estates appear. You can still detect the old rivalries, scrawled across the map. The Royalists name their plantations after themselves, or their fancy friends at court. The Roundheads, on the other hand, prefer something more apocalyptic, such as Succoth, Gilgen or Beersheeba.

Only the slaves suffer, but at least their role will be remembered for ever: Aphra Behn calls by, and produces *Oroonoko: or, The Royal Slave*. It will be the first English novel to emerge from the continent.

But then the Dutch appear. After several inconclusive wars, the English agree to swap Willoughbyland for a cold, wet slab of North America called New Amsterdam. It's a terrible transaction. Even with a catchy new name (New York), nothing grows up north. It will be another fifty years before the American colonies can produce even half as much as the island of Barbados. What's more, England will lose its new colony in just over a century, whereas Holland will keep hers until 1975.

Despite the protests from people such as Bolingbroke and Aphra Behn, the deal is done. In 1674 the Roundheads and Cavaliers burn down their mansions and leave the colony, soon to be forgotten. They are not the key to the story from here.

Instead, it's their slaves, now scattering into the forest. They will vanish for a while, like a secret world within, the nucleus of modern Suriname.

As my ferry shuddered through the currents, I realised how little I knew of the country ahead. For months I'd been gathering books and statistics, and touring the Web. Of course, I had the components but I could never make sense of the whole. It was like viewing a gallery by looking through the keyhole. One minute I'd have a perfect view of the eighteenth century, and the next it would all be swept away in a torrent of languages, or I'd find that there were fifteen separate Marxist parties, each saying something different.

Sometimes Suriname seemed almost to shrink out of sight. This wasn't hard for a country the size of Florida, the smallest on the continent. I read that, at night, it all but disappeared, producing too little light for the satellite maps. Its population, at half a million, would barely fill a London borough. But I realised it wasn't just size. Suriname seemed somehow to court oblivion. It had few diplomatic links and was often tangled up in sanctions. Visitors were deterred with a labyrinth of visas and a dearth of information. I never found a guidebook, and the only map I had was gleefully approximate.

The world, it seemed, had repaid Suriname by forgetting all about it. This must be one of the few countries that's produced at least five famous people without anyone knowing where it is (they are, incidentally, all footballers: Clarence Seedorf, Patrick Kluivert, Frank Rijkaard, Jimmy Floyd Hasselbaink and Ruud Gullit). Meanwhile, Suriname often ends up on the wrong continent. The Discovery Channel once placed it in Africa, and in the film, *The Silence of the Lambs*, it pops up in Asia. Things were no better under its temporary name, Dutch Guiana. Evelyn Waugh said it conveyed nothing to him (but then nor did anything Dutch). Even the Dutch thought it sounded too *Deutsch*, and in 1938 changed it back to Suriname.

These days, few places are so energetically misspelt. Voltaire called it 'Surinam', and ever since the French have followed suit. On Google there are now almost as many Surinams as Surinames. Even my map gets it wrong, and so does the national airline. But I like 'Surinam'. It has a mysterious quality which describes a land that's everything this isn't: ancient, rich, exploding with life and tucked into the margins of Indochina.

On the far bank I found a prophet to drive me to Nieuw Nickerie. He said that the taxi was only a temporary measure, and that for years he'd been waiting for someone like me. 'I want you to tell me what language this is', he said, slotting a tape into his deck.

From the speakers came the sound of muttering and birdsong.

'I don't know,' I said. 'Surinamese?'

The man grinned and shook his head.

As he was Indian, I tried Bengali.

'No, not Indian, not Dutch, not any words I know.'

'But it's your voice, isn't it?'

'Yes!' he said triumphantly, 'but I don't know what I'm saying!'

'So the words just came to you?'

'Exactly! I think they come from God.'

I'd been in Suriname an hour and already I could feel veils of incomprehension beginning to descend. At first everything had seemed normal: houses on stilts, oxen pulling carts of manure, canals cutting away to the horizon and wetlands bulging with rice. But then words appeared, and people. *LET OP!* said the road signs, and every little shack had *Kippen te koop*, or 'Chickens for sale'. Even more intriguing were the things that were forbidden. What pleasure, I wondered, was prohibited by '*Verboden voor Fietsers en*

Bromfietsers'? Bicycles and motor bikes, according to the Prophet. But there was another sign that said, '*Verboden te plassen'*. It seemed to mark the start of Nieuw Nickerie.

'Ah yes,' said the Prophet, 'that means "No wild pissing."'

Now we were among people and long rafts of vowels: Gouverneurstraat, Landingstraat and Oostkanalstraat. Everything dangled over water, and the canal banks were shored up with panels torn from cars. It was pretty, with its pink lilies and long waterways lined with palms and hatbox houses, and enormous creaking churches. I remember the sound of hymns coming from a bar, and an old crashed plane now serving as a nightclub. This is how Amsterdam would look if it were made from spare parts. It even had its own *zeedijk*, or sea wall, and a fleet of skiffs that sailed through the market. Water got everywhere. One area was called 'Bangladesh', because it was perpetually soggy. People didn't seem to mind this. In 1879 their entire town had slithered into the sea, and they'd simply retrieved what they could and anchored further up.

But most surprising of all were the people themselves. Where were all the Africans, with their flutes of bubbly and button-down collars? Almost everyone was Asian. I could see Chinamen in the shops, and Indonesians out in the mud. But the majority were Indian. The Prophet told me that, although *Hinduestanen* made up only a third of Suriname's population, here they ran the town. They also ran the rice fields, the gold claims, two television channels and dozens of political parties. This was like a corner of Bihar, translated into Dutch.

'You want me to give you a tour?' asked the Prophet.

'Thanks,' I said, 'but I've got a friend here.'

He frowned and switched off the birdsong.

That was the end of my encounter with the Prophet. Part of me still regrets not going on his tour. Suriname might have looked so much clearer through the lens of a seer. I often wonder at the experience I'd missed: two days, perhaps, of wild piss and wishful thinking, and a hotline to God.

It was true I had a friend in town, or at least a friend of a friend. Archie Kaw was a bootlegger, journalist and trader in old computer parts. Like Suriname itself, he was a composite of races. His great grandfather, he once told me, was from Uttar Pradesh, and had been so rich he'd ridden around on a white horse throwing coins to the poor. This was obviously a popular ploy, because soon there were Africans in the family tree, together with Scotsmen, *boeren*, Lebanese, Pathans and the occasional Sephardi. 'Shake a Surinamese tree,' as Archie would say, 'and a Jew always falls out.'

All this had left Archie looking oddly nondescript. This was useful, as he ducked around between his lives and wives. He always wore black sandals and black jeans, and shirts of forgettable orange. He also carried two mobile phones, which rang alternately every few minutes. One was for calls from the television station and required a voice that was solicitous and urgent. The other was for wives and clients, and required ridicule and charm. Archie always had to pause at the sound of the chimes. It was like being with a man with two heads, never quite sure which one he was. Then, once he'd found the person he needed to be, he either slumped in his chair or ran for the door. Often he'd be away for hours and would then slip back in as though nothing had happened.

It was obviously a delicate matter, being a mixture of colours. As in Guyana, status was a matter of shading. Being too dark would have made Archie merely a half-breed, known as a *Moksi*. Among other Indians, he'd have been lumped together with criminals, the Guyanese and those that pick bananas. But being too light, as Archie was, could also be a problem. It made him an outsider, both superior and slightly suspect. In this respect journalism was a perfect pedestal. It gave him just the vantage point he needed to administer the necessary levels of flattery and scorn.

Soon after we met, Archie took me to his television studio.

'What's the story today?' I asked.

'One of our leaders is making a donation, to repair the road.'

I nodded appreciatively. 'And what about crime?'

'A bit of smuggling, that's all ...'

He said they hadn't had a murder for years. That was impressive, I thought, for the nation's second city. 'Not really,' said Archie, 'they're all alcoholics. Can't get up without a rum.'

He was an unusual reporter. I soon realised that most of Archie's life was a matter of repackaging. Here in the studios he'd download a few hours of BBC, dub it in Sarnami and then send it back out. It was the same in his shop. The shelves were stacked with music that had been reclaimed, transferred onto disc and wrapped up in porn. Even the computers were re-packaged. Archie would take an old hard-drive, strip off the casing and replace it with a new one. 'There,' he'd say proudly, 'who's going to know?'

No one, it seemed. Nieuw Nickerie was full of fakes and counterfeits, fizzling cigarettes and clothes that shrivelled up and shrank as soon as you put them on. But none of this was making anybody rich, and – despite his own industrious contribution – Archie remained obstinately poor. Tourism was just his latest scheme, and that's where I came in. For a modest fee he'd feed me for two days, drive me around and put me up in his garage.

So that's how I ended up with a large pink room in a yard full of dogs. Whenever I went out, Archie had to gather them up and drag them to the side. I dreaded the telephone going at moments like this, and had visions of Archie dropping everything, vaulting the gates and leaving me alone with the pack. The only building within screaming distance was a brothel. It was made of old wet wood and had a neon sign across the front. *ALLEEN VOOR GASTEN* ('Only for Guests'), it proclaimed – rather needlessly, I thought. Archie once let slip that the girls were mostly Brazilian and charged twenty bucks an hour.

The next two days were partly Indian, and partly something else. At dawn I'd be woken by a muezzin and the response of the frogs. For breakfast we'd eat fried chickpea and samosas, dipped in ketchup. Then we'd be out in the rice, which Archie called the *achterland*, or boonies. Usually the farmers were already out, half-naked on the polders. Once we visited the creek where the water monkey lives and found it planted with prayer flags. Although we never saw the ogre, we did come across a pond full of giant crabs, and a tiny prehistoric fish called the *kwie-kwie*, which is like a rhinoceros with fins. Another time we went down to the *zeedijk* to drink some beers and ended up in a temple with the goddess of water, Ganga Mai.

Archie often talked about his ancestors. I was never quite sure whether he admired their enterprise or despised their credulity. He said they'd been coaxed here after the abolition of slavery in 1873. Many believed that they were coming to the Land of Ram. 'Can you believe it?' said Archie. 'They thought they'd come to heaven!'

Tens of thousands of Indians had followed. This great misconceived migration ended only in 1916, at the insistence of Mahatma Gandhi. But there could be no question of going home, or turning back the clocks. 'We were told,' said Archie, 'to make lots of children, and take this country over.'

Archie's own attempts at population had been somewhat sporadic. He had families, but never quite where he wanted them. Now there were the ringtones, a constant reminder of the pitfalls of the past. His latest girlfriend was called Shafiqah, and happened to be Javanese. 'The Indonesians,' he once told me, 'were the new slaves, imported to replace us.'

On my last morning Archie disappeared for hours, and so Shafiqah took over. She drove me out to her father's farm in a *kampong* on the padi. It was like life on an island, lapped by green. The family had only one modern possession, and that was a tiny car that gleamed like a jewel. Shafiqah's mother fried up some peanuts and liver, and then her sisters appeared, and giggled very neatly. I suddenly felt rather big and ungainly, as though I'd taken 'EAT ME' pills and ended up in Wonderland, among rabbits dressed in *klimbis*. We saw their father only once, way off in the rice. On his back he had a large tank of pesticide. '*Salaam alay-kum!*' he squeaked, and then faded away, beneath a billowing incubus of spray.

Shafiqah said it was time to go and look for Archie.

'Tomorrow, you'll see more rice,' she said, 'so much it makes you mad.'

It was indeed a lot of rice, but no worse than open sea.

I spent most of the next day sailing east in a minibus called Destiny. The driver was a friend of Archie's, known as 'Garage Ivan'. He was also Javanese, and had two pigtails and a tiny beard, no bigger than a coin. I think he liked the idea of a foreigner aboard and was always stopping for photographs and plunging off the road. The other two passengers, however, seemed to disgust him. One was an ancient Indian lady who was very publicly dying and had already turned pale green. The other was a prostitute returning to Brazil. She'd somehow managed to scoop herself into a bodice of crimson spandex and was now trying to explode her way out of it, on a diet of Coke and crisps. I often caught Ivan studying her in his mirror, as though she were some rare creature that had wriggled from the swamp.

For hours the view didn't change. Just occasionally we'd spot factories, like great silvery cathedrals, thrusting out of the rice. At some point we reached Wageningen, which was once – I'd read – the biggest fully mechanised rice farm in the world. We were still skimming over its land an hour later, and for an hour after that. Then, slowly, things began to change; lilies reappeared, followed by shrubs, bushes, scrub, trees, woods, cattle and then great, red patches of scorching savannah. By now the huge parallels of rice had fallen apart, and nature had reasserted its control. Ahead lay the other 90 per cent of Suriname, richly smothered in forest.

Soon there were signs of human life again. It wasn't much at first: a hut like a bonnet, or a child selling fish. But then, we were among *winkels* and *drempels*, or corner shops and speed bumps. The people here were different, I noticed: no longer Asian, but African or Creole. It was beginning to feel like another country, severed by the rice. I also noticed fishing boats, sailing through the trees, and a wooden church with a dainty little spire. A thought suddenly occurred to me. I'd once read of an improbable Utopia, known simply as 'Seacoast'. Perhaps this was it, or at least the start?

Garage Ivan said he'd never heard of Seacoast.

'Sorry, *baas*. You wanna stop?'

From the back rows there were sounds of pouting and pain.

'No, it's OK. But what are these villages called? This one, for instance?'

'This one?' said Ivan. 'This little place called Oxford.'

The tale of Seacoast is like that of Willoughbyland, except a century later, and without a New York.

It all begins with a beautiful idea. Britain will quietly expand into Dutch Guiana, to keep Napoleon out. At the same time honest crofters will be persuaded to leave their shabby, overcrowded islands and come to Guiana. Here they'll settle in lavish, scarlet soil and soon be lairds themselves. Their slaves will drain the land and carve out estates as big as any at home. It will be a beautiful Presbyterian land, rich in sugar and cotton.

By 1816 the plan is well under way. The Nickerie coast is now covered in polders with magnificent names like Waterloo, Hazard and Botany Bay (which will puzzle people for centuries to come). There is also a new Scotland in Coronie, beginning in Oxford and spreading out east. Here the Scots' slaves have been hard at work planting Scottish sugar. Among the cane there are now Scottish villages, each with a little spire: Burnside, Totness, Clyde, Inverness, Hamilton, Moy and Perseverance. The crofters are happy to be alone again, and accessible only by sea. They call their colony Seacoast because that is all it is.

But, the same year, the Dutch recover the land, under the Treaty of Paris. Most of the Scots, however, decide to stay. They have no Manhattan to swap, the profits are good, and the cotton grows high. All that troubles them is the malaria, which – would they only knew it – is now the most deadly on the continent. So it is that they live well here – and die rich, if long before their time. But, it won't last for ever, and the end comes when the price of cotton crashes. By then there are so few crofters left that they merge with the slaves. Eventually, all that will be left of them is a string of Scottish spires, and some curious African tribes, such as the MacDonalds and the McLeods.

But England – and its neighbours – have left Suriname with more than just a litany of names. Englishness haunts every aspect of this country's life. It's in the newspapers and on the radio; it percolates politics and contracts; it's at the heart of every love affair and the root of every murder; it's blown up on billboards and sprayed over walls. Often, it's all you'll hear from Coronie eastwards, and for 300 miles inland.

At first, it doesn't sound like English, but a simple babble of home-made slang. Then you realise it's both. Amid the syntactical chaos and the warm, round vowels of Africa something familiar emerges. A door's a *doro*, a boat's a *boto*, tomorrow's *tamara*, and enough's *onofo*. In English, the Surinamese will declare both their love for their country (*Mi Kondre Tru*) and their love for each other (*Mi lobi yu*). In English, too, they'll say they don't understand (*Me no ferstan*) or that you need to hurry (*Mekie hesie!*) or that everything's fallen apart (*alasani fuk-up*). Although Dutch may be the language of officialdom, Talkie-talkie, as it's called, remains the language of the hearth.

All this ought to make life easy for the Anglophone, and yet it doesn't. The chatter still sounds bewilderingly African, with its drumbeat accent and echoing words. Without an ancient vocabulary, things that are *fugufugu* and *kruwakruwa* become simply mysterious, instead of 'hairy' and 'half-done'. But it's not just African. Talkie-talkie is also riddled with Hebrew, French, Portuguese and *Spanyoro*. Rabbits, money and children (*Konkonis, plaka* and *pikins*) all owe something to the Spanish, and so does being thin, or *mangrimangri*. There's no real pattern to it; a hill may be Dutch (*bergi*) while the river is English (*liba*). Different languages seem to erupt everywhere. The Surinamese will greet the day in Dutch (*Morgu!*), meet their friends in Portuguese (*Odio!*), say goodbye in Spanish (*Adyosi!*), and then go to bed in English (*Ku'neti!*). Sometimes they'll hitch languages together to create highfalutin words such as *Grantangi*, the expression of great thanks.

But, at its core, Talkie-talkie is English. Often it's simplified English, with the words pared and rounded, or given an African echo. 'Noise', for example, becomes *bawli-bawli*, and 'knife' becomes a *neefi*. Sometimes this can give the language a nursery feel, as when things happened a long time ago (*langa langa*) or a very long time ago (*langa langa langa*). But it can also be both touchingly poetic ('good friends' are *skin-skin*) and brutally blunt. Requesting a drink, for example, may involve the phrase '*Watra osu killame*' (literally, 'Water or kill me'). This is clearly no ordinary English. It's the sort that's either spoon-fed to children or beaten into adults.

And that's the clue as to how it came about. It would be nice to think – as some do – that Talkie-talkie is merely a relic of Willoughbyland or Seacoast. But the English were never here long enough to leave their language behind. Instead, it's an idiom created not in Guiana or Africa but somewhere in between. It's the language of what was once the world's greatest industry, slavery – a matter in which England excelled. Simplified and abbreviated, it became the language of command. You can still hear the sound of the seventeenth century in the words that remain. A garden gate is a *nengre-doro* (negro door), the police are still 'scouts' (*skowtu*) and a young woman is a *wenke*.

That this slave argot survived is perhaps surprising. The Dutch, however, did little to discourage it and merely called it *Negerengels*, or Negro English. Then, for a while, it became a mark of ignorance, and children would have to wash their mouth out for speaking Talkie-talkie. But now, since independence, it's become a source of pride and is known as *Sranan Tongo* (or 'the tongue of Suriname'). It's even started growing again, to meet the demands of the modern world – although its neologisms still sound bosky and antique. A

Paramaribo slaves, circa 1830. In Suriname, slavery only ended in 1870, just short of the Age of the Car.

machine gun is a *dagadaga*, a plane is an 'iron bird' (or *isrifowru*) and all vehicles have become 'wagons' (or *wagis*). You know it's all over when the hearse turns up, otherwise known as the *dedewagi*.

It's surprising, too, how difficult, in its simplicity, this English has become. I realised from the start that I'd never really understand it. It was almost easier to admit defeat in Dutch: '*Het spijt me, Mijnheer, Ik spreek geen Talkie-talkie.*'

As Destiny rattled its way east, I moved up front and sat with Garage Ivan. I think he liked this arrangement. It was an opportunity for him to vent his full range of likes and dislikes in language that no one else would understand. As we sped along, through the enormous stands of coconut palms and the wreckage of old plantations, I was treated to his full spectrum of prejudice and preference. On the plus side, he liked Arsenal, Toyotas, his mother's cooking, all *Javaans* (except the songs recorded in Holland), dogs, Pringles and Mariah Carey. He wasn't sure about President Obama and detested

Michael Jackson. In fact, Africans were top of his other list, along with bicycles, spiders, the president, Ruud Gullit and all the Dutch. Everyone despised Holland, he said, and in Sranan it was known as *Patata Kondre*, or 'Potato-land'. They had no nice girls, just *Patata-umas*, or 'Spud-women'. 'And you know what? Holland has the best bridge-builders in the world, and they never built us one!'

At that moment a vast bridge appeared, across the Coppename.

'Then who built this one?'

Garage Ivan shrugged sulkily. 'Dunno. Maybe Cuba.'

Soon he was back on safer territory, railing at the Creoles. He said that all Africans ever thought about were drink, sex and coconuts. 'They just buy a couple of trees and some rum, and then settle down with a girl.' This rather pleasant-sounding idyll irritated Garage Ivan so much that he couldn't even bring himself to smile when people waved from the roadside. After a while I began to suspect that news of his hostility had travelled ahead of us up the coast, and so – by the time we got to the great Saramacca River – there was no one waving at all. The countryside had emptied once again. Those who'd once worked this land had now become city-dwellers, or *Stadsnegers* (as the Dutch called them) – or had long since fled, deep inland.

Since the collapse of Willoughbyland, the slaves who'd escaped had been quietly flourishing.

No one seemed to care that there was a little Africa re-forming, with its own languages and tribes. Over the next twenty-six years – to 1700 – they'd be joined by another 5,000 runaways. Some had come alone, some had fled after a revolt in 1690, and others had escaped from a powerful Jewish owner called Machado and called themselves 'The Matjau'. Another wave came after the French pirate Cassard sacked the coast in 1712. Soon there were so many of them that they became like tiny, truant nations, with their own kings and captains, and fancy names. Here, on this river, they were the Sara-maka, or Saramaccaners.

It wasn't long before the fugitives were forming little armies and plundering the farms. In time they'd have their own firelocks and lances, and could raid the coast at will. By 1726 the rebels were, as our old friend Bolingbroke noted, so numerous 'by accession of fresh runaways and by the natural fertility of their women, that they rendered the prosperity of the whites very insecure'. To English-men like him the runaways were also known as 'maroons', from the Spanish word *cimarrón*, meaning 'wild or untamed cattle'. But to the Dutch the loss of slaves had a more permanent feel – like a change to the landscape – and so they became known as the 'Bush Negroes', or *Bosnegers*.

So began what is known as the Age of Heroes. As with all heroic ages, there was plenty of random bloodshed. Outnumbered twenty to one by their slaves, the Dutch were forced to rule by fear. They were always lopping off tongues and testicles, but in 1730 they held a spectacle of horror: two girls were decapitated, six women were broken on the rack, two men were roasted alive, and another had an iron hook stuck through his ribs and was hung from a gibbet. Across the colony the slaves were outraged, and the maroons sought revenge. As Bolingbroke put it, 'white planters were in their turns hooked on trees or roasted alive'.

What followed was merely an age of mutilation. Suriname became a byword for brutality in the name of profit. In *Candide*, published in 1758, Voltaire's hero arrives here to be robbed by judges and sea captains, and to meet a slave who's been shorn of his limbs. ('That,' he says, 'is the price of your sugar in Europe'.) It's a moment of utter despair, the literary obverse of the road to Damascus. Candide finally renounces his faith in Providence and decides to head for home.

The Dutch, meanwhile, had no intention of giving up their sugar, although they would find an alternative to war. They suddenly realised the maroons could be bought – or 'pacified' – and that vast tracts of the jungle could be harmlessly signed away. It was gruesome diplomacy. The runaways now had leaders with names such as Zam-Zam and Captain Boston, who'd lived in the forest for much of their lives. At first, in 1757, the Dutch tried to fob them off with trinkets and baubles. The response of the fugitives was stark. 'Do Europeans imagine that Negroes can survive on combs and looking glasses?' replied Captain Boston, and the war began again. News of the Dutch weakness, meanwhile, filtered west, prompting – eventually – the revolt in Berbice.

It was another five years before the Saramaccaners signed a treaty. This time the Dutch provided proper gifts (muskets, ammunition, checked linen, canvas, beef spirits, saws, salt and hatchets), and the parties had to swear oaths and drink each other's blood. The formalities done, the Europeans were then treated to the best of the warrior women.

Under the treaty the Saramaka acquired a kingdom within a colony. The interior and the upper reaches of the river would devolve to the Saramaccaners, and each year the Dutch would recognise their sovereignty with not only gifts but also the flummery of office; for the captains there'd be uniforms and black canes with silver tops, and, for the *granman* a breastplate and a kingly tricorne hat. In return, the Saramaccaners would be faithful allies, they'd return all deserters and would never enter the whites' city, Paramaribo, in groups of more than six. Apart from two European emissaries who lived among them, the Saramaccaners had little contact with the outside world. Soon people could forget all about them, as though they'd never existed.

As we drove along the river, I asked Garage Ivan what had become of them.

'Go see for yourself,' he said. 'It's like Africa in there.'

Two weeks later I took this advice and flew up the river.

I'd managed to join a small group heading for a tributary of the Saramacca, known as Gran Rio. It was 170 miles inland, and as I rode along I realised how much the Saramaka had craved their solitude. Below, the trees looked like clubs of broccoli, packed tight from horizon to horizon. I could see the river, now thready and deranged, and tiny pocks of orange, gouged from the forest. These were gold mines, I realised, scraped away by miners, or *garimpeiros* ('One Brazilian and two girls', as people used to say). But then the broccoli would close in again, sucking out the light. Over the last year, I read, twelve previously unknown species had emerged from this vegetable wilderness, including a brand new frog that glows fluorescent purple.

Among our group there were several Dutch tourists, a Chinese girl called Mary (who worked for the government) and a photographer called Toon Fey. No name better describes this man. He was like a brilliantly animated shambles: Pooh with more punch, or Popeye without the spinach. Everywhere he went, he left a trail of passports, pens, memory sticks, anti-malarials and lenses. To some extent he'd dealt with this by covering himself with pockets. But, coupled with the fact that he was completely bald, this only made him look stranger still, like some sort of military egg. Despite all this – or perhaps because of it – I took to Toon, and he and I have been friends ever since.

It also turned out that he'd been married to a maroon for almost thirty years. Although nowadays she seldom left Holland, Toon was always popping over, to gather up the story. He'd now written three books about the maroons, and taken thousands of pictures. Few people had such a window on their remarkable world. Toon said there were over 50,000 maroons still living in the interior, making them easily the largest-ever group of runaway slaves. Although the Saramaccaners accounted for almost half of them, there were five other tribes: the Kwintis, N'Djukas, Bonis, Paramaccaners and Matawais. Until modern times they'd had nothing to do with each other and had never inter-married, and trespass had been a sure-fire cause for war. As for their relations with the coast, the anxiety has never really ebbed. The Creoles have spent over two centuries trying to pretend the maroons aren't there and only gave them the vote in 1963.

'Should we be anxious?' I asked Toon.

He smiled. 'Just careful. The Saramaccaners are good people. Maroons for beginners.'

No sooner had we landed than an eerie society seemed to fold in around us. Most of the men on that savannah wore short togas and carried rifles. For a while they closed in to watch us. They had hard, glossy limbs, and their hair was woven into thick braids like ship's rope. Some carried heavy loads on their heads – like chainsaws – and the braids acted as cushions, protecting the scalp. As for the togas, or *banjakoosus*, they were startlingly bright, and embroidered with bursts of colourful geometry.

For a moment no one said anything, and I had a sense of time standing still. Then the men gathered themselves and padded away, still watching us like cats. 'No photos,' muttered Toon. 'Not unless they say so.'

With the men gone, the women came forward to gather up the freight. They wore not togas but long strips of linen. It was checked linen, I noticed (just as Captain Boston had ordered in 1762). One piece, the *hangisa*, fastened round the waist and was a repository for babies and knives. Another piece was tied around the breasts, with a little tail down the back. 'Beautiful women,' said Toon approvingly, 'and – look – there's one not married.'

'How can you tell?' I asked.

'Ah,' he said, 'it's all in the length of the tail.'

At that moment the tribe's guide appeared and introduced himself as Heer Nootje, or 'Mr Nut'. He was well bellied, short and powerful, and had an enormous, wiry moustache. I don't think he noticed how few of us there were, and began to address us as a rally. Although I'd come to enjoy Nootje eventually, I didn't just then. As he embarked on his not very welcoming Welcome, it occurred to me that this is how Stalin would have looked if he'd been black and had worn a toga with rolled-down rubber boots, a pea-green shirt, a string of glass beads and a flat cap. Perhaps I shouldn't have been so surprised by the nonchalance of this first encounter. Here is what the American anthropologist Morton Kahn had to say about his experience of the Saramaccaners, in 1929: 'The traveller is struck by the fact that Bush Negroes are not subservient in any degree. While they are not inhospitable, one feels one is being tolerated rather than welcomed ...'

A hint of indifference seemed to follow us upriver. It was a beautiful day, and Nootje marched us through the grass and down to the reach at Kajana. There a dugout was waiting. It was made from a single tree and was patched with tin and decorated with brass nails. Beside it sat the crew, who, when they saw us slithering down the bank, rose slowly to their feet. There were no greetings, just functional shrugs and grunts. The head boatman couldn't even bring himself to glance at us and simply stood at the prow looking heroically detached. I noticed that, beneath his toga, he wore white canvas breeches and a cutlass. It was Toon who broke the ice, addressing him in formal Saramaccan.

'*U dë nö?*' he asked. Are you still alive?

The boatman swung round sharply, and almost smiled.

'*U dë oh!*' Yes, he said, I'm still alive.

The crew held out like this for almost two days, hardly acknowledging our presence. It was the same on the river. Up in the rocks we could see people scrubbing pans, and naked children casting lines and cleaning catfish. No one ever waved back; they just looked at us as though we were bad weather or hard work. Even when – later – we got to the tribes' guesthouse, the mood was barely more than that of tolerance. The manager had left a message saying that, although he would like to have met us, he had much too much to do. That left only the cooks to register our arrival, which they did by bursting into song. Clearly, the entertaining of *baccras*, or whites, was the work of the women.

Only one man seemed to like us, and he was candidly insane. Pingo, or 'Peccary', was one of the boatmen and had a misshapen skull and a face too small for his tongue. Although he couldn't speak, he was lavishly affectionate, and for some reason I became his favourite. He was always finding me giant ants and caterpillars, and one day he brought me a magnificent skull, which had once belonged to a tapir. I liked the idea that he was the only Saramaccan who'd ever forgiven the whites. For everyone else the disdain was congenital, and *patata-men* were now eternally malevolent. It was impossible to see them in any other way – except, of course, through the prism of insanity.

The little Africa created by Captain Zam-Zam and others is still a world of secrecy and refuge. Apart from the children and the pot-washers, we could see little from the river. Occasionally we might glimpse a cluster of canoes, with their tiny, spear-shaped oars, or an archway made of leaves, but then the water would catch our keel and hurl us back into the currents. The trees gave nothing away, except the steely squeal of insects. Once we saw a sloth, like a sniper in the branches, and another time there was an explosion of blue sparks, which turned out to be kingfishers, scattering over the water. I began to wonder what had happened to the villages marked on my map.

'They're all around,' said Nootje, 'you just need to look.'

After that, he started shouting names at the shadows. Some way back was Logolio, he said, the only Christian village, but this was Deböö, the one that means 'I'm Free'. Then there was Godowata ('The Wasp Nest on the Water'), and a tall, steep bank of weeds that was supposed to be Stonhuku. Suddenly I realised that we'd just ridden through the heart of Saramaka territory and barely seen a thing. We hadn't even spotted their fields.

'They're deep in the forest,' said Nootje, 'way out of sight.'

After that I saw nothing until we reached the guesthouse, seven miles upstream. It was a pretty place called Awaradam, built on an island of granite and grass. Along one bank, under the kookoo trees, were a cluster of huts and a great hall, woven from paralu and tash. Whenever it rained, toads clambered out of the bushes and stood on the paths belting out their songs. But most of the time it was hot, and lizards held the stage. They were usually tegus – each four feet long – and would spend all day on the lawns, taxiing up and down like little airliners, waiting for their wings.

Along one wall of my hut was a beautiful toga, behind which lived a colony of bats. At some stage during the night they'd stop squeaking, and then all I'd hear was the mesmerising rumble of water. Silly *baccra* huts, I thought, as I drifted off to sleep. Zam-Zam would never have built here, so open to attack.

At dawn we were woken by a pounding sound, which Nootje said was 'the talking drums'. The river was already busy. We could see the gunmen coming home, with a monkey or some toucans, all extravagantly dead. It was said that the maroons ate whatever their ancestors had eaten but were suspicious of creatures unique to this continent. The ocelot, for example, was associated with leprosy, and the armadillo was a god.

'I'd like to see their village,' I said.

'That could be difficult,' said Toon, 'We're going to need some gifts.'

Visiting the Saramaccans has never been easy. There have always been protocols, rituals, hierarchies to be consulted and demands for penitence and presents. (Even within living memory the Dutch were still paying tribute.) At the heart of all this was the desire to be aloof. Modern anthropologists, such as Richard Price, say that their flight from slavery still defines the Saramaccans. They suffer a collective dread of re-enslavement, and so solitude is like an affirmation: we are because we're alone. In fact, they've now been separated so long they don't even speak the same Talkie-talkie, but one more tuneful and introverted, and richly suffused with old West African languages, such as Twi and Kromanti.

When we told Nootje about our plans, he listened carefully and then made a speech. In it he stressed the need for deference and gifts, but particularly the gifts. He also said that he would have come with us, except he was far too busy. Instead, he'd find us a canoe, and a boatman called Edi. Another canoe would go on ahead to warn the village we were coming. Meanwhile we busied ourselves assembling a tribute and came up with a Hacketts shirt, a Swiss Army knife, a packet of Polos and a bottle of rum. It was a good haul, we felt, although in all probability it wouldn't stop a war.

We stopped first at the bank of weeds and clambered up to Stonhuku. At the top of the slope there were two paths, one for women and the other for men. Edi put us on the right path, and we set off through the forest, wondering how different a female path could be. According to Kahn, women in Saramaccan culture are like alien beings. For a start, they own everything, and – paternity being such an uncertain science – all property passes down the female line. But they're also dangerous. A woman's uterine fluids are potentially lethal, and during menstruation she cannot touch babies, skin game, clear forest, carry water or share a man's canoe. Small wonder she has her own path.

After ten minutes we came to another arch made of leaves.

'The beginning of the village,' said Toon.

The arch, or *azanpau*, was a sort of spiritual security check. All visitors had to pass through it, and if they didn't they were immediately suspect. Maroons, it seemed, lived in a constant state of mystical alert. Treachery was everywhere, says Price, and revenge could reappear at any moment, having lain dormant for centuries. Existence was a constant struggle to right the wrongs of the past. Even the killing of animals required atonement, and as we came to a clearing we passed the shrines built to snakes. Each was like a tiny temple, built from oil drums and furnished with old Dutch gin flasks and glasses for the ghosts. Although there is a greater being (the *Gran Gadu*), Edi said that all animals were sacred, particularly the caiman and the boa.

That was as much as we ever saw of Stonhuku.

'Wait here,' said Edi, 'while I go find the captain.'

After fifteen minutes he returned, alone.

'I have found a man who knows the *basia* …'

'Great,' said Toon, 'then perhaps he can ask?'

'No. The man has no authority to summon him.'

There our visit stalled. We walked back to the river, got back in the boats and moved on to Kajana. Just as before, there were the snake-shrines and an arch, and a walk through the forest. We also came across a much larger altar, which included a crucifix mounted with a bony wooden head, and draped in shredded togas. Toon said it was hard to know what the Saramaccaners believed, because they seldom explained. When the first anthropologists arrived, people thought they were thieves who'd come to steal their stories. 'The white man steals everything,' said Toon, 'even their words.'

Then, suddenly, we were in the village. It was like being in a field of furniture. Each house was made from rattan and polished hardwood, and had tiny cupboard doors. Only the lintels were decorated, with brocades of fretted wood. Every design was a work of perfect symmetry and yet rigorously abstract. The same patterns were repeated on ladles and drums, and on elaborate combs with four-inch teeth. How could people who lived such wild, approximate lives be so geometric in their thoughts? But it wasn't an unbroken pattern; menstruating women had their own cabinets outside the village, and the collapsed houses belonged to the dead and could never be touched again. There was also a small shop, or *winkel*, which sold beer, copper kettles and gaffer tape.

'And this is the *basia*,' said Edi formally.

The village captain lived near a big tree, where the togas dried. He had a large radio, and through his open door I could see he'd decorated his hut with pictures of white girls, torn from a calendar. I could also see an old champagne bottle and a solar helmet hanging from a nail. The captain, meanwhile, was sitting on a large winged stool, like the one that appears on the flag of Ashanti. He didn't move as we approached, and, although he must have been eighty, he was wearing a glossy new football shirt that seemed to shimmer in the heat. Toon greeted him in Dutch and explained that I was an *Englesman*. Although the captain was clearly unsure about the implications of this, he said he'd once worked in Cayenne, and so I could address him in French.

'*Nous avons rendu des cadeaux*,' I said.

The captain surveyed the gifts and nodded. He apologised for not wearing his uniform but said he'd not been expecting visitors. He told me he had a brown uniform and a black cane with a silver top. He also said he was proud to have served his people and sent his greetings to Queen Beatrix. He hoped his sons would be captains too. He had eight of them, and they had all married well, although the virgins were expensive.

'*Voulez-vous voir les femmes dansantes?*'

I said I'd like it very much, to see the women dance.

The captain seemed pleased, and told us to come back at sunset. There were only a few hours to wait. Meanwhile, the women assembled at the shop. The oldest of them was around seventy and the youngest about ten. I recognised some cooks from the guest-house, and a beautiful girl whom I'd seen skinning monkeys.

Soon everything was ready. As darkness fell, unseen drums burst into life, and the women began to dance. First, they did the *Sëkëti*, a secretive ritual from the days of slavery. One lot of dancers would clap a message with their hands, and the rest would reply, stamping their feet. After that, the men danced, hurling each other high in the air on a pair of parallel poles. Then the women were back, more lethal than ever. Their last dance, the *Bandamba*, was a display of unexpurgated sexual prowess. In perfect time to the drums, the dancers would roll their buttocks and abdomen, and thrust out their breasts. Soon even the children were drenched with sweat, but the rhythm never faltered. When Kahn saw this dance in 1927, a man was inveigled into the group and worked up into a state of 'actual coitus'. I don't know what this says about Saramaccan women: that they're exploited, perhaps? Or no better than slaves? Kahn didn't think so. Women were in charge of their sexual destiny, and a good woman had to be earned.

After this, the talking drums throbbed away till midnight. At some stage we slipped away and returned to our canoe. It was an uneasy journey back, with the rocks sucking and gurgling, somewhere in the dark. But Edi didn't seem to notice the night and took the rapids at full tilt. According to Nootje, only one aspect of the river worried the boatmen and that was the *ogri*. He described it to me once. It was like the water monkey anywhere, except this time brutally white.

On our last day death intervened, and life on the river came to a halt. The cooks didn't sing, the drums stopped and the hunters disappeared. Nootje turned up in satin baseball pants and a sombre waistcoat, and Edi didn't seem to recognise us, as though we'd never met. Even Pingo picked up the mood of the day and cried like a cat.

Nootje said that today was the funeral of an old lady.

'When did she die?' I asked.

Nootje thought for a moment. 'Three weeks ago.'

'Three *weeks* ...!'

'Sure. We kept her preserved in oil and herbs.'

'Well,' whispered Toon, 'it's probably good we're moving on.'

All death, I learned, revives the spectre of revenge. No man's death is natural, and the death of a woman is an insult to the accepted order. Every death is therefore a crime, reaching out from the deeds of the past. With their obsession for justice, no Saramac-caner can ignore this crime, and so each death prompts an inquiry. These days the quest is more ceremonial than forensic, but the body is still kept until it's so putrefied that the fluids run clear. In Kahn's time the fluids were offered to all – as a drink – and it was felt that, by his refusal, the murderer would reveal himself. Nowadays this divination takes a slightly healthier form, with the carcase merely hauled from house to house. 'Is this the man that killed you?' says the sorcerer, as they stop at every door. It's a long and gruesome day.

'And then what happens to the corpse?' I asked Nootje.

It's buried, he said. No one ever visits it again, and the site becomes taboo.

So it was that the river emptied, the forest fell silent and the Sara-maka disappeared. Just as they had in 1762.

But that year was not the end of the struggle. One lot of maroons may have been rendered compliant, but there was far worse to come. Ahead lay a tribe so neurotic and lethal that they would bring them-selves almost to the brink of extinction. The war that they re-kin-dled has never truly ended, and the country that should have been paradise still shudders at their memory. By 1768 they were poised to fall on Paramaribo, perhaps the world's most fanciful city.

7

PARAMARIBO

Paramaribo is handsome, rich and populous; hitherto it has been considered by far the finest town in Guiana.

Charles Waterton, *Wanderings in South America*

All the luxuries, as well as the necessaries of life, abounded; every sense was apparently intoxicated with enjoyment; and to use the figurative language of a sacred book, Surinam was a land that flowed with milk and honey. But this delusive felicity lasted not long ...

John Stedman, *Expedition to Suriname*

I once read that sex is the most popular pastime in Suriname.

Andrew Westoll, *The River Bones*

IF I WERE TO DESIGN THE PERFECT CITY, it would be white and have a river running through it. There'd be plantations and fruit trees all around, and little canals would come seeping through the centre. There'd be no business district or overbearing banks, and nothing would be taller than a church. At the heart of it all would be a little purple fortress, like a hat full of mansions. There'd be no trains or tubes or public toilets. This would be one of the greatest cities of the eighteenth century. Everything would be built from wood and handmade bricks, and next to the fort there'd be a huge palm garden, where once an army planted beans. By day the presidential palace would glow like a wedding cake, and then by night it would turn green and flare like a planet. As for embassies, there'd be only nine, including a tiny bungalow for the entire United States. Temples, however, would spring up out of the foliage, along with stupas, pagodas and funeral ghats. There'd also be a mosque and a synagogue, huddled so close that they'd share a car park. This would not be a city of ghettos or new ideas. Over half the country would live here, and between them they'd speak over twenty different languages. Without parental consent no one could marry until the age of thirty, and it would be quite common to have giant rallies protesting at obesity. Meanwhile, the police would be called the *korps politie*, and would wear white gloves and ride around on bicycles. There'd also be an alligator living in the city's pond, eating all the strays.

That, broadly speaking, describes Paramaribo. So what went wrong? How did it get forgotten?

I spent my first day falling in love with Paramaribo, and then the rest of my time wondering quite why. It wasn't that I ever fell out of love, just that after a while things stopped making sense. Although the city was never conspiratorial like Georgetown, it could still be mind-bogglingly obscure. How had it ended up with square coins, for example, and a banknote for 2½ dollars? Why was the newspaper called the *Times of Suriname* and yet published in Dutch? And why were all the advertisements in 'English' English, a language only a few understood? The big poster at the time depicted a woman in a state of advanced ecstasy, under the banner 'Did you already find spice?' I simply couldn't imagine what she wanted me to buy. Her tiny dress? Condoms? Delay spray? Or just marjoram and dill?

Everything began well when I booked into a guesthouse called Albergo Alberga. It was a large Victorian building with a slave-house at the back. For the first few days, until he flew home, Toon had a room on the ground floor. My room was up in the eaves, and from it I could look all the way down Heerenstraat. This was a street of little wooden banks, and each night a small army of gunmen would appear and settle in the porches. We even had one on our porch, who took a shine to the pretty black actress in the room next to Toon's. She was also from Holland and was here to discover her roots. It can't have been an edifying experience, because after a week her hair began to straighten and her face broke out in spots.

Other guests, however, were Surinamese, just visiting the city. One had a very young baby which she once left on reception. As the girl on the desk had never handled a baby before, she asked me for help. For a while we debated whether to give it a carton of milk, and then decided we should. The baby seemed to thrive on this and was slightly disappointed when, an hour later, her mother returned, covered in parcels and gratitude and a large statue of Ganesh. 'This place gets worse and worse!' she panted. 'You can never get what you want!'

When I told Toon about this, he merely smiled.

'But isn't that odd?' I insisted. 'Don't you think that's strange?'

'Everything's a bit crazy here. You should try the shopping.'

I soon found out what he meant. Up behind Heerenstraat was a neighbourhood of shops. They all looked relatively normal at first, large clapboard buildings selling jeans and drums and camouflaged crossbows. But then I noticed that the largest shop sold only Christmas baubles, and that some places only opened at lunchtime or on Wednesdays or for a few hours at dawn. They never seemed to open together, and even when they did, that's when the confusion began. Things often cost half as much as it said on the label, and occasionally double. Worse, some items, such as cloth, were still measured out in Rhenish *els*, or they'd slip you an extra three-eighths of an inch by trading in Dutch feet. I once tried to buy something and found myself sucked into a Soviet queuing system, joining a line to pay, a line to get a receipt and then finally – twenty minutes later – a line to pick up my biro. Far more straightforward was the witches' market, where you could buy anything from a cure for husbands to a bundle of tampons grown in the forest.

Turning right out of the guesthouse, the street led downhill towards the river. This was the Paramaribo I loved. The street opened up into a large grassy field known a little grandly as Independence Square. Around the edge were palm trees and mangos, the wedding cake palace and a splendidly crooked old courthouse, the Hof van Justi-tie, which looked like the backdrop to a Rembrandt.

At first I was troubled by the thought that perhaps the only reason I liked all this was because it was familiar, and that I might simply be homesick. But then I noticed that everyone else loved it too, and that each afternoon people would appear with kites and easels, or would dance in the grass. It was hard to think of a city that looked so readily happy. Sometimes the army would appear, thrashing their drums and tootling pipes. Or it might be a troupe of kung fu fighters, or the Rastafarians, with their buckets of cold sweet mush, keenly known as *schaafijs*.

Because I looked so foreign and unhurried, people often talked to me. I never knew what they really wanted, although their requests were intriguing. Usually they wanted to know whether I had a mobile, but once someone asked me if I'd come and change the oil in his car. Another time I was questioned about the snow in England, and whether we had *wintis*, or spirits. Occasionally I was approached by maroons, in their breeches and checked linen. Although they spoke only Talkie-talkie, they were enthusiastic salesmen. One tried to interest me in a live boa constrictor, and, when that failed, he started mimicking an ape. It was quite common to see monkeys chained up to trees, but he kept insisting, '*Yapiyapi switi! Yapiyapi switi!*'

'No *ferstan*,' I'd say. '*No ferstan*.' I don't understand.

Eventually he gave up and moved off, still muttering '*Yapiyapi*.'

That evening I asked the girl at the Alberga what he'd been saying.

'Nothing really,' she said sweetly, 'just that monkey tastes delicious.'

At the far end of the grassy square was the little purple fort. For some reason people didn't like it down here, under the trees. There was something about it that seemed to repel them, and so I often had the riverbank all to myself. It became my favourite place in the city, with its abandoned cannon, its biscuity ramparts and a scattering of marble heads. It also happened to be the last remnant of Willoughbyland, the original Fort Willoughby, and the beginning of Dutch Guiana. On 27 February 1667 Abraham Crijnssen had scrambled over its shellstone walls and claimed the fort for Holland. After that, it would get a new name – Fort Zeelandia – and a new little town inside, like a miniature Amsterdam.

It took me weeks to get inside. Although it was now a museum, its opening hours were – like the shops' – impressively quixotic. All I could do was walk around the outside peering up at the walls. It was a pentagon, I noticed, with its two biggest bastions thrusting into the river. No one would tell me what it was about the fort that so appalled the city, or why everyone shrank away. Most people I met said they'd never been inside and probably never would. So, with little else to go on, I simply assumed that the *wintis* had been at work, and that the place was somehow cursed. A far less easy explanation would just have to wait.

At night the city was like a theatre closing down, and then secretly reopening. First the actors stepped into the wings, then the audience left, and then out went all the lights. I've never known a place so dark. A few of the main streets were lit, although even then it was more like orange gas than light. Often the only way I could get around was by starlight or by the glint in the canals. But it was still a perfect city, or almost perfect. The air crackled with bats and nightjars, and the darkness smelt of earth. Eventually, even the distant traffic would die down, and so there'd be no sound but the hum of the forest.

That's when the new cast appeared. There weren't many of them: scavengers and cleaners, the watchmen with their little fires, the maroons that lived in the *palmentuin,* the drunks, the lovers, the conscripts with nowhere to stay, and the wild girls who tottered out of the bushes, hissing in Sranan. Occasionally, I'd bump into someone who didn't seem to belong in this scene at all, such as a pedlar selling hammocks, or a lone rackler, out with his songbird.

What puzzled me was where everyone else was. Downtown, almost everything shut as soon as it got dark, including the restaurants. There were only a few places open. One was called Café 't Vat, which was popular with the Dutch, who liked to huddle together, like a wagon train under the lights. Another was an old warehouse, with a vast pair of scales. According to Toon, a lot of people thought these were for weighing slaves, and so no one used to go there. That left only the old harbour wall, the 'Red Steps', down on the Waterkant.

The Red Steps were like a stage within a stage. Odd characters were always pitching up here with things to sing or sell. One man had a trolley covered in love-hearts, and another sold little stuffed alligators, wearing hats and bras, and with huge glass eyes. It was also the place to buy something to eat and a *jugo,* or bottle of beer. I always liked ordering food from these stalls because everything sounded like jazz. There was *Olie Bollen, Pom, Bami Kip*, and *Pinda Soep* with *Tom Tom* (or, more prosaically, oily bread, yam, chicken noodles and peanut soup with plantain). On Toon's last night we went down there to find that we had ten food stalls all to ourselves.

'Where is everyone?' I gasped. 'Don't people ever eat?'

'Not at night,' said Toon, 'they go to the casino.'

'What? Everyone?'

'Not quite. But the city's pretty hooked.'

'And who's paying for it all?'

'I don't know. Holland, probably.'

'Holland?'

'Sure. We got an aid package worth over a billion dollars.'

This has to be seen, I thought. A game of development poker.

Toon refused to come with me. He said he hated the casinos and was too much of an old hippy. A few days later, however, I sought them out myself. They weren't hard to find. In this star-sprinkled city they were their own galaxies, exploding with light. Or were they black holes? It seems that everyone had been sucked in: Indians, Creoles, Javanese, the old, the young, the witless, matrons, manikins, whole families of suits, wives like carthorses and mistresses like ponies, a priest, a man with no nose, a table of schoolgirls, an elderly Jewess trimmed in rabbit, and a pair of twins, both famine-thin and wearing matching bodices of rubber. I could also see waiters battling their way through this gaudy throng, with more trays of *pom* and *bami kip* and flutes of champagne. Then I spotted Mary, the Chinese girl I'd met on the Saramaka trip.

'What a surprise,' I said.

'Yes,' she beamed, 'except we're here every night!'

Behind her were her family, glittering with accessories and whisky.

'Oh, is this your family's business?'

Mary laughed drily, 'Don't you know what this place is?'

'A casino?'

She leaned her face into mine, so close I felt her hair on my cheek.

'A washing machine,' she whispered. 'Cleans up the drug money.'

I didn't know what to say, but Mary carried on.

'It's all imported,' she said, glancing at the rubber twins, 'even the girls.'

After that I didn't go back to the casinos, although this left me with a problem. With everyone squashed inside, how would I ever experience Paramaribo at night? I had only three contacts. One ran a tug-boat company, and the other two were revolutionaries, old comrades of Dr Roopnaraine in Georgetown. I tried one of the Marxists first. All I knew is that, after one of the military coups, he'd become some sort of minister. After that the trail went cold. They told me at the Alberga that he was dying of cancer. But then someone told me he'd been in court on a sex charge, perhaps involving children, and so I abandoned the search.

Ah well, I thought, every Garden of Eden has to have its snakes.

The excesses of today were nothing, I realised, compared with the decadence of 1769. Not even Demerara and the Berbice could compare, despite all that Malmsey and sausage. That was just hoggishness, over-sexed bumpkins and a surfeit of grog. Paramaribo was altogether different. It was like Rome at the moment it ruptured, except a fraction of the size and ten times as torrid. It even had Roman law, citadels, colonnaded courts and a society of slaves. There were few other places with such a concentration of wealth and such a dearth of restraint. Whenever the governor had a banquet, the gentlemen at his table would enjoy the best crystal and silver, and his most beautiful girls, perfumed and half-naked.

Amid such bacchanalian splendour a wealthy man could want for nothing. He might live on Heerenstraat, or down on the Waterkant, which was paved in seashells and planted with tamarinds and lemons. His would be no ordinary house but a fine wooden mansion, furnished with gilt mirrors and chandeliers, and richly panelled in cedar. The master would sleep in a magnificent hammock, over which there'd be a fine awning to deter the insects, or a slave would appear and take off her blouse to swat away the gnats. It's often mischievously thought that the great fires which so often swept the city were acts of retribution, directed by God. Today only a few of these great houses remain.

But more remarkable than the great Paramaribo mansion was the appearance of the merchant himself. It wasn't just the absence of vitality, or the excess of everything else. Visitors from Holland had never seen so much bling. As one put it: 'Their carriages and dress are truly magnificent: silk embroidery, Genoa velvets, diamonds, gold and silver lace, being worn daily, and even the masters of the trading ships appear with buttons and buckles of solid gold ...' As though all this dressing up wasn't enough, our baubled knight even had his own theatre, in which he could entertain his friends. In fact, his whole life was like a very short play, in which he'd make a dramatic entrance, debauch all the extras and then die in Act I.

Naturally, while he was alive, he could have whatever he wanted, and very often did. Like today, everything was imported, from carriage clocks to women. If, for a moment, his needs weren't met, he had only to blow his ivory whistle. Across the city there were some 75,000 slaves attending a mere 5,000 Europeans.

In the stew of Paramaribo slavery was always the volatile component. As in Rome, all that sustained it was the idea of disproportionate dread. No transgression could ever be worth the penalty that inevitably followed. Here the colony surgeon was as busy as anywhere, lopping off limbs at £6 a go. But the merchants could not rely on amputation alone. That year, 1769, slaves would not only have spikes driven under their nails; they'd also be impaled on hooks and pulled apart by horses.

It wasn't just men doing this, but also Dutch women. Frustrated by their husbands' Olympian feats of infidelity, the wives often took it out elsewhere. 'They are also rigid disciplinarians,' wrote a diarist of the day, 'as the backs of their poor slaves, male and female, sufficiently testify.' In one incident a pretty slave girl was given a hundred lashes for breaking a piece of china. It was quite common for slaves to kill themselves, usually by jumping out of a window. The Dutch women were never punished for their excesses. One used to get particular satisfaction from beating the breasts of her girls, while another once stabbed a 'quadroon' with a red-hot iron, killing her at once. It's hard now to imagine how they worked up such hatred, and I've often wondered whether in the Sranan term 'potato-women' there isn't a lingering hint of revenge.

Slavery, however, wasn't just killing slaves; it was also killing the slavers. The abundance of everything was suffocating. There was even talk of a 'vortex of dissipation'. Men would do whatever they dreamed and then drown in their fantasies. Drink and the pox killed most, but some just faded away. Meanwhile the wives seemed to survive. Often they were widowed two or three times before they found another rake. It was almost as though the city was about some gruesome masque, dancing itself to death.

Then, amid the fiddles, came the sound of Rome, catching fire. Maroons had surrounded the city, and were closing in for the kill.

The arrival of maroons in the city still caused anxiety. I couldn't always tell who was a maroon and who wasn't. Some were easily recognisable by their togas and breeches, or by their bags of herbs and snakes. Or it might be the slightly superior strut, and the air of defiance. But even when maroons wore jeans and a smile, the Creoles still knew who they were. 'They talk like animals,' said a man I met on the foodstalls, 'and they act like them too.'

I said that didn't sound like the Saramaccaners.

'They're not so bad,' he said. 'The N'Djukas are filthy.'

Many maroons now lived in the city, although there were plenty just visiting. They called Paramaribo '*Foto*', as though it was still just a fort. I often saw the new arrivals on Saramaccastraat, at the end of the Waterkant. This was the drop-off point for the country buses, little *wagis* all crudely daubed in girls. Often the maroons just seemed to settle wherever they alighted, making their home on the street. Some sold back-scratchers or bushmeat, but others just issued their demands: cigarettes, drinks, attention, menaces or money. They were fascinated by the girls and were always panting and squeaking at them, even the children. But it was worse for shopkeepers. They'd now dreaded the maroons for over two centuries (ever since the first treaties, and the arrival of Saramaccaners – six at a time – swaggering around with their silver-topped canes). In 1960 V.S. Naipaul wrote that only violence would resolve the tension between the city and the country. They were prophetic words for a man only passing through.

Although I couldn't distinguish them, I probably saw maroons from almost all the different groups. The only tribe I wouldn't have seen were the Bonis, or Alukus. They were different from the others. It was said that they even had their own impoverished language, Aluku-tonga, with no word, for example, for 'yellow' (they had to describe things as 'bird fat'). By reputation, they were also shorter and less affable: bold soldiers but poor carriers. According to the Danish explorer Henry Larsen – writing in the '50s – every Boni had a beautiful, tender childhood until the age of ten and was then jolted into adulthood. After that it was a life stripped of affection. Men were even despised by their women, for whom love was rare and infidelity began early. ('It was the sensual experience that was

valued,' wrote Larsen, 'and the identity of the male who provided
it was a matter of minor importance'.) Perhaps that's why the Boni
version of the water monkey was female and sexually insatiable. It
may also explain why the tribe were often thought of as a lost generation. They were maroons at their most extreme: quarrelsome,
volatile and persistently vindictive.

Later I'd catch up with the Bonis – but not here. They'd never
signed a treaty or drunk blood with the Dutch. They hated the other
maroons and had never emerged from the forest. The last time they
came to Paramaribo was in 1769, when they'd held the city by the
throat.

The Bonis see themselves not as delinquent but as a cleansing
scourge.

While the planters were drinking away their faculties, this new
group of fugitives gathered in the swamps along the coast. They'd
found a perfect natural hideaway, a spur of jungle 100 miles long,
bounded on one side by the sea and on the other by a river called the
Cottica. At the heart of their refuge was a citadel called Boucou, or
'Mould' (it would rot, they said, before it ever fell). It was a daunting little fortress, defended with mantraps, stolen swivel-guns and
underwater paths. Getting maroons out of there would be like trying
to winkle shadows from a maze-within-a-maze, to say nothing of
the disease and heat, the constant bog and the benighted forest.

Encouraged by the success of the Saramaka, the Bonis rose in
revolt. Here, in the words of a Dutch soldier, is what happened:

The most beautiful estates in the settlement, called plantations, were
once more seen, some blazing in flames and others laid in ashes,
while the reeking and mangled bodies of their inhabitants were scattered along the banks of the River Cottica, with their throats cut
and their effects pillaged by their own negroes, who all fled to the
woods, men, women and children, without exception.

By 1769 the 'Cottica Rebels' (as the Dutch called them) had reached
Paramaribo and were setting fire to the edges of the city.

Bloated and luxurious, the planters were unable to respond.
Although the company that ran the colony, the Society of Suriname,
had its own army, they were the 'outcasts of all nations', with barely
anyone fit enough to fight. So the company did what any good

company would, and paid someone else. As the only men left were slaves, it was slaves that they employed. This ought to have been the end of Suriname, and yet in some ways it was only the beginning. Even today, it is a country with two minds: one urbane and slightly dissolute, the other wild and ascetic.

The Society's gamble paid off. The Neger Vrijcorps (or 'Negro Free Corps') was never short of volunteers. For some, it was the simple promise of food and freedom. For others, it was about self-preservation; they didn't want to throw in their orderly, relatively prosperous lives and become like the savages within. But there were also a few who just wanted their old lives back, Africa's cycle of warfare and booty. The Dutch promised them 25 florins for every hand that they recovered, dried and smoked in the normal way.

By 1772 the colony had a force of over 300 'Black Rangers'. They would prove to be better than any Society troops, and just as loyal. (The entire Vrijcorps was commanded by four white men, known as 'Conductors'.) They were also perfectly adapted to this swamp warfare. Each ranger was armed with a sabre and a flintlock, which he mastered with ease, and – out of preference – he tended to fight naked, except for breeches and a scarlet cap which bore his number. He was assiduously obedient and wore an amulet of metal and bones that made him both invincible and euphoric in the fight. Before long, the Red Caps, or *Rode Mutsen*, were fanning out along the Cottica, hacking off hands and gathering florins.

Later that year they arrived at Boucou itself. After a short but inconceivably violent struggle the hideout was captured. It was not, however, the end of the rebellion – far from it. After this, the Bonis would disperse throughout the Cottica basin, losing themselves in over 2,000 square miles of primary forest. Just to prove that the war was only just getting dirty, they captured twelve rangers as they left. Eleven of them had their throats cut, and the twelfth was sent back to his comrades, with his ears, lips and nose all crudely sliced away. He was just able to convey the horror of the day before he also died.

The Dutch weren't sure which worried them more: the Bonis or their reliance on the rangers. In desperation they appealed to the Staten-generaal in Holland. It was months before anything happened, but then, on Christmas Day 1772, a large expedition set sail. It was a typical Dutch army of that time: an unruly body of over 1,200 marines, mostly Germans, Scots and Swiss. They'd never fought together before, and by the time they reached the tropics they were struck with such lassitude that, when the bosun's mate fell overboard, no one bothered to rescue him. Eventually, however, after five weeks of scurvy and lice, they pulled into the Suriname estuary and gratefully dropped anchor.

One clear, bright day I borrowed a bicycle and hurried out to meet them.

There was still a great star fort ten miles downstream, in the mouth of the river. It was called New Amsterdam, like the city that became New York.

In the estuary I hired a ferryman to take me across. The fort didn't look much from a canoe, but once I was up on the bank, I could see the beginnings of La Rochelle, or the foundations of Corfu. Huge, rounded hummocks of turf splayed out in all directions. I imagine that for a passing parakeet it might still have looked like a star, although it was no longer much of a fort. Two British invasions, one American landing and 300 years of tropical rain had left it looking lush and herbaceous. The moats were now full of lilies and little alligators, and along the old earthworks were luxurious clumps of mango and palm. It was all beautifully sleepy and exotic. Deep in the grass I found a complete armoured car, now more vegetable than metal. There was also a little empty prison, with pictures of girls still pasted to the walls. But what surprised me most of all were the cannons, which lay everywhere. They were like little fat men, asleep in the turf.

Right in the middle of the star was an old, white gunpowder house. It was exactly the same as it had been the day the great expedition landed on 2 February 1773. With so much of their hardware still around, it wasn't hard to picture them strolling through the camp. They must have been a heartening sight; new marines in smart leather hats and natty blue jackets turned up with scarlet. They too were happy and thought they'd landed in heaven. A cargo of fresh fruit was sent out to them, and from the plantations all around came the gorgeous scent of spice. Only two things marred this, their glorious arrival. One was the jiggers they'd picked up around the fort (and which could only be removed by bathing in fresh lime). The other was the sight of a slave girl who'd just been given 200 lashes, and whose skin had been colourfully shredded. Heaven, it seemed, was a complicated place.

Amid all the celebration, no one had any idea of the trials ahead. Of the 500 marines that arrived that day, almost 90 per cent would never make it home. Of the senior officers, only two would survive. One was the expedition's commander, 'a Swiss Gentleman of the Alpine mountains', called Colonel Fourgeoud. He was a veteran of the Berbice revolt ten years earlier, and although he was now sixty, he's still this story's psychopath. He's like Robert Duvall's Colonel Kilgore: a thundering, bare-chested killer who will eat nothing, feel nothing and fear nothing. He would be brutal with the maroons but equally brutal with his own men. In the words of one of them: 'He was not cruel to individuals, but was a tyrant to the generality, and caused the death of hundreds by his sordid avarice and oppression … few men could talk better but, on most occasions, few could act worse.'

The other officer to survive was Fourgeoud's opposite in every respect. He was gregarious, humane, proud, passionate, occasionally silly and always impetuous. He was for ever fighting duels and, in Paramaribo's taverns the brawls he'd start would be remembered for years. ('Hats, wigs, bottles and glasses flew.') But he was also poetic, and his account of the insanity that follows would be the *Apocalypse Now* of the eighteenth century. He was Captain Stedman, lately a *luitenant* in the Prince of Orange's most loyal Scots Brigade.

John Gabriel Stedman was born in the wrong place, and 200 years too early. His own era constantly irked him, like a skin that doesn't fit. It infuriated him that soldiers were flogged, that leadership was a birthright and that the poor were so dispensable. Slavery too would disgust him, although he was never quite old enough to imagine abolition.

But worse than being born in 1744 was being born in Holland. There, warfare was almost a constant feature of everyday life. The country's frontier was so insistently violated that the States-General could no longer muster the soldiers to guard it, and so instead employed mercenaries, including the brigade of Scots. That's where Stedman's father came in. He was a hapless lowlander who'd arrived in search of his fortune, joined the brigade and then lost all his money. The only sensible thing he'd ever done was marry Antoinette van Ceulen, who was by all accounts indomitable. She'd had nine miscarriages by the time she delivered John, and then two years later she was right in the thick of it, bandaging the wounded at the Battle of Roucoux.

But for her, being shot at wasn't nearly as bad as being Catholic. So great was her fear of John's papal pollution that she eventually sent the boy to his uncle in Scotland. There he spent his time stealing pigeons, raiding orchards, street-fighting, killing cats and dogs, breaking windows and firing off pistols behind old ladies' backs. Eventually, at the age of twelve, he was returned to Holland with all the education he'd ever need.

After that Stedman drifted for a while. One moment he wanted to be a priest, and the next he wanted to become an artist and go and live in Italy (a scheme regarded as altogether far too Catholic). He took to wearing coloured shoes and crimson breeches, and strutting around with his face painted and his hair 'elegantly frizzed'. It couldn't last, and so, in 1760, he did what he'd been signed up to do since the age of three, and that was join the army. But just as he was drifting into the Scots Brigade so his father was drifting out of it. After falling off his chair one day, Stedman Senior began to lose whatever was left of his marbles. He'd spend the rest of his life sitting by the hearth composing little ditties. When he eventually died in 1770, all that John inherited was a steel penknife, a crucifix and some books (which he was obliged to sell for £10 to pay off the debts).

Meanwhile, life in the brigade was surprisingly unstructured. Sometimes Ensign Stedman turned up for duty, and sometimes he didn't. He was supposed to have been guarding the frontier but was often to be found sprawling anywhere but. 'Heusden', he wrote, 'was a town where I offered incense to Bacchus; Nijmegen to Venus, and at Breda I used sometimes to rattle the dice.' He was drifting again, except this time in uniform. From Amsterdam he 'escorted the Whores like a wild man to Rotterdam', and once he got so drunk that he lay in the street until daybreak. In his rare sober moments he read Plutarch, Fielding and Smollett, and posed as a doctor to pay off his bills. At one point he left the country altogether and set off for Carolina, to make some money. However, this adventure got no further than London, where he fell in love with a sail-maker's daughter and decided to stay. For nine months he made his living playing a fiddle in a bar and heaving ballast on the Thames, until eventually he was arrested for fighting in Kensington Gardens. In

1771 he returned to Holland and the Scots Brigade, only to find that – rather surprisingly – he'd been promoted to *luitenant*.

When, the following year, volunteers were sought to quell a slave revolt, it seemed like a tempting offer. Stedman again abandoned the Scots and joined the marines, taking the rank of captain. As he set out for Suriname, his mother gave him everything she thought he'd need: two blue shirts, a hammock, a silver spoon, two lumps of Spanish sugar and a small but powerful bottle of medicine.

Five weeks later he was sailing into the estuary. He would recall how, at the sight of Fort New Amsterdam, the men in the rigging burst into song. 'But', he adds, 'how miserably these poor fellows were mistaken in their reckoning shall soon be seen.'

After a promising start, the expedition soon began to falter. A week after their arrival in the estuary, the three great transports docked at the Red Steps. For Stedman it was an enchanting moment; the country was 'delicious', and the city 'uncommonly neat and pleasing'. As he and his men disembarked they were thronged by the crowds and fêted as saviours. Soon every man had his uniform adorned with sprigs of blossom. Colours flew, a band played and the little fort burst into life with an eleven-gun salute. The governor had even ordered one of his half-naked banquets, and women of all races turned out, looking powdered and expectant.

The marines marched up the Waterkant to the Oranjeplein, that great grassy space now known as Independence Square. There they formed up in lines. Some had been below decks for almost two months, and in their tight uniforms they began to faint in the heat. Together they made a curious spectacle, of uncertain talent. There were the Swiss, of course – such as Fourgeoud – some formidable Germans and an affable Dane called Baron de Gersdorph. But there were also plenty of Scots. They'd made respectable border guards, but how would they fare in the swamps? Of the subalterns, a few would still be around twenty years later, but Messrs MacDonald and Campbell would perish in the early sorties, and Mr Small, who was as fat as Falstaff, would very soon go mad.

The Scots, however, weren't the only imponderable soldiers. There were also two drummer boys with a well-earned reputation for treachery and killing. They're not new to this story but are old acquaintances from the revolt in Berbice. It's Okera and Gowsary, who'd betrayed their comrades in 1763 and then joined the marines. Now they were back, in the theatre that they knew, and in time they'd prove useful, as they could read smoke and interpret the drums. Fourgeoud would love them like he loved no one else. They were what every soldier should be: inexhaustible, functional and pitiless. Okera wasn't even perturbed when, by coincidence, he came across his brother, still working as a slave.

Only the governor cast a slight cloud across the day. He was thinking about money, and what all this would cost. Although the United Provinces were to meet half the expense of the expedition, the Society of Suriname was coughing up the rest.

Out on the estates, the planters felt the same. 'They hesitated not,' wrote Stedman, 'to call us the locusts of Egypt, who were come to devour the fruits of the colony.' Even before the expedition had arrived, the colonists were planning its departure. Over the next four months the marines would not set one foot in the jungle, and yet three times they were shown to their ships and told they could go. Each time all that ever stopped them was the rumour of maroons.

And the demands of the women.

It's no great surprise, perhaps, that the fate of this easy, languid city was determined by sex.

For those first four months Stedman could think of almost nothing else. From the very beginning there was the promise of sensual adventure. He discovered that slave girls 'exult in the circum-stances of living with a European', and that some would happily bestow their favours 'for a dram or a broken tobacco-pipe, if not for nothing'. Even the clergy would take advantage of these 'customs', and the whole city, it seemed, was maddened by its itch. By the end of his first fortnight Stedman had been offered a wife of fourteen, and almost anything he wanted. He even found himself, on his very first night, at the house of one Mr Lolkens, being bedded by the maid. Having planted an ardent kiss on his lips, he says, she 'insisted upon pulling off my shoes and stockings, and in a moment disen-cumbered me of that part of my apparel ...'

But it wasn't just slave girls mobilised by this great surge of men: so were the whites. For Dutch women, the expedition offered the prospect of a lover. The slave society had never brought them

For the first two centuries, most of *de Wilde Kust*, or 'The Wild Coast,' fell under the control of the Dutch. Although they looked impressive, they only ever visited about four per cent of the land they claimed. Their 'Court of Policy' was, in reality, merely a parliament of ants.

Into the great Surinamese slave revolt of 1769–77 came a Scotsman, Captain John Stedman (above). His account of five years of jungle warfare reads like a Georgian rendering of *Apocalypse Now*. But it was an unlawful marriage to a beautiful slave, Joanna (above), that caught the eye of abolitionists. This tragic tale would bring slavery one step closer to the end.

In Paramaribo, the Dutch are still remembered at a great annual lampoon, the Snow Ball.

Often Suriname still feels like a place forged from turmoil of Stedman's day. Out in the Hinterlands, his illustration of a rebel arouses great interest (above left), whilst at Alkmaar (above right), the author uncovers the tomb of Stedman's great friend, Charles Godeffroy. Meanwhile, between campaigns, Stedman took a house on the Waterkant in Paramaribo (below). In the revolts and fires that followed, the houses may have changed, but the grandeur's just the same.

Deep in the Surinamese interior, the maroons created a world of secrecy and refuge. Having extracted a treaty from the Dutch, they were in no mood to give up their African lives, and nor are their descendants. The Saramaccaners (above) still speak a vivid, seventeenth-century slave language, *Talkie-Talkie*, and have never abandoned their drums or their gods.

To the maroons, all animals are sacred (even those of a strange new continent, like this one, the tapir), and all violations of their territory are an invitation to war.

In 1986, an old war re-started, more vicious than ever. The N'Djuka maroons, led by Ronnie Brunswijk (left), took on the coastland forces of Marxist dictator, Desi Bouterse (right). During the next six years madness ensued, fuelled by heroin and voodoo. Brunswijk's rebels, known as 'The Jungle Commandos' (below), wore amulets against the bullets and, once again, the Amerindians were sent in to flush them out. Eventually, France brokered a truce, although everyone kept their guns.

French Guiana, or Guyane, had never enjoyed much success with slaves. Two years after abolition in 1848 a new experiment began. The colony became a giant penal settlement, killing almost every other convict. In France it became known as 'the dry guillotine', and is now a matter of public shame. At its heart was St-Laurent-du-Maroni (depicted above by the convict Lagrange). It had its own 'Little Paris', and a vast camp for processing human beings, 3,000 at a time. The camp only closed in 1946 and has lain empty ever since (below). It was the very antithesis of El Dorado: a city of mud, built to impoverish, in the worship of work.

Although once considered salubrious, the Iles du Salut became a prison within a prison. They were both idyllic and lawless. On Royale (above), a convict might grow vegetables, or make souvenirs for passing cruise ships, and yet only two per cent of the murders were ever resolved. The punishment for killing another inmate or assaulting a *surveillant* was, of course, the blade (bottom right). But tougher still was Devil's Island (at the centre of the picture above). Its most famous prisoner was Captain Alfred Dreyfus (below left), who was here from 1895 to 1899. 'So profound is my solitude,' he wrote, 'I often seem to be lying in a tomb.'

The solitary confinement block on St-Joseph. A man could spend up to five years in here, hearing nothing but the surf. The penal colony only finally gave way to international outrage on the eve of World War Two. Over the next six years a quarter of the convicts died of malnutrition; the settlements were finally closed in 1946. The last prisoners – Indochinese rebels – remained however until 1963. The land was then handed over to the European space agency, in whose hands it remains.

adventure. (If a white woman was caught with a slave, he would be shot, and she would be branded and expelled from the colony.) Now, with such a shortage of lawful, potent men, the arrival of the transports was – to the 'fairer ladies' – like a dream come true. With little dignity and even less restraint they threw themselves at the marines. Two women even fought a duel over a particularly angular specimen, and another offered Stedman unlimited access to her slave girls if only he would marry her. Although he was generally impressed by this ardour, he was less impressed by their offering. White women here, he noted, were 'languid, sallow' and 'shrivelled'.

But, with or without Stedman, the women had their way. The marines, they told the governor, were to stay where they were.

As might be expected, vice and disease were soon thinning the ranks. During those first four months of inactivity the marines drank and fornicated, and then drank all over again. It didn't seem to worry anyone that there were still rebels round the city. It was easier not to think about it, just to swill back the gin and take another lover. Some died of yellow fever – or 'The Seasoning' – and some died of heat, but many just melted away. 'Now,' wrote Stedman, 'our common soldiers fell the victims of idleness and licentiousness, and died frequently six or seven in a day …'

By July 1773, five months after its arrival, a quarter of the force was either dead or unfit, and they hadn't even left Paramaribo. The cemetery where the dead were buried is still there, looking weedy and abandoned, right in the heart of the city. Even now, no one ever goes inside or walks among the tombs. The gates are padlocked, and people say it's haunted by *wintis*. This is hard on those who did nothing worse to Suriname than arrive here and die. Among them there were the expedition surgeon and two lieutenant-colonels, including the affable Baron de Gersdorph.

Even Stedman came close to death. 'I became a member of a drinking club, I partook of all polite and impolite amusements, and plunged into every extravagance without exception. I did not, however, escape without the punishment I deserved.' On 17 May he developed a fever and took to his hammock, preparing to die. But dying was a cumbersome business in the Paramaribo of 1773. One whiff of mortality and all the neighbours would turn up with cures and unguents, cordials, quacks, lamenters and professional wailers. Death was like a last great public appearance, and yet for Stedman this was a defining moment. Afterwards, he was never again quite the rake he had been. This was partly because he'd peered into the abyss, but there was also something else: a beautiful slave had just walked into his life, by the name of Joanna.

The story of Joanna would one day nudge history off course, or at least the history of slaving. Twenty years later – long after her death – Stedman would bring her to an English readership, and this little tropical tragedy would seep, insidiously perhaps, right to the heart of political society. Abolitionists would even extract her tale from Stedman's journals, to create a book of her own, the *Narrative of Joanna, an Emancipated Slave of Suriname*. It was an important tale for the way it recast slaves. A good slave was not merely loyal or strong but also compassionate, intuitive and inexplicably humane. She could also be a lover, and not merely a helpless victim.

Joanna herself made a perfect heroine. She was only fifteen, and her blind grandfather had once been a kingly figure in an unknown country. Although she'd never been to school and could barely read, Stedman gave her the voice of an English queen. ('Yet though a slave,' she once told him, 'I have a soul, I hope, not inferior to that of a European, and blush not to avow the regard I have for you.') It's hard now to distil reality from the fondness of Stedman's old age, but one thing is clear: Joanna was impressively expensive. At £200 she must have been not only bright but profitably handsome. At the sight of her, even Stedman, normally such a trenchant observer of the female scene, was rendered shamelessly soppy: 'Her face,' he wrote, 'was full of native modesty, and the most distinguished sweetness. Her eyes, as black as ebony, were large, and full of expression, bespeaking the goodness of her heart ... Her lips, a little prominent, discovered, when she spoke, two regular rows of teeth as white as mountain snow ...'

Her beauty would kill her in the end, and had dogged her all her life. She was born at Fauquemberg, the property of a planter, known only as 'DB'. Her father was a Dutchman who'd spent years trying to buy her off her owner. But DB was a man of reptilian warmth and had always refused. It was said that eventually the refusal killed her father, and that all Joanna had left of him was her magnificent outfit. According to Stedman, she was festooned in gold chains, rings and medals, and wore a red chintz petticoat, with a shawl of India muslin covering one breast, and 'a beaver hat, the crown trimmed round with silver'.

The unlawful affection that she'd felt for her father would be repeated with Stedman. The slavery was always there, like a frontier between them. But at least at Fauquemberg there would be some kind of justice. Eventually, most of DB's slaves rose in revolt and ran away. Without his labour DB went bust and fled the colony for Holland. The liquidator then put the whole plantation on the market, including Joanna and the last of the slaves. But with the revolt raging there were no takers, and so for the next five years she remained in commercial limbo, bankrupt stock as yet unsold. Meanwhile, her uncles had run away and joined up with the rebels.

A hint of her family's defiance survived in Joanna. Despite the obvious affection she felt for Stedman, she never truly surrendered. She would court him carefully; she'd send him secret gifts after first spotting him at the house where she worked; she'd nurse him through his fever; she'd keep him going through the foul campaigns ahead, with crates of fruit and claret; she'd maintain his house and his bed, and would love him even when he returned from the forest, stinking and purulent; she'd be his friend, his mistress, his confidante and his saviour, but she'd never be what he wanted, and that was his equal. Stedman was always trying to liberate her, and she was always defiant. It was almost as though she feared a white man's freedom more than his slavery. As a precious possession, she lived the life of an exalted concubine. The same could not be said, she realised, for the wives of the Dutch.

For Stedman her humility was tantalising, and made her more irresistible than ever. As he lay recovering on his sick bed, in May 1773, he knew that here was a girl who, in every sense, he simply had to own. The problem was how. On his current captain's pay he'd never be able to pay for her manumission. The only way this could change was if he somehow managed to distinguish himself, and that meant hoping for a war.

Meanwhile, Stedman decided on one of his great, impetuous gestures. If he couldn't buy Joanna, at least he could marry her. Although the arrangement would be invalid under Dutch law (as were all contracts with slaves), she accepted his proposal, and so – two weeks after they met – the couple were married, with all the ceremony that Stedman could muster.

Paramaribo still mocks the pomp and fanfare of the Dutch. People
were always dressing up in top hats, gloves and 'bum-freezer' jackets.
The biggest of these mock pageants was 'The Snow Ball', which
happened to be on while I was there. This wasn't a private party but
an enormous free-for-all, in the tradition of the slaves. One moment
I was quietly enjoying a grassy snooze on Independence Square, and
the next I was surrounded by hundreds of neo-Georgians all dressed
in brilliant white. It was like waking up in the middle of a variety
show deep in the Afterlife. There were dazzling trumpeters, shimmering drummers, a parade of large, lacy ladies, dandies in starched
frock coats, a fleet of white limousines like a motorcade for hair-
dressers, a master of ceremonies in pearly tails and a troupe of gorgeous, skinny dancers, wearing nothing but their smalls.

Next to me, a man was whistling through his teeth.

'Nice girls,' I said, assuming he spoke English.

He nodded, still transfixed by the dancers.

'That's all this country has,' he sighed, 'nice girls and cocaine.'

On 15 June 1773 festivities like these were interrupted by news from
upriver. For most, it was the moment they'd dreaded. The revolt had
restarted.

The story of what had happened would be a grim foretaste of
the war ahead. Some weeks earlier a detachment of Society troops
had set off up the Cottica. At their head was a former Life Guard
called Lieutenant Lepper. Nowadays he'd be described as 'dashing',
in the sense of ornamental and rash. Some months earlier, he'd
fled Holland after killing a friend in a duel. While some men might
have paused for reflection at this point, Lepper didn't. Instead, he
was still desperately in search of heroism, which is how he and his
men found themselves in a swamp, up to their armpits in mud. For
the Bonis, it was like shooting apples in a barrel. They killed thirty
soldiers, captured six prisoners and took Lepper's head as a prize.
The captives were then taken to the rebel camp, where the Bonis
stripped them and beat them to death 'for the recreation of their
wives and children'. Lepper's handsome (if slightly empty) head was
then mounted on a pole and would adorn the Boni village for several
months, until it was recovered by the Dutch.

Only a handful of soldiers survived. When Stedman found one

of them, weeks later, dying in the jungle, the survivor described how the Bonis had moved among them, cutting and butchering and hacking off heads. He himself was only saved because, as the rebels came close, their leader had shouted: '*Sonde go sleeby, caba mekewe liby den tara dogo tay tamara*' ('The sun is going to sleep, we must leave these other dogs till tomorrow'). After that, the survivors had wandered the forest for ten days until they stumbled into a Dutch camp, half starved, witless and 'our putrefied wounds full of live worms'.

Paramaribo reacted to this reverse with a mixture of fluttery outrage and downright sloth. It was three weeks before the marines were dispatched up the Cottica, in a collection of 'crazy old sugar barges'. Stedman said these boats were like the colliers on the Thames, except roofed over with boards ('which gave them the appearance of so many coffins'). He himself had two under his command, *Charon* and *Cerberus*. Each was rowed by ten slaves and carried about thirty soldiers. Both boats were armed with swivels and blunderbusses, and Stedman called his 'the wooden walls of the colony' or, less charitably, his 'hen coop'.

Still, he was relieved to be under way. War was good for his love life.

A few days after the Snow Ball, I also said my goodbyes to Paramaribo and set off in a barge. For months it had troubled me, how I might follow Stedman into the swamps. On the map I'd been able to see nothing but a snaggle of enormous rivers spread over 2,000 square miles. There were no roads through this scribble, and no marks except the heart-sinking symbol for bogs. Back then, the *Charon* and *Cerberus* had paddled down the estuary to Fort New Amsterdam, where on 4 July 1773 they'd turned right into the Commewijne River. This bit was easy: several times I'd been out there on a combination of bicycles and boats. But after that, things looked more difficult. Beyond the Commewijne, the vast, empty weed-world began, and it was still another seventy miles along the Cottica to the Coermotibo River, and the seat of the revolt. How would I get there? Rent a boat? Buy a canoe? No man can easily imagine his own demise, but I did have a sudden vision of myself, inextricably lost in this enormous labyrinth of water.

Then I remembered my friends at the tug company, which happened to be English. Did they know the Cottica River? Sure, they said, every day one of their tugs headed up to Coermotibo or returned with a load of bauxite. It was a round trip of 232 miles, but I was welcome to join them. 'Just give us a call,' they said, 'when you get to Paramaribo.'

So that's how I ended up aboard the MT *Kite*, as it gnashed its way down the Suriname River. Unlike the *Cerberus*, this was no hen coop. Everything about it had a deep, industrial bellow. Out at the front were two hoppers, or barges, each 200 feet long. When they were empty, as now, they drew only three feet of water, and so they bobbed along like vast rectangular balloons. When full, they'd carry 3,500 tons of bauxite each, and sink to the depth of a house. As for the *Kite* itself, it was ninety feet long and three storeys high. From the bridge I could see Paramaribo shrinking into the mangrove, and a wartime wreck – the German freighter *Goslar* – way below. The Master told me that, up here, we were further above the river than the river was deep.

'A comforting thought,' I said, 'if ever we sink.'

'Yup,' he replied. 'Just sit tight. You won't even get your feet wet.'

8

THE HINTERLANDS

The colony of Suriname is reeking and dyed with the blood of African Negroes.

V.S. Naipaul, *Middle Passage*

Farewell, ye shady woods, thou pleasing gloomy forest, pregnant with so many wonders and so many plagues, and which in the opinion of so many sufferers, even surpassed the ten plagues of Egypt.

John Stedman, *Expedition to Surinam*

Son sma no man gi den srudati pardon fu den hat' sani san den ben du den sma.
('Some people cannot forgive the soldiers for the painful things they did to people.')

Surinamese phrasebook, 2009

THE HINTERLANDS HAVEN'T ALWAYS LOOKED so empty. If anyone really wants to know what lies out there, they need a map from the 1760s. It would show over 800 plantations along these rivers – in places, one every 500 yards. Among them there are cacao farms, palm oil plantations, little forts, French settlements (such as Mon Désir and Groot Marseille) and a Huguenot colony, called La Providentia. Linking it all up are the rivers themselves, canals, ditches, dykes and a few paths cut through forest, each marked *cordonpad* and as straight as a gunshot.

But now it's almost all gone. These days, whatever was there before can only be appreciated by satellite or plane. It's not much, just a vague waffling of the earth's surface, or the spectral outline of some vast endeavour. In places this great watery forest extends almost fifty miles inland, and it's all largely empty. How different things were in 1699, when Maria Merian, a German artist, came out here to sketch and visit the plantations, getting over her divorce. She stayed for two years, and her botanical illustrations, published as *Metamorphosis Insectorum Surinamensium*, are some of the most glorious ever produced. Today, the same work would be almost impossible. Once you get to the Cottica, there's barely a school or a shop, let alone a mansion.

On this, our crowded planet, such dereliction is remarkable. It's as though humankind's been forgotten and virginity's returned. Not that nature's complaining. I'd heard that the sea cows, or manatees, were back, and that there was now a rich society of turtles. Only the Creoles were unhappy. They thought the emptiness was devious and that the Cottica was cursed. People often told me there was a cocaine laboratory upriver, run by a former president. Some even took the view that these days only fugitives inhabited the swamps.

Perhaps they were right. No one seemed to take any chances. Even the crew of the *Kite* were prepared for the worst, and, the day we left, they had a full-scale practice of their piracy drill.

Quite soon, life aboard settled down and became somehow quaintly British. Cups of milky tea appeared, with bacon sandwiches and bottles of HP sauce. Up and down the companionways there were pictures of great London tugs, and in my tiny cabin I had a bar of Lifebuoy, and a panel of awkward English sockets. Even the smells were British, the fried bread and the loos. It didn't seem to matter that six out of eight of the crew were Indonesian: the *Kite* was like a little British factory, clanking down the river. As though this British-ness wasn't enough, there was also the Master, who was strict and gingery, and expansively Welsh. 'Went to sea at fifteen, I did,' he once told me, 'working the paddle steamers on the Bristol Channel.'

I used to like sitting up in the wheelhouse with Captain Mans-bridge. It felt as though we were sitting in a tower, enjoying two lives at once. Down there was Suriname, sliding by, looking steamy and lush. Up here it was cool, and we had big aircraft seats, the Welsh teas and almost fifty years of seagoing tales. As he eased us through the shipping lanes, the Master hardly seemed to notice the world beyond, and so we pootled along as though we were off to the Mumbles. I heard all about Mrs Mansbridge and her top-notch cooking, about the caravan, about the best tugs and the best rum, about the best fights in Cardiff docks, and the foolish magistrates and fiercest captains, about Bantry Bay, and about the young cabin boy who'd had his face whipped off by a hawser, and all the men who'd been crushed or drowned. Lester Mansbridge was a human repository of lives at sea.

'And how long have you been here?' I asked.

'Thirteen years. Know this river like my hand.'

For the operator of such a hulk, he also had an extraordinary

Stedman's armoured barge: harmless to its quarry but lethal to those inside.

insight into the little lives along the shore. On the Suriname River he knew all the unseaworthy boats, the homes of the drug barons and the politicians-for-sale, the captain who'd not washed in thirteen years, and the villas of the rich. He also knew the Hindu fishermen, who'd head out to sea in open boats and stay away for weeks. Then there were the 'sand-dancers', the tiny dredgers in the mouth of the estuary. They were always being mown down and smashed to bits. 'Imagine that,' said the Master, 'getting yourself killed for a boat full of sand.'

We'd now reached the star-fort and veered right, up the Commewijne.

A short way ahead Stedman was finding his barges difficult. He was only a day out of Paramaribo and yet already he'd renamed them: *Sudden Death* and *Wilful Murder*. Beneath the boards, the heat was crushing. Then it rained, and everything began to rot: hammocks, tunics, black bread, knapsacks and biscuit. The mosquitoes didn't help, or the fug of tobacco. Already men were beginning to sicken and bicker with the slaves.

Stedman realised that to survive he had to adapt. His orders were to patrol the rivers for a month, to prevent rebels crossing, to harry them inland, to kill them and generally to make the prospect of another African homeland seem hopelessly remote. At this rate,

however, he wouldn't last a week. He wasn't even in enemy territory yet, and the patrol was beginning to fail. Only slaves knew how
to survive in conditions like this, and so Stedman did the unthink-
able and sought their advice. Strip down, said Caramaca, the oldest
slave, swim every day and get rid of your shoes. Stedman began
immediately and plunged into the river.

From now on he became known as *Le Sauvage Anglais* and, out
on campaign, never wore shoes and fought only in linen. Every
morning he took a swim in the river, and – his own refinement,
this – he finished each day with a generous glass of claret. By the
standards of today's bushcraft this may sound a peculiar regime,
but it worked for Stedman. It would sustain him through three and
a half years of sweltering warfare, including seven forays into the
Hinterlands of up to five months each. No one else would fight like
Stedman, and perhaps that's why they died.

Meanwhile, he was glad to be among the last, surviving plantations. The barges stopped at each one, taking on fruit and wasting
time. Stedman had often been out here before and knew most of
the estates. These had not always been easy visits. At Sporkesgift
he came across a slave who'd been hamstrung, or surgically crippled, and at 'Schovnort' he found a 'fine old negro' chained to a
furnace, consigned to 'the intense heat of a perpetual fire night and
day, being blistered all over till he should expire'.

Now, it seemed, revenge was all around. Almost all the planters
knew of friends who'd been lashed apart with billhooks and displayed in the trees. At Elisabeth's Hope the owner, Mr Klynhams,
had this advice for Stedman:

> As for the enemy, you may depend on not seeing one single soul
> of them; they know better than to make their appearance openly,
> while they may have a chance of seeing you from under cover.
> Thus, Sir, take care to be upon your guard – but the climate, the
> climate will murder you all.

As the soldiers pulled away, they caught one last sight of Klynhams's
daughter. She was unforgettably beautiful, and she stood on the pier
waving, the tears streaming down her face.

The *Kite* didn't stop for the plantations, or what was left of them. But a few days earlier, I'd ridden out here on my bicycle and taken a boat across the Commewijne.

I hadn't expected to find much – even here, a good ten miles before the Cottica begins. The land was sodden and ripe, and the mangrove had swelled up out of the river and reclaimed the dykes. There were roads still, but sometimes they led nowhere, except into the swamps. At one point I found myself walking through the skeleton of a vast sugar factory, with cattle now grazing among the machines. Everywhere smelt of earth and steam, and crumbling wood. Occasionally I came across the great open spaces of the past, now shrinking under the trees. But the slave-yards had all gone, of course, leaving nothing but the stragglers. One of these little shanties was still littered with large pieces of artillery. Another had a *dede-osu*, or morgue, on which someone had painted 'WAKE UP AND LIVE'.

Even more surprising, I'd found two old plantation houses. The first was on the south side of the river. Plantage Zorgvliet dated from Stedman's time and was a large, wheezy clapboard house, mounted on enormous brick piers. It looked like Noah's Ark, waiting for the flood. The other house, Fredericksdorp, was on the north bank and was built a few years later. This is just how I'd imagined an old plantation, with lawns and fruit trees and a view of the river. As it happened, the whole place had been restored by a more recent Dutch soldier. Captain Hagemëyer had arrived in the '60s, fallen in love with the emptiness of Commewijne and stayed ever since. He'd been so faithful to the original *plantage* that he'd even resurrected its statutes and spruced up its prison.

'Let me show you this,' he said.

At the back was a wide stone pavement, for drying coffee.

'You know how they knew the beans were ready?' he asked.

'Tell me.'

'When the slaves burned their feet.'

I could have spent all day pottering around with old Captain Hagemëyer, but it was soon time to go. I'd got one more place to visit, back across the river. It was the home of the Godeffroys, known as Plantage Alkmaar. In Stedman's torrid tale few people emerge with much decency, apart from the Godeffroys. The family were German, a cut above most, and had a magnificent crest, replete with eagles and lions and a hefty coronet. Perhaps it was their blue blood that affected their attitude to slavery. It always seemed more feudal than commercial: at Alkmaar, said Stedman, 'slaves are treated like children', and 'here were no groans to be heard, no fetters to be met with, not any marks of severity to be seen – but all was harmony and content.' Slavery never got more enchanting than this.

A few miles upstream I'd found the Alkmaar dykes. Charles Godeffroy had designed most of them himself, over the last thirty years of his life. By the time Stedman arrived, he was sixty-nine, and the sheer effort of draining the Hinterlands had taken its toll. He died on the very day the revolt restarted. But his family had never forgotten Stedman. Widow Godeffroy would lend him a home, encourage his writing, pay for his book and look after Joanna, whenever he went away. She even bought the girl herself, so that no one else could have her. Joanna, of course, was effusively grateful, although – as a matter of honour – she insisted on remaining in Mrs Godeffroy's service until the widow herself was repaid. In the meantime Mrs Godeffroy gave Joanna her own house, her own garden and her own little complement of slaves.

Enchanted Alkmaar had, I realised, all but disappeared. Of the big house there was now nothing left but a field of cinder and weeds. It horrified me how completely the Godeffroys had vanished, having transformed so much of the landscape. I wasn't even sure that this was Alkmaar, rather than the next plantation, 'Nyd en Spyd' (or 'Anger and Sorrow'). But then an Indian woman emerged from the grass. She looked frightened at first, until she saw the pencils and bites, and my old tape-recorder, and realised I was harmless. Although she didn't speak English, we somehow scraped by in Talkie-talkie.

'*Plantage?*' I tried, pointing at the weed.

'*Me no sabi.*'

'*Plantage Alkmaar?*'

'*Disi Alkmaar,*' she nodded. '*Disi Alkmaar, dyaso!*'

'Godeffroy?' I tried, and then pranced around like a king.

'Godeffroy? *Yu wani see?*'

'Yes! Yes, *me wani see,*' I said, without being sure of what.

The woman then called her daughter, who came with a cutlass.

'*Kon un go!*' they said, and so I followed them into the grass.

Some way in was the wreckage of an old wooden house that had buckled and collapsed. The women started tearing at the beams and throwing them aside. They were immensely strong, and soon we'd cleared away half the house and were down to the sand and ash.

Then, as we started digging, there was the perceptible clink of stone, and an eagle appeared, followed by two lions and a hefty coronet. The Indian got up and stood aside.

'*Disi Masra Godeffroy ...*', she said, as though by way of introduction.

It was old Charles himself, magnificently entombed at the heart of his estate. The date on his gravestone was '*9 Juny 1773*', almost exactly four weeks before Stedman sailed past, in search of uncertain glory.

Night fell, but the *Kite* carried on rumbling upriver. From the mast two brilliant rods of light, sparkling with insects, felt out the shoreline ahead. In the wheelhouse all the dials and screens came twinkling to life, and the Master hauled himself off to bed. He was replaced by the First Mate, called Saiman, who added to the electrical effects with a boom box and the sound of *Javaans*. Although he was Indonesian, his family – unlike those of the deckhands' – had worked this river for almost a hundred years. 'My father was a fisherman,' he told me, 'but now I'm up here, I'm so happy ...'

In the darkness, everything closed in. I was no longer conscious of the enormous boat, or the enormous river all around. Ahead, the water looked like tar, sleepy and deceptive. Occasionally we'd hear a faint bump, and a tiny shiver would ripple through the *Kite*. It was the tree trunks, disintegrating under 15,000 tons of steel. At some stage we passed into the Cottica, but nothing seemed to change. Stedman had described a little fort here, owned by the Society. Its cannon had commanded the river, and I noticed that it was still marked on the chart: Post Sommelsdijk.

I asked Saiman what happened there now.

He laughed. 'Just *bush-bush*!'

'And ghosts?' I joked.

Saiman frowned. 'Yes, yes. Everyone afraid of the ghosts ...'

More sandwiches arrived, together with the night watch. I sat with them for a while, peering into the beams. It was mesmerising, and soon I couldn't make sense of anything, whether it was shadows or reflections or trees with arms and heads. I decided to go to bed and clambered back down to my cabin in the hull.

There I lay on my bunk, leafing through Stedman. From this

point on, he'd said, every plantation lay in ruins. Looking at the chart, I was surprised that so many names had survived. I could see Nieuw Klarenbeek, where Stedman had found a military hospital overrun with rats, Charlottenberg, where he'd treated his men to a feast of twelve ducks and thirty-six bottles of claret, and Groot Marseille, where the slaves themselves had fought off the rebels. I was just beginning to wonder whether, since then, anything had ever happened in these places when sleep began to merge with history, and soon I could feel myself grinding through my dreams, as though they too were powered by diesel and jolted by the logs.

At about dawn the engines stopped and I woke up. I went up on deck, and found that overnight the river had narrowed, and that we were now in the mouth of a small tributary. The forest was so close that huge shoots of mocco-mocco leaned nosily over the decks. It was a bewitching place, and I could now see why Stedman – when he wasn't dying – had loved these swamps. The river was like liquefied sky, and the trees seemed to hover above it, without any land beneath. In the steamy early morning warmth I was tempted to do something Stedmanesque and plunge into the water. But then the Master appeared with a story about fishing here, and an alligator so big that it broke the rod in two. Instead, I had bacon and eggs and the news from the BBC.

Saiman was still up in the wheelhouse, wearing his Breton cap, with his uniform all pressed and neat. He told me we were waiting for the tide, that we'd done sixty miles since Paramaribo, and that he always stopped here. 'My favourite place,' he said, 'They call it Koopmans Kreek.'

It had obviously been a popular *ankerplaats* for several centuries because the *Charon* and *Cerberus* had moored here, at exactly the same point, on the fourth evening of their fateful excursion.

For the *Charon*, that night was almost her last. By now, Stedman and his men were deep in rebel territory. Sometimes they could hear the Bonis at night, calling to them or 'talking' on the drums. Occasionally the men even managed to get a shot in, but all that ever fell out of the trees were giant snakes and monkeys. Once, everyone rushed to arms in the middle of the night, only to find a sea cow snuffling round the hull. Perhaps Farmer Klynham was right, and they'd never see the rebels? No one had any idea where they came from, or where they were going, or how they managed to be everywhere at once. The marines didn't even know how their enemy managed to land or negotiate the river. The woods looked as though they floated on the water, with no sign of any riverbank beyond. 'Not a footstep of land could we find,' wrote Stedman, 'where we might cook our salt provisions safely.'

Unable and unwilling to land, the marines were imprisoned in the barges. Every function and every disease they shared with the slaves. The soldiers now looked sallow and taut like drum-skins. Cooking on board had already proved difficult, with the men packed so tight (one marine had fallen foul of the kettle and lost most of the skin on his back). At Koopmans Kreek they tried again, and this time the *Charon* caught fire. Fortunately the blaze was contained, and disaster narrowly averted.

Another day of this, and the men would have started dying at Koopmans. The next morning, however, they managed to row another two miles to a Dutch camp and started dying there instead. Despite its perky name, 'Lands Welvaren', or the 'Welfare of the Nation', it was a verminous spot. It had once been a plantation, but it now seemed to be a place where soldiers came to die. Nothing thrived here except mosquitoes and jiggers, and half the garrison were already in the hospital. There, wrote Stedman, 'I beheld such a spectacle of misery and wretchedness as baffles all imagination.' To alleviate the suffering of the sick, he went out and shot a twenty-two-foot anaconda, returning with 'four gallons of fine, clarified fat'. But despite his thoughtfulness, most patients died. Within weeks the 'pesthouse' had claimed all the best Scottish officers, together with his ensign, Mr Cottenburgh, Mr Owen and Mr Stromer, the commander of the *Cerberus*. With such a grisly record for 'intolerable unhealthiness', the fort would be known from then on as Devil's Harbour.

For the next seven weeks the barges sallied forth from the fort on their sickly patrols. They ranged over thirty miles upstream, and sometimes the men left the river altogether and tramped up the 'communication paths', abandoning those too weak to walk. Along the way, they experienced 'ring worm, dry gripes, putrid fevers … horse-flies, wild bees and bats, thorns, briars and alligators … burning hot days, cold and damp nights, heavy rains and short allowance'. They planned mutiny, shot more snakes and supplemented their salt beef with monkeys, which Stedman said reminded him of children, 'especially with their little hands and their heads'. By the end he had only twenty-one men left out of an original party of fifty-four. But the

Once a Dutch stronghold, Devil's Harbour has now sunk back in the litter.

loss was mostly in vain. During the entire campaign they hadn't seen a single rebel. In fact, apart from captives and stragglers, Stedman wouldn't see a rebel on the next campaign either, or the one after that. It would be another two years before he came face-to-face with the mysterious Bonis.

Meanwhile, after seven weeks Stedman was recalled to Devil's Harbour and put in command. By now everyone's sanity was beginning to totter. Disease was still thinning the ranks, and yet among the slaves the revolt seemed to flourish. To the south another three plantations were torched, and their owners cut up or skinned. Each night there was talk of a massed attack on the fort. Stedman calculated that he needed 300 healthy men to defend the perimeter, and yet all he had was twelve. When they heard of the revolt, however, even the sick rushed to the defences. 'For this whole night', wrote Stedman, 'we again watched under arms, and in the morning found two more of our little party dead on the ground.' But no attack came, and the marines would die fighting shadows. By 2 September 1773 there were only seven men left fit to fight. It seemed that, if the Bonis waited long enough, their enemy would simply perish of their own accord.

Eventually, however, reinforcements appeared, and Stedman finally cracked. In a state of 'distraction' and 'agitation' he was bundled into a canoe and paddled back to Paramaribo. There he discovered that he'd already been given up for dead, that his house had been re-let, and that the insects had eaten all his clothes, including twelve pairs of shoes.

Devil's Harbour is still a cursed place, courting human failure.

The river was even narrower now, and seemed to curl back on itself before swinging round in a series of hairpin bends. It must have been a brave man who first sent the tugs down here, with their barges out front, 500 feet long. It was like trying to squeeze a warehouse down a woodland path. At any moment we could have become jammed fast or torn in two. The Master said that these were some of the most difficult waterways he'd ever known. At least one captain had lost a barge out here, and another had lost his wits. 'Just couldn't handle it,' said the Master. 'They had to send him home ...'

At Devil's Harbour – now on its third name, Cabanas – the *Kite* slowed. As we came into the bend, I peered into the foliage, but the clearing had gone, along with the officers' mess, the powder store and the 'pest house'. I was just trying to imagine all those Germans and Scots laid out in the sub-soil when the *Kite* suddenly lurched. We'd hit a mudbank, and all around us in the black water great blooms of khaki came floating to the surface. Up ahead, the leading barge skated to one side and smashed through a tree. No one said anything, the engine snorted and struggled for a moment, and then we were back on our way. Meanwhile, the deckhands moved up front, checking for damage. 'And looking for snakes,' said the Master, 'which sometimes fall out of the trees.'

Further up, there were more bends and the first signs of life. We hadn't seen anyone for almost sixty miles. Now there were breaks in the trees, and the occasional figure appeared; a maroon fishing, or a woman on the bank, peeing in the sand. Then there were two tiny clusters of timber and tin, marked as Agiti Ondro and Wanhatti. When the villagers heard us, they came running out, shouting '*Bari! Bari!*'

I asked Saiman what it meant.

'Barrels. They want our old oil drums, for collecting water.'

'And who are they? What kind of maroons?'

Saiman craned over, studying the people below. 'N'Djukas mostly.'

'So, no Bonis?'

He'd smiled, as though I was joking. 'No, no Bonis, not here.'

Saiman had no particular affection for his neighbours upriver. He told me that they ate 'tree chicken' and 'water chicken', or iguana and caiman. During the bad times, twenty years ago, they used to come on board the tugs. 'They looked like madmen,' he said, 'and I guess they were on cocaine or something. One of them was wearing a pair of Nikes and had like a machine gun, a *German* gun. I think he was the leader, and I also heard he had a hideout right here in Wanhatti. He kept asking if we had any soldiers, and they broke open all the lockers. They wanted food and radios. I remember the leader … He was killed eventually, by the Amerindians.'

'You must have been frightened.'

Saiman shrugged. 'Nobody liked it. But it's my job. Maybe they'd kill me? I don't know, but the insurance would pay my family …'

Two hours on, we turned into the Coermotibo. The *kreek* here was so narrow that it looked like silver trickling out of the forest. The trees were close enough that I could almost reach out and pick the livid orange fruits. One tree, the tafrabon, was taller than the others and completely white, like some lanky arboreal ghost, and sometimes we could see lines of monkeys spilling through the branches, way overhead.

But the strangest figures in the foliage were the herons, who stood ramrod straight in their shabby uniforms of royal blue. They had the look of deserters, hoping not to be seen. Stedman and his men had hated the Coermotibo more than anywhere else. 'A most dismal solitary place,' he wrote. 'Here we saw nothing but water, wood and cloud.' It was funny, I thought, how often the world's most beautiful places (Afghanistan, Tennessee, the Dolomites …) were its most unforgiving in times of war.

Just when I was thinking how much he'd have liked the creek today, we arrived at the mine. Strangely, Stedman himself had long predicted the presence of metals here (and had urged the Dutch to search 'in their bowels'). But what he can't have predicted is the sheer volume of output, or that its aluminium would one day make flying barges that would soar over Germany and pound it to gravel. Even now Coermotibo produces almost 2 million tons of bauxite a year, and – to get it to civilisation – the little fleet of tugs travels the equivalent of four times round the Earth. None of this makes for a pretty sight. Up at the wharf, the forest looked as though it had been gored and then crudely dissected by mechanical monsters. As bowel-searching goes, even Stedman would have been suitably impressed.

While thousands of tons of pink porridge bubbled into the hoppers, the crew had a rest. It was about then that I became aware of the tug's chief engineer, a Scot called McLwraith. He'd spent most of his life below the waterline, and this had left him looking slightly wary and nocturnal. But he was a kind man and told me that he'd always been more at ease with engines than with humans. I asked him why there were so many Scots in Suriname's story, what with Seacoast and the Scots Brigade. He said he didn't know, but that no place had ever made him feel happier and that he was about to marry an Arawak. This we celebrated with mugs of Earl Grey and Glasgow-sized bacon butties.

Then the hoppers were full and it was time to go. Ahead of us lay another twenty-hour voyage, and we were seen off by swifts, nipping the water all around. It would feel like a different journey in the failing light. The Coermotibo was now a canyon of trees, and then we were back on the Cottica, which had become a huge pink ballroom, lit by millions of candles. It was the fireflies, enjoying their first and last fortnight of life. Then, just as darkness finally descended, I caught a glimpse of a gaping hole in the wall of forest: the entrance to Barbakoeba Kreek.

Little had anyone known it, but this dank, overgrown aperture led right to the core of the revolt. Several days walk from here – north towards the coast – lay the Bonis' last great hideout, called Gado Sabi (or 'God knows'). There they kept their families and grew their cassava and rice. It was a pretty place ('in the form of an amphi-theatre,' as Stedman wrote later, 'romantic and enchanting beyond conception').

Slightly less enchanting were the rebels themselves. By now there were probably several hundred of them, here and elsewhere. They had two leaders, both of whom would lend the group their name. One was Aluku, who soon fades from view. The other was Bonny, or Boni, who was altogether more memorable. He was a *bos creool*, born on the Barbakoeba, and his father may even have been the local planter, called Heer van der May. His mother, however, had run away in about 1730, and Bonny had spent the next forty-odd years adapting to the forest and cultivating his own brand of terror. He wore 'a gold laced hat', trusted no one, kept a retinue of women and ruled by voodoo and fear. It was like old Africa again, the men believing they were invincible and eating their enemies.

But they were also adept fighters. Colonel Fourgeoud's marines had already discovered how the Bonis could be both everywhere at once and yet also elusive. The maroons would never engage the Europeans head-on, but they could always spot weakness: an unguarded plantation, perhaps, or a platoon crossing a swamp, their guns held high and dry. They'd even rigged the jungle with traps, digging pitfalls of sharpened bamboo and poisoning the swamps. All they lacked was shot. By 1775 they were loading their guns with coins and buttons and bits of stone.

For years the marines had ignored the entrance to Barbakoeba Kreek. Stedman and his men had moored here countless times, wondering where to go next. He'd even stood here in October 1773, just a month after his little brush with madness. But instead of going up it, he'd travelled east for four months, reaching almost as far as French Guiana and nearly starving to death. Then he was back again in early 1775, marching almost a hundred miles inland. As always, men had died, although nothing was found. But then, the following August, news came through of an enormous rebel camp right under their noses, up the Barbakoeba.

This time the prospects for a kill were so good that even Colonel Fourgeoud came, along with 200 soldiers. By now, the old Swiss was almost as charmless as the rebels themselves. According to Stedman, he'd become 'impetuous, passionate, self sufficient and revengeful'. Even his own men weren't spared his brutality. He insisted that salt rations would harden them, and when the City of Amsterdam sent them food parcels, Fourgeoud confiscated the treats, sold them and trousered the proceeds. 'Hannibal', he once told Stedman, 'had lost his army by too much indulgence.' He himself, however, maintained a box of fresh provisions, but his real secret, he insisted, was *tisan*, a brew of Jesuit's bark, liquorice and cream of tartar so foul that no one else could stomach it. On campaign, his only other luxury was his wig, freshly powdered every day.

He must have made a daunting sight on Barbakoeba Kreek, right at the head of his column. 'His dress', reports Stedman, 'consisted of nothing but a waistcoat, and through one of the button holes he wore his sword; on his head he wore a cotton night cap with a white beaver hat above it and in his hand a cane; but he seldom carried his musket or his pistols. I have seen him all in rags and barefooted like the meanest of soldiers.' The slaves thought Fourgeoud was mad and would kill them all, whereas he considered himself a military figure somewhat akin to the Duke of Cumberland. He once asked Stedman to paint his portrait in full 'bush equipage', believing such a picture would advance his prospects in The Hague.

Back on the *kreek*, the raiding party was ready. At dawn on 15 August 1775 they set off, with the pioneers cutting a path. It was slow going. That day they cut their way through 'briars' and 'brambles' and covered a mere eight miles. The next four days were worse, a torment of drums and yelling, lice, fire-ants, horse-flies and hairy spiders. By night the mosquitoes were so bad that Stedman was forced to sling his hammock in the tree tops 'near one hundred feet above my companions'. To begin with, the odd soldier disappeared, but then 'our poor men were dying in multi-tudes' and 'thrown promiscuously into one pit like heaps of loath-some carrion'. At one point a Boni sprang up out of the leaves and then bolted like a stag. The men were too surprised or spent to get a shot in and were only cheered when a hundred 'black rangers' overtook them, all spoiling for the fight. 'One of these negroes', noted Stedman, 'is preferable to half a dozen white men in the forests of Guiana.'

On the fourth day the marines reached Gado Sabi, and there was a sudden flurry of colourful, polyphonic violence. Both sides used *tutus*, or trumpets, and there was a spirited exchange of curses and insults. Amid the screams came explosions and crackling as the greenery burst into flames and the forest turned white with smoke. In the confusion the Bonis slipped away and became invis-ible again. Coins and buttons sizzled through the air, ripping at the skin but leaving muscle and bone intact. Then, at some stage, a rebel climbed down from the canopy and started calmly reload-ing his gun. Stedman was fascinated: he'd never seen the enemy in action. The man was covered in amulets and charms, and clearly thought nothing could harm him – until the moment a musket-ball smashed through his femur. Then, as he lay there, reassessing his invincibility, another soldier put a musket in his ear and 'blew out his brains'.

At some point the screaming and the smoke subsided. The flames had left Stedman's men no spoils, except some broken spoons and a few half-eaten heads, mounted on stakes. Piqued by the lack of booty, the Vrijcorps rangers toured the dead and injured, found a few rebels and prised off their heads. When they started playing bowls with their trophies, Stedman protested, but they just insisted that it was 'the custom of their country'. Later, they would snip off the lips and ears and smoke them, as gifts for their women.

All night the battle of words continued. Both sides were now almost out of powder, and they goaded each other to come out and fight. The Bonis taunted the rangers as 'poltroons and traitors'. In reply, the Red Caps 'damned the rebels for a parcel of pitiful skulking rascals', too lazy to work. Then Fourgeoud joined in, offering the maroons 'life, liberty, victuals, drink and all they wanted'. The rebels hooted with laughter and said they wanted nothing from the half-starved Frenchman, and that his soldiers were scarecrows, hardly worth good ammunition. They were just 'white slaves hired to be shot at for four pence a day'. Bonny, said the rebels, would soon be governor of Suriname. Then, just to reassure everyone that they weren't finished, they tinkled their bill hooks, fired off a volley and scattered into the forest. Fourgeoud was furious and swore to pursue Bonny 'to the world's end'.

And that, broadly speaking, is what he did. It took the marines three days to march back to the entrance to Barbakoeba Kreek, and they then spent the next four and a half months scouring the jungle. Although they wouldn't find Bonny, they'd cover hundreds of miles and would find themselves in places that few people have visited since. By the end, Stedman was not only half naked and half starved, he also had 'a bad foot, a sore arm, the prickly heat and all my teeth loose with the scurvy'. He was also deeply depressed by the 'constant train of tortures to which I could see no end'. Maybe the Bonis were right, and he was merely a scarecrow, barely worthy of powder and shot? In early January 1776 Stedman was granted leave and boarded a barge bound for Paramaribo.

When I woke the next morning at dawn, we were well over half-way back. The Indonesians were in the galley cooking noodles, and the Master was on his bunk, an enormous pair of boots keeping watch at his door. Saiman was up on the bridge, sitting back in his huge chair, enjoying the sprawl of water ahead. He'd got rid of the tinny music and now wore his cap perched on the back of his head, as though he were Huckleberry Finn. All around us the river looked like a photograph slowly developing, its long, pale shapes gradually seeping from the morning mist.

I asked Saiman where we were.

'Just leaving the Cottica. Coming to the Commewijne.'

Ahead lay the junction of the two great rivers. We were heading off to the right, where the Commewijne widened again and arched away towards the sea. But off to the left it veered into the bush, where, according to the chart, it wriggled inland for over a hundred miles. I could still see the names of the plantations that Stedman had known: Fauquemberg and L'Espérance. In all the madness of the Boni War it was here that he'd found what he'd least expected, and that was happiness.

'How do I get up there?' I asked Saiman.

'You can't. No ferries. No boats any more.'

'But what about this road I can see?'

'OK, you can stand on the bridge and see the river.'

'But all the old houses are gone?'

'All gone. Burned down in the Hinterland War.'

I was puzzled. 'What? Two hundred years ago?'

Now Saiman was looking at me strangely.

'No, the Hinterland War,' he said, 'the one we just had.'

Ah yes, that one, I thought. An old war in new skins.

A few days later I would go out to the bridge and look down on the river.

Although I knew it was a forlorn enterprise, I found a driver who spoke English and asked him to take me out to the Commewijne. Jupiter was part Chinese and part N'Djuka, and had been born in the Hinterlands. He told me that the Chinese traders used to buy their wives off the maroons but that now he hated everything Chinese. After an hour of paddy fields and jungle we came to the bridge.

'See?' said Jupiter. 'Just a river.'

It was the same river I'd seen earlier, except blacker and clustered with trees. Somewhere in among the roots there'd be the remains of tiles and dykes, and hardwood piles. There were once great country houses all along this river, and in February 1774 Stedman had sailed

L'Espérance, the scene of something like happiness in a savage and eerie war.

up here, and – finding one abandoned – had made it his home. The war was almost forgotten for the rest of that year. Stedman restored L'Espérance, clearing the dykes, rebuilding the roof, driving off the rats and then, finally, calling for Joanna. She arrived in a tent-boat, rowed by eight slaves, and so began the only perfect part of Stedman's life. For the next ten months he and Joanna walked, bathed, ate, tended their garden and made love. 'I was never so happy,' he wrote many years later. Towards the end of 1774 their son, Johnny, was born, and was immediately bathed in Madeira for his contentment and health. Just at that moment it didn't seem to matter that – as the son of a slave – he was also a slave, and the personal property of somebody else.

Nor did it really matter that the war still went on. Stedman may have found contentment on the upper Commewijne, but it was never quite tranquillity. By night there were the drums, and the alarm guns all along the river. Then there were marines billeted near by, 'so very disorderly', noted Stedman, 'as to oblige me and my officers to knock them down by the half dozen'. Although he and Joanna were always planning a beautiful future, as Stedman's journals show, the madness of war was never far away. 'A marine drowned himself,' reads one of the entries, 'in one of those phrenzy fevers which are so common in Guiana ...'

'Jupiter,' I said, 'there's one more place I'd like to see.'

On my old map there was a path leading up from L'Espérance.

'I know this path,' said Jupiter, 'but it's all *broko* now.'

He was right: at the point where the path had joined the road there was nothing left but a house made of twigs. When we stopped outside, three very old people emerged, shaking the sleep from their filthy clothes. 'If they're maroons, they won't tell you anything,' whispered Jupiter. 'That's the tradition.'

But they weren't maroons and they chattered away in Talkie-talkie. *'A pasi gras'grasi,'* they said. The path's overgrown.

L'Espérance had gone, they told Jupiter, and no one lived there any more except a few N'Djukas. But the talk of war excited them. The two old women said their brother still had a bullet lodged in his skull. It's been there since Korea, they said. At this the old man drew himself very close and squinted into my eyes. I need this bullet, he said; if they take it out now, I'll probably die.

As the *Kite* passed through Paramaribo, I asked the Master what he'd do when the trip was over.

'Turn her around,' he said, 'and do it again.'

I'd almost forgotten that my river adventure was merely part of a cycle. There'll probably be tugs shuttling along the Cottica for ever, or for as long as the bauxite holds out. And what if it stops and the cycle ends? I had a sudden vision of the trees knitting together and the forest healing over.

It was different for the Bonis and Fourgeoud's marines. For them the cycle did end, although it wasn't the end of the war. By 1776 the pillage had all but ended, and the relentless rounds of manhunting had slowed to a grind. Both sides were exhausted. There would be no treaty, and no one could claim victory. The Bonis didn't have the weaponry to hold the forest, and the Dutch didn't have the manpower to sieve it. Stalemate ensued. If there was one lesson to be learned from the war, it was that only the Surinamese could properly fight in Suriname. From now on all maroon revolts would be dealt with by the Red Caps, or Vrijcorps. In time they'd become the Corps of Black Guides, and were only disbanded in 1863. At that point, it's said, they became maroons themselves, and their descendants still live on an island, far up the Marowijne River.

Meanwhile, Fourgeoud's marines were utterly spent. They'd covered thousands of miles of waterways and paths, and had burned twenty-one villages and over 200 fields of rebel crops. True, they'd contained the revolt, but they'd never captured the Boni, and the cost was catastrophic. Of the original detachment of 1,200 men, only a hundred remained. Of them, many would never get over the trauma, and remained, according to Stedman, 'in a state of incurable insanity for ever'.

As for the maroons, they'd continue their resistance but without the Bonis. The 'Cottica rebels' would abandon the Hinterlands. They could always cope with the loss of their villages, but not the loss of food. The final straw came in January 1777, when Fourgeoud discovered them on the Marowijne and burned everything they had. This time the Bonis crossed the river into French Guiana, leaving Suriname for ever. For Fourgeoud this was as good as success. The old colonel was now sixty-five and declared that 'having ransacked the forest in every direction and driven the rebels over the Marawina into Cayenne, he was determined no more to return to the woods'. He would never get the honours he felt he deserved, but died shortly after his return to The Hague, attended only by his slave.

Bonny too perished, after leaving the Hinterlands. For a while, all had seemed well in Cayenne. The French had often been accused of supporting the revolt, and now Bonny swore them an oath and even acquired his own little village (known, of course, as Boniville). But there was still fighting to be done and, in the end, Bonny was killed by rival maroons. It's said that as his killers fled down the Marowijne, they reached some falls where Bonny's severed head suddenly bounced up out of their canoe, grinned and then vanished in the rapids. The falls are, even now, known as Lèssé-Dédé ('Leave the Dead'), after Bonny. Right to the end, he'd given everyone the slip.

A few weeks later I was on the Marowijne and caught up with the Bonis. They still lived on the far bank, near where they'd landed. At first, their village didn't look very different from other maroon villages I'd seen, with its geometry and togas, and triangular huts. But then I noticed that, in the detail, it was French. Each hut had a blue enamel number; there was a small triangular town hall; all the canoes were painted in the colours of French football teams, such as

Paris Saint-Germain; and even the shrine to the *Gran Ouata Sinecki*, or Great Water Snake, was draped in a tricolore.

The Bonis had always loved the novelty of France, with its guns and its gadgets and its hoity-toity language. According to my guide (who was Surinamese), there were now almost 6,000 *Bushi Nengués* living in Guyane, enjoying all its trimmings. He said that at one time the Bonis had even given their children fancy French names such as Bateau, Champagne and Bicyclette. Not that names mattered. At any moment a Boni can shake off whoever he is and become someone else. This horrified the Surinamese. 'The people don't have laws,' said the guide. 'They don't care about work or marriage. No one controls them! France thinks it does but, to them, France is just … useful.'

There was still something of the warrior about them. The men on the jetty were all daintily cloaked and coiffed like Tudor men-at-arms. Their hair was lavishly plaited into wavy puffs, and they watched us with studied indifference. The Bonis have always unsettled outsiders. In 1948 the American explorer Hassoldt Davis wrote of the 'cold war' that characterised his travels with the Bonis. They had 'little heart and no ambition', he wrote, and would happily have killed him. Perhaps it was just contempt passing through the genes.

One of the men got up, and ambled over.

'*Téléphone?*' he asked.

I showed him my feebly blinking screen. '*Pas de signal.*'

He spat and looked away towards the far bank.

I asked him whether he'd ever like to live over there again, in Suriname.

He hauled his cloak up and glanced at me over his shoulder.

'*Pourquoi je voudrais? C'est merdique. J'habite ici. Je suis français.*'

(Why would I? It's shitty. I live here. I'm French.)

At the end of the Cottica campaign Stedman returned to the city to ponder his future. His first priority was his health. After months in the forest he was a 'miserable debilitated tatterdemalion', a mass of boils and bites. But he also had many months of back-pay, and so he rented a 'very neat small house' on the Waterkant, opposite the

Red Steps. There he settled down with Joanna and Johnny, almost as happy as they had been out at L'Espérance.

But there were no easy options from here. On the one hand, it was tempting to stay on in Suriname, as a dozen soldiers would. He had his family here, and the governor had offered him 400 acres of land. On the other hand, there was the problem of money. Stedman knew no other trade except soldiery and had no funds to develop the land. With what he had, he could only just afford the freedom of Johnny. This was more than most marines could manage. At least forty other children, the offspring of the expedition, would remain behind, in a state of perpetual slavery.

Then there was Joanna. It wasn't just that she was unafford- able or the property of someone else; she herself was still wary of freedom. She dreaded the prospect of becoming valueless, of being nothing, and of losing her status as a prestigious slave. For months Stedman tried to persuade her to come with him to Holland. There were tears and letters and long nights of pleading, but Joanna had decided. She'd give up everything, but not the dependence that defined her. Eventually Stedman realised it was hopeless and pre- pared himself for the loss that lay ahead. He placed Johnny under the guardianship of two Scots who were staying behind and gave instructions that, when the time was right, the child was to be baptised.

By the end of March 1777 the troopships were ready to sail. Stedman spent his last few days with Joanna and his son, and then, on 1 April, the order was given for him to embark. 'Joanna', he recalled, 'was unable to utter one word. The power of speech also forsook me, and my heart tacitly invoked the protection of Provi- dence to befriend them. Joanna now shut her beauteous eyes – her lips turned the pale colour of death ... Here I roused all my remain- ing fortitude and leaving them, surrounded by every care and atten- tion, departed and bid God bless them.'

Soon the transports were under sail. 'Motionless and speechless,' wrote Stedman, 'I hung over the ship's stern until the land quite disappeared.'

Much of his life after that savoured of regret and remorse. It was as though, in Suriname, he'd lived life so intensely that the years after that were merely a time of reflection. For a while he hung around in Holland with the Scots Brigade, slowly divesting himself of the previous five years. He stopped drawing and writing. He then gave away his enormous collection of maroon artefacts to the Royal Dutch Cabinet of Curiosities. (They were later sent to the Rijksmuseum voor Volkenkunde in Leiden, where they remain to this day.) He also remarried, recognising that not only was his first union invalid but that – after five years – it was also part of his past. His new wife, Adriana Wiertz van Coehorn, was well heeled, saintly and severe, all of which were qualities that, in her marriage to Stedman, she'd need in abundance.

Then, in 1783, Joanna seemed to reappear in Stedman's life. News came through that, at the age of twenty-four, she'd been poisoned, a victim of envy. Stedman had clearly never forgotten her, and now he seemed to feel the pain all over again. This time he called for Johnny and the boy was shipped to Holland along with a draft for £200 (his mother's legacy and, coincidentally, her value as a slave). That same year Holland allied itself with the nascent American colonies, and the Scots Brigade was disbanded. Stedman left behind his country of birth and took his family to England.

There they settled in Tiverton, in Devon, and became famous for fighting their neighbours. Stedman also made regular trips up to London, attending theatres, dances and bawdy houses. Adriana was constantly threatening to return to Holland, but in the end she settled for low-grade warfare with the English servants. She also bore Stedman another six children, including a Joanna. All of their sons would die on military service, including Johnny, who was drowned off Jamaica at the age of seventeen.

Somehow, amid the threads and ructions of his tumultuous life, Stedman managed to assemble a memoir. The first draft of *Narrative of a Five Years' Expedition against the Revolted Negroes of Surinam, in Guiana on the Wild Coast of South America* was so explicit that, when it first appeared in 1790, it had been vigorously bowdlerised. It was another six years before an unexpurgated version appeared, but the result was a triumph. With illustrations by William Blake, the book was underwritten by – among others – the Archbishop of Canterbury, Warren Hastings and the good Mrs Godeffroy. It ran to several editions and was translated into Dutch, French, Italian, Swedish and German. Everyone seemed to find something different in it; to many it was a rollicking adventure; to the abolitionists it was an inspiration; to Charles Kingsley the story of Joanna was 'one of the sweetest idylls in the English tongue'. Only V.S. Naipaul seemed

to find it all too much to stomach. It was, he said, 'a nauseous catalogue of atrocities' like those about the Nazis.

But, idyllic or emetic, the success of *Expedition* came too late for
Stedman. He died the year after publication, on 5 March 1797. He was
only fifty-two, but – after all he'd been through – even that felt like a
generous allowance. He'd made careful plans for the afterlife and asked
to be buried in Bickleigh churchyard, next to Bampfylde Moore Carew,
the self-styled 'King of the Gypsies'. Perhaps in Carew he thought he'd
find a fellow-wanderer and rebel. Clearly, however, Adriana was having
none of it, and so now the two old rogues find themselves at opposite
sides of the graveyards, with the church in between.

After my return from the Cottica I also found lodgings on the Waterkant. It was a large wooden house, white and clinker-built, with big
sash windows, dark green sills and drainpipes, and verandas up the
front. At first I'd rather quaintly imagined the Stedmans sitting up
there, sipping their punch, with a view of the river. But then I discovered that the entire quarter was burned down by maroons in 1832,
and that this house had only risen from the cinders.

I never discovered who owned it, or who the other guests were.
Occasionally, I'd find that my room had been cleaned, or that cur-
tains had been opened or that bits of furniture had vanished or been
replaced by something else. But the only person I ever saw was a
woman called Felisie, who used to come in at night and sit in the
hall, answering the phone. She was one of those Surinamese who
could be either mostly African or mostly Indonesian, or perhaps
even Jewish, depending on the light. 'I'm Dutch,' she told me, 'I only
came back to discover my roots.'

The other odd thing about the house was that at some stage it
had been completely scooped out and then fitted out in plastic. It
had vinyl walls and a glossy floor, and even the air was chilly and
false. Only the stairs were original, worn down by six generations of
sea-boots and two generations of slaves. Right up in the roof was my
room. It was clammy and white, like a sandwich box, and whenever
I opened the door there was a faint hermetic hiss. Up here I couldn't
hear or smell anything of the city. Once I opened the window but
was so startled by the blast of heat and roasted street that I never
opened it again.

That night I sat on the bed trying to work out how things had come to this. At first the city had seemed so expansive and open. Then I'd begun to notice that people disappeared or could only be found in casinos. Now here I was unable to taste or smell anything at all. It was almost as though the experience of Paramaribo had left me swaddled in film, deprived of my senses. But was it me, or was it Paramaribo? I'd often read about the city's opacity. No one ever seemed to know exactly what was happening. According to one writer, Andrew Westoll, even the truth here was never absolute but always democratic.

Something had to be done, and so I decided to call the last of my contacts. It was the other Marxist, the second of Dr Roopnaraine's comrades. From the start I had a feeling that I'd never get to meet him but that the quest would be intriguing and that, along the way, I'd get to peek beneath the surface. The man was already something of a myth, who'd emerged from nothing and was now disappearing again, hardly ever seen in public. People said that he'd been a chicken farmer and long-distance runner, that he was part Amerindian, that he was pale-skinned, that he never looked at anyone directly and that, in the army, he'd never been more than a sergeant-major, teaching PT. Still, I thought, he shouldn't be difficult to find. On 25 February 1980, at the age of thirty-four, Désiré Delano Bouterse had seized control of the country.

Downstairs, I asked Felisie to help me find his number.

'Desi?' she gasped. 'You know him?'

'No, I'm just trying to get in touch …'

She studied me for a second. 'You know he's a powerful man?'

I said I'd read a bit about him.

'OK,' she said, 'we'll try,' and, with a tiny tremble she found the number for his office. She dialled, spoke for a moment, listened, spoke again and then hung up. 'They say he'll call us back.'

'That was his office? So he's still in politics?'

Felisie nodded, avoiding my gaze. 'Yes, he's very strong.'

'But he frightens you a little?'

Felisie shook her head. 'No,' she said.

'Then why are we whispering?'

Across the city I'd come across several reminders of Desi's coup. There were the old barracks on the waterfront, now no more than a burned-out carcase. The Ministerie van Financiën had also been charred a little later, and all that remained was an outline. There was even a monument to the day, a large bas-relief made from slabs of concrete. It depicted soldiers with hunting rifles, and was made with so little conviction that now the slabs were peeling away and tumbling into the street.

Everyone now thanks Holland for what happened, or blames it. Five years earlier, Suriname had been a bubbly little colony, with guilders splashing around and more bauxite than it knew what to do with. But then came a call for autonomy, and in 1975 – in a fit of over-indulgence – Holland granted not only independence but also passports for anyone wanting to leave. Over the next five years a third of the country took up the offer. Businesses closed, millions of dollars left the country, and so did a whole generation of graduates, taking with them whatever chance the country may have had of surviving on its own. Instead of leadership, it was left with two decrepit factions known as the Ruziemakers, or 'Troublemakers', and the Oude Ratten, or 'Old Rats'.

During the shambles that followed, Suriname was easily overwhelmed. In all the press cuttings Desi has a beard and a hunting rifle and looks like The Deer Hunter, except that he knows about nothing except chickens. But people would still believe him. He declared a *revolutie*, and marched his enemies out onto Independence Square, dressed only in their underpants. Democracy, he promised, would follow, and out on the wall of the barracks he left a box labelled 'Suggestions'. Even The Hague seemed to like him at this stage, and – say some – may even have put him in power. In the hands of the Chicken Hunter, Suriname seemed secure.

But it wasn't long before Desi was burning books, and everything that follows. Parliament and the constitution all failed in the ensuing months. Paramaribo seized up with strikes, and even the palace was reduced to using candles. Only Desi seemed to flourish, and made himself a colonel. Although he wasn't a natural Marxist, he was soon closing down papers and punishing the bourgeoisie. 'We have stooped long enough beneath the yoke of capitalism,' he declared. By 1982 his only friend was Cuba, and it had no money to spare.

Then events took a turn for the worse. Dr Roopnaraine told me that until that time the 'Caribbean Left' had supported Bouterse. 'He was one of us,' said my Guyanese friend, 'but then something happened, and things got much worse. We never saw him after that.' What caused the change? Who knows, perhaps a visit from Maurice

Bishop, the Lenin of Grenada? 'The Surinamese revolution is too friendly,' he told Desi. 'Reactionary forces are too strong. You have to eliminate those who are not with you.'

When I got back later that evening, Felisie was there by the phone.
   'Has Bouterse called?' I asked.
   'No, he won't call back.'
   'Why?'
   'He'll think you're the CIA.'
   'Maybe I should visit him, just turn up?'
   'Better to call,' said Felisie.
   'Why is everyone so scared of him?'
   She pretended not to hear. '*Desi for Presi*, that's what we say.'
   I smiled, letting a little silence gather between us.
   'The fort,' she said quietly, 'you need to look inside the fort.'

The next day I walked down the waterfront to Fort Zeelandia and, for the first time, found that it was open. The inside was even stranger than I'd imagined, like an acre of Europe that had somehow got lost. Everything was made of rock or bricks, which made voices sound different and gave footsteps a dry, unfamiliar ring. Around the courtyard was a small pentagon of mansions, housing an apothecary, dining-rooms, state apartments and some hot, stuffy gun-decks up in the attic. Nowadays it was a museum with a pitiless tale to tell. No one, it seems, had ever benefited from possession of the fort. The man who captured it from the English went bust. His successor, Lord Sommelsdijk, was dragged up onto a bastion by his own men and shot like a sheep. The fort hadn't even withstood a good siege, and eventually it was reduced to a jail.

The dungeons were still there, deep below the mansions. Its inmates must have felt they'd been bundled away to die in the drains. Countless visionaries had perished down here, reconsidering their perspective with the help of pincers or racks, or just years of neglect. A candle still burned for them, the room's shadows trembling in the glow. Stedman had always hated the fort and called it 'the gloomy mansions of despair'.

Just below the east bastion, Bastion Veere, was the kitchen. Not long ago, in 1982, it too had become an oubliette. With such an impressive record for persuasion, the fort had seemed perfect to Desi. It would be his Tower of London, or a miniature Bastille. That year he snatched it back from the museum service and began filling it with those who opposed him.

By 7 December the kitchen was like a little parliament, an assembly of all the best brains the country had left. Later, Desi's men would struggle to justify the round-up. 'It was them or us,' said one of his prime ministers, Wim Udenhout. But the prisoners were hardly desperadoes – just unionists, journalists, the dean of the university and a few of their lawyers. Desi called them 'the Underworld', and at midnight they were marched up the stairs onto the bastion itself.

At the top of the stairs it was dark, and I became aware of someone else, standing in the shadows. He was stooped and had narrow, rheumy eyes, and skin like a date. Despite the heat, he was wearing a cardigan and suit, and I had a feeling he wasn't supposed to be there. He explained how he'd once been a teacher, and that now all he did was show people round. 'OK,' I said, 'then perhaps you can show me the Bastion Veere?' And, with that, we stepped outside into the sunlight.

It was still a crime scene, with a temporary fence from wall to wall.

'That's where they was standing,' said the old teacher.

Just like Sommelsdijk, I thought: lined up, facing soldiers and wondering how all this would end. Some say that Desi himself appeared, hauling a belt of twinkling cartridges and some dire weapon, which he unleashed on the group. Others say it was the fort's commander, or that the men died trying to escape. This was the explanation that Desi preferred, and the one which, the next day, he broadcast over the radio. It was never a great story and looked even shakier when fifteen corpses turned up at the hospital, bruised and beaten, and spattered with gunfire from front to back.

The shellstone rampart was still deeply scarred and pitted. I asked the teacher about the groove around each hole.

'Dutch detectives. A few years ago, they cuts out the bullets.'

'And did they discover anything?'

'Yes, my friend, they did. None of this was planned.'

'How could they tell?'

'Because the killer weren't standing here at all.'

I was puzzled. 'Then where was he?'

'Right up there. In the roof.'

Nothing about the killings would, I realised, make much sense. They'd become known as the *Decembermoorden*, or 'December murders', a historical riddle at the heart of Suriname. A few years later a detective had tried to investigate them but had himself been hauled in front of the fort and shot through the head. Even now the case was fraught with distortion. All the pieces of the jigsaw were there – scene, motive, weapon and killer – and yet nothing seemed to fit together. There was even a murder trial, which Desi occasionally attended. He had his own courthouse, with its own new road, and the trial looked set to become an institution that would trundle on for ever. It hadn't even got beyond the wearily procedural and had already scrambled the wits of three different judges. Every now and then Desi appeared on television, silvery now and slightly heavier around the jowls. He seemed quite sure that one day he'd be president once more.

'Do you think he will be?' I asked the teacher.

'We all got blood on our hands.'

'I don't understand …'

'We lived with this so long, we don't believe anything no more.'

After the killings Suriname would never be the same again. At first, it was merely isolated. Each of its neighbours shrank away, except Brazil, which moved 20,000 troops up to the border. Meanwhile, the Dutch pulled out, taking all their money. At the funerals of those who'd died in the fort the mourners stopped outside the embassy and shouted 'Help us! Help us!', but there was nothing the Dutch could do. Desi was already recruiting new bedfellows. China built a stadium, and the Iranians called by in the hope of something cheap. Then came the Libyans, looking for rice, but even they found Desi too cranky and drifted away. In desperation Desi turned to private enterprise, and by 1985 the country was floating along on the profits of Colombian cocaine.

After that, Suriname seemed to slip deeper and deeper into a moral malaise. It became a sort of narco-dystopia, a Colombian Guiana. Airstrips were rented out at the rate of $1 million a year, and there was always a general to help things through. At one point Suriname was filtering cocaine into Europe at the rate of twenty tons a year. Once Desi himself went to Brazil to buy the necessary ether (and was only accidentally arrested because he had so much cash that the whores thought he was a robber). Meanwhile secrecy thrived, and so too did fear. The streets started emptying at night, and bodies appeared, wrapped in plastic and blasted with shells. A new order had developed, under the cover of government. In Holland, Desi and a few of his lackeys were tried in absentia and convicted of trafficking. They all had guns and boats and planes of their own.

Most of this had gone now, and Suriname's a much better place than it was. But it's said that on every flight to Amsterdam there are still a few 'mules'. The Desi years explained everything: the casinos, the poverty, the fear of darkness and the politicians driving around in Humvees on $20,000 a year. Even now there were still occasional reports of ministers importing girls or building drop-sites in the bush.

But in 1985 there was far worse to come. The talk of booty had awoken a giant. It was the Hinterland War, about to restart, more vicious than ever before.

By now I was phoning Desi four times a day. I realised I'd never find him, but the hunt was intriguing. I always got someone different, usually a woman. '*Who?*' they'd say. 'What you wanna ask him? He gonna call you back.' He never did. Felisie gave me some more numbers, and I'd phone them all sequentially, to find that Desi was in three different meetings all at once. One woman even said he was abroad, a thrilling idea for a man now wanted all over the world. But I never gave up and hounded him down from number to number. Felisie said he had houses everywhere, although what I suspect she meant was girls. Desi was notoriously demanding.

In some ways his persistent inability to get to the phone came as a relief. What do you say to a man who's been found guilty of war crimes and trafficking drugs? Would I become shrill or just silly with nerves? And if he asked me to meet him, would I go to his house, hidden away behind the razor-wire and trees? I decided that, while I'd keep pestering Desi, I needed someone else, calmer with the facts. But who? Would anyone talk about the new rebels, and the new Hinterland War, and how it all began? Then I discovered that Desi's old prime minister, Wim Udenhout, worked around the corner. Between 1984 and 1986 he'd fronted an unhappy coalition, but then – as the regime corrupted – he'd found himself miles away, as ambassador to Washington. Nowadays, he ran a conservation organisation and was a model of reform. Surely he'd put everything in place? I gave him a call.

'OK,' he said, 'I can see you for an hour.'

When I first met Udenhout, I was so fascinated by his appearance that I hardly absorbed a word. Although a little older, he was exactly like those Surinamese I'd seen on television all those weeks before: slim, black, buttoned-down and suave. We were sitting in his office on huge velour sofas, mine so deep and plush that it made my handwriting bounce all over the page. It was like being in one of those adverts, everything verging on perfect. There was only one unsettling feature, and that was Mr Udenhout's tie, which hung on a hook above his desk. It was all looped and ready-knotted, as though at any moment he might throw it over his head and bound off into a crisis.

I don't think he'd noticed my lapse of concentration, and was already in full swing. '… when I first saw maroons, they were like curiosities …'

Next to us was a large map of Suriname, and across it a red laser dot darted backwards and forwards, picking out the tribes. Mr Udenhout explained how the maroons now lived in harmony with the coast, how they were developing and becoming urbanised, how their women were going to university, and how old structures were changing. It would take time; nothing would happen overnight. 'If you want to educate a man,' he beamed, 'you have to start with his grandfather.'

I smiled back, uncomfortably conscious that I was a congregation of one.

'You make it all sound very simple,' I said.

Udenhout laughed and then leaned forward, talking with politician's hands. 'Yes, of course the old tensions are still there. They go back years. The coast and the maroons. But, after independence, it was different. The Creoles began to discover their identity. We began to appreciate our blackness. The maroons, however, weren't interested, not at all. They'd never had an identity problem! They didn't even accept the leadership of this country, and had no interest in independence. They said their treaties were with the Queen of Holland, and no one else. It caused a lot of resentment on the coast …'

'Just resentment?'

Udenhout held out his palms. 'They don't trust us, we don't trust them.'

'You've often been criticised for your treatment of maroons …?'

'In the foreign press, you mean?'

'Well, yes, and all those judgments in the Inter-American Court …'

The little red eye flickered angrily over the room. 'Outsiders,' said Udenhout, selecting his words with care, 'still seem to believe in a noble savage. It's far from the reality, really it is! This is not about human rights, it's about politics. The maroons just use these false, idealist arguments for their own political gain … They say they want communal rights. But we say the state protects the rights of individuals, and, by joining the electoral process, they've elected to be part of our state! Believe me, give them an inch and they take a mile …'

'But they've lost a lot of land, hunting, gold …?'

Udenhout shook his head, and said that whatever was out there was never theirs. 'The crux of the problem is that a people happy in isolation have discovered that it's not really their country and that the resources don't belong to them …'

'And under your administration it led to a war?'

'The maroons were led by a bank robber …'

'But with quite a lot of support?'

'That was the Dutch,' said Udenhout, 'the Dutch Secret Service.'

'And what about Desi? Didn't he once say he'd wipe out the maroons?'

Wim Udenhout looked at his watch, and sighed. 'I think if we're going to talk about Mr Bouterse,' he said, rising to his feet, 'it'll have to wait until another time.'

When I told Felisie that I no longer needed my room, and that I'd be going in the morning, she seemed almost relieved. It was as though, at last, she could say what she wanted, safe in the knowledge that her thoughts would go with me, travelling west and harmlessly leaving the country. It was such a sad valedictory that I wrote it down almost word for word.

'I'm also leaving soon,' she said, 'I can't live here any more. I can't stand it. I had such high hopes when I came. I was brought up in Holland but I always felt different. There was something missing. So I came here. Do you understand that? Maybe not, why should you? I thought it would be paradise. But it isn't. It's hell. No one is who they seem to be, and beneath the surface everything's a lie. I now know something I never knew before: I'm not African. I can't connect with Africans. I'm Dutch. Maybe it's all about slavery? We were fed and housed. We never had to think, never had to use our initiative. This place is mad. You know the politicians here? They fight in their parliament. They actually kick and punch! How can I live here, and teach my children how to behave? People here have no respect for anything, not even your life. I hate it. I hate it here.'

As I read these words back, I still don't know what to think. Did other people feel like this? Perhaps it was a mark of the superficiality of my travels, but I was sorry to be leaving. I'd never quite fallen out of love with Paramaribo, even if, the longer I was there, the less I felt I knew it. So did Felisie really mean what she'd said, or believe it with such vehemence? I'd often wondered how well she'd known Desi, and whether they'd ever been lovers. How did she have all those numbers, and how did she know what he'd say?

As I was leaving Udenhout's office, he'd said something to me that I'd taken as admonition: 'In Suriname,' he'd warned, 'take nothing at face value. Nothing is what you'd expect.'

The last stage of my Surinamese journey took me west, through the sweltering forests of the new Hinterland War. This time the war was fought not along a river but along a road: the Oostwestverbinding, or East–West Highway. It was a battlefield two lanes wide and 144 miles long, ending on the Marowijne, the border with Guyane. Although the killing was supposed to have ended in 1992, it was said that there were still a few stragglers, fighting on. There were also minefields scattered through the verges. Never travel at night, people said, and never leave the road.

I rang up Jupiter and asked him if he'd take me.

'OK, man. Sixty euros. Pick you at 4 a.m.'

The great thing about travelling with Jupiter was that I always knew when he was telling the truth. It didn't take long to work out that he'd organised his honesty geographically. In Paramaribo, Jupiter was inventive and sly. Until we got back out to the

Commewijne bridge, everything he said had to be carefully assessed. He told me he was ex-special forces, that he'd travelled with the president and that he could kill a man with a single blow, driving the nose up through the brain. At one point, about an hour out of Paramaribo, we came across a large anaconda, lying dead across the road. 'The Chinese will come and eat this,' he said. 'They eat everything. They even ate my dog.'

But beyond the bridge Jupiter changed, and became more self-assured. The flippancy went, and with it the drawl of the street. Perhaps being back on ancestral lands made him feel he no longer needed to impress. At the very mention of the N'Djukas he became serious, even fleetingly withdrawn. They were the poorest of the maroons, he told me, but probably the oldest. There were still 25,000 of them, scattered through the forest. 'Once we had double that,' he said, 'but then they all run away ...'

The jungle too was different after the bridge. Jupiter loved the way it seemed to wrap around us, and talked about his childhood. All the best bits were about trees. He remembered hiding for weeks, and hunting for monkeys. There were seeds that could knock you out, and wood that could make a chainsaw spark. There was even a palm nut with juice just like a mother's milk. 'And this leaf here,' said Jupiter, 'this is bush papaya, which we make into tea.'

At that point he spotted a stake in the verge, mounted with a gourd.

'Good, someone selling *podosiri*.'

With that he veered off the road through a leafy tunnel and out into a large clearing of blackened stumps and sand. At the far side was a village made of grass, and, as no one was around, we got out and walked through the huts. I felt sure that we weren't alone, and were being carefully studied from out in the shadows. There was a monkey tethered to a post, and fresh fruit on all the altars (bananas and cassava, said Jupiter, left out for *mama-bouchi*, the goddess of the bush). There was also a cage full of peccaries, who squealed at us and made themselves as unappetising as possible with a collective fart of rotting vomit. The foul acid reek caught me right in the gullet. 'Shit!' I gagged. 'How can anyone eat that? I'd rather have roadkill, that old anaconda ...'

'We don't touch *snekis* ...'

'But all that oil ...?' I said (thinking of Stedman).

'Too dangerous. The *sneki* is a friend of the water monkey ...'

At that moment an old woman appeared. She looked as though she'd been chemically shrunken, or packed in ash. She wore only a thin, dusty dress, and around her neck she had a string of seeds that seemed fat and voluptuous against her shrivelled skin. Her eyes were yellow, and the pupils swivelled nervously between us. She told Jupiter there were no children, she was too old to find the pina fruit, and so there was no *podosiri*. She then stood there, her hands shaking, willing us to leave.

'She looks very frightened,' I said, as we got back to the car.

Jupiter nodded and tried to explain. These were difficult times for the N'Djukas. Many of them had only just returned. The dead had not been properly buried, and some had never been found. Their spirits would wander the forest for ever. Mama-Bouchi was angry, and the land was *broko*. Once, only little things – such as a knife – became *paiyé*, or cursed. Now it was everything. People wondered if the soldiers would come back. You don't forget that noise, the *boom-boom* and *dagadaga*. The worst, however, was the Alouette. It was like the water monkey except it came from above.

Further down the highway we crossed the Cottica river.

'This is where I was,' said Jupiter, 'when the war began.'

Just off the highway was a small town, Moengo. It had been built by a bauxite company and had a spry, American feel. Everything was widely spaced and dusted in pink, and occasionally large contraptions rumbled through, coughing up smoke and ore. Most of the shops were Chinese, but there was also a mosque and a glossy, incongruous bank. It was here, in 1986, that the old war of the Hinterlands had restarted, with what seemed like an ordinary bank raid. The robber was only twenty-four, an N'Djuka called Ronnie Brunswijk. He'd been one of Desi's bodyguards until they'd fallen out over money. After that, he'd taken his guns and headed back to the forest, where he'd become an army of one. His friends had called him Ronbo.

'I remember him then,' said Jupiter, 'I was only a kid ...'

'I heard he was just a thief ...'

'No. He was the only man who cared about maroons.'

I'd often seen pictures of Brunswijk in his extravagant togas. Although he was meaty and powerful, he'd always been a man of outfits. During the fighting he'd affected mirror glasses, a crossbow, a full-length wig and a fancy holster. The maroons had loved him; he was brash, generous and brutal. He'd also realised that there was more to running away than robbery. He became the focus of N'Djuka discontent. Desi was an impostor; the interior belonged to the maroons, along with everything in it. By the end of that year Brunswijk had rallied over 300 fighters, enough to call themselves an army. At first they were the SLA but, as this didn't sound like a movie, they changed it, and became the Jungle Commandos. Brunswijk even found them their own flag, and amulets to ward off the bullets.

'That's his house,' said Jupiter, as we pulled out of Moengo.

Set back in the bush was a large dirty-white villa, surrounded by an eight-foot wall. Behind the wall I could see a watchtower and a haze of aerials and wire. Once, the medieval equivalent of this fortified house could be found all over Britain. Everything about this war, I suddenly realised, was beginning to feel feudal and old. In time, Brunswijk's men would control an area the size of Wales but without any law at all. Only the weaponry would be state-of-the-art. Every other aspect of modern life would falter, and for the next six years the western hinterlands would once again seal themselves off from the outside world. All communication would fail, and so would the rivers. The tugs would run for a while, but then the pirates would bring them all to a halt. Moengo too would empty, forcing families such as Jupiter's into a city for the first time in their life. 'And once we did that,' he said, 'we forgot how to live, and we've never come back.'

Meanwhile there was still a national army to be defeated. The N'Djukas began by raiding the mines and stealing all the dynamite. They then crept back to the highway and started snuffing out the present.

From now on there was always some reminder of the upheavals on this road. It was either buildings, charred and black like empty hearths, or whole villages, reduced to their stumps. At one point the road itself had been viciously gashed up the middle and then repaired with new white concrete. For almost twenty miles we followed this gash as it wriggled away in front of our eyes. 'It was the Jungle Commandos,' said Jupiter. 'They once steal a digger, and dig up the road.'

Elsewhere, the road fell away in holes, but Jupiter kept up his speed.

'Never stop for the potholes, or they going to rob you.'

'Who's they?'

'Just people. They don't have much.'

Almost everyone was diminished by this war. Some merely lost everything, while others were stripped down to their screaming, primeval selves.

Among the Jungle Commandos there had never been much idealism. A few Hindu officers had ended up among them, but at the first whiff of voodoo most had drifted away. They could never understand the amulets and effigies, and the strange decisions, divined from smoke and offal. Even those that stayed often found their loyalty taxed and would slowly fall apart, and then be killed as traitors.

For the N'Djukas warfare had seemed a bold enterprise at first. Most of the rebels had happily joined up, although a few had needed beating. Some had almost no experience of guns, while others – such as the infamous Django – were notorious criminals, pleased to be killing. In the first surges the N'Djukas fought like the Bonis and almost reached the city. But then the war slowed, and their squalor seemed to gather in around them. Weapons rusted, garbage mounted, camps were scattered with faeces and the men reverted to wearing feathers and bone. To secure even the most incidental compliance Ronnie would have to flog them hard, with an old steel cable.

But after a while the N'Djukas no longer seemed to feel their own pain. Perhaps that's why they were so curious about the pain of others and were always trying to prise their captives apart with sticks and bayonets. As for themselves, they were invincible, or so their shaman told them. He also gave them magic talismans – made from reinforcing rods – and herbs with which to make themselves invisible. They'd become their own little gods, oblivious to mortality.

The drugs didn't help. There was marijuana for the hunger, and heroin for everything else. Some N'Djukas could shoot so much of this stuff that it would make their eyes glow red. That's when the trees started walking and the sky turned to snakes. On Langatabbetje Island they began worshipping a severed head that had been set on a stake still wearing its helmet. But nearer the enemy the constant zip and thwack of bullets seemed only to amplify the trip. At a place called Frontline the warriors would baptize themselves in a large drum of human soup, made of body parts and water. Once, on a high like this, Django and the shaman set off to take on the National Army and were immediately captured, to be slowly and thoughtfully killed.

Even Ronbo was diminished by the war. By the end he was no longer the muscly, guns-blazing video star but a retiring figure, greedy and compulsive. He spent most of the conflict way up the Marowijne, out of reach of the government planes. There he whiled away his days playing Space Invaders, and trying to rekindle his vigour with other men's wives. Having blown up all the bridges and power lines, he had no idea what to do next. For months nothing happened. 'It's kind of hit-and-miss,' he told journalists, 'we don't have the weapons ...'

Things were little better on the other side. At the height of the war Desi had only 2,535 men at his disposal, mostly Creoles. They were terrified of the Hinterlands, and the N'Djukas, whom they thought of as ghosts. Most would only enter the forest behind an armoured car, with its .50 cal blindly pumping cannon fire into the trees. They did the same on the river, gunboats blasting away at anything: villages, manatees, mudbanks and monkeys. It's said that one in ten of the soldiers deserted and fled to French Guiana. As for the rest, they soon lost sight of what the war was all about. It infuriated them that they could never find the enemy, and so they started killing maroons wherever they could. They pulled them off minibuses, or tracked them down in the city, and paid them visits at night.

It was even better when the helicopters arrived. Villages were easy to spot in an Alouette. A man didn't even need to get his boots wet. He could just sit there, above all the terror and stink, delivering death from above.

Ahead was a small settlement, more like a camp.

'Alfonsdorp,' said Jupiter.

Amid the tin and grass I spotted something familiar: bluish hair and Asiatic faces. Amerindians.

'Yep,' said Jupiter, 'put there by government.'

'You don't sound as though you like them?'

He sighed and then reached over for his mobile phone. 'See this? The Amerindians think this is a god. They live all natural in the forest, right? But you promise them one of these, and they do any-thing you want. Anything. Give him a cell phone, he's gonna do what you say, even kill anyone you want …'

Like a game of chess where every move is stalemate, the war had soon seized up. Both sides needed champions to punch their way through to the other.

The maroons had hired theirs in Amsterdam. They offered $500 a week, and $1 million if the revolt succeeded. This brought out all the riff-raff of the gun world – Rhodesians, Belgians and Afrikaners. There was even a band of fourteen Americans at one stage, although they never made it beyond New Orleans, where they were arrested with a cache of weapons and *Fodor's Guide to Suriname*. But most of the mercenaries were British, former soldiers drifting around in search of a high. Few of them thrived. At least one drank himself to a standstill. Another was shot by his fellow Britons, in some Byzan-tine intrigue. ('Why are you doing this to me?' he pleaded, as they reloaded their weapons and fired again.) But the most notorious of all was a Liverpudlian called Karl Penta. In his memoirs he happily admits to having tortured his captives and claims to have built his own rockets and crippled the government all by himself. It's a bold claim from such a stagnant war.

Desi was more cunning in his choice of champions. He realised that they'd been there all the time, living in the forest. Only the Amerindians could survive this fight. Desi put out a rumour that he was one of them and made a grandiose promise of land. The tribes already had their own little armies, such as 'Tucayana Amazonas', and soon they'd be hunting maroons again, just as they'd done for the Dutch. But, unlike the Dutch, Desi was never much good with his promises. The Amerindians never got their land, just the odd little slum, like Alfonsdorp.

A few miles up the road, the Alouettes had been at work. The day they landed at Moiwana, 29 November 1989, is still the most per-plexing day in Suriname's history. Never before had so many died in one morning or so pointlessly, and there's been nothing like it since. Today Moiwana is no longer just a village but a byword for disbelief and horror. For years the forensic pathologists picked over the bones, but they never found a killer. The Inter-American Court would order the state to pay millions in compensation, but no one has ever worked out who did what, or why. Desi, of course, was never very far from the smoking gun. He's often been quoted demanding an end to the maroons, or saying that it was he who ordered this mission. But now he denies everything, and you can even watch him on YouTube, beaming with innocence and hurt.

The court did, however, establish what happened. From the blizzard of sand and whirring blades, men appeared. Most of the N'Djukas panicked and scattered into the forest. There was the faint *snap snap* of gunfire and the giddy reek of gasoline. Then the soldiers busied themselves among the stragglers, lopping the children, felling the women and wrenching them apart. 'I just ran and ran,' said one girl, then aged eleven, 'and somehow I survived …'

Many of the dead were butchered, chunked with machetes. It was like the old war, except for the gasoline and Alouettes. There was the same loathing, the same perfunctory rape and the same eerie sense of detachment. 'Another soldier,' recalled one witness, 'grabbed a six-month-old baby and put the barrel of his gun in its mouth. The baby took it eagerly like a baby bottle. The soldier pulled the trigger …'

Thirty-nine people died that morning, most of them children. Some were doused in fuel and burned, and the rest tossed into pits and left until the end of the war.

Jupiter hesitated at the edge of the clearing, and so I walked ahead.

Out in the sand were the monuments, ordered by the court. Each victim had his or her own huge polyhedron, either a cube or column or a rectangular prism, made from concrete and steel. Each one was different, like a sarcophagus for someone who'd vanished. Few remains had been found. These shapes were now all that was left of the village and the villagers. To maroons the geometry may have been perfect, but the emptiness was a constant reminder of something else. Along this road a way of life had died. After Moiwana, 10,000 N'Djukas fled to the city, and about the same number to Guyane.

'They never coming back,' said Jupiter, back at the car.

'Because Desi's still around?'

Jupiter ignored this, and started up the car.

'Because burning people,' he said, 'is the worst you can do.'

'So what would get you all to come back?'

Jupiter looked out over the clearing and the huge blocks of rust. 'Nothing,' he said at last, 'except revenge.'

At the end of the road was a small town that's always felt like an island. In front of it is the Marowijne, like a strip of ocean, and behind it – on all three sides – there's the forest, as dark as the sea. But along the waterfront there's sand and little coves of shell and powdered coral. The first settler here was German, who thought it all so pale and *gemütlich* that he named it after his wife, Albina.

There were still a few traces of the little lives that had prospered here. I spotted what had once been an esplanade, a line of *boetieks* and a fancy cinema called the Apollo. Trading with maroons had obviously been good business. By the 1930s all that had troubled Albina was the sight of French convicts swimming over the river. It had dealt with the problem by hiring a militia to shoot them on sight.

Only for a moment did the town feel linked to the outside world. That was when the highway came nosing through the forest, bringing with it cars and tourists and the Paramaribo rich. For a while, in the '70s, Albina became a little Acapulco, and there were villas and tarts and a glittery casino. But then came the war and the closure of the road. For years Albina was once again reliant on the sea. Meanwhile, the maroons vented their fury on the town, torching the villas and taking potshots at anything that moved. That's why Albina looks like a camp again, and why the Apollo now has a jungle growing up through the foyer.

By 1989 the war that surrounded Albina began to look different. If it had ever been a struggle over land, it was now a war of turf. Even Brunswijk had realised that, in wartime, there were better things to do than fight. Planes started appearing, packed with cocaine, and there was talk of millions of dollars in counterfeit notes. While the foot soldiers slogged it out in the forest, the leaders cut a deal and shared out the spoils. Not even the little flurries of democracy, in 1987 and 1991, could reverse the decline. Desi was soon back at the levers, wielding control. Towns such as Albina became miniature kleptocracies, doing whatever made most money.

'Be careful,' said Jupiter, 'there's still bad people here.'

It was time for him to return to Paramaribo.

'I got to be off this road before it gets dark.'

So it seemed Albina was an island once again, encircled by the night. I was happy to be leaving that same afternoon.

I spent my last few days in Suriname on a journey of revival. The trees grew back, the river opened out, and people reappeared. I'd needed this, the perspective restored. Travel is so often a series of snapshots that gives us not a whole but a sequence of viewpoints. Could I really let my Surinamese travels end in empty tombs and ploughed-up roads? This was one of the most enchanting, enchanted countries I'd ever known, and here I was creeping out through the wreckage of its long-lost war. Almost half the population were now too young to remember it, and much of the horror had long since merged with the leaf mould.

Even before leaving Paramaribo, I realised that another journey was needed. This time, I'd travel right to the far side of the Hinterlands, through the tail-end of its wars, and emerge in the present. It would be a journey up the Marowijne, and for this I'd managed to join a group of Germans and Dutch, departing from Albina. Our guide, as you'd expect in Suriname, didn't seem to belong in this story at all and was a Lebanese, called Zaahid.

Ahead, a beautiful river unravelled towards us. Although the Marowijne was almost two kilometres wide, it was barely navigable. The water looked as though it had been ploughed and then thrown down the stairs. Along the length of the river there were eighty-seven sets of rapids, each one a squall of gnashing and froth. According to Zaahid, these falls all had names such as 'Spill your Wealth', or *Petrosoengoe*, 'Peter Sank'. Until the advent of the engine, the Marowijne was almost useless to Man, except as a refuge.

Sometimes we saw whole islands of vegetation hurtling past, like gardens on the move. Or it might be tree trunks or other *korjalen*, loaded with oil drums. Our own canoe wasn't much more than a tree trunk, split down the middle and sharpened at one end. But when it came to the rapids, the boatman, Jacobus, simply gunned the engine, and we lumbered up over the torrents. It felt as though we were climbing an escalator the wrong way, with the river in our faces and bulging over the gunwales. But it was all second nature to maroons. Jacobus seemed to feel his way through the currents, and if ever we touched a rock, the boat just grunted and carried on up. Everyone used these *korjalen*, even the *gendarmes* over on the French side. We could often see them skimming over the water to see who we were.

At other times the channel took us right across, and we could peer into their lives. It might be a brand new school, or a television mast, or a line of soldierly pants drying in the sun. To the maroons this strange, rich world was known simply as 'France'. Most of the villagers, however, were – just like them – *les marrons noirs*. After two centuries of Hinterland wars, almost a third of all bush negroes were now holed up in French Guiana, and probably would be for ever. At Apatou we stopped to visit the oldest of all the refugee communities, that of the Bonis.

I asked Zaahid what the Bonis now thought about the Creoles.

'Same,' he shrugged. '*Baccra slaaf*. The white man's slave.'

I turned to Jacobus, but he hadn't understood.

'That tooth,' I said pointing to the fang on his necklace.

'Jag-u-ar. *Mi kiri en,*' he said, and then never spoke again.

Beyond Apatou the river narrowed and became fiercer than ever. But despite the ferocity, there were still gold-dredgers bobbing around in the froth. They looked like little factories, complete with their floating slums. Nestled in among the drums of mercury there were always girls, and babies with faces like old men. For the time being this, I suppose, was the future of the river: a quick buck and poisoned fish. It was probably better than war. The Marowijne had proved an enthusiastic participant. It had even got revenge on the Alouettes by sucking one into the rapids and smashing it to bits.

After an hour we passed Langatabbetje Island. This was where the Jungle Commandos had worshipped the severed head. It looked quiet now. In a last fit of rage the government had bombed it with phosphorus, crisping anybody left. After that, the war just petered out.

Peace came from an unexpected quarter: France.

For years the French had encouraged the Jungle Commandos. But then, after 10,000 refugees and the occasional bomb, they decided enough was enough. The Treaty of Kourou, in 1992, was a shameless pact. The maroons kept what they'd always had, which was a little autonomy, and Desi kept his booty. He remained in power, off and on, until 2000, when democracy finally prevailed. But by then Desi was rich, and had houses and girls all over the country. At his last election all he could offer was irony, and a heartless slogan: *Niks no fout*, or 'No Harm Done'.

Ronbo, too, prospered in the aftermath. He retired to the forti-fied house and built up a logging company, a football team (called Romeo Bravo) and a political party with the splendidly vague name, Algemene Bevrijding en Ontwikkelingspartij', (or 'The General Lib-eration and Development Party'). He'd also managed to squeeze in a conviction in Holland – in absentia again – for trafficking cocaine. Not that it bothered him. In Paramaribo, Ronbo was often being arrested for beating up referees and rivals, and it always ended in red tape.

'How does Suriname put up with these two?' I asked Zaahid.

'What do you mean?'

'Two big men, the drugs, the stupid names, and terrible pasts ...'

'Sure,' said Zaahid, 'but everyone did terrible things.'

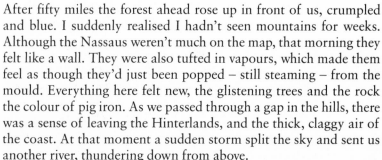

After fifty miles the forest ahead rose up in front of us, crumpled and blue. I suddenly realised I hadn't seen mountains for weeks. Although the Nassaus weren't much on the map, that morning they felt like a wall. They were also tufted in vapours, which made them feel as though they'd just been popped – still steaming – from the mould. Everything here felt new, the glistening trees and the rock the colour of pig iron. As we passed through a gap in the hills, there was a sense of leaving the Hinterlands, and the thick, claggy air of the coast. At that moment a sudden storm split the sky and sent us another river, thundering down from above.

The canoe filled with water, and the engine spluttered for air. Sometimes we seemed to slide sideways into the currents, and the prow would rise up and then slap down with a sound like a cannon. At other times the river beneath Jacobus would disappear, and the propellers would squeal with rage. The Upper Marowijne, it seems, had always defended itself like this. The Dutch had seldom ventured this far, and until the 1940s almost every expedition had ended in disaster. It wasn't just the water and the malaria. The

The Surinamese forest is as awesome as ever. Whilst, these days, we appreciate its beauty, the early Dutch saw only monsters.

river had its human guardians too, such as the Roucouyenes and the mysterious 'Long Ears', or Oyaricoulets. In their most productive purge, at the turn of the twentieth century, they ambushed a French expedition and slaughtered forty-nine men, and had never been heard of since.

Zaahid said that the maroons here were different too.

'They live on islands,' he said, 'away from the snakes.'

They were mostly Oucas, he said, or Paramaccaners. They'd never had much to worry about, except the Long Ears and The Monkey in the rapids. In 1761 they'd signed a treaty with the Dutch and then padded up here, to their bold new world, and shut themselves in. Once we stopped to visit some, on an island called Skin. Their lives were partly Amerindian and partly like those of maroons elsewhere. There were the tethered animals, the same prismatic pictures and the altars covered in togas. But there was also a persistent aura of abstraction. I remember a generator producing nothing but Techno, and a clearing decorated with old toilet bowls like the garden of Marcel Duchamp.

Zaahid appeared. 'This is the chief.'

Beside him stood an old man in a camouflaged smock.

We shook hands. 'A soldier?' I said, and Zaahid translated.

A long time ago.

'Do you ever see the Jungle Commandos now?'

Not any more. They once had their hideout near here.

'I heard they handed in their guns.'

Just the muskets, not the *dagadagas*.

'But I thought they had to hand over everything …?'

Would you? What if the treaty's no good?

During those last few days in Suriname nature was at its most insistent, and I could feel my affection restored.

We stayed opposite Skin Island, at a place called Loka Loka. It was a collection of painted wooden huts, high on the banks. By day the entire landscape seemed to slide past, steaming and restless, and at night there was the constant rumble like some great migration of watery hoofs. The owner of the huts was a Paramaccaner, who was proud of their design. He said it was from Africa, a place called the Ivory Coast. All his pots and pans, I noticed, were polished up like silverware, and he also had two canoes, called *Lobi Sweet* (or 'Love is Sweet') and No Harm Done.

Each day his boatmen took us out on the river. Once we went swimming in the rapids, which was like plunging into a washing machine that's rinsing out old trees. But most of the time we went on forays into the jungle. I always liked the idea that this was only the edge of a wilderness, and that beyond it lay 90 per cent of Suriname, barely explored. Even here creatures lived their lives largely unmolested. Some were so surprised to see us that they didn't even move. Poison dart frogs just sat there, waxy and orange, tempting us to touch. ('So deadly,' said Zaahid, 'they can only be handled with gloves'.) At one point we also came across a labaria, peering over its coils with a look of slight disgust. Everything was fabulously toxic. Even the trees had their own sophisticated weapons. One was covered in tiny brittle needles that sheared off in the skin. It took me hours to pick out all the pieces, which was, I suppose, one way of ensuring you'll never be forgotten.

Nature was still bidding for attention back at the camp. In the shower block there was always a tarantula up in the rafters, like a thin, hairy hand. Elsewhere things sang, copulated, stank, ate each other, whirred, preened and glowed. I shared my hut with two tiny rival frogs, who would belch at each other for hours. Then at the end of these brutal librettos they'd launch themselves into the darkness, collide softly with my mosquito net and tumble back to the floor to start all over again.

On our last morning, the chief paddled over to say goodbye. The island is being washed away, he said. Soon we must move.

'Maybe you could live in France?'

The chief shook his head. They'd lock him up. Two weeks in jail.

'Two weeks?'

Two months if you go back again.

'But that's terrible …'

No. It's good food. Everyone likes the appetisers.

'But where will you live, and how will you survive?'

Most of the men had a girl across the river.

'And how does that help?' I asked.

It's France. If you have babies there, they give you some money.

9

THE LAST OF THE COLONIES: GUYANE

'Let us make for Cayenne,' said Cacambo, 'we shall find some of those globe-trotting Frenchmen there, and they will be able to help us.'

Voltaire, *Candide*

Cayenne was unfit even for a dog ... [and] is now a blot on Guiana and a danger to the other colonies.

J. Rodway, *Guiana*

You feel as though you are entering the kingdom of the Sleeping Princess. It's dead country.

Raymond Maufrais, *Journey without Return*

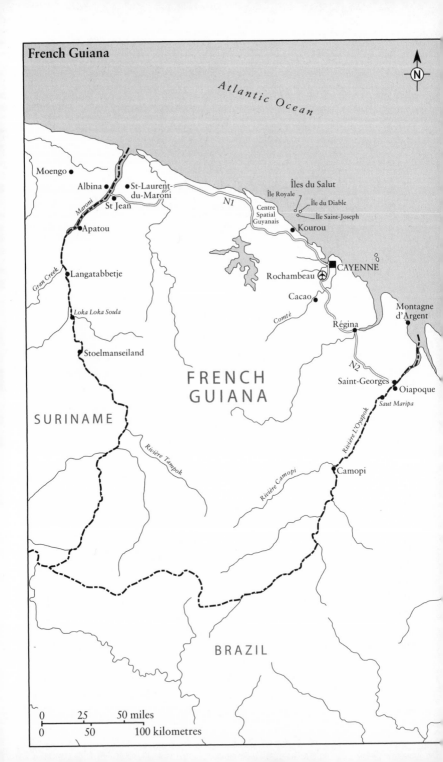

BACK IN ALBINA I hired a *pirogue* to take me over the river. It was three miles across, and ahead I could make out a town and a crinkly, black sliver of forest. I could also see a haze of canoes, swarming over the water, and some tall brown studs, like columns of rust. As we got closer, I could see that they were wrecks – Victorian wrecks of steamships and barges. One of them had even sprouted palm trees, like some ludicrous hat for Carmen Miranda.

The sight of it all still made the boatman laugh.

'*Une cimetière*,' he squealed, '*pour les français!*'

This river has seen plenty of disaster but nothing so odd as the long, slow suicide of Raymond Maufrais. The probability that French Guiana would kill him was so great that he'd recorded it, in the style of a novel. Although it would shape the views of a whole generation, there was no science to Maufrais's journey; he set out with only a back pack, a canoe, a rifle and little dog called Bobby. His travels would prove only that, in the heart of Guyane, you either miraculously survived or, more predictably, you died. It would be a thorough death, a complete disappearance. Guyane is a forest a sixth the size of France and is ploughed by hundreds of rivers, three of which are as big as anything in Europe. For readers of Maufrais the only question is: what would get you first? The loneliness, the hallucinations, or the surfeit of geography? Maufrais discovered all these things and perhaps little else. Here is his tale.

Maufrais begins his journey here on the river, almost exactly sixty years ago. He's only twenty-three, and there's already something about him fatally heroic. A vicious war still haunts him, and the bombs and the Gestapo return each night. He was a boy when he got his croix de guerre, and he will often reflect on the violent currents that have brought him here, and on the fighting in *Indochine*. He still wears his paratrooper's uniform and has a soldierly disregard for the frailty of life. Within months of arriving in Guyane, his boots and watch have perished, and he's sold his best gun to pay for food.

By September 1949 he's on this river, known in France as the Maroni. Ahead of him lies 35,000 square miles of jungle, only delicately scattered with people. (Even now, there are only 202,000 people across the whole of Guyane.) 'He'll never come back,' say *les guyanais*, but Maufrais shrugs them off and sets out into the bush. Within a fortnight he has no money left and only two cartons of food.

It will be a remarkable journey on an empty stomach. Maufrais will haul his boat hundreds of miles inland and then set off on foot across the watershed, to the rivers of the east. Along the way he'll eat iguanas and dried fish, and then lose it all in candid bouts of diarrhoea. His legs ulcerate, and he starts panting specks of blood. But even when he meets some Bonis, he refuses to turn back. 'You'll die …' they tell him, but still he presses on. There will be no more people after that, and the walk will slow to a mile a day. By now Maufrais is eating raw snails, and little birds softened in gun oil. He is too weak to hold his gun steady, and most of his kit has rotted away. At night he sees the dead from Toulon, wrapped in thin white paper, and he weeps for his mother. Even Bobby is now feral with hunger, and so Maufrais kills him and sucks the meat off his bones. It does nothing for his dysentery and brings on a night of excruciating cramps.

Despite all, however, Maufrais somehow crosses the watershed after seventeen days walking and reaches the rivers of the east. It's still another fifty miles to the main artery heading back to the coast. He tries to build a raft, but the wood is sodden, and it just falls apart and sinks. Despite his malaria, Maufrais decides to wade down the river. He will strip down to his shorts and perhaps kill a caiman, using his knife. Before he sets out, he eats two tiny fish, and writes a message in his journal, which he leaves on the rocks. It's a message to his parents, full of affection, and is dated '*13 janvier 1950*'. After that, he wades into the water and disappears for ever.

A month later the diaries are found by an Amerindian, and a search begins. The rescue party discovers that somehow Maufrais had managed another thirty-five miles, but otherwise they find nothing. Only Maufrais's father keeps hope alive. He gives up his job at the Toulon arsenal, and over the next twelve years he launches eighteen expeditions, covering over 7,500 miles of barely charted paths and rivers. It is an extraordinary gesture of paternal love, almost as forlorn as his son's ambition. He pays for it all by publishing the diaries, just as they are.

Aventures en Guyane horrifies France and remains in print today. For those who can still find Guyane on the globe, it confirms what Frenchmen have always felt: this land's a white man's grave, a green hell. *L'enfer vert*.

Over in St-Laurent, however, it wasn't notoriety that worried them but the prospect of oblivion.

The boatman dropped me at a small metallic booth. It was like an inhabited fridge, and inside were two cold, pink officials. They were obviously French, and so were their uniforms and badges, and all their laws and rules. Even the booth had been shipped out from *la métropole*. By passing through it, I hadn't just entered some scabby remnant of empire, but – politically at least – I'd tumbled down a rabbit hole and ended up in Europe. This wasn't merely an outpost of France but one of its *départements*. Everyone here was therefore as French as the Gascons and Savoyards, even the Bonis. They could fight for France if they wanted, or pick up its benefits or settle in Cannes. They could even vote in its elections, and at any moment there were always two deputies shuttling backwards and forwards, being extravagantly Gallic. All this, of course, meant that Guyane didn't belong here at all. Physically, it may have been South America's smallest mainland territory, but administratively it belonged to another continent altogether, 4,000 miles to the north. In fact, it was now the largest chunk of the European Union detached from the whole.

All down the long, hot road into town, St-Laurent proclaimed its Frenchness. Yellow triangles told the traffic what to do, and there were tight little *rond-points*, and boxes for dog poo. Most of the older houses were made of corrugated iron – but painted mock-Tudor as though this were Normandy, rendered in tin. Billboards depicted naked women holding yoghurts, and then there were blue vans for cops and yellow for the post. Even the public housing, or *les bidonvilles,* looked French, with its tubular playgrounds and cement coloured Revlon-pink. Eventually I came to the wide boulevards and fussy red-brick villas of the old colonial quarter. In here was a large sprawl of barracks, named after Marshal Joffre, and when I peered through the gates, there were the gendarmes, obstinately dressed in black.

But Frenchness wasn't only in the streets. It also got into all the shops and heaped itself up on the shelves. Everything was imported, every last *Yop* and *Cola Zoulou.* Guyane, I'd read, imported almost six times as much as it exported. But at least it was cool in the super-market, and so I ambled around, lingering over the names. (Who, I wondered, had come up with Cat's Tongues and Jellified Croco-diles?) In the end I settled for a lump of cheese, which I'd not seen for months, and which I paid for in Euros. Even the currency belonged somewhere else.

Not everything, however, was French. I could often hear the tin yawning in the heat, and – beyond the town – the jungle, still whis-tling and whirring. Occasionally, huge lime-green iguanas came plodding up the street – the original *Crocodiles Gélifiés* perhaps. At the cemetery I noticed that many of the old colonial tombstones were now tottering, and that some had collapsed in the sand. Maybe St-Laurent's Frenchness was like this, merely a scattering over the surface? In the weeks to come, I'd often feel that – with all its checkpoints and soldiers and bladders of fuel – Guyane was more a campaign than a settlement. I imagined that, if for a moment the importing ever faltered, the forest would rush back in and smother it within days. Perhaps that explained the exclamatory architecture and the stentorian French. It was just a fear of being forgotten.

GUYANE FRANÇ.ᴱ
POSTES
2ᶠ50
+1ᶠ
GENDARME COLONIAL
P.A. LEROUX   HELIO.VAUGIRARD.PARIS

The French-American writer Albert Guerard once said that the French had colonies but no colonists, and that – even if they had colonists – they wouldn't know how to colonise. 'They import nothing into their overseas dominions except damaged officials,' he wrote, 'and they export nothing from them except the same officials, worse damaged.'

Sixty years on, the imports might look different but there was still a torrent of officials. Almost one in every ten inhabitants of Guyane was born in metropolitan France. The Creoles call them *métros*, which I've always thought makes them sound dinky and effete, whereas actually they were part of a large army of technicians, soldiers, carpetbaggers, bigwigs, big shots and bureaucrats. Their task was to keep everything French. Sometimes, it seemed that the sole purpose of Guyane was just to be French. Ever since 1763, it's been France's only holding in the American New World, give or take the odd little island and a short stint in Louisiana.

It's now almost 400 years since France first started importing itself along this boiling, swampy coast. The results have usually been disastrous. The first wave of settlers, in 1613, unwisely picked a fight with the 'savages'. The second wave, in 1635, went collectively mad and became savages themselves. The third wave, eight years later, looked more robust, under the swaggering Sieur de Brétigny. But then the heat got to him, and he started breaking his men on the wheel for offences such as 'having a disturbing dream'. Eventually, however, the savages returned, and everyone died in a shower of arrows. The same fate befell the fourth wave, in 1652: 800 men cut down and eaten.

But the most conspicuous imports of all were the settlers of 1763. There were 12,000 of them, mostly peasants who believed they were heading for a city of gold. They arrived in the wet season, and many of them would never again experience the sensation of being dry. This time dysentery devoured them. By the time the expedition pulled out, a year later, over 10,000 people were dissolved in the mire.

Guyane would prove a hard mistress. For a long time the colony didn't seem to produce anything except arrows and disease. It was also too far from the French Caribbean, and the trade winds were wrong. Worse, it didn't have a natural harbour; the forest just seemed to continue into the sea. Even as late as 1947 freight from abroad was still being landed by lighter. But still France persisted, pouring in money and men. Nothing seemed to thrive. After three centuries the population was still only 25,000 souls, and all that had emerged was a new kind of pepper.

These days even the drama was imported, as I discovered at The Star.

The Star was a small concrete hotel with a garden full of spines. Around the walls there was a thick growth of razor wire, and at night the owner used to drive his car inside and park it by the pool. Apart from that, The Star was entirely forgettable, which may explain why the French secret service had always enjoyed it. During the Hinterland War they were often here, stirring up trouble, and back in Suriname they'd be known for years as 'Room Sixteen'.

Rather less forgettable were the people round the pool. In the mornings there was always an American who was here to collect scorpions, which he sold as pets in New York. Then came the Pentecostalists, the Chinese and a *sage-femme*, who sat in the shade telling people's fortunes. Occasionally soldiers appeared. These weren't like the British ones, with their displays of nakedness and drinking, but ham-faced, Velcro-headed men who made fighting look like a job. They always swam up and down very fiercely, as though wrestling the water.

Then there were the actors. They were a troupe from Lyon,

and two of them I soon got to know. Jean-Luc was a magnificent smoker, and lived his life as though it were a movie, shrugging his way from scene to scene. His friend Zi-Zi had more about her of the kitchen sink, a sort of homely doubt and a large handbag containing everything she'd need for the disasters of the day. They'd been on the road all their lives, picking up government grants. Now their art had brought them to Guyane. They were part of the huge cultural army – like the postmen and soldiers – shoring up everything French.

'It must cost France a fortune.' I once remarked.

Jean-Luc smiled and watched his smoke tumbling lazily into the air.

'*Chaque année,*' he murmured, '*un milliard de dollars.*'

And did anyone think that it was worth a billion bucks?

'It's land', he said, 'and it's French. We don't often give that up.'

I used to enjoy my walks around town with Zi-Zi and Jean-Luc. They never made light of anything when there was a drama to be had. Often we walked along the riverbank to the old Chinese landing, the Dégrad Chinois. Jean-Luc loved everything here: the shudder of drums, the maroons with their long knives, and the huge grey sea-monsters quivering away the last of their lives. In all that space and sound he was convinced something big was about to happen, and he was often almost right. Once we heard a sound like a meteorite coming in to land, and a huge object came crashing through the reeds and buried itself in the sand. It had black, lifeless windows, but the bodywork was still babbling away in electronic squeaks. I half-expected aliens to emerge, but all that got out were four little boys, none of them older than twelve.

Another time a very old Chinese woman stepped out of the grass.

'*Cigarette, monsieur,*' she said to Jean-Luc, touching his sleeve.

He rolled her a thick white finger of tobacco and gave her a light.

'*Tu me rappeles quelqu'un,*' she said tenderly. You remind me of someone.

For a moment Jean-Luc was lost for lines, but she'd already vanished, back in the grass. Perhaps his life really was a film, at least in Guyane.

Zi-Zi was less happy. Being black herself, she'd expected to feel more at home among the Creoles, and yet she found herself more foreign. People were suspicious of her Frenchness, and her cold, improbable accent. It also pained her to find here the same sense of alienation as that back in Lyon. Wasn't this supposed to be a land of black people? *'NON A L'ECOLE POUBELLE!'* read the graffiti, *'FUK POLICE!'* I could tell it upset Zi-Zi. It often feels, she said, as though slavery's only just ended.

In Guyane the end of slavery was famously untidy. Some say it was like the end of another experiment. There'd been a settler phase, an African era and even a sampling of Chinese. ('White, black, yellow …' as one wag put it.) But none of this had transformed the landscape. You only need to click on a satellite picture to see that there are no rectangles, no neat little oblongs of sugar. Even the coastal strip is still the bog it was when the French arrived. Slavery had added nothing except a tiny population, and a way of life that's never been replaced.

Looking back, emancipation ought to have been a glorious affair. The slaves were first liberated during the French Revolution, in the giddy, free days of the Terror. But then, as the economy collapsed, they were re-enslaved for another half a century. Eventually, however, in 1848, slavery was finally abolished, and within days the plantations of Cayenne had reverted to weeds. A new idea was needed.

Two years later another experiment began, as bold as any before.

Just beyond the Dégrad Chinois a great scheme still rises out of the reeds. It covers an area of almost seven acres and is enclosed by a stone wall, sixteen feet tall. Everything around it has been cleared away, and so this structure stands alone and gaunt. Apart from a small industrial chimney there are no features to it – no windows or doors – it's just a vast, lifeless block of diminishing parallel lines.

The only way in is through a small gateway round the side. The gate itself is made of iron and painted prison-grey. Above it are the words 'CAMP DE LA TRANSPORTATION'.

The idea of transporting unwanted people to Guyane wasn't entirely new. The French Revolution had often sent its enemies here. Among them were seventeen deputies, Marie-Antoinette's lawyers, the president of the Conseil des Anciens, and the playwright Collot d'Herbois. In all, perhaps a thousand came. The likelihood of them dying here was so great that banishment became known as *la guillotine sèche*, the chop without the mess.

The concept of a penal colony was revived in 1848. By then, France had over 6,000 prisoners locked up in its penal system or *le bagne* (the word came from the 'bathhouses' once used as lock-ups for prisoners of war). Now reformers were beginning to question the utility of such a punishment. What benefit was there in able-bodied men rotting away and then emerging worse than ever? It was English jurisprudence that provided a solution. Transportation, wrote Sir William Blackstone, offered the prospect of 'a new homeland, a new existence, hopes of fortune and the prospect of forgiveness'. It would be a scientific solution to the moral decline of France. Men would be transformed by hard work, civilised and cured, and at the same time they'd replace the Africans and bring new hope to a benighted colony. Guyane would be *'Le Botany Bay français,'* rebuilt by the 'slaves of the law'.

What's more, Louis-Napoleon liked the idea. His coup d'état had created another 27,000 detainees, and here was a chance to kill several birds with one stone. In 1850 he signed an order for the creation of *la colonie pénitentiaire*. Within eight years the great *bagne* at Rochefort had closed, and over 8,000 *bagnards* had been transferred to Guyane. What was now needed was a new settlement, designed especially to punish. In 1858 a site was selected at St-Laurent du Maroni, and later that year building began.

Soon, rising out of the reeds, was a vast mill for processing people.

The camp still feels like a factory, empty and abandoned. I went there several times during my stay in St-Laurent, sometimes with the actors, sometimes alone. Now these visits have all merged into one. Only the light ever changed. There was no view of the outside world, and none of the usual punctuation that marks out the day. The symmetry was devastating; the sharp lines, the rows of barracks and the rectangle all around. I tried to imagine what it would be like to be boxed up in here for a week, a year or even for life, breathing hot sand and never knowing anything but the walls and the sky.

The barrack blocks were like silos for human beings. Housing over 3,000 convicts, everything about them had a dull industrial clank. They had concrete walls and iron roofs, iron bolts, iron doors and then iron stairs leading up to another warehouse, just like the one below. It was here that men were broken down. They'd already lost their names and become a number. Now their lives would be reduced to a peg on the wall. The pegs are still there, although the numbers have faded. They, and the striped uniforms and straw hats, were all a man had left. Until the 1930s he didn't even have his own hammock, just a stretch of canvas, shared with everyone else. '*Sans dignité,*' as Jean-Luc put it, '*et sans futur.*'

Although every surface was now crusted with mould and damp, a system had survived. The erasure of personality had been so thorough that there was no sign left of the men who'd lived here: no words, no art, just a mottled wash of pink and grey. Between 1858 and 1946 over 67,000 *bagnards* had passed through the camp. These were not ordinary people but France's most colourful and violent criminals. Among them were assassins, gangsters, psychopaths, forgers, pimps and racketeers. Most famous of all was Henri Charrière, alias Papillon. But there was also Dieudonne, of the Amiens gang, the first thug to use a machine gun in France; Baratand, a millionaire who brought Limoges out on strike when he was spared the guillotine for murder; and the Comte de Bérac, who'd killed the child he'd fathered by his maid. Then there was the man who lost his arm when his mistress bit it as he hurled her out of a window, and the barber who bludgeoned his wife's lover with a bottle and then cut up his face with some shears. There was even the odd Englishman, such as George Seaton. 'Even I, the effete socialite,' he wrote, years later, 'acquired a sinewy brutality ... I slid back several centuries and obeyed the law that said, "If all else fails, I shall survive" ...'

Now all that remained of them were these stark units, built for bashing out new citizens and dismantling the old. With all its iron and parallels and tight-fitting hatches, the camp had been callously efficient. It may even have inspired later regimes, wanting to automate people or just make them vanish. Guyane at that time was still famously unhealthy. During the first thirty years of the penal colony disease claimed over half the convicts. The combination of confinement and humidity was lethal. In 1867 it was considered so insalubrious that whites weren't sent at all, and until 1887 only Arabs and Annamites arrived. After that, however, death was treated as merely incidental to the experiment in hand. Malaria, yellow fever and dysentery all played their part. In some barracks men slept on perforated planks to drain away the fluids. Even in the 1920s one in ten men died each year.

But production, rather than extermination, was always the object of this camp. Here men were channelled and sorted, and selected for work. *Transportés*, the regular convicts, wore red stripes, and *relégués*, or repeat offenders, wore blue. One lot went one way, the others went another. The great experiment, however, was always a failure. The convicts were never trusted with initiative, and the work they did was pointlessly brutal. In St-Laurent they dug holes or made bricks. I still have one of these bricks, which I found in the river. It's stamped 'AP', or *Administration Pénitentiaire*. St-Laurent is built of bricks like this, all fabulously over-deployed, just to absorb the endless output.

Was this what Blackstone had meant by 'a new existence'? Or the 'prospect of forgiveness'? It was almost as though, in St-Laurent, France had created the very antithesis of El Dorado: a city of mud, built to impoverish, in the worship of work.

Along one side of the camp was a walled-off area, more abattoir than factory. One day Jean-Luc and I hired a guide from the town hall to take us inside. He was an Amerindian, bow-legged and stooped like a sturdy chair. With a large bunch of keys he led us through two armoured doors and a guardroom into a system of darkened pens and cages. Once whole consignments of men could be herded through here, and then the whole place flushed clean. Now everything smelt of bats, and across the concrete was a litter of droppings and plaster. This was where they brought the hard cases, said the Amerindian.

'*Y compris les évadés?*' asked Jean-Luc.

'*Oui,*' said the guide. Including anyone absent more than twelve hours.

Out in the work camps, four out of five *bagnards* attempted escape, and on average 150 men a year were never seen again. That's not to say they all found freedom. As the commandant told new arrivals, 'The real guards here are the jungle and the sea.' Meanwhile, the rest were hunted down by trackers. People like my grandparents, said the Amerindian, who were paid for every man they returned.

Back on the camp, *les évadés* were known as 'the returned horses' (*les chevaux de retour*) and were funnelled through these gates. Ahead lay the consequences of their actions, set out in channels; the court, the cells and the *quartier disciplinaire*. Above each gate I could still make out the words all *bagnards* dreaded: *BLOCKHAUS* or *TRIBUNAL MARITIME SPECIAL*. These weren't simply labels; they added to the sense of inevitability and process. In this court, said the Amerindian, escape was generally punished with twelve months solitary, and even murder trials lasted no longer than a day.

One gate here was marked '*Libérés*'. It led to a long, narrow yard, with cells around the edge and a concrete washtub in the middle. This is where the 'free men' served their sentences. They were some of the sadder characters in this tortured system. Although they'd already served their main sentence, the rule of *doublage* required that every man serve the same period all over again, as a 'free man' in the colony (and if his original sentence was more than seven years, he could never go back to France). Entrepreneurship was forbidden, and yet each was expected to support himself. Some worked as gold-washers, or *orpailleurs*, and a few made a living mounting butterflies, but over three-quarters of them died of malnutrition. It was almost as though, having survived their sentence, a long, slow death penalty still lay ahead. As the Amerindian put it, '*Le bagne commence à la libération.*'

Turning the other way, we came to the punishment yards. Here, men were either herded into the *blockhaus*, a hundred at a time, or singled out and brutalised alone. In the *blockhaus*, every night, the *bagnards* were shackled to one of two central rails, and yet they still managed to punish themselves and each other. Tethered a few feet apart, the men would settle old scores by slashing at each other with tiny handmade knives. Or they might introduce the new boys to the love life of the colony, which was always swift and violent, and administered over the toilet. The little pen at the end of the room was known, said the Amerindian, as the *chambre d'amour*.

It was better in the cells, with only the prospect of madness. There was no view out, and now the walls were bristly with fungus. Here, however, something of the *bagnards* had survived, at least in their scribbles. Not much of it made much sense. There were occasional dates (1934 was a big year for doodling), and one cell had a large picture of a frigate in full sail. In the 'death row' cells, someone had spent his last hours carving '*ADIEU MAMAN*' in his plank. Others had opted simply for a name. *PAPILLON* was the most common, I noticed.

Was any of this the work of Charrière? Maybe, said the guide, but there were butterflies everywhere.

Perhaps that's the key to Henri Charrière. I've always wondered whether he was as innocent as he insisted, or as heroic as he claimed. As autobiography, *Papillon* is magnificently improbable. (A hayseed from the Ardèche is convicted in 1931 of a murder he didn't do and ends up in Guyane. There he is witty and resourceful, and finds himself at the heart of everything that happens. He escapes nine times, beds half a dozen women, leads mutinies, kills several people with great style and flourish, and then finally gets away in 1944. Meanwhile, he's forgotten all about his wife and daughter in Paris and writes them out of the plot.) But it's in the detail that *Papillon* falters, with our hero experiencing things that in reality he's unlikely to have seen: ants eating men alive, oysters yielding a pearl every day, lunatics howling at the moon. That said, his descriptions are those of a man who was almost certainly here, and it's likely that most of the stories he tells really did happen – but just not to him. According to one French researcher, the official record of Charrière's sojourn shows only that he never got into trouble, and that he kept the latrines.

That's why it's probably better to think of him as a collector of stories, rather than their hero. *Il y avait des papillons partout*, as the Amerindian would say. But Charrière hasn't always been seen this way. In the 1960s his book sold over a million copies in France alone. One minister even blamed him for the country's moral decay, along with mini-skirts and pop. Charrière would have enjoyed all this, being at the heart of a real revolt. There's a memorable picture of him, taken in 1969, four years before his death. He's back in the Ardèche, wearing a cream polo-neck jumper, looking sleek and self-assured, every bit the novelist.

At the far end of the secure quarters was a killing machine. All that remained of it were five pads of concrete. Like the penal colony itself, the guillotine was supposed to have been a rational solution to the conundrum of punishment. Science would give barbarism a spurious humanity. Here there had been three devices, each one well greased and tested every week. The last time one was used was 1942. The condemned man was an Arab who'd killed a local woman while out on parole. For weeks he'd tried to cheat the machine by stealing pins and pushing them deep into his chest. But then the day came, and the final meal and litre of wine. Before he was decapitated, the Arab was ordered to sign a prison discharge, just to complete the papers.

Around the yard, the other prisoners were gathered. Perhaps Charrière was among them (he certainly described a scene like this). We're all here to die, they'd think, but just at different rates. Then the blade fell, and the executioner reached down and picked up the head by the ears. '*Au nom de la République,*' he proclaimed, '*Justice est faite!*'

In the name of the Republic, justice has been done.

Beyond the camp was an area known as 'Little Paris'. It was like a slice of *la Belle Epoque*, served up in the tropics. Arranged around a tiny park were mansions in caramel and pink, civic halls, a palais de justice, and a hotel, magnificently ribbed in Ionic columns. Most of the mansions had louvred fronts, to suck in the breezes that came off the river, and every spare surface was either fluted or fringed or covered in friezes. There were gods and gymnasts tussling up in the pediments, and garlands of laurel over everything else. The best house of all went, of course, to *le Directeur du Bagne*. He was the most important man in the colony, and his residence had a pagoda roof, pyjama-striped stonework and a chorus of Ottoman arches. Here was the Third Empire at its most outrageous, demanding attention at whatever the cost.

Little Paris was like the capital of a country that didn't really exist. It even had its own national bank, I noticed, built by the convicts from imported stone. Across the front they'd built two grand staircases, like arms outstretched to scoop up the wealth. But the profits had never materialised. Right to the end *les pénitenciers* absorbed 90 per cent of the colony's budget. Too late, France realised that there was no money to be made enslaving burglars and pimps. Most *transportés* just made their bricks and died. Few settled, and in the first decades only 10 per cent of them ever made it home. In economic terms, Guyane was just an expensive means of having men put down.

The Amerindian said only the work camps had paid their own way. I asked him if there were any left.

'*Seulement St-Jean*', he said, '*à dix kilomètres d'ici.*'

Then let's go, said the actors, as soon as we can.

According to the map, St-Jean was now a military camp.

'No problem,' said Jean-Luc. 'I know an artist. He'll get us in.'

At first, it looked as though we were too late for St-Jean and that it was already deep in the realms of archaeology.

Scattered along the riverbank was the wreckage of an ambitious past: old trucks, railway cars, giant canoes and the last straws of a great Amerindian *carbet*, or hall. There was also a huge clump of rust, nosing up out of the creepers, like some strange industrial growth. It was composed mostly of cranes and bulldozers, and right in the middle lived an old engineer and his long-suffering wife. They were like characters from a children's story, with their patched clothes, an ancient gun and a dog that could sing. It's so beautiful here, the wife told me, we never felt the need to move.

They weren't the only ones living in the ruins. Further along, under the trees, we came across a tribe of maroons. They said they'd been here for generations and that they manned all the boats that ran upriver. The failure of the penal colony had obviously suited them well, and they now had a village made of old iron beds and plundered bricks. But more surprising was the artist's shack. It looked like several houses that had been smashed up and then thrown together as one. There was no door, so we scrambled in through a hole in the wall. Inside was a large area, waist-deep in feathers and oil cans, and lumps of cardboard. I also counted ten battered refrigerators. They'd clearly just had a brawl, and some were huddled up one end, while others lay on their backs choked with landfill. I was beginning to wonder whether the artist had survived this riot when there was a rustle among the papers, and a spiky head appeared.

'*Enfin!*' said Jean-Luc, '*Voici* Jérôme Rémont ...'

Jérôme clambered over and covered the artists in kisses. He was dog-bone skinny, and wore only a vest and some pale yellow trousers. He reminded me of an old sepia print I'd seen for sale in St-Laurent. Now it had sprung into life, and out had popped a startled, sleepy convict.

Jérôme was a Norman, and had come from Lisieux. I said I'd like to see his work. He smiled and waved a bony arm over the chaos all around.

'*Voilà!*' he said, '*l'art essentiel!*'

From the shambles of his studio a curious tour took shape. At the edge of the trees a gateway appeared, guarded by soldiers. When they saw the shrunken figure of Jérôme lolloping towards them, they stood by and wafted us inside. Immediately everything changed. We were now among avenues with whitewashed kerbstones and long, frilly walls of brickwork like lace. There was a chapel with an entrance for warders and another for convicts, and a parade ground, now covered in drab-green trucks. Pairs of agoutis grazed the lawns, like giant red hamsters (or were they miniature deer?). 'This is where the prison bread was made,' said Jérôme, 'and this is where they killed their cows. We're always finding bones.'

Over the hill were the convicts' sheds. It wasn't like a prison, more a compulsory village. It had no great wall, and, said Jérôme, there'd only ever been thirty-two warders for 2,000 men. But the convicts here weren't the ordinary *transportés*; they were *relégués*, recidivists banished for life. This hill is all you'll ever have, they were told, so you might as well make it flourish. Each man was given four hectares of land and made to plant it for France. He wasn't even allowed to read or write, just to think about the land. As always, nothing came of it. St-Jean was merely one colony deep within another, and when, in 1931, the *relégués* went on strike, the outside world didn't even notice.

It could have gone on for ever, said Zi-Zi.

Maybe, said Jérôme. There were still cows here in 1951.

I asked him whether it was the last place to close.

No, he said, that was the Iles du Salut. First to open, last to close.

'*Et la plus belle!*' said the actors.

Yes, said Jérôme, and probably the worst.

These days a road soars through the swamps, off to the isles. It was a long, flat ride, through a soggy landscape of roots and knotted scrub. I was sorry that the actors couldn't be persuaded to throw in their lives and come along too. They'd have enjoyed the roadblocks. About every fifty miles my minibus was stopped by some or other militia, and something always happened. But France has so many militias that it's often hard to say whether you've offended the navy or the tax man, or just parked where you shouldn't. These ones always found someone to question or to take off and search. I think they'd have worried me more if it wasn't for their shorts. These were always half a dozen sizes too small, making them look magnificently gay, as though Village People had taken over the bush.

'What are they after?' I asked the driver.

'*Brésiliens,*' he whispered, '*les brésiliens illégaux.*'

Then we'd get the nod, everyone would breathe again, and we'd be off.

Behind us, the roadblocks sank back into the plain. In a rather bored way I tried to imagine what an earlier generation of officials would have made of their successors. The shorts would have raised a few eyebrows. In all the pictures I'd seen, the colony's warders or *surveillants* are wearing sharp white drill and look passionately grim. It's said that the French prison service was an offshoot of the marines, and that its foot soldiers regarded imprisoning as just another form of war. It would also have surprised them, the way things were done in modern Guyane. They'd spent their lives trying to keep people in, and now here was the army trying to keep them out.

Eventually we arrived on the coast, and there, wrinkling the horizon, nine miles off shore, were the Iles du Salut.

They've never raised much hope in the hearts of Frenchmen. Originally they were just a nautical feature, the Triangle Islands – three great lumps of granite on the way to somewhere else. But then, after disembowelling one too many passers-by, they became known as the Islands of the Devil. It was a good name for such a lifeless place, without even water. Sailors could hear it heaving and groaning for miles. There was only one moment of grace, and that was in 1763. It was the great expedition, now in the final stages of dysentery and damp. The last few thousand survivors had sought out the islands, just to feel dry. It would never be much of a home, but at least there were no mosquitoes. In their feverish gratitude they renamed the archipelago the Salvation Islands, and somehow the name has stuck.

But there wasn't much salvation in the years to come. For a while it was a leper colony, but then in 1852 the first convicts appeared. Suddenly the islands had a role. There was Royale for the incorrigible, and St-Joseph for punishment. Then, for those who'd courted oblivion – France's rebels and its traitors – there was Diable, or Devil's Island, the ultimate oubliette. Although none of these islands was more than a mile long, in the popular imagination they'd have the stature of Hell. *L'enfer au Paradis*, as the actors would say.

Take your own food, they'd warned, and plenty of water.

'*Et faites attention aux trous …*'

'*… et aux mille-pattes!*'

I now pondered this advice. It was easy to stock up on cheese, tins, ham and a flagon of water, but preparing for the holes and the centipedes was harder. Instead, I bought a bottle of wine and a hammock, and booked my passage on the boat to Royale.

The next day, at dawn, it set out, breasting a truculent ocean swell. We were barely out of the estuary before huge curls of silt were bursting overhead. Then the whole boat would be lifted up and we'd have a dizzying view of the islands before burrowing back in the waves.

Throughout 1938 there's a constant traffic of new arrivals on Royale. Among them is a forger from Lille, called Francis Lagrange. He is scraggy and twitchy, slightly arched, with quick, beady eyes, thick glasses and more than a touch of the rat. He's also a terrible forger – so bad that, at the age of thirty, the police were beating down his door. He has now been in the camp at St-Laurent for seven years and has taught himself to paint. Like his banknotes, his work is crude, or *naif*, and his people have tiny heads and swollen shoulders and hands that look like spam. But cowardice has made him a shrewd observer, always watching to see how things turn out. His pictures are scandalously detailed, like a window on the life of the camp. There are the fights, the work camps, the escapes, the executions and the *libérés* lying in the street, dying and drunk.

Lagrange also has an impressive memory, especially for women. He never forgets a well-rounded body and will remember Lille's girls for years, long after they've hustled him out, followed by his trousers. This makes him a formidable pornographer, and in the scrawny world of St-Laurent he accumulates a little fortune. He uses the money to pay a boatman to row him over to Suriname. But the Dutch always send him back. Eventually, after an attempt on the commandant's mistress, the court declares him '*inco*', or incorrigible, and sends him to Royale.

Lagrange likes the island more than he'd imagined. It's like a trilby covered in jungle. The sides of the hat are covered in hanging gardens and neatly cobbled roads. He is marched uphill, under the shade of the coconut trees. There are huge retaining walls of orange and purple granite. Everyone has a little job up here, growing vegetables or selling fish – and there's Papillon with his oxen, slopping out his buckets.

At the top of the hill there's a little plateau and a clearing in the trees. Even up here Lagrange can hear the surf, like the storm in a seashell. The plateau is shady, and around the edge there are houses, a church with a Norman spire, barracks, the lock-up and a shiny new lighthouse, built out of iron. At one end the convicts have cut a reservoir which is so vast that they call it *la mer*, or the sea. At the other end there's an old stone hospital, with a brand new ice-machine that clanks away all night. Next to it is *la maison des fous*, or the madhouse, from which every morning a man emerges and clambers down to the rocks to assemble his stones in the sea. He's building a causeway, he explains, along which to escape.

Lagrange is taken to his barracks. These are like the sheds in St-Laurent, but older and with thick walls of stone. They're called 'the Crimson Barracks', and life inside is never quite as breezy and wholesome as it is across the hill. Lagrange watches and paints. Gambling powers a miniature economy, run by Parisian hoods and the Corsican *milieu*. The big shots, or *truands*, wear suits made of flour sacks. Everyone has a racket, usually in drink or boys. It's not unusual for the strong-arm men to have several 'wives', who are known as *les mômes*, or 'the brats'. Arguments are settled with home-made blades, and when a person's sliced open over the concrete, there are no questions asked. It's said that more murders have been committed here than in any other building in the world.

Alongside the barracks is the *quartier des surveillants*. It's a compound of squat pink bungalows. An uneasy truce exists between them and the barracks. The *surveillants* will leave the convicts to their own devices, provided the convicts don't escape. If they do, the warders will lose six months' leave and their colonial allowance, and they'll come smashing through the barracks, breaking everything they can. They have become brutalised by their proximity to the *bagnards*, although each insists he's addressed formally as '*Monsieur le surveillant*'.

Lagrange paints a wistful picture of warder life, called *Le Garçon de famille*. In it, the surveillant stares from the window of his little pink house. Outside, a 'houseboy', in red-striped uniform and pinafore, pegs washing on a line. Beneath him, with her back to her husband, the warder's wife gazes up dreamily, with her breasts deliciously exposed. The *bagnard* is so distracted by her gaze that his head is now twisted round, facing backwards. Everyone is distorted by being so compacted together. As George Seaton, the English convict, put it, the warders are just as imprisoned as he is. They suffer the same 'blistering heat and the savage rains', and they're just as likely to get leprosy and TB. They're like animal trainers in a circus, never daring to relax. 'In the *bagne*,' he writes, 'one half watches the other ...'

Although it was now over fifty years since the last *bagnards* left, much of their lives remained. There was still a great stone break-water, the walls and the lanes up the hill. The hanging gardens were overgrown but still scattered with coconuts and fruit. A small menag-erie of animals – monkeys, agoutis and giant iguanas – now snuffled around among the roots. Sometimes I'd get a flash of macaw, and shreds of guava and mango would come fluttering down from the branches above. In the lower forest there were long-legged pigs, as bristly and crude as the convicts before.

Up on the plateau there was still the same settlement clinking in the heat. Only the madhouse had been overwhelmed by creepers and torn apart. The pink bungalows were still there – now chalets for tourists – and the barracks and the cells and the mango trees for shade. The hospital floors had turned to dust and sifted into the cellars, and the ice-machine had rusted up, but the reservoir still worked. It now had a sign, saying '*ATTENTION CAIMANS*', and down in the ponds below I could see a pair of old crusted lags sleep-ing off their kill.

These days there were only two policemen. Every evening they ate at the old mess, a huge monastic place now used as an auberge. It was cool and fresh up here, right on the peak. Both officers were from the Alps and said they'd never imagined a job like this: *une ville déserte*, said one, a deserted town.

And a network of empty roads, said the other.

Just one old truck!

And a population of pigs!

I slung my hammock in the old Crimson Barracks. Someone had given my block a new tin roof, but otherwise not much had changed. I had a room for 120 men all to myself, although at night there was always something rustling in the rafters. As I lay there, I could also hear the surf all around, breathing on the rocks, and the drowsy tick of the lighthouse. It still emitted long spokes of light, which eventually found my window and sent the bars wheeling round the room. On my first night I realised that I was not a natural hammock-dweller and had bought a rope that was slightly elastic. Instead of dangling nicely out of reach of the wildlife, by 4 a.m., I was back down among it, scraping the concrete and beginning to itch.

I was grateful for sunrise, got up and sat out on the steps. I ate a tin of mussels and dried the sea mist from my clothes. The agoutis were already out, under the mango trees, looking enjoyably absurd. They had too much bottom, I decided, and not enough head. When a peacock arrived and screamed, they all panicked and ran off into the cemetery. Being Royale, this graveyard was not quite as easy as it first appeared but was exclusively for children.

Then someone came out and unlocked the church, and I wandered inside. It was a bland interior, despite a few murals over the altar. I hardly noticed them at first, but then, in a biblical scene behind the door, I thought I saw people I recognised: the cuckolded officer, some girls from Lille, the boy in the pinafore and Jesus Christ, with spammy hands. It was Lagrange, trying to purchase a little redemption. He'd even painted throughout the war, foregoing colour and making brushes from his hair. The effort had paid off, and in 1946, after eight years on Royale, he was finally freed.

Lagrange never went home, or showed any sign of reform. He carried on painting but drank away his money. For a while he lived in Suriname, but in 1949 he was expelled when his atrocious forgeries once more let him down. Then he was discovered by an American journalist and invited to the States. It suited him for a while, rediscovering white women and getting married and divorced. But there was too much space in America, and too much insistence on playing it fair. He was soon on his way, this time to Martinique.

He died, still painting and cheating, in 1964.

Across a narrow neck of water was a far less lenient island. It was geography much better suited to the infliction of pain. The sea around St-Joseph was said to be incessantly violent. I've never seen the Atlantic looking so furious and brown. It was like old concrete that's been brought to the boil. If the island wasn't such an obstinate sprig of granite, it would have vanished millions of years ago and been spattered over the seabed. No doubt this infuriated the waves, which came rolling in with a noise like buildings and bridges and ground-up roads. Some days it couldn't be reached at all, and on Royale people just watched and waited for the anger to subside.

On my second day the boatman decided we'd probably get across. 'I won't stop,' he said. 'When we get to the quay, just jump.'

Between the islands the sea heaved and arched, and I could feel the little boat being spun in the current. It would have been perfect for the disposal of bodies, like one of those sinks that glugs away the waste. Once every convict expected to end up here. Only warders and their families earned a place in the soil. For everyone else there was a bell and a rowing boat, and a plunge in the current. Lagrange called this ceremony *le mouillage du forçat*, or 'mooring the old lag'. It's said that the sharks got so used to the bell that they always turned up, like Pavlov's dogs.

At the quay I waited for my moment, and jumped.

'*Trois heures!*' shouted the boatman, as he was hauled off into the swell.

Like Royale, St-Joseph bristled in palms, but it was smaller and more vicious. There were no hanging gardens and churches, just a bright red road of hand-crushed granite. At the far end, the Chapeau du Gendarme, where the surf impacted with the cliffs, the air seemed to stand still and shudder. It was like being struck suddenly deaf. There was only one beach, of six-foot breakers and pulverised shell. The wind here crackled with grit and had lashed the names off all the tombs. To the leaders of the *Troisième République* there was no better place to re-tune the errant human being, or to have him forgotten.

I left the red road and followed a cobbled lane uphill. In the forest the sea soon became a dull, disorientating groan. Apart from the palms, the trees in here were sinewy and lean, with a tendency to strangle. At the top of the rise was a large sprawl of ruins, made of brick and stone. The trees were already among them, wrenching out the walls as though they were teeth. I climbed in through an old iron gate. The roof had long gone, and inside it was damp and the jungle was thicker. Dwarf palms erupted out of the brickwork, and long waxy trunks extended down from the canopy, like molten trees, trickling into the mortar. There were iron bars tufted with epiphytes, and across the walls marched huge formations of gingery ants. I realised that I was in a corridor, and that beyond it lay another and another. Along each corridor there were perhaps fifty cells, each a little box of captured forest. Here in 1904 France had developed the ultimate punishment, on an industrial scale. It was known as 'The Man-Eater' or, more formally, *La Réclusion.*

Behind this complex of cells was the idea of inertia. In these tiny, blank spaces men would be deprived of all sense of the world around. There was hardly any light, and the silence was ruthlessly enforced. The men wore soundless canvas slippers and were forbidden from reading or smoking, or any form of human contact. They'd see nothing, hear nothing and do nothing, and – left only with their thoughts – they'd gradually come to a halt. It was like being buried alive, a sort of judicial suffocation of the mind. But it wasn't something that happened overnight. Time was the punishment here, anything from six months to five years.

The cells had bars instead of ceilings. Above them I could just make out the rusted stumps of a gantry. From up here the warders had kept watch on their charges without ever needing to enter the cells. Meanwhile, most of the old steel doors had gone, stolen or taken off for scrap. They were never opened during a man's sentence. All food and waste went through a *trappe,* or hatch in the door, and once a fortnight the prisoner would put his head out to be shaved. He'd have just enough food to survive but not enough to enjoy. His simple, bland diet never changed, although if he ever broke the rules it could be reduced or watered down.

In Lagrange's picture of this scene, *Réclusion cellulaire à Saint-Joseph,* the faces at the hatches are ghostly and brittle. They look as though they're being processed, merely numbers in a line. Perhaps at the heart of revolutionary French thought there was always a weakness for solutions that were grandiose yet brutal. Places such as La Réclusion even survived the age of Auschwitz and Belsen, if only just. During the war the Vichy regime held out against an American blockade, and the *bagnard*'s bread ration fell to just 14 oz a day. Almost half of them died. Only after that did France finally lose its appetite for these distant penal camps. In 1946 the *bagne* was closed, and most of the prisoners set loose.

Here at *La Réclusion,* the doors lay open, and the jungle crept back in.

But the end of this experiment began much earlier, with *l'affaire Dreyfus.*

One day I took my provisions out to a cove called L'Anse Legoff and sat on the headland. It was a beautiful place to ponder what had happened. Below me the convicts had built a pool, which was calm and black like an eye in the surf. From here I could also look out across Devil's Island, the last and most exposed of the trio. It was also smaller than the others – not so much a hat as a soup plate. But, like them, it was densely tufted in palms, and among the trees I could just make out some tiny stone cottages. Other than that, there was nothing to the island except the beating of the sea. Huge rollers would come tumbling off the Atlantic and explode in the forest. I couldn't see anywhere to land. The ocean was like a hammer, constantly smashing away at this little anvil of granite.

'*Il est défendu de visiter …,*' said the policemen.

'*… Trop dangéreux.*'

I asked them if anyone ever went there.

Just officials, they said, to repair the Dreyfus house.

But no one actually sees it?

'*C'est vache,*' they shrugged. That's how it is.

Next to me were the remains of a tower. Once a cable had run from here to the island, carrying a hopper for warders and supplies. It was never much of a place. Until 1895 Devil's Island was merely a dump for the colony's lepers. But then, that year, news came of a new inmate. The lepers were removed, and their huts burned. Any tree capable of making a boat was cut down, and the cottages were built. One of them had a wall around it so that the special prisoner would have no view of the sea. The *surveillants* feared that one day a huge Prussian fleet would appear on the horizon and spring him from his cell. He was, of course, Captain Alfred Dreyfus.

Dreyfus is an odd man to find at the centre of this scandal. He is dowdy and neat, and has a stiff Alsatian accent. Clemenceau will describe him as a 'pencil salesman'. But he's a good officer, and when, in 1894, French military secrets start turning up in German hands, he's not an obvious suspect. But the investigative officer, a thoughtless oaf called Paty de Clam, thinks differently. He's not looking for an obvious candidate, simply a Jew. The evidence against Dreyfus is trimmed into shape, and he's convicted, and, at the age of thirty-six, he's sent to Devil's Island.

He arrives in April 1895 and soon the great punishment machine is grinding him down. The island is like a *bagne*-within-a-*bagne*.

Dreyfus sees no one except his guards, and they are forbidden to talk to him. Most of his time he spends in solitary confinement, and at night he's shackled to his bed. 'So profound is my solitude,' he writes, in a letter to his wife, 'that I often seem to be lying in a tomb.' All he has to comfort him is Shakespeare, and he starts learning English.

Meanwhile, in Paris, the novelist Emile Zola is outraged and stirs up dissent. On 13 January 1898 he publishes his famous letter to the president, entitled '*J'accuse*'. 'These, Sir, are the facts', he writes, 'that explain how this miscarriage of justice came about. The evidence of Dreyfus's character, his affluence, the lack of motive and his continued affirmation of innocence combine to show that he is the victim of the lurid imagination of Major du Paty de Clam, the religious circles surrounding him, and the "dirty Jew" obsession that is the scourge of our time.'

It is a well-aimed blow, and everything will be different after this. Zola is forced into exile, but the following year Dreyfus is returned to France and eventually freed. He will never mention Devil's Island again but will rejoin the army, show himself a diligent Frenchman at Verdun and die peacefully, in his own bed, in 1935. France is also changed, although no one's quite sure how. (It's said that, among other things, the legacy of Dreyfus includes Zionism, the wedge between church and state, *les Pétainistes* and the Tour de France.) But Devil's Island too will never be the same. To the establishment it's proved the perfect political deterrent, a blend of oblivion and terror. From now on it will house all France's public enemies – its dissidents, traitors, spies, New Caledonians and mutineers, and the Viêt Quôc. Consignments of Vietnamese are still arriving, miserably beaten and starved, in 1931.

To liberals, however, Devil's Island becomes a symbol of all that's wrong with *la patrie*: the secrecy, the perverted science and the excess of authority. Zola and Clemenceau extend their protest to the entire settlement and demand that it's closed. The movement is helped by a rash of foreign books, embarrassing France: *The Dry Guillotine, Horrors of Cayenne, Hell on Trial, Loose among Devils* and *The Isle of the Damned*. Eventually, in 1938, the government of the Popular Front announces that no more transports will be sent and that the colony will die a natural death, gradually withering away.

All that's needed is a good war to help the withering along.

After three days on the islands I took a boat to Kourou. There was
nowhere on this journey that I liked so little. It was a cruel, hard-
baked town, with its origins in pain. Although little of the old penal
camp remained, there was still the road, known as '*Route Nationale
1*'. The convicts had called it '*Route Zéro*', as though nothing better
expressed the futility of their lives in Guyane. The road was supposed
to have linked Kourou with Cayenne, sixty miles to the west. By 1906,
after half a century of work, only fifteen miles had been completed.

After landing, I asked a taxi-driver to find me somewhere to stay.
'Hotel des Roches?' he asked.

Fine, I said, let's give it a try.

The driver was a Creole, covered in ropes of gold.

'Les Roches is full of pigs,' he said. 'Their barracks are next door.'

It was also painfully expensive, too much for concrete.

'And I'm sorry,' said the receptionist, 'the café is only for police.'

'*Allons-y!*' I told the driver. We'll try somewhere else.

'*OK*,' he said agreeably, '*Un petit tour de Kourou …*'

Beyond Les Roches the town still hadn't lost its temporary feel.
It had the layout of a great city, but with the buildings yet to arrive.
Around the edge was a scattering of tyre shops and stores. The
roundabouts were bald, and the ponds looked like pits. For the more
upmarket whites there was a little, prefabricated Nicetown, with
street names such as rue Degas and rue Van Gogh. Then there were
the shanty towns. Every distant upheaval seems to have produced
another one; there were straw shacks for the Amerindians, cement
for the N'Djukas and tin for the Bonis. Everywhere there was broken
glass, always a sign of people moving on. At one point we came
across an entire slum, blackened with soot. '*KOUROU ENSOR-
CELÉ!*' said the graffiti: 'Accursed Kourou!'

Eventually we ended up where we'd begun, in *le vieux bourg*.
It was a rickety quarter of sticks and peeling paint, built by the
convicts. The houses here had rooves like pagodas, which will have
pleased the Chinese, who owned all the shops. Outside one of them,
called Proxi, there was a stippling of blue, flashing lights.

'*Encore un vol,*' said the driver. Another robbery.

The police were standing around with their hands in their
pockets. I asked whether it happened a lot.

'*Peut-être deux fois chaque jour.*'

Twice a day? How can anyone put up with that?

The Creole just smiled.

'It used to be worse,' he said. 'We once had a gang that stole little kids.'

Eventually, we found a house that rented out rooms.

Call me if you need me, said the driver, and left. On his card it said: '*JEANNOT COSMIQUE – VA OU TU VEUX*' ('Cosmic Johnny – Go anywhere you like').

The house was made of concrete, and the owner was a *métro*.

'Actually, I was born in *Indochine*,' he said, 'I could never live in France.'

My room had metal furniture and steel bars, just like a cell.

'It's safe,' said the *métro*. 'If I hear anyone, I'll shoot them.'

That evening I negotiated the shutters and gates and headed for the cafés. It was an unsettling walk, through the roundabouts and plots of dried-up mud. Across one plot there were some cars, all well spaced out. It was a sort of impromptu flea market, selling only sex. Each little Citroën and each little Clio was its own little brothel on wheels. As I passed by, the driver's doors would open and long, dark legs would unfold to the ground. I could still hear the voices tumbling after me even as I reached the street. '*Mon cheri ...un moment ...!*' Officially most of these girls were Brazilian, servicing an outbreak of AIDS wholly unrivalled on this side of the globe.

The cafés on Charles de Gaulle looked as though they'd never got over the end of the *bagne*. Along one wall was a mural of Montmartre, complete with hoods and tarts and 'swallows', or cops. I chose a bar run by some Vietnamese. All the other customers were *métros*: sallow, stubbly men, who sat at the zinc with their *pichets* of plonk. I suppose some of them had been farmers and soldiers but to me – raddled and hungry – they just looked like the remnants of an earlier age, a bunch of old cons.

After the closure of the *bagne*, life wasn't easy for those left behind. France still had no idea how to fill so much space. It certainly wasn't keen to drain it of people and send the convicts home. After the war it even offered Guyane as a homeland for the Jews (only losing out to Israel). There was also a plan to fill the camps with 'displaced persons', such as Romanians and Poles. A few came. St-Jean was

Polish for a while, until its football team drowned and everyone went home. The colony was bankrupt, and there was nothing there to keep them. In 1947 there were already 1,800 *libérés* demanding to get home. Most were Arabs, just keen to die in Muslim soil.

After them, the government dragged its feet. It took seven years to get the last 2,000 home. In the end it was the Salvation Army who helped the convicts out. That still left the political prisoners, such as the Indochinese. Some of them would remain in their camps until 1963.

Not everyone left. Some *libérés* saw no future in France or had been here so long they knew no other life. It's said that about 400 stayed. Everyone had stories about 'the old boys'. There was the one who spent his time writing to the Queen of England, demanding a pension. And the Russian who told everyone he'd designed a rocket, and who was carted away when the Cold War began. I once saw some pictures of these people, taken in the '90s. Shrunken and damp, they looked hopelessly benign. Gradually they all died out, and the great experiment finally came to an end.

Meanwhile, France had found a new breed of settler. In 1964 they took over all the old camps and the Iles du Salut. This time they weren't slaves or convicts, but a colony of spacemen.

Behind Kourou stretched a wilderness, often referred to as the Gateway to Space. It didn't look much like a gate, at least not on my map. It was more of a hole, filled with saltgrass and estuaries and 800 square kilometres of swamp. Roads seemed to shy away from it, and those that still wandered through it had turned white, like little bones in the sun. There were no villages any more, just names from the past. Amid all the symbols for moisture and bog, I could see nothing except a few masts and beacons and the words 'CENTRE SPATIAL GUYANAIS'.

Before leaving Kourou, I got Cosmic Johnny to drive me out there.

'Centre spatial *Européen*,' he corrected.

Jeannot had never seen the point in *Le CSG*.

'It just brings trouble,' he said. 'More police and more of *les métros*.'

I was puzzled. 'Doesn't the CSG bring in the money?'

'For some. They earn three times what we do, and then go home.'

'I heard they make up a third of the town.'

'True. They've got their own little quarter: *La Ville Blanche*.'

'But isn't there work for locals too?'

'Just a few cleaners. The rest are from Europe.'

Ahead of us was a wire fence.

'Entrée inderdite aux guyanais,' joked Jeannot. Even the Amerindians had been cleared out, he said, and dumped back in Kourou. From now on there was nothing but whites and rockets, and wild animals. With no hunting, the place was crawling with *serpents et tigres*.

Then a rocket appeared, towering out of the trees. It was a mock-up of Ariane. This wasn't the delicate, streamlined dart that turns up in films. It looked more like a child's crayon, fifteen storeys high. Jeannot conceded that it was a beautiful sight as it set off over the sea. It was odd to think that Guyane was now the start of a journey instead of always being the end. Once it had taken ships months to get here from Africa. Now Kourou could lob one of these office blocks up through the stratosphere, and twenty minutes later its working parts would be floating over Kenya.

At the *centre de contrôle* I joined a little tour. It was like being miniaturised and then climbing round an aircraft with a member of the flight crew. Everything was outsized. There were giant ashtrays, giant lampshades and giant trolleys, which all turned out to be parts of Ariane. At one point we found ourselves in a room like a Zeppelin shed, except finished off in giant wallpaper and carpet as deep as turf. Even our hostess was having trouble, in her dainty Parisian heels. She was better when she leaped up into the furniture and brought all the monitors to life. Suddenly we were enveloped in the history of French rockets. The first ones didn't look too promising and flopped into the bog. But then someone tweaked the design, and in 1979 Ariane was launched. Since then it hasn't stopped launching, and now the screens were full of burning crayons spurting off to Kenya. The CSG, said the hostess, now launches over half the world's commercial satellites.

'Pourquoi ici?' someone asked her. Why here?

'We're on the equator,' she replied. 'A shorter trip into orbit.'

'So even the Russians launch from here?'

'Oui, Soyuz aussi. Et les italiens …'

'I bet it makes some money?'

'*Evidemment*', she said sweetly. About a billion euros a year.

'And do the locals like it?'

'*Oui, bien sûr. Avant le CSG, ils n'avaient même pas de frigos.*'
(Yes, of course. Before the space port they didn't even have fridges.)

Then we were out in a bus, touring the launch pads. I still felt like one of the Borrowers Afloat. From a distance the rocket silos and propellant plants looked like cartons scattered through the bush. Up close they still looked like cartons, but we looked like ants. The biggest silos were called BIL and BAF, and were linked by some outsize Ivor-the-Engine rails. None of this did anything to dispel my suspicion that space travel – with all its journeys into nothing – is as much about fantasy as about science. France's first rocket was called *Astérix* and was said to have been modelled on the cartoon spaceship in *Destination Moon*. That afternoon I still felt the hand of Tintin guiding things along. The jungle even had its own little army of khaki guards, and a fire brigade lent by the city of Paris. Then, as if that wasn't enough, there was also the French Foreign Legion, to fight off whoever might invade.

France had searched hard for this patch of rocket-lovers' heaven. It had previously considered Algeria, Madagascar, Polynesia and the Seychelles. Rockets, it seems, had much the same requirements as convicts: wasteland, a vast body of open water and a dearth of human life.

At last, Guyane was wanted, for being of no value at all.

I once met a Welsh legionnaire who'd spent three years in Kourou.

'It was OK, like. Pay was shit. Heat nearly killed us …'

Most of the time they were out patrolling the forest.

'Everything wants to eat you in there, even the fucking trees …'

His regiment was one of the last to keep *un bordel militaire*. 'We had four girls on camp. They changed them every month.'

It wasn't a bad life, he said. There was even a bit of fighting down in the town. 'Nothing much. Just the local dickheads. No big deal.'

To get to Cayenne, I hitched a lift with a physicist called Christian. He had long white hair and an ancient hatchback that creaked like a galley. Across the back seat were reams of figures, graphs, calculations and tables. If we'd ever had to stop suddenly, I'd have been crushed to death under a wave of mathematics.

'You shouldn't hitch-hike,' said Christian.

I noticed that he had a slight American accent.

'Oh,' I said, 'it looked OK to me.'

'No, my friend, this place is still pretty wild.'

Christian said he was constantly surprised by how wild things were. 'I've been here many years, working on Ariane. I must have watched – I don't know – a hundred launches? And I've seen billions of francs and euros poured into this land. But does it look any different? Has anything changed? You turn your back, and everything's covered in rust, and all the bridges have collapsed. We have an army out there, trying to keep out the immigrants and find the cocaine. But does it make any difference? It's like trying to turn back the tide! This crazy coast will be whatever it wants to be. France has been here almost 400 years, and yet it looks like we just arrived! All around, what do you see? *La forêt, les bambous, les étrangleurs ... la terre sauvage!*'

Ahead of us the road sped away through the endless whips and barbs.

'Some people,' I ventured, 'say France has too much control.'

'Of course they do. They talk about *l'apartheid guyanais*. They say they're ruled by scientists. Imagine that! What would it be called? *Un régime pédagogique*? A technocracy, I suppose. But they don't know how little control we've got. Most of this country we can't even get to. All we can do is throw a bit of hardware into space so that on the other side of the world people can chatter on their mobiles. That's all! One day people won't need mobiles any more, and then we'll be gone. The space port will disappear into the forest, and who knows what the *guyanais* will do. They'll probably come to France, and this will all be forgotten. It'll be just another ruin – *une énigme pour les archéologues ...*'

'Yes, it will seem odd,' I said, 'especially BIL and BAF.'

Christian gave a sort of Gallic huff of laughter. 'Exactly. They'll think we were talking to God instead of chatting to each other.'

'So this isn't the beginning of a golden age?'

'No, it will never be mentioned again, just like *le bagne*.'

'*Le bagne*?'

'Yes, a subject you don't talk about in France.'

'So you think Space-Age Guyane will become taboo?'

'*Oui*, just like every other plan for this magnificent land.'

I spent four days in Cayenne. Most of the time I felt like an onlooker at some strange, slightly manic party. It helped that all the houses were pink or orange and had bright blue doors, rattly roofs and lace around the door. For ages nothing would happen, and then it would suddenly flicker into life. Feathered dancers would appear, and girls in sequins and masks. Somewhere, deep in the tin, hundreds of bands would begin to play, and people would drive around with their music so loud that it would set off the car alarms and make all the glasses rattle. Large crowds would gather on Les Palmistes, smelling faintly of anxiety and rum. Then the clouds would burst, everyone would scatter and huge rivers would appear, bringing with them branches and bottles and luxuriant waves of paper cups.

For a while the party would fizzle on. The night would throb away, the lights would crackle and the rain would guzzle down the streets. It was always more a sensation than a spectacle. Cayenne could be fabulously flashy one moment, but then it would all vanish at the touch. This, I suppose, was partly because there was never much there to start with. The city was trying to have a superpower party with the population of a tiny country town. Often I'd rush out in the hope of a carnival, only to find the square all quiet, *Le Roi des Frites* packing up his stall, and the chair-o-planes whirring emptily overhead.

But what bothered me was not that there wasn't a party but that it was going on somewhere else. Everyone seemed to have spectacular hangovers, and yet I was never there when they got them. Few of the restaurants ever seemed to open, and even when they did the waiters looked as though they'd been up all night, and the service was dreamy and languid. Obviously Cayenne was not a town for outsiders. The real action seemed to happen deep inside or well out of sight. I noticed that it was supposed to be an island, but whenever I went in search of the sea, all I ever found was mangrove and pungent, sticky swamp. Maybe this made it even more of an island, a world of its own.

As to what people were celebrating, I never really discovered. Half the town didn't have a job, and *les métros* ran everything from the sewers to the police. They also owned all the bars, cut the grass, made the water taste like swimming pools and built all the round-abouts. Apart from roundabouts, old Cayenne hadn't seen much new building for 200 years, and with its wooden *quartiers* and chunks of fort it looked much the same now as it did back then. Among the twelve 'monuments' listed by the tourist office there was a roundabout, three squares, a fountain and a fruit market. Since the abolition of slavery little, it seemed, had happened. (Cayenne had never had the convicts, like St-Laurent, or the spacemen, like Kourou.) Perhaps that in itself was a reason to party.

The festivities were continually starting and stopping. But it was the gaps in between that were always so surprising. In the heat and silence of the day *les cayennais* could be crapulously strange. No one would bat an eyelid at the sight of voodoo charms, straining spandex or unauthorised body parts breaking cover. I remember once seeing a man taking a bath in the old marble fountain outside the *préfecture*. He was enviably oblivious to the world around and had even brought a piece of soap and a towel. Another time, I came across a girl high up on the ruins of Vauban's fort. She was about sixteen, white, freckly, creepy and conspicuously pregnant. '*J'adore Cayenne,*' she said. '*Je me sens une femme*' (I love Cayenne. It makes me feel like a woman). Perhaps strangest of all was the Musée Départemental, which was like a collection of all the weirdest moments in Cayenne's past. Among the exhibits were a crucifixion scene etched on a skull, a mutant palm tree with buttocks, some bottled toads, and the plaster cast of a condemned man's foot, made under torture.

At this odd feast there were plenty of skeletons, and as an outsider I often seemed to find myself among them. Usually, they just hung around the square. Most were drunks, whites and blacks, levelled by undiscriminating drink. But others were Guyanese who, with no claim on the largesse of Paris, were candidly wasting away. The Cayennais had a way of looking through them ('Never give them anything,' I was told, 'they don't forget a face'), but it was not a skill that I ever came to terms with, and so whenever I crossed *Les Palmistes* I had an escort of skeletons and waifs. Of all the people I met, it was they that troubled me most, because everyone wanted them gone. 'I'm hungry,' one of them told me, 'but I'm never gonna steal.'

A few blocks away was a whole quarter of rejects and outlaws. It was called La Crique or 'Chicago', and sat on a narrow, muddy river that led off into the bush. Originally this was where the Indochinese settled at the end of their sentence. In the water I could see fish like ghosts, with huge white eyeballs and thin, translucent bones. Just as I was wondering how these little wisps of gristle survived, I felt some one touch my sleeve. 'You don't want to be round here,' said a voice.

It was one of the fishermen, an Indo-Guyanese.

'Thank you,' I said.

His head wobbled. 'There's a lot of bad people here ...'

'Bad people?'

'This where the drugs come in. Not even the police is here.'

I thanked him again and picked my way back through the shacks.

By now I was used to the idea of being uninvited. It was therefore even more of a surprise when someone tried to put me on parade. It was the old seamstress next to my hotel. She was also Guyanese, and on my last day I'd wandered into her workshop to see the costumes in progress. She immediately decided I was just what the carnival needed and started measuring me up for a ballgown and wig. 'Oh my God, man, you gonna be perfect. I gonna make a Touloulou!'

'I'm sorry,' I told her, 'my journey's come to an end ...'

'Stay longer!'

'I'd like to,' I said, unsure if I meant it, 'but I have to go home.'

I think she was genuinely disappointed to see her plans fall apart, and so in a way was I. Since then, I've often wondered how I'd have fared as a carnival queen. A few days later I watched the parade on television. The first dancers to enter the Place des Palmistes were tossing a young woman high in the air. As they passed the grandstand, they seemed to forget about the girl, and she tumbled through their outstretched arms and landed flat on her face.

Guyane's most recent settlers are probably the most exotic of all. The new colonists had set out from here in September 1977, travelling by truck. They had a hard journey ahead, fifty miles into the hills. *Les guyanais* already hated them. When they'd heard they were coming to Guyane, they were out on the streets, shouting '*Méo dehors! Métro déro!*' (Barbarians out! Down with the French!) They feared they'd be swamped and that their world would turn yellow. That's why the new arrivals were travelling at night, protected by the army.

They are curious people to encounter on this journey. They've been fugitives most of their existence. Nobody knows where they originally came from. Some say Mongolia, others Tibet or even Lapland. But it was in China that they were first called *Miao*, or 'The Barbarians'. They appalled the Chinese, living in the mountains, sacrificing dogs and practising magic. For 2,000 years they were ignored and, left to themselves, they became the producers of opium. But then in the nineteenth century they fell foul of the Manchu dynasty, and thousands of them were forced to flee again, scattering south. They took with them their silver ingots and their neck-rings, and headed for Laos. There they settled in mountains even more remote than before and became known as the Hmong.

The newcomers of 1977 weren't the first Hmong in Guyane. They'd always been enthusiastic guerrillas, tormenting the French. In the Lao highlands they'd made the best knives and crossbows and home-made guns, and they even looked like an army in their black pyjamas and coloured bands. Their greatest uprising was in 1919 and was known as *La Guerre des Fous*, the War of the Mad. Many of them ended up in prison hulks to Guyane, and then on the road to the hills. These days nothing remains of the old *pénitencier* up there except a ring of stones. But in 1977 France decided on a new scheme. By a strange coincidence it also involved the Hmong, and so, once again, they were back on the road.

'How do I get up there?' I asked.

No one knew. *'Pas de bus. Pas de train. Rien.'*

In the end I departed from principle and hired a car. I've always hated cars, and this one was no exception. I'd rather meanly hired the smallest one I could, and it was like riding along on a sewing machine. I was also convinced that it didn't have enough windows or that they were all in the wrong place. Everywhere I looked there were blind spots, all of which seemed suddenly to fill up with crows and tractors and trucks of legionnaires.

Fortunately the traffic soon fell away, and in the slot up front a beautiful landscape began to take shape. It reminded me of a book I'd had as a child, a lavish edition of *Robinson Crusoe*. There were well-feathered forests and tempting blue peaks, and clearings quilted with buttery yellows and strawberry pinks. Then I left the main road and began thrumming uphill. The way ahead now had all the makings of a mountain, and I don't think the foresters had ever seen such a small car clambering over the ruts. But eventually I reached a ridge, and there – on the other side – was a pretty Lao hill station, known as Cacao.

It so happened I'd been in Laos the year before. This was hard on the internal compass, tumbling over a hill and ending up back on the opposite side of the world. I recognised the black pyjamas, the big farms on stilts and, of course, the Hmong themselves, sturdy and squat. Most of the farmers had the same knobbly home-made guns, and rolled-down boots as protection from snakes. There were three stores, and they each stocked incense and rice steamers, and all the essentials of life in Laos. There was also a market that sold tapestries of either great battles or B-52s trickling bombs on people's heads. Cacao even had an old cutler, grinding out knives in steel and bronze.

But it wasn't all Laos. The opium days were over, and so were the wandering farms. I asked one of the farmers what he hunted. *'Tatous et tapirs,'* he said, slightly bemused. Armadillos and tapirs.

The settlement was also keenly Roman Catholic. Few people worried any more about Nplooj Lwg, the divine frog, or the poisonous caterpillars of Otherworld. The day after I arrived I went to listen to morning Mass. The farmers arrived in their best embroidered shirts, and the old ladies, after climbing the hill, hawked up the dust and spat in the bushes. Then there were psalms in Hmong, and a rich arpeggio of notes floated off over the forest. The priest didn't understand the prayers but had an altar boy that did.

'Sib Hawm Teev Ntuj,' chanted the boy. Our Lady of Peace.

'As les lus yas!' replied the farmers. Alleluia!

I stayed at the town's inn, the Lotus d'Asie. It was popular with the farmers after work. They always tipped a little beer into the dirt, to propitiate the spirits. I had a room in a lean-to at the back, furnished with a car seat and some hooks for my hammock. The owner of the inn was called Madame Maysy Siong. She once showed me her mother's dowry, a hoard of ingots and neck-rings. Her parents had spent much of their life on the run, she told me, and wherever they went they always buried the silver at night.

René, her husband, was a hunter and had a crossbow he'd made himself. Soon after I arrived, he appeared with three huge fish and a small *bak*, or porcupine. As a child, he'd been brought up in refugee camps and could still remember his English. He said that people didn't often talk about those experiences any more, but – over the next few days – this is the tale that emerged.

I was born in lowland Laos in 1965. Our village didn't have a name. We grew hill rice, and when the soil was spent, we moved somewhere else. But my parents were Catholics and fought for the French. They called us the *montagnards,* the mountaineers. I was too young to remember how the war began. But most of our men joined the fight, against the Pathet Lao. We had a general called Vang Pao, who wore a hat like a cowboy. My father said we also helped the Americans, picking up their pilots and doing hit-and-run. You say it was called 'The Secret War'? It didn't feel very secret to us. Our camp at Long Cheng was the second-biggest settlement in Laos, and the only city the Hmong have ever had …

But then, when I was ten, we had to leave. The communists had won, and they started to hunt us down. We had to escape through the forest, walking for weeks. I'll never forget that. There were a lot of landmines, and many people were killed. It's a terrible sight, a person killed by a mine. Eventually, however, we got to the Mekong and crossed into Thailand. We then spent two years in the camp at Ban Vinai. That was my childhood really. It was a long time before they found us somewhere to live. Obviously we could never go back to Laos. General Vang Pao went to America, and a lot of us went with him. I don't know how many, maybe a quarter of a million? Others went to places we'd never heard of, like Iceland and Bangladesh. But then, one day, some French missionaries turned up and said they'd found us a home. We were taken to aeroplanes and flew to Paris, and then on to Cayenne. I'd never been on a plane before, and have never been on one since.

I've always loved Cacao. I suppose, with the jungle and the red soil, it reminds me a little bit of Laos. (What's Laos like now? I heard they're very poor.) We had to do a lot of work here, to make it what it is. By the end of our first year we'd built over a hundred houses, and had started to plant the fields. People even said Vang Pao should buy the whole country and make it a homeland for the Hmong. But there have never been many of us. Altogether about 2,000 came. We still make up only 2 per cent of the population. Still, we work hard. Almost all the fruit and vegetables in Guyane are grown by the Hmong.

Sure, we had a bit of help from the French whites, the *fabkis dawb*. We never knew how much the blacks disliked us. They called us *'le péril jaune'*, and thought we were Chinese (who weren't popular in 1977). They still don't trust us, *les guyanais*. Personally,

I don't really understand it. They refuse to cultivate their own land, and have never fought for France. We lost 400,000 people fighting the communists ...

I don't know whether there'll always be Hmong up here. It's not easy: the land here's too steep for machines. It's a constant battle with the jungle and the fire-ants. Even the children work one day a week. And now there are robbers, out in the forest. My parents found it tough – too tough – and left. They now live in France, near Rennes. Maybe others will leave. They can afford to now. Perhaps we'll all go, and that will be the end of the Hmong in Guyane? We've always moved around. Our homeland is our money.

My last few hundred miles of Guyane felt like a long goodbye.

The people I travelled with were terrified of the forest ahead. I'd got rid of the car and found a minibus leaving from Cayenne. Most of the other passengers were heading for Brazil. There were three *garimpeiros* with their girls, and an Amerindian travelling with an enormous bale of Huggies. Had she already had her babies, I wondered, or was she planning on half-a-dozen? One of the miners had snakeskin shoes and a brand new jacket, with a label still on the cuff. His girlfriend was already hating this journey before it had even begun, and whenever the junkies came near, she hopped about like a little bird at the approach of a cat.

She asked me if I was going all the way to St-Georges.

I told her I was.

Good, she said. Then we can all go together.

But the journey was never as gruesome as she'd feared. The most serious threat was from the music, great shattering waves of *brega* that exploded from the speakers. The long ride through the forest did, however, bring something else to mind. It was like an affirmation of all that had happened, or perhaps a parting shot. The superlatives necessary to express the density of forest simply don't exist. The roadside was like night-time, packed with spikes and armour. As for the canopy, it looked equally defiant, a thick phalanx of huge brain-like structures, riding at anchor. I'd lost count of the schemes and colonies that had foundered under this magnificent vegetable onslaught. It's been a long farewell, lasting hundreds of years. Across the Guianas not a single railway or canal or cattle trail still functioned, and only one fort. Countless airstrips had come and gone, and thousands of plantations had vanished for ever. The sheer difficulty of living on this coast meant there were now as many 'Guianians' living abroad as there were here. And that's only the coast. Inland there were thousands of square miles that had hardly been touched at all.

During the construction of this road, in 1994, French ecologists protested that this was the beginning of the end. They said that the last primary Atlantic forest would be destroyed, with the loss of 450,000 trees. This time *les guyanais* reacted with anger. They said that, since slavery, France had never invested in Guyane, and that in 400 years it had laid only 260 miles of paved road. The ecologists were like slavers themselves and their science was rotten. The new road would absorb less than 0.001 per cent of the forest. The only endangered species were the Guyanese themselves. 'We think we're old enough to make our decisions,' said one politician, and the road went ahead.

It was an incongruous sight, a European road in the South American forest. It had metal barriers and neat little signs, all made in France. Occasionally we passed through road blocks set up by the gendarmes, or saw troops of soldiers training on the verge. Then, near St-Georges, we found something else: the roadsides cluttered with burned-out cars.

'Qu'est-ce qui s'est passé?' I asked.

But no one knew. The Brazilians seemed to think that the wreckage was more normal than the road. Maybe it was the Amerindians, said the bird-girl. This didn't sound very likely, but at that moment the idea was pleasingly symmetrical: the Wild Coast, still as wild as ever.

I was sorry to be leaving. During these few months in the Guianas life had become thrillingly arrhythmic. I was never able to look ahead or guess what was coming. Each time I emerged from the darkness, everything around me was different. Perhaps the soil had turned scarlet, or the language had changed, or a new race had appeared. It was always remarkable, and often chaotically beautiful. I don't suppose that I shall ever see such dramatic rivers again, whether they're gnashing with fury, or sliding along like a land in the mirror.

I also love the idea that much of this world isn't even known to those that live here, and that its creatures – mad, gaudy, toxic and exotic – are safer here than anywhere else on the planet. Other places may feel more magnificent than the Guianas, or perhaps even emptier, but nowhere feels quite so unconquered.

I think I understand better now the rawness of its human history. Along this coast mankind has always been made to feel a little frail. It's not just the flora and fauna, but the sheer scale of the forest beyond. Ghosts and magic have always thrived and had often been a daily feature of my travels. But what had always seemed so odd about the supernatural life of the Guianas was the sheer consistency of its ogres. Everywhere I went the same fiends cropped up, particularly the water monkey. In a land comprising three different countries, three different cultures, three official languages, three currencies, myriad religions and umpteen different races, this was remarkable. It was almost as though, in cultural terms, the only thing that linked the Guianas was a fear of the unseen.

Freud once said that if you accidentally leave something behind, you don't really want to leave. I now had lots of things I could have left behind. Although I'd given away most of my clothes, I'd accumulated over 3,000 pages of notes, ten hours of taped interviews and 1,000 photographs. I'd also acquired a bow and arrow, a Dutch wine bottle, some maroon togas, several clay pipes, a few yards of bead necklaces, various coins, feathers and rocks, and a small cannonball. The fact that I'd somehow hung on to this lot was a reminder that this was just a journey, and that – at heart – I wanted to get back home.

At the last minute, however, I did leave something on the minibus. It was my marked-up copy of Raleigh's *Discoverie*. As the minibus didn't look as though it had ever been cleaned, I suspect that this curious volume is still there, and that it will trundle up and down the coast for ever, or at least for the life of a South American bus.

In St-Georges I asked around about the burned-out cars. The town sat, very neatly, on the banks of the Oyapok. It was like a last vestige of old France, tottering on the edge of a loud, new world. It had a bakery, a war memorial, a little town hall, a hotel made of corrugated iron, a tin church with a spire, two grocery stores, a gun shop, and a Chinese *bibelotier*, or purveyor of fancy goods. There was also a garrison for thirty soldiers, just as there had been since the French first arrived. I tried to get inside the church but was seen off by a stray, giving birth to puppies all over the vestry. From the Brazilian side came a constant clunk of drums, like a heartbeat but faster.

I stopped by at the hotel. It had lemon-yellow shutters and was decorated with plaques from all the great *régiments* who'd called in for coffee. That afternoon it was full of gendarmes. President Sarkozy had just announced a big campaign against illegal migrants. Across the Guianas there were now almost half as many *garimpeiros* as there were lawful natives.

I asked one of the officers about his work.

'*Nous sommes debordés,*' he said. We're being swamped.

And what about the Brazilians, the ones that he caught?

They're OK, he told me. '*Ce sont surtout de bons gens …*'

'And they work hard?'

'*Oui, plus durs que les guyanais.*'

'And what about the cars?'

'*C'est aussi les brésiliens …*'

It transpired that the vehicles were stolen in Cayenne, driven down Route 2, stripped of their parts, and then set on fire. It happens all the time, said the officer. '*Chaque jour, trois ou quatre voitures …*'

'So Brazil's now here to stay, warts and all?'

'*Oui, bienvenu dans le futur,*' he said. Welcome to the future.

EPILOGUE

My friends, there is no more beautiful or richer country under the sun than this one. It is yours.

The governor's words to Cayenne's first convicts, 1852

The leather will rot in your shoes, and the seams of your clothes will come undone, and the material will be torn into shreds. Your instruments will fall to pieces. Everything you have will rot. Your brow will turn to water, and mushrooms will breed in your flesh.

Raymond Maufrais, Journey without Return

AT SOME STAGE DURING MY RESEARCH I'd realised that Oyapok
had played an uncomfortable role in my family history.

As the last river in these travels, it was obligingly ferocious. From
St-Georges the Oyapok looked merely huge, like a lake speckled
with canoes. But everything I'd read suggested that, within twenty
miles, it became a monster. Along its length (310 miles) there were
said to be 120 sets of rapids. Even here the tide was constantly piling
up sandbanks and then sucking them away. The river also had its
own mist – called 'The Shroud of the Europeans' – and an entire
population of mini-monsters from *sucurís*, or anacondas, to fish-
eating rats.

Being so surly, the Oyapok had seldom been colonised. Most of
the people living on its banks were Amerindians, tribes that had
been here for thousands of years. They've never made easy neighbours. The biggest group were the Galibis, who were once known as
the Caribs and who'd made a name for themselves by eating everyone else. Then there were the Karipunas, the Oyampis and – way
upriver – the Emérillons, who were almost extinct. There was also
talk of a tribe of women, who, once a year, coupled with the men
of the Taïras, and then killed any males they produced. Raleigh had
loved this story and had included it in his catalogue of Guianese
delights, recasting the tribe as 'The Amazons'.

With such strong allusions to the origins of Guiana, it felt right, ending my journey here. But there was another sense in which I was ending my travels where they'd begun. It had suddenly dawned on me that the Oyapok of today and the 'River Wyapoko' of 1629 were one and the same. That meant that Robert Hayman, my airy-fairy, ditty-jotting forebear had finished up somewhere near here. Of course, I had no way of finding him, but, having followed him down from Newfoundland, I did at least owe him the courtesy of an excursion: a little tour around the scene of his final disaster.

Which is how I ended up in a dugout heading for Brazil, with an Amerindian aged eleven, my rucksack, the bag of notes, my bow and arrow, and a very cold little piglet.

On the far bank we got out at Oiapoque. I made signs for a bigger canoe, and pointed upriver. The Amerindian took me to a gold-dealer, who spoke a little French.

'*Visitez* Rona,' he said, through a slot in the wall.

He gave the boy some directions, and we both set off, with the pig on a piece of string and me dangling history and weapons. After Cayenne, Oiapoque was like six towns compacted into one. I could suddenly feel all my senses abruptly jolted into action. Everything here seemed to howl or stink or glare or slosh around under the feet. In this part of Guiana – known as Amapá – only one house in fifty is connected to the sewers. It struck me that an earthy Stuart like Hayman would have understood it all much better: the streets like rivers, the waggons glooping through the mud, the banter of music, the hawkers with their ointments and gew-gaws, the chickens being cooked in the road, the public displays of insanity, the poor without shirts, and lives slowing down to the pace of a slouch. On the other hand, in Hayman's day there'd have been nothing here at all, except a few Carib huts. I wondered what 'Oiapoque' meant. 'Water-logged', perhaps, or 'The Place of Mating Dogs'.

At the edge of the town we came to some mangrove and followed a boardwalk out through the swamp. If birds had designed this planet, it would be covered in mangrove. All around us in the gloom was a fizzy black goo, humming with insecty treats. We also came across a small dead coral snake, and a sign that read '*Perigo – abelhas*' ('Danger – Bees'). I was glad when we re-emerged in the light. Ahead was a beach, and a clearing planted with bananas and coffee.

'*La Chácara du Rona!*' announced the boy, who then took his money and his piglet, and left.

Rona appeared. '*Bom dia! Como vai?*'

'*Tudo bem!*' I replied, in my schoolboy Portuguese.

Rona smiled and offered to speak in French.

He said he had rooms to let and boats on the river. Although in his sixties, Rona was still immensely solid, with tufts of thick black hair erupting at his collar and cuffs, as though he'd been padded. One of the first things he showed me was his hatchlings, tiny turtles he'd rescued from the hunters. While I always had a sneaking feeling that Rona's ancestors had made life hell for mine, it was hard not to like him. He was as I imagined a good quartermaster during *la conquista*, and could fix up almost anything. Under the trees there were giant canoes – all ready and waiting – together with barrels and oil drums and a crew of Caribs. Not only did Rona have the plantation and the huts, but he also ran cargo, right up the river.

I told him about Hayman, and his long-lost farm.

Rona was intrigued. '*Quand est-il arrivé?*'

'*Le dix-sept fevrier 1629.*'

There was a whistle of surprise. What was Hayman growing?

Sugar and cotton, perhaps. Certainly cassava.

In that case, said Rona, he was probably near here.

How could he tell?

Because, downstream, the soil's too salty.

And upstream?

Rapids. You can't get a ship past.

Hayman, I said, took a canoe upriver. Twenty days.

That's to the headwater. Now, with a motor, it's seven.

Had Rona got a boat free tomorrow?

Sure, he said. Where are you going?

The Maripa Falls.

'*OK, não tem problema.*'

I chose the Maripa Falls for a particular reason. Looking at the river, I now realised that, for all his airs and fancy ideas, Robert Hayman had undertaken an astonishing journey. With almost no experience of the continent he'd tackled one of its most violent stretches of water. He had no map, no medicine and no prospect of rescue. With his little crew he'd be constantly pulling the dugout out of the water and carrying it up through the rapids. His outfit may have been all right for a jaunt round Bristol or for filching gull's eggs on the edge of the Labrador Sea, but it was hopeless in the tropics. He didn't even have a spade, in case anybody died.

With him were three Caribs and his servant from Wessex, and together they travelled hundreds of miles inland. The idea was to 'traffique' with the Norrague people, who've long since disappeared and who lived three weeks upriver. What could they possibly have had, to make all this worthwhile? In years to come, explorers would come back with all sorts of wonders: a grass that could stop bleeding, mind-bending mahogany apples, and a leaf for entrancing fish. But what was Robert after? It's one of the frustrations of this extraordinary journey that his shopping list, like everything else, has completely disappeared.

Particularly galling is the fact that there's no way of knowing where this voyage began or even where it ended. Nowadays Robert would have his itinerary up on the web and would be tweeting his poems all round the world. But back then there wasn't even so much as a handwritten log. The only evidence that this journey ever took place is a deposition, written by a friend, as proof of Robert's death. 'During theire stay at wyapoko', it begins, 'the said Robert hayman about the moneth of October last past and a servant of his called Thomas Duppe with Axes, bills, cassada irons, strong waters and diverse other Commodityes went up the river from his plantation ...'

And that's it, as far as geography goes. If my journey was to become intertwined with Robert's – even if only at the end – I needed to find a spot where our paths were funnelled together. The Maripa Falls looked just the job.

Rona said that his boatman would drop me on the French side, at the foot of the falls. From there it was an hour's walk up through the jungle to the upstream side. Hayman must have done much the same. The river here was about 300 metres wide, and dropped the height of a tree. There was no other way through, except overland.

Good luck, added Rona, and beware of the bees.

The boatman was, like Hayman's, a Carib or Galibi. Although he was impressively po-faced, he wore a T-shirt that said 'I AM THE

NEW IN YOUR WORLD OF NEW'. Apart from this slightly puzzling sentiment, it would be a trip without words. If the boatman wanted me to do anything, he merely tilted his head or made some subtly anguished grimace. There was also a nod for 'sit down' and a scowl for 'get out'. Three weeks of this, I decided, might have got rather trying. But at least the Caribs no longer regarded their visitors as lunch. In Oiapoque I'd seen some of their old war clubs. They were works of art, with huge diagonal teeth. The victim would've been not only knocked senseless but flattened and tenderised, ready for the grill.

Ten miles upstream the water began to buckle and heave. Ahead was what looked like an avalanche of crumbling snow and mud. Just to demonstrate that no one had ever paddled up here, the boatman opened the throttle, and we crawled through the froth to the bottom of this wall. For a moment we hung there, and then the water caught us and sent us spiralling off downstream. It was exhilarating in a way, like jogging through ten lanes of traffic and somehow surviving.

On the French bank the boatman scowled, and I jumped out into the forest. Amid the trees there was a miniature rail track that led up to the other side of the falls. All cargo used to come this way on a *pousse-pousse*, or handcart, but now the track was abandoned. Saplings were pushing up through the sleepers, and the bridges were rotting away. As always, the jungle was healing over. In places trees had fallen over the track, and I had to climb through the springy branches, listening carefully for bees. Soon it began to rain, and everything around me seemed to scream with pleasure. Songs belched out of the undergrowth, which sagged under the downpour. Then suddenly behind me there was a deafening crack, followed by myriad splintery explosions. I walked back to see what had happened and found that a vast tree had collapsed across the track, just where I'd been moments before. It wasn't exactly a close shave, but it was a reminder that falling trees kill more people in the Guianese jungle than any other peril. I once heard a story in Guyana of a bulldozer driver who was so emphatically crushed that he had to be buried in his cab.

After an hour I came to the head of the falls. The forest opened out onto a small, sandy savannah, smouldering with rain. Beyond it I could see the Oyapok, now looking less like a tropical river than a strip of angry North Atlantic. I took refuge in an old, rotting shack and was surprised to find that I wasn't alone. Out on the porch was a *légionnaire* with a machine gun, keeping watch on the river. If he was surprised by the sight of an Englishman, streaming water and covered in scratches, he didn't look it. I didn't trouble him with my ghost-hunt. Instead we talked about poisonous frogs and Madagascar, which was where he came from.

I also asked him why he'd joined the Foreign Legion.

'Pour le passeport,' he said frankly.

And, for that, he'd be here five years?

The soldier nodded. All he wanted was to get a degree.

I stared out across the rumbling tussocks of slate-grey water. Funny thing, ambition. Hayman had done all this for a little fame and fortune at the court of King Charles. Of course, he'd never found it. According to his friend, on the way back downriver 'he dyed in the said Canoo of a burning fever and of the fluxe'. It wasn't a great end to his trip, excreting blood and boiling in his skin. The Caribs and the servant, Thomas Duppe, had then dug a grave 'close by the waters side, with paddles and Cassada irons'. Under the terms of his enterprise, Hayman's worldly goods passed first to his partner, Charles Hellman – who also died a Wyapoko death – then to 'one William Knevett, of london, ffishmonger'.

Poor Robert. In death he'd realised something that Europeans would take several centuries to appreciate: that Guiana would exact a terrible price for its beauty, and would rarely share out its wealth. In fact, Robert had come away with nothing, not even a single line of his jangling verse.

AFTERWORD

In November 2009 Guyana and Norway signed a historic deal in which Guyana placed its forest under Norwegian supervision in return for an aid package worth $250 million over five years.

DR ROOPNARAINE continues to struggle for social justice, although the days of armed revolt are long behind him. In 2010 he issued his prospectus for change, titled *Call to Citizens.*

LORLENE JAMES remarried and still lives in Georgetown, where she campaigns for civil society.

JANET JAGAN, the dental nurse who became Guyana's first and last white American president, died in March 2009.

DEBORAH LAYTON, who escaped from Jonestown and brought the world news of its excesses, later became a stockbroker and still lives in California. Her brother LARRY was sentenced to life imprisonment for his part in the shootings at Port Kaituma but was released in 2002.

In November 2009, the Guyanese government erected a plaque at JONESTOWN, its first memorial to those who'd died thirty-one years before.

I continued to ring DESI BOUTERSE after my return to London but I never got an answer. In July 2010, he and his party ('Mega Combination') won the election, and Bouterse became Suriname's president. Meanwhile, his trial in relation to 'The December Murders' continues, and Holland has withdrawn all non-essential aid.

French Guiana is still busily lobbing rockets into orbit. The latest, in November 2010, took with it Hylas-1, a satellite made in the old seafaring city of Portsmouth. It promises Britons greater broadband access, and thus even more chatter.

Meanwhile, as the world gold price rose, there was more violence in the forest. In December 2009, Brazil despatched a military plane to Albina to rescue its beleaguered miners. The lure of gold, it seems, continues to vex this coast.

SOURCES

The Guianas

Finding books that provide an overview of the Guianas was surprisingly difficult. Few authors and historians have ventured into comparison. Perhaps the earliest, and easily the most imaginative, description of the region is provided by Sir Walter Raleigh's *The Discoverie of the Large, Rich and Bewtiful Empire of Guiana* (reprinted by the Hakluyt Society, London, 2006). However, as he never actually set foot in the lands with which I'm concerned, his great work makes for a somewhat unreliable guide. Richard Hakluyt's *Voyages and Discoveries* (London, Penguin, 1972) also provides a few early insights into the region, if equally second-hand.

One of the first English-language histories of the Wild Coast was *Guiana British, Dutch and French* (London, T. Fisher Unwin, 1912), written by the curator of the Georgetown museum, James Rodway. It's a surprisingly even-handed account, despite some trenchant observations about the French ('Cayenne was unfit for even a dog'), and is still in print today. Now, however, apart from the usual websites (CIA, BBC and Wikipedia), *The South American Handbook* (Bath, Footprint Handbooks) is as good a source as any for the basic comparative data.

I could find few other travel writers who have made the journey through all three Guianas. However, V. S. Naipaul provides a rich and damning account of the region's colonies in *Middle Passage: Impressions of Five Societies – British, French and Dutch – in the West Indies and South America* (London, Andre Deutsch, 1962).

To understand the military resources of the late 1980s, a period of great significance to newly-emerging Guyana and Suriname, I turned to Adrian English's *Latin America Regional Defence Profile* (London, Jane's, 1988).

Guyana – General

For an overall guide to the country, I was indebted to my friend, Kirk Smock's book, *Guyana* (Chalfont St Peter, Bradt Travel Guides, 2008). However, for a general history of Guyana (or British Guiana, as it was), I turned, as everyone does, to Vere T. Daly's *A Short History of the Guyanese People* (Oxford, Macmillan, 1975) and *The Making of Guyana* (London, Macmillan, 1975). Although well-written and useful, both books tend however to reflect the nascent nationalism of the 1970s.

Three remarkable accounts of life in Georgian Guyana (then the Dutch colonies of Essequibo, Demerara and Berbice) are provided by Edward Bancroft's *An Essay on the Natural History of Guiana* (London, 1769), Henry Bollingbroke's *A Voyage to the Demerary* (Norwich, 1807) and George Pinckard's *Notes on the West Indies* (London, 1806). In my research on the Dutch forts of this period, I was also greatly assisted by the Journal of the Walter Roth Museum of Anthropology, *Archaeology and Anthropology*, volume 10, 1995 (Georgetown, Walter Roth Museum, 1995). Some interesting Afro-Guyanese perspectives on slavery can be found in *Emancipation* (*The African-Guyanese Magazine*, volume 2, No 15, 2007–8), and Alvin Thompson's *The Berbice Revolt* (Georgetown, Free Press, 1999) provides a helpful Guyanese analysis of the slaughter of 1763.

Meanwhile, Victorian British Guiana is subjected to splendid analysis in Graham Burnett's *Masters of all they Surveyed: Exploration, Geography, and a British El Dorado* (University of Chicago Press, 2001). It's a perfect companion to Robert Schomburgk's sombre memoir, *Travels in British Guiana 1840–1844* (London, 1847). There's also a worthy study of Guyana's early Indian heritage in Dale Bisnauth's *The Settlement of Indians in Guyana 1890–1930* (Leeds, Peepal Tree, 2000).

As far as indigenous or Amerindian culture is concerned, there has – over the centuries – been a wealth of interest. Raleigh was one of the first to document the various rumours, but it was left to the Georgians to provide rather more scientific accounts. Aside from Bancroft and Bollingbroke, Charles Marie de La Condamine makes some fascinating observations about the lives of the aboriginal people (and, in particular, their use of curare) in '*Relation abregée d'un Voyage fait dans l'Interieur de L'Amerique Meridional &c*'. A little later, Edward Goodall provides us with a last glimpse of a way of life that was becoming rapidly extinct with his *Sketches of Amerindian Tribes 1841–1843* (Oxford, Macmillan Caribbean, 1977). I was also drawn to a slim and rather impenetrable volume by an old missionary hand, W. Grainge White, called *At Home with the Makuchis* (Ipswich, Harrison & Sons, 1920). But for a more modern exposition of Amerindian culture, I turned to Janette Forte's *Amerindian Testimonies* (Georgetown, Janette Forte, 1989) and *Iwokramî Pantoni: Stories about Iwokrama* (edited by Janette Forte, Makushi Research Unit, 2001). There are countless other anthropological texts on the subject but I would particularly single out William Brett's *Legends and Myths of the Aboriginal Indians of British Guiana* (Whitefish, MT, Kessinger Publishing, 2003).

The modern history and politics of Guyana, however, proved a difficult subject to grasp, if only because it's steeped in obscurity and loyalties based on race. Former president Cheddi Jagan provides waspish accounts of everyone else's failings in *The West on Trial: My Fight for Guyana's Freedom* (Antigua, Hansib Caribbean, 1997) and *A New Global Human Order* (Harpy, 1999) but there is little analysis of his own unfortunate rule. For a more detached view, I often found myself relying on the findings of judicial enquiries such as the *Report of the Commission of Inquiry into the disturbances in British Guiana in February 1962* (London, HMSO), or – more recently – the report of the Canadian Research Directorate of the Immigration and Refugee Board, *Guyana: Criminal Violence and Police Response* (Ottawa, July 2003). As for the unhealthy life spawned by the gold-mining industry, I would strongly recommend Marc Herman's *Searching for El Dorado* (New York, Doubleday, 2002).

Guyana has a rich legacy of travel literature. Anthony Trollope penned some charming sketches of the erstwhile colony in his *The West Indies and the Spanish Main* (London, Chapman and Hall, 1860). Then there was the redoubtable Edward Knight, who describes a short but typically colourful visit in *The Cruise of the Falcon* (London, Sampson, Low, Marston, Searle & Rivington, 1887). Another visitor was Paul Zahl, who explored the interior by air just before the war (an experience described in *To the Lost World*, London, George G. Harrap, 1940). But perhaps best known of all is Evelyn Waugh's gruelling account of his 1933 journey, *92 Days: Travels in Guiana and Brazil* (London, Duckworth, 1934). Not only is it a deeply unflattering picture of the colony, it also provides the setting for one of the greatest English novels of the century, *A Handful of Dust* (London, 1934). V. S. Naipaul (above) provides an equally bleak view of British Guiana but more recent travel writers – particularly the naturalists (to whom I shall return) – have found things much more to their liking. Not all of them make great literature but there's much to enjoy in Margaret Bacon's *Journey to Guyana* (London, Dennis Dobson, 1970), W. M. Ridgewell's *The Forgotten Tribes of Guyana* (London, Tom Stacey, 1972), and Stan Brock's *All the Cowboys were Indians* (Pelham, AL, Synergy South 1999).

This is not to ignore the local contributions. Matthew Young's account of a life spent in the bush, *Guyana: The Lost El Dorado* (Leeds, Peepal Tree Press, 1998) is earthy, occasionally raunchy, and often surprising. Former mayor Hamilton Green has provided a wonderfully eccentric take on his city in *Georgetown – an anthology of Georgetown* (Georgetown). But it is perhaps in their fictional descriptions of their country that the Guyanese excel. I would particularly recommend Brenda DoHarris' *A Coloured Girl in the Ring: A Guyanese Woman Remembers* (Lanham, MD, Tantaria Press, 1997), and Pauline Melville's wonderfully torrid novel, *The Ventriloquist's Tale* (London, Bloomsbury, 1997).

Guyana – The Natural world

Again, however, it's the writer-naturalists who've always got the best from Guyana. Leading the way is Charles Waterton, with his brilliant and chaotic journal, *Waterton's Wanderings in South America* (London, Macmillan, 1880). And, as to his Yorkshire legacy, I am indebted to Richard Bell's *Waterton's Park* (Wakefield, Willow Island Editions, 1998). In the final years of British Guiana, this was followed by three other enormously popular books: David Attenborough's *Zoo Quest to Guiana* (London, Lutterworth Press, 1956), and Gerald Durrell's *The New Noah* (London, Collins, 1955) and *Three Singles to Adventure* (London, Penguin, 1964).

Balram Singh's *An Introduction to the Birds of Guyana* (Georgetown, Guyana in Colour series, 1994) does exactly what the title suggests, and has the additional merit of being very slim and light.

Jonestown

The literature surrounding the People's Temple grows daily, thriving mostly on wild conjecture. It's hard to know exactly what's reliable, and even Deborah Layton's eye-witness account, *Seductive Poison* (New York, Doubleday, 1978), has to be viewed with a little circumspection.

That said, there is solid material there to be found. A good starting point is *The Assassination of Representative Leo J Ryan and the Jonestown Guyana Tragedy* (Report of a Staff Investigative Group to the Committee of Foreign Affairs, US House of Representatives, Washington, DC: Government Printing Office, 1979). Rather more lively is reporter Charles Krause's compelling account of the last few days, *Guyana Massacre* (New York, Berkeley Publishing Corp, 1978). As to what happened afterwards and why it happened at all, Shiva Naipaul provides as sober an assessment as any with *Journey to Nowhere: A New World Tragedy* (New York, Simon and Schuster, 1980). I should also mention as worthy of reading Gina De Angelis' *Jonestown Massacre: Tragic End of a Cult* (Berkeley Heights, NJ, Enslow Publishers, 2002).

Suriname – General

Again, I struggled to find useful material in English on Suriname. This is surprising given the country's early appearance in European literature. It features in both Voltaire's *Candide* (translated by John Butt, London, Penguin Classics, 1947), and Aphra Behn's *Oroonoko: or, The Royal Slave* (London, W. Canning, 1688).

That said, I'm indebted to the work of another friend, Toon Fey, for his lavishly illustrated *Suriname Discovered* (Schiedam, Scriptum, 2007). Also, in addition to the usual internet sites, I found helpful insights into the country in V. S. Naipaul's *The Middle Passage* (above) and Nicol Smith's slightly bizarre work, *The Jungles of Dutch Guiana* (New York, Blue Ribbon Books, 1943). The only recent work of travel writing that I could lay my hands on was Andrew Westol's excellent *The River Bones* (Toronto, McClelland and Stewart, 2009).

I did however find plenty of material specifically about the Maroons and their history, and I shall return to this below. The Maroons aside, I found that the *Journal of the Suriname Museum (Mededelingen van het Surinaams Museum)* was a good source of historical material, particularly volumes 27, 29, 30, 33, 38,

40, 42 and 44 (published by the Suriname Museum, Paramaribo. Note: it is published in both English and Dutch).

In relation to the civil war of 1986 to 1992, I found reliable and useful material in the judgement of the Inter-American Court of Human Rights, dated 15 June 2005, in the case of *Moiwana village v Suriname*. I also read the heartless, amoral memoir of the mercenary, Karl Penta, *Have Gun will Travel* (London, John Blake, 2003), although it's hard to know whether all he says is true. An idea of Desi Bouterse's own warped perspective on his seizure of power can be seen in an old government publication *Suriname in Ontwikkeling: 25 Februari 1980* (Paramaribo, Dubois, 1980).

Suriname's Maroons

The Maroons have – deservedly – attracted a great deal of interest from both historians and anthropologists.

However, for me, the starting point had to be the work of a soldier and traveller, John Stedman. His memoir, *Expedition to Surinam, Being the Narrative of a Five Years' Expedition against the Revolted Negroes of Surinam, in Guiana, on the Wild Coast of South America, from 1772 to 1777 (&c)* (Reprinted by the Folio Society, London, 1963) is a fabulously exciting and compassionate account of the most turbulent time in the country's history. In providing the context for the book, I was also greatly helped by Louise Collis' *Soldier in Paradise; The Life of Captain John Stedman 1744–1797* (New York, Harcourt, Brace and World Inc, 1966).

As to the history, however, I relied heavily on Wim SM Hoogsbergen's *The Boni Maroon Wars in Suriname* (Leiden, Brill, 1990). In addition, I found useful supplementary material in John Thornton's *Africa and Africans in the Making of the Atlantic World, 1400–1800* (New York, Cambridge University Press, 1998).

As to the anthropology, I owe much to the leading authority on this area, Richard Price and his two works, *The Guiana Maroons: A Historical and Bibliographical Introduction* (Baltimore, Johns Hopkins University Press, 1976) and *First Time: The Historical Vision of an African American People* (Chicago, University of Chicago Press, 2002). In relation specifically to the Saramaka people, however, I also found fascinating – if a little outdated – material in Morton Kahn's *Notes on the Saramaccaner Bush Negroes of Dutch Guiana* (*American Anthropologist* volume 31, number 3, 1929). I should also mention Melville and Frances Herskovits' *Rebel Destiny: Among the Bush Negroes of Dutch Guiana* (New York, Whittlesey House, 1934).

French Guiana – General

Aside from the general histories already mentioned, I found the following helpful: Richard Burton's *French and West Indian: Martinique, Guadeloupe, and French Guiana Today* (1995) and Jean-Michel Tissot's *Guyane: Des Hommes en Amazon* (Paris, Les Créations du Pélican, 2003). As to the early colonial history, and the background to my own ancestor's unfortunate sojourn, I am indebted to the work of Joyce Lorimer, *English and Irish Settlement on the River Amazon 1550–1646* (London, Hakluyt Society, 1989).

Peter Redfield's *Space in the Tropics: From Convicts to Rockets in French Guiana* (Berkeley, University of California Press, 2000) was interesting for its study of the relationship between the old penal colony and the modern space port. I also enjoyed a number of works by explorers, all dating from the immediate post-war period: Hassoldt Davis' *The Jungle and The Damned* (London, The Travel Book Club, 1955); Henry Larsen's *Behind the Lianas: Exploration in French Guiana* (Edinburgh, Oliver and Boyd, 1958). Perhaps the most compelling of all, however, was Raymond Maufrais' deathly tale, *Journey without Return* (London, William Kimber, 1953).

For some understanding of Hmong culture, I drew on Robert Cooper's *The Hmong: A Guide to Traditional Life* (Lao-Insight books, 2008). The arrival of the Hmong in Cacao is described in Pierre Dupont-Gonin's *L'operation Hmong in Guyane Française de 1977*.

Meanwhile, John Young's *The French Foreign Legion* (London, Thames and Hudson, 1984) provides a background to the legion, and its role in Guyane

The penal settlement of French Guiana

It was the literature generated by the *bagne* that finally brought about its closure. During the 1930s and 1940s there was an outpouring of books describing the iniquities of the French penal settlement, most famously René Belbenoit's *Dry Guillotine: Fifteen Years amongst the Living Dead* (New York, Blue Ribbon Books, 1938) and his *Hell on Trial* (New York, Blue Ribbon Books, 1941). In the 1960s, the subject was revived by Henri Charrière, with his memoir *Papillon* (translated by Patrick O'Brian, Granada, 1970). The storyline may be contrived but the descriptions of settlement life are accurate enough. Later, of course, the book became the basis for a highly successful movie.

A more sober overview of the *bagne* is provided by Marion F. Godfroy's *Bagnards* (Paris, Editions du Chêne, 2002). There is also a local, and slightly eccentric, guide to the islands by Eugène Epailly, called *Les Iles du Salut* (Cayenne).

ACKNOWLEDGEMENTS

I would like to thank the following for their help with this book.

In Guyana – Major General (Ret'd) Joe Singh, Judge Patterson, Suria (Teri) O'Brien of Wilderness Explorers (www.wilderness-explorers.com), Gwendoline Tross, Zaman Bachus, Dr Rupert Roopnaraine, Premchand Dass (Deputy Archivist at the Cheddi Jagan Research Centre), Krishna Mandata, Mr Arjun and Kelvin George at the Wales GUYSUCO factory, Joey Jagan, Nigel and Cathy Hughes, Gary Serrao of the Toucan Inn at Meten-Meer-Zorg, Leon Moore on Baganara Island, Judy Karwacki of Small Planet Consulting, Indranath Haralsingh of the Tourism Authority, Godfrey Chan-a-Sue and Jud Wickwire of Mabaruma, Denise Duke and Caroline George of Port Kaituma, Fr Hildebrand Green and Brothers Matthias Farrier and Paschal Jordan of the Benedictine Monastery near Bartica, Bradford Allicock (the headman of the Makushis in Fairview), Archer Moses and Cassius Williams of Iwokrama, Colin Edwards of 'Rockview' near Annai, Paulette and Daniel Allicock of Surama, Fred and Francisca Allicock, Sidney Allicock, Diane McTurk, Ashley Holland of Yurupakari, Brian Li, Dr Marta Ware of Manari, Gordon Forte of Lethem, Ester Parks, Duane and Sandy de Freitas of Dadanawa, Oswald Isaacs, the *capataz* at Dadanawa, Cyril Andrews, the tanner, Alex Mendes of Peereboom, Mrs Georgiana Grimmond, the caretaker at Fort Nassau, Gloria and Edmund Kertzious of de Velde (Berbice), Colin Kertzious of New Amsterdam and his sister Maylene.

In Suriname – Glenn Firama, former prime minister Willem Udenhout, Mike White of J. P. Knight and Co, Erik Kuiper of METS, Hilda Neus, Lester Mansbridge (Captain of the *MT Kite*) and Chief Engineer Ian McLwraith, Guinio Zebeda and Charlie Beck.

In Guyane and metropolitan France – Alain Hermes at Tikari travel agents (Cayenne), Philippe Soler of 'Le Planeur Bleu' in Cacao, M and Mme René and

Maysy Siong, Christian and Cathy Gomis, Patrick Monier of Kourou, Jérôme Rémont (the artist of St-Jean), and Christophe Allwright of *Les Compagnons de Route*.

In Israel – Paula Betuzzi for her help in establishing contacts in Guyana.

In the USA – Kirk Smock for his friendship and advice, and of course for his excellent book, *Guiana: The Bradt Travel Guide*.

In Australia – Tony Thorne of Wilderness Explorers (www.wilderness -explorers.com), for his invaluable logistical and moral support in putting this journey together.

In Holland – Annemarie Slotboom, Arnold Karskens (the distinguished radio reporter who covered the Hinterland War), and Toon Fey for his companionship and wisdom on my visits to the maroon areas.

In England – thanks first to those travel experts who provided logistical support for the Guyanese section of these travels, namely Cox and Kings (www .coxandkings.co.uk), Andean Trails (www.andeantrails.co.uk), and Wildlife Worldwide (www.wildlifeworldwide.com). Special thanks, however, go to Claire Antell of Wilderness Explorers (www.wilderness-explorers.com), for her tenacity and ingenuity in getting this project going.

Also thanks to Col John Blashford-Snell, Dr Ahmed Jethu, the Surinamese Honorary Consul, Dr Claire Fuller, David Kerry, Martin Forde, QC, Richard Knight of J. P. Knight and Co, Sheila Markham (the wonderfully knowledge-able librarian at the Travellers Club), Bruce Hubbard, Samantha Tross, FRCS, Fraser Wheeler (the British High Commissioner to Guyana) and his wife Sarah, Yvonne Constantinis, Keith Waithe, Emmanuelle Simon, Judith van Holten, Dan Linstead at *Wanderlust*, Michael Kerr at the *DailyTelegraph*, my agent Georgina Capel, Diana Coglianese at Knopf, and Peter Carson at Profile. I also extend my special thanks to my parents, Dr and Mrs TMD Gimlette, for all their help and encouragement with this book, and for their invaluable suggestions on the draft manuscript.

Some of the episodes in this book first appeared – in a rather different form – in *Wanderlust* and the *Daily Telegraph*.

Finally, there's my wife, Jayne, and daughter, Lucy. As before, Jayne has been a source of tireless inspiration and support, and Lucy has borne my long absence with great understanding and curiosity. My gratitude therefore comes, as always, with all my love.

ILLUSTRATIONS

INDEX